The Past in the Present

The Past in the Present

Women's Higher Education in the Twentieth-Century American South

~Amy Thompson McCandless~

The University of Alabama Press
Tuscaloosa and London

designed by Lucinda Smith

∞

The paper on which this book is printed meets the
minimum requirements of American National Standard
for Information Science-Permanence of Paper for Printed
Library Materials, ANSI Z39.48-1984.

Library of Congress Cataloging-in-Publication Data

McCandless, Amy Thompson
    The past in the present : women's higher education in
the twentieth-century American South / Amy Thompson McCandless.
        p.   cm.
    Includes bibliographical references and index.
    ISBN 0–8173–0945–4 (cloth, alk. paper)
    ISBN 0–8173–0994–2 (paper, alk. paper)
    1. Women—Education (Higher)—Southern States—History—20th
century.   2. Women college students—Southern States—Conduct of
life—History—20th century.   3. Universities and colleges—Southern
States—Sociological aspects—History—20th century.   I. Title.
    LC1756 .M24 1999
    378.1'9822—ddc21
                                98–40089

British Library Cataloguing-in-Publication Data available

Photographs on the cover of the paperback edition are published by courtesy of the
following institutions:
top, front cover and spine: McCain Library and Archives, University Archives, University
of Southern Mississippi.
bottom, front cover, left to right: Office of Public Relations, Sweet Briar College; Avery
Research Center for African American History and Culture, College of Charleston;
University Archives, University of Richmond.
spine, bottom: Woman's Collection, Blagg-Huey Library, Texas Woman's University.
back: W. S. Hoole Special Collections Library, University of Alabama.

With love to
my parents, Eleanor and Jack Thompson,
my husband, Peter McCandless, and
my sons, Alastair and Colin McCandless

~ Contents ~

Photographic Section   *159–176*

~ Preface ~

My interest in the higher education of women in the twentieth-century South is both personal and professional. I have a baccalaureate degree in history from Sweet Briar College in Virginia, have a master's in business administration from the University of South Carolina, and have taught history at the College of Charleston in South Carolina for twenty years. Although I left the South to earn a Ph.D. in modern social history from the University of Wisconsin–Madison, it was the academic preparation and personal encouragement I received at a small Southern women's college that enabled me to handle graduate school at a large Midwestern university. My undergraduate experience did not, however, prepare me for the culture shock of moving from a protective, nurturing, and conservative environment where "ladies" wore dresses, hose, and heels to football games at neighboring men's colleges to the impersonal and activist milieu of a huge urban campus where even the clergy were involved in social protest. Conversations about college life with classmates who hailed from all corners of the globe confirmed my own suspicion: the South was different. There were, of course, many experiences shared by college women of my generation, regardless of the type or the location of the institution, and yet there were others unique to the region. As a historian of women, I wondered how traditional categories of historical analysis such as gender, race, class, geography, and time period affected educational philosophies and practices. An investigation of women's higher education in the twentieth-century South, I concluded, would help me understand my own collegiate experience as well as the "if" and "why" of Southern distinctiveness.

As for most authors, my debts are many. There are my parents, who encouraged me and funded my own Southern education; my family, who spent many of their summer vacations near college archives (I remember my husband asking, after a particularly grueling July tour of women's colleges in Alabama, Mississippi, and Louisiana, why I couldn't study Canadian women); my professors, who encouraged me to set my sights on graduate school; my colleagues, who read and commented on papers and chapters; my friends in the Southern Association for Women Historians,

Preface

who inspired me with their own research and writing; and my students, who shared their college experiences with me. Librarians and archivists throughout the region have been uniformly kind and helpful. The National Endowment for the Humanities, the College of Charleston, and the Institute for Southern Studies at the University of South Carolina have all helped fund my research. Anne Hawkes, Peter McCandless, Joseph Coady, Karen Offen, Walter Edgar, Nan Morrison, Patricia Johnson, JoAnn Diaz, Mary Martha Thomas, and Marcia Synnott have all read parts of the manuscript, and I am enternally grateful for their help and support. It has been a joy to work with the editors at the University of Alabama Press—Nicole Mitchell, Mindy Wilson, Sue Jane Smith, and others.

Introduction
The Past in the Present

*T*he history of women's higher education in the twentieth-century United States is a complex story, incorporating many of the themes of women's, racial, ethnic, regional, and educational history. Unlike Aristotle's perfect drama, this story does not observe the unities of time, character, or place. For much of the twentieth century, the higher education of women in the South[1] has differed significantly from that of other Americans. Gender, race, ethnicity, class, religion, and geography have all made a difference in the nature of admissions standards, curricular offerings, campus life, and postgraduate opportunities. The demographic, economic, social, political, and cultural characteristics of the region have accounted for many of these educational variations. African Americans have composed a higher proportion of the population than in any other area of the country. Southern students—white and black—have been more Protestant, more rural, more conservative, and less affluent than their Northern and Western counterparts. Southern institutions have been slower to raise matriculation and graduation standards, to revise the classical curriculum, and to eliminate in loco parentis than schools in other regions of the country. Southern administrators and legislators have opposed coeducation and integration longer and harder than college officials elsewhere. Certain types of institutions such as all-black colleges, public women's colleges, and separate agricultural colleges have been more prevalent in the South than elsewhere in the nation. In no other part of the country have events from the past played such a large part in the educational policies and practices of the present. Although many of these differences are not gender specific, all have contributed to the distinctive educational experience of women in the American South.

Introduction

Southerners have long viewed themselves and their institutions as unique. Historian Carl Degler has commented on the "twoness," or dual identity, of white Southerners. They think of themselves both as "Americans" and as "Southerners." W. E. B. Du Bois found a similar "double consciousness" among blacks in the early twentieth century: "One ever feels his two-ness—an American, a Negro; two souls, two thoughts, two unreconciled strivings."[2] Although African Americans longed to merge their double selves into a single identity, Du Bois wrote, they did not wish to lose either the African or the American component of their personality in the process. Gender differences complicated the picture still further. As Dorothy Salem has noted, black women "possessed a triple consciousness because they were American, Black, and women." Historian Darlene Clark Hine has argued that a "multiconscious" model would come closer to capturing the realities of black women's identities. If Du Bois had considered women in his analysis of American society, "instead of writing 'One ever feels his twoness,' he would have mused about how one ever feels her 'fiveness': Negro, American, woman, poor, black woman."[3] Similar difficulties emerge when we attempt to characterize white Southern women with a single descriptive variable. As Elizabeth Fox-Genovese observed in her history of women on the antebellum plantation, being white was not enough to make one a "lady." Whether we employ the term "double consciousness" or "twoness" or "multiconscious" to describe the many factors that affected Southern women's perceptions of themselves and their environment, we must constantly remind ourselves of the diverse voices that narrate our story.[4]

The Southern setting provides an equally complex yet important backdrop to this history. Although most cultural historians associate the creation of a self-conscious Southern identity with the Confederate defeat in the Civil War, European proponents of colonization noted differences among the various regions of North America as early as the sixteenth century. Richard Hakluyt, in his *Discourse on Western Planting*, presented to Queen Elizabeth in 1584, described the South Atlantic soil as rich in natural resources and perfect for plantation agriculture—a veritable paradise. Later immigrants to the Southern colonies agreed. New England might claim to be God's City on a Hill, but the South was the new Garden of Eden.[5]

The rich, lush environment of the South Atlantic region seemed to extend endlessly westward, giving settlers a "frontier" mentality. As long as there was land, there was life, and the land and the life were good. This view of the colonial South as an extension of Eden, W. J. Cash has argued, accounted for many of the "dominant traits" of Southerners: they possessed an "intense individualism" and a "tendency toward unreality, toward romanticism, and . . . hedonism."[6] Unlike their European ancestors who had only dreamed of a Golden Age, they had found paradise and intended to enjoy it.

Plantation slavery soon became an integral component of the Eden myth. European settlers knew little about tropical crops and often succumbed to regional maladies such as malaria and yellow fever. After unsuccessful attempts to employ Native Americans and Europeans in the fields, large planters resorted to the forced labor of African slaves, whose skill and industry had brought considerable wealth to European colonists in the Caribbean.

The Africans who were uprooted from their homelands and forcibly enslaved hardly considered themselves in Eden. Few Africans tasted the fruits of the Southern Garden. For most Africans in the New World, paradise had been lost. Christianized slaves soon adopted their own mythical view of the promised land—one in which they were delivered by Moses out of bondage into freedom.[7]

The development of the plantation brought the serpent into the Garden. Slavery seemed incompatible with the revolutionary principles of liberty and equality espoused by the founding fathers of the new American republic. The ideological differences that led to the three-fifths compromise in the constitutional convention of 1787 would widen in the nineteenth century into a cataclysmic conflict over the South's peculiar institution.

The war created a Southern "nation," and the Confederate defeat increased perceptions of regional differences. It also gave the region a history of its own: "For Southern history, unlike American," C. Vann Woodward noted in a 1960 essay on Southern identity, "includes large components of frustration, failure, and defeat. It includes not only an overwhelming military defeat, but long decades of defeat in the provinces of economic, social, and political life."[8] The gates to paradise appeared to have closed.

Introduction

Even after the Fall, memories of Eden were hard to erase. "We Southerners are," Jonathan Daniels wrote in 1938, "a mythological people. Supposed to dwell in moonlight or incandescence, we are in part to blame for our own legendary character. Lost by choice in dreaming of high days gone and big house burned, now we cannot even wish to escape."[9] For many whites, Daniels argued, the Civil War became a convenient scapegoat for sectional problems: "The South was poor; the war caused it. The South was ignorant; the war made us too poor to educate. The South was slow; well, after what the damnyankees [*sic*] did it wasn't any use to stir."[10]

Visions of a past that could have been and never was haunted the Southern imagination in the decades after the Civil War, giving Southerners a special sense of time and kind of vision. *Fugitive* writer Allen Tate and his fellow "agrarians" at Vanderbilt in the 1920s thought that Southerners shared a "unity of feeling . . . which came out of . . . a common historical myth." They yearned to look forward to a New South, and yet they continued to look backward to the Old. Much like Janus, the ancient Roman god of doorways, Southerners seemed to face two opposite directions at once and were peculiarly "conscious of the past in the present."[11]

The "twoness" of Southern society thus involves a complex sense of time as well as of character. An examination of this multiconsciousness is crucial to an understanding of Southern women's educational experiences in the twentieth century. A peculiar mixture of national and regional philosophies and practices has made Southern higher education unique. Howard Odum, in his 1936 study *Southern Regions of the United States,* described the Southern pattern of education as "essentially 'American,' with its own racial and regional variations."[12]

The region has not been immune to American educational trends. Progressive ideology transformed schools in the South as it did in the rest of the nation at the turn of the century. The First World War expanded educational opportunities for white women throughout the country, as many private and public colleges sought to maintain their enrollments by becoming coeducational. The Harlem Renaissance of the 1920s led black students throughout the South to demand reforms in the administration of their institutions. The Great Depression brought the educational problems of the poor—white and black—to the attention of the nation, and the New Deal provided funds for badly needed college facilities and programs.

World War II further increased the percentage of women and blacks in institutions of higher education. The civil rights protests and the antiwar and women's movements democratized institutional structures and gave students more control over their academic and extracurricular lives. Southern education was affected by all these national developments.

But Southern history has provided the region with unique educational experiences as well. The South lagged behind the North in the development of free, public schools, and as a consequence the education of the masses was largely neglected. In a 1909 examination of the "Educational Ideals" of the Old South, Professor Philander Claxton, of the University of Tennessee, concluded: "The rural life, the large plantation, the labor system and the predominant traditions of the South all tended to aristocracy and away from the democracy of the public school."[13] Unlike New England, the South had few towns or areas of concentrated population. But demographic reasons were not the only factors that retarded the establishment of community-supported schools in the antebellum period. The large planter, who controlled the political as well as the economic life of the region, tended to share the presumption of the English aristocrat that education should be the responsibility of the individual family.[14]

In the antebellum South, higher education was the preserve of the planter elite. Originating in the desire to train young men for the professions of law, medicine, and the ministry, Southern colleges offered a traditional liberal arts education with a heavy emphasis on the classics. Private tutors or private academies taught Latin grammar, which prepared youth for the university. As one historian quipped, "It has been said that in the Old South there were more people who could read Latin and fewer who could read English than in any part of the country."[15]

Individual Southerners were sometimes complimented for their knowledge of natural science and the practical arts, but Southerners as a group were thought to have less interest in the abstract life of the mind than Northerners. In his autobiographical essay, *The Education of Henry Adams*, the New Englander Adams characterized Rooney Lee, his Southern classmate at Harvard in the 1850s (and the son of Robert E. Lee), as representative of the Southern student: "[T]he Southerner had no mind; he had temperament. He was not a scholar; he had no intellectual training; he could not analyze an idea, and he could not even conceive of admitting two; but in life one could get along very well without ideas, if one had only the social instinct." Although Southerners such as Lee attended Northern colleges and universities, few Northerners were educated in the South in the nineteenth century. Southern educational institutions were usually regarded as "inferior" to Northern ones.[16]

Vanderbilt professor and progressive educator Edwin Mims attributed the region's disdain of academic accomplishments to plantation conceptions of manhood and womanhood. Because "[s]lavery put the badge of inferiority on work of all kinds," Mims wrote, intellectual effort was viewed as demeaning. The Southern planter was a horseman, a hunter, a farmer, even a businessman; he was not a scholar. His feminine counterpart was the lady on the pedestal, elevated for all to admire and none to touch, sheltered and protected from the harsh realities of life by her lord and master, and indulged and adored by her black slaves. She was noted for her domesticity, purity, and piety, not for her independence or intellect. The stereotype of the "lady," Mims concluded, affected Southern ideas on women's education: "As domestic and social accomplishments were considered of first importance, any education aimed at any other object was considered unnecessary and undesirable."[17]

Only a few, upper-class white women received an education outside the home before the Civil War. And most of the women who attended such private academies were "confined to the acquirement of certain accomplishments, such as music, painting, wax-working, and fancy needlework." As one historian of antebellum South Carolina explained, "The educational machinery of the state was geared up to assure the dominance of the male in most of the relations of life. Education for the female was to equip her to adorn and ennoble society, and to supply a background for the more aggressive male."[18]

Yet, paradoxically, the antebellum South was also "an innovator in collegiate education for women." As Christie Anne Farnham has shown in her study of the schooling of the Southern belle, elite Southern fathers were much more willing than their counterparts in the North to expose women to the classical curriculum of the men's college. Because the education of the planter's daughter was to prepare her for a life of gentility and not for a profession, there was little fear that her training would provide "the means for mounting an attack on the sex segregation of the professions." Instead, a classical education became for Southern women what it was for Southern men—a symbol of "class."[19]

The majority of Southern women did not even have a finishing-school education. Public schools were few and far between, private education was expensive, and state laws forbade the education of slaves. Most rural families believed that young girls could learn all they needed to know at home from their mothers. As a consequence, the antebellum literacy rate for Southern women was the lowest of any group of women in the nation.[20]

The gap between Southern and Northern education widened in the late nineteenth century. The devastation of Civil War and the failure of Reconstruction, the persistence of one-crop agriculture, the development of a segregated, biracial culture, the slow growth of industrialization, the large proportion of school-age children to tax-paying adults, and the continued dominance of the planter elite meant that the South did not have the human or financial capital to keep pace with educational changes elsewhere. Standards of scholarship continued to be set in the North.

Demographic factors have long contributed to Southern distinctiveness. Despite the rapid industrialization and urbanization that occurred throughout the nation in the late nineteenth and early twentieth centuries, Southerners continued to live in rural areas and to make their living off the land. In most of the postwar South, cotton was still king. Its production was labor intensive, competition was stiff, and forces beyond a farmer's control determined the yield and profit. Yet cotton was what the Southern farmer knew how to grow and grow well, and the agricultural marketing system of the region was geared to its production. It was one thing for New South proponents to call for diversification; it was another thing to get farmers to give up the only sure cash crop they knew.

There were numerous educational consequences of this cotton economy. Many turn-of-the-century farm families saw little use for book learning when children could learn vocational skills and contribute to the household by working with their parents. Because of crop demands, there were only three or four months of the year during which children were "free" to attend school. The dominance of sharecropping also meant that there was very little ready cash for educational purposes (indeed, for any purposes). The distribution of the population on far-flung farms and the lack of good roads and transportation facilities resulted in a plethora of one- and two-room schoolhouses, where a few poorly paid teachers struggled to teach children of all abilities and ages in the months between the planting and the harvesting of the crops.

Southern economic conditions continued to discourage immigration to the region. Most of the European Americans who resided in the Southern states were from northern and western Europe and had settled in the South during the colonial and early national periods. The massive immigration from eastern and southern Europe that occurred at the turn of the twentieth century had little impact on the southern United States. There was no shortage of unskilled or semiskilled agricultural labor in the South, and there were few manufacturing establishments outside the cotton mills. Most immigrants went west, not south, when they left the northern ports. The South did not have to cope with assimilating new immigrants, a necessity that inspired numerous educational innovations in other parts of the United States in the Progessive Era.[21]

Almost the entire population of the South was Protestant. The region's few Catholics were concentrated in southern Louisiana and its few Jews in coastal cities such as Savannah, Charleston, and New Orleans. Most Southern Protestants were Baptists or Methodists, fundamentalists who were primarily concerned with personal salvation. Those who professed their faith and were saved were expected to behave accordingly. Drinking, dancing and partying, smoking, and breaking the Sabbath were frowned on. The church was one of the most important institutions in the community, and pastors were concerned with the education as well as the behavior of their flocks. The earliest educational establishments in the region were the creations of various religious groups, and by the twentieth century, the major Protestant denominations had established at least one college for white men, one for white women, and one for blacks in every Southern state.[22]

Another distinctive feature of the Southern population for most of the nineteenth and twentieth centuries was its youth. Birth rates were higher in the region than in the country as a whole. Southerners tended to marry earlier than Northerners and to have larger families. Southerners also tended to have a lower life expectancy. As a consequence, there were fewer wage earners and taxpayers to support an educational system that contained proportionately more school-age children.[23]

The black population of the South has been more numerous than the black population elsewhere in the nation. The plantation system had brought large numbers of Africans to the region as slaves, and in the coastal areas along the Atlantic and the Delta regions of the Deep South, there were more blacks than whites in the late nineteenth century. Not until the mass exodus of blacks to Northern cities in the years after World War I did South Carolina or Mississippi have a white majority.

9

Slavery and, later, racial segregation have long been associated with Southern distinctiveness, and educational developments in the twentieth-century South are intricately interwoven with matters of race. Before the Civil War, there were no institutions of higher education for blacks of either gender in the South. Slaveholders believed that the education of blacks would foment rebellion, and even free persons of color had to leave the region to attend college.[24] Slavery also affected the education of whites. As attacks on the South's peculiar institution increased in the early nineteenth century, Southern leaders called for the creation of indigenous colleges that would protect Southern youth from the corruption of Northern ideas.

Numerous analysts of the prewar South have noted the connection between the defense of slavery and the suppression of dissent. Drew Faust, in her examination of the dilemma of the intellectual in the antebellum South, concluded that the growing regional tension over slavery made it impossible for individual Southerners to speak their minds with impunity. The protection of its peculiar institution from the attacks of Yankees, W. J. Cash wrote in *The Mind of the South*, "turned the South toward strait-jacket conformity and made it increasingly intolerant of dissent." Historian Catherine Clinton thought that the Southern elite assumed a "bunker mentality," whereas economist William Nicholls found a "general intolerance of intellectual progress and the intellectual process."[25]

With the defeat of the South and the emancipation of the slaves, the education of the new freed men and women became a primary concern of most of the Reconstruction governments of the region. As F. L. Cardozo, an African American delegate to the South Carolina Constitutional Convention of 1868, explained, "We know that when the old aristocracy and ruling power of this State get into power, as they undoubtedly will, because intelligence and wealth will win in the long run, they . . . will take precious good care that the colored people shall never be enlightened." The South Carolina convention subsequently included a statewide poll tax to finance a system of compulsory elementary education, and similar provisions for public elementary and secondary education were made in other Southern states.[26]

Whether or not these new public schools should be integrated was a controversial issue throughout the South. South Carolina established separate schools for whites and blacks. Reconstruction governor Robert Scott told the South Carolina General Assembly that "in legislating for . . . two distinct, and, in some measure, antagonistic races, . . . [statesmen] must . . . take cognizance of existing prejudices among both."[27] An attempt by the South Carolina legislature to integrate the University of South Carolina after the war was a total failure; white faculty and students departed en masse when black students were admitted. Nor was the South Carolina experience unique. De facto segregation existed in the majority of the educational institutions in the region in the 1870s and 1880s. Only in New Orleans did Reconstruction governments succeed in integrating the public schools.[28]

To provide teachers for the new black schools, missionary and philanthropic societies founded numerous institutions of higher education for African Americans throughout the South. By 1870 the American Missionary Association alone had established seven colleges and thirteen normal schools. There was considerable debate among Northern and Southern educators about whether the higher education of blacks should be similar to or different from that of whites.[29] Although both liberal arts colleges and industrial training schools were established for African Americans in the late nineteenth century, many white Southerners feared that too much education of any kind would "ruin a good field hand."

With the passage of Jim Crow legislation in the 1890s and early 1900s, the de facto segregation of Southern educational institutions became de jure. When the Supreme Court ruled in 1954 that separate educational facilities for the races were inherently unequal, Alabama, Georgia, Florida, Mississippi, and South Carolina had state laws mandating segregation in their public and private colleges and universities.[30] And in education, as in public accommodations, separate was never equal. Black colleges, like black elementary and secondary schools, had smaller budgets, poorer facilities, fewer programs, and inadequate staffs.

The agrarian economy of the South has also contributed to the region's postbellum educational distinctiveness. The Morrill Acts of 1862 and 1890 made provision for the establishment of land-grant institutions throughout the nation. In the North and West, agricultural programs were generally combined with liberal arts studies in a single state university; in the South, separate agricultural and mechanical institutions were created in Virginia, North Carolina, South Carolina, Georgia, Alabama, Mississippi, and Texas. Because these agricultural and mechanical colleges were initially for white men only, separate women's industrial and normal institutes and black agricultural and industrial schools were established with land grant funds to provide for the educational needs of "farm wives" and "colored farmers."[31]

Men's agricultural and mechanical colleges and women's normal and industrial schools were institutions designed primarily for the middle and lower classes, whereas liberal arts colleges were viewed as the preserve of the region's elite. The socioeconomic differences between various types of public institutions in the South meant that legislative battles for appropriations often degenerated into class conflicts.

Religious conflicts also characterized Southern educational developments in the twentieth century. Many denominational colleges opposed the granting of public moneys for any type of higher education whatsoever. Church leaders thought that it was unfair for the state to subsidize the education of youth attending secular institutions when undergraduate education was readily available at denominational schools. Most thought that the state university should confine itself to professional and graduate preparation.

As the bitter debates between advocates of secular and religious education indicated, higher education could not be separated from regional politics. In the 1880s and 1890s, populist demands for agricultural and industrial programs that would benefit poor whites led to the establishment of agricultural and mechanical institutes for white men and industrial and normal institutes for white women. Federal requirements that land-grant funds be distributed equally between the races led to the establishment of separate agricultural and industrial institutions for blacks in the region.

Southern politicians have consistently interfered with the operation of state universities. Ben Tillman tried to destroy the University of South Carolina in the 1890s, and Theodore Bilbo wreaked havoc with the public colleges in Mississippi in the 1930s.[32] White legislators often used the "threat" of integrated schools as a weapon against their political opponents. The "educational awakening" of the Progressive Era, for example, was associated with universal education for whites and the mass disfranchisement of blacks. In the 1960s, public officials in several Southern states blatantly obstructed the integration of their public universities.[33]

Cultural differences have also separated Southern educational institutions from the national pattern. The shock of the Civil War and Reconstruction led to the propagation of a romantic view of the Old South— a land of moonlight and magnolias and the home of chivalrous planters, pampered ladies, and faithful servants. The plantation system, or so it was claimed, had brought whites prosperity and blacks security. The myth of a lost Eden made Southerners look wistfully to the past.

Conceptions of gender, race, and class growing out of this plantation ideology (and idolatry) affected educational philosophies and practices in the South for much of the twentieth century. For white women, the ideal remained the lady on the pedestal. The "lady" was to be dependent on men. Despite the increasing number of women who sought employment outside the home to support their families, the "ideal" woman did not have a career (or even a job). Many twentieth-century parents continued to view colleges for women as nineteenth-century finishing schools—places where adolescent women could be kept safe from the corruption of the outside world and where they could acquire the grace and bearing of a "lady."

The aristocratic nature of this image of the "lady" excluded most whites and all blacks. Most Southern women were expected to help support their families and wanted training that would enable them to do so. Nonetheless, the normal and industrial colleges, which were established to prepare women for jobs in teaching and in "suitable" female industries, were determined to graduate women who looked and acted like "ladies."

Racist ideology further defined the educational horizons of black women. The plantation was idealized as the best "school" for "savage" Africans. Postwar educators argued that because emancipation had freed the slaves from the control of the master, schools needed to "supply all the elements of training which the plantation under the old order [had] afforded to the slave, and in addition must fit the negro for freedom by energizing his will, conscience, respect for law, and desire to live at peace with his neighbors."[34]

The preoccupation with antebellum conceptions of gender, race, and class created all sorts of difficulties for Southern educational institutions in the first half of the twentieth century. Howard Odum found numerous problems associated with the "dual load of dichotomous education for Negroes and for whites, for men and for women, technical and liberal, public and private, and for geographical and denominational representation."[35] A poor region, with the lowest per capita wealth and the highest ratio of children to adults in the nation, was trying to run too many separate institutions. The result was "overlapping duplication, [needless] competition, inadequate support, low standards, outmoded arrangements, lack of concentration of needed bodies of knowledge and services, [and] uniform deficiencies in the techniques and tools necessary for the development and utilization of the human wealth of the region." This division of effort, Odum concluded in his 1936 study, hindered the establishment of first-rate universities in the South.[36] Plantation conceptions of womanhood dominated fictional and nonfictional accounts of Southern women's education in the early 1900s. In Ellen Glasgow's novel *Virginia*, the star student at the Dinwiddie Academy for Young Ladies was described as "a docile pupil" and educated according to "the simple theory that the less a girl knew about life, the better prepared she would be to contend with it." Dinwiddie rewarded conformity and compliance, not creativity or sagacity: "To solidify the forces of mind into the inherited mould of fixed beliefs was . . . to achieve the definite end of all education."[37]

Louise Boas, in her 1935 history of women's colleges, maintained that occasionally "parents sent daughters to Southern schools to acquire the languid grace and the perfection of manners of the Southern lady, but in general education meant Northern education, in the educationally advanced states."[38] Boas was not the only writer to dismiss Southern colleges as substandard. Most educational historians chose to focus on the women's colleges of the Northeast, the coeducational institutions of the Midwest, or both. The education of African American women in the region was largely ignored. Thomas Woody, in his two-volume *History of Women's Education*, published in 1929, did not mention a single black college.[39]

Even modern histories of higher education have tended to dismiss Southern institutions as poor imitations of their Northern counterparts. Authors have commented on the time lag between developments at Southern schools and elsewhere, but they have often ignored other regional factors that have made the South "different," not just "slower."[40] Recent studies of women's collegiate experiences by Barbara Solomon, Helen Horowitz, and Lynn Gordon have noted Southern exceptions to national patterns of educational development, but they have not examined the causes of Southern educational distinctiveness.[41]

Southern women and Southern colleges have shared many of the "burdens" of Southern history. The image of the South as a poverty-striken, guilt-ridden, and benighted region has tinged portraits of its people and institutions for generations. Southern women have been dismissed as "belles" more concerned with marital prospects than with mental accomplishments, and Southern colleges as bastions of "good ole boys" more interested in booze than in books. Southern women's colleges have been characterized as mere "finishing schools" for the wealthy, and Southern black colleges as outmoded "trade schools" for the poor. More often than not, the term "educated Southerner" has been viewed as an oxymoron.

The consequence of this diminution of Southern schools and omission of the Southern experience is, of course, an incomplete picture of the American educational scene. The impact of higher education on the lives of Southern women has not been as uniformly negative as critics would have it. For some women, the culture of deference and dependence that pervaded Southern institutions did, unfortunately, stifle aspirations and reinforce the status quo. For others, however, higher education provided the wherewithal for them to expand their intellectual and social horizons, to understand their regional heritage, to ameliorate its worse aspects, and to build on its best elements.

Stephanie Shaw, in her book on professional black women during the Jim Crow era, described the ways in which black families, schools, and communities transcended the "multiple disabling factors . . . of race, class, and sex" in the education of their daughters. Young women were raised in an environment of "socially responsible individualism" that inspired them "to use their education in a socially responsible way."[42] Instead of focusing on what they could not do, they were constantly reminded of what they could do.

15

From the campuses of twentieth-century Southern colleges emerged women who became the teachers, leaders, and mothers of the modern South—women who worked tirelessly in their clubs, churches, and communities for social, economic, and political reform. Educators such as Mary McLeod Bethune, Elizabeth Avery Colton, and Clyda Rent; suffragists such as Rebecca Latimer Felton, Nellie Nugent Somerville, and Ida B. Wells-Barnett; civil rights activists such as Ella Baker, Septima Poinsette Clark, Rosa Parks, Mary Modjeska Simkins, and Ruby Doris Smith-Robinson; journalists such as Katie Couric, Jane Robelot, and Charlayne Hunter-Gault; writers such as Nikky Finney, Zora Neale Hurston, Alice Walker, and Eudora Welty; club leaders and social reformers such as Jessie Daniel Ames, Janie Porter Barrett, Sallie Sims Southall Cotten, and Mamie Garvin Fields; and feminists such as Anna Julia Cooper, Paula Giddings, and Pauli Murray—all received some, if not all, of their education in the normal schools, colleges, and universities of the South.

The Scottish writer James Boswell once compared a woman preacher to a dog "walking on his hinder legs." "It was not done well," he commented, "but you were surprised to find it done at all." Much the same has been said about educated women in the South. Yet if we cavalierly dismiss Southern educational institutions as finishing or trade schools, how do we explain the accomplishments of thousands of alumnae in the region? Were such women anomalies who miraculously escaped the limitations of their education? Or did their education enable them to overcome the restrictions of their environment? Was the rebellion of some women against traditional mores and values as much a consequence of their education as the conformity of their classmates?

Even in the antebellum period there are examples of Southern women who used the language and demeanor of compliance and conformity to undermine paternalism. Three of South Carolina's most famous "rebels"—Angelina Grimké Weld, Sarah Grimké, and Mary Boykin

Chesnut—received their education in the private homes and academies of antebellum Charleston. The Grimkés doffed the mantle of piety and probity characteristic of a Southern lady and used it against the violence of their proslavery opponents. Mary Chesnut, by observing the social conventions of her class, was respected when she spoke intelligently on politics and literature. As she herself had once commented about a classmate: she was so beautiful in appearance and manner that "men would [forgive] . . . her cleverness."[43]

That conformity and rebellion are often two sides of the same coin has been noted by historians of slavery. Peter Wood in *Black Majority* and Eugene Genovese in *Roll, Jordan, Roll* have suggested that the apparent accommodation by slaves to paternalistic values may have been a subtle form of resistance to the system that exploited them: "Accommodation itself," Genovese wrote, "breathed a critical spirit and disguised subversive actions and often embraced its apparent opposite—resistance." Genovese found this particularly evident in the development of a black version of Christianity: "It rendered unto Caesar that which was Caesar's, but it also narrowed down considerably that which in fact was Caesar's."[44] This, of course, was what the Grimkés did when they used their religious education to attack the very foundations of paternalism. They accepted the premise of biblical authority but used it to draw very different conclusions about the rights of women and blacks. Mary Chesnut found her physical activities limited by traditional views of a woman's place, but she refused to allow her intellectual freedom to be similarly fettered. She gathered her mental resources to create a world of words and ideas the patriarchy could not touch.

Black women, as Evelyn Brooks Higginbotham has shown in her analysis of the metalanguage of race, similarly used concepts of race as a "double-voiced discourse." Although race was a means of oppression for some African Americans, for others it was an agency of empowerment. Race came to represent pride in a shared African American culture and history, not the stigma of biological inferiority. "When the National Association of Colored Women referred to its activities as 'race work,' " Higginbotham explained, "it expressed both allegiance and commitment to the concerns of black people."[45]

In the story "Everyday Use" and the essay "In Search of Our Mothers' Gardens," Alice Walker recounted the important lessons that black women learned from their "uneducated" foremothers. In their quilts and in their gardens, generations of black women created something out of nothing and inspired their daughters to do likewise. As literary critic Barbara Christian explained in her introduction to Walker's works, "[T]he figure of this older African American woman who knows the patterns of the past and therefore knows how to stitch together patterns for the future—a perspective first enunciated in 'Everyday Use'—is central to our understanding of African American culture as well as that culture we call American."[46]

A knowledge of the "twoness" of Southern culture is also essential to our understanding of Southern women's educational experience in the twentieth century. "Any college," Marjorie Nicolson wrote in 1930, "is a cross section of the society which produces and supports it. It is inevitable that it should reflect within its gates the world outside."[47] Odum came to a similar conclusion: "[E]ducation reflects far more of the effect of politics, religion, and sectionalism than it appears as modifying influences upon them," he wrote.[48]

The South, John Boles noted in a 1983 essay on the region, has been "both American and something different, at times a mirror or magnifier of national traits and at other times a counterculture."[49] If we are to interpret the American experience in its entirety, we need to consider the ways in which Southern people and institutions have both differed from and resembled those in other regions of the United States. The history of women's education in the twentieth-century South is, like the history of the region, both similar to and different from the national pattern. This study examines the ways in which the story of women's higher education in the last 100 years has been shaped by this "twoness" of character, place, and time. The nature of admission standards, of curricular offerings, and of campus life at institutions throughout the region has reflected the demographic, economic, social, cultural, and political history of the South. As William D. Piersen concluded in his examination of the African legacy to American culture: "History works best when the past has something to say to the present. By looking backward, we should indirectly come to a better understanding of our own lives in the here and now."[50] If the purpose of education is to know ourselves, we must seek, as *Fugitive* poet Allen Tate reminds us, to be ever "conscious of the past in the present."

17

1

The Forgotten Woman

The Higher Education of Southern Women at the
Turn of the Twentieth Century[1]

" **N**o aspect of social reform in the South during the progressive era," historian Dewey Grantham wrote, "touched the lives of more of the region's inhabitants than the great educational awakening soon after the turn of the century."[2] But as C. Vann Woodward and Edward L. Ayers have shown in their studies of the New South, progressivism did not touch the lives of all the region's inhabitants equally. In education, as in politics and economics, factors of race, gender, and class largely determined the nature and the extent of reform.[3] Southern educational developments in the Progressive Era and the response of educated Southern women to these developments illustrate the ways in which the "double consciousness" of Southern culture affected educational and social reform.

The expansion of higher education in the years between 1890 and 1920 created unprecedented personal and professional opportunities for white women in the region, but the recipients of that educational largess were in turn expected to conform to chivalric images of womanhood promulgated by their benefactors. Although the emphasis on feminine domesticity and docility stifled the aspirations of some Southern women, it led others to employ the protective mantle of ladyhood to effect change in their communities. These educated white women used their all-female clubs and associations to win male legislative support for educational and social reforms. Unfortunately, public efforts to improve educational standards in the schools and colleges of the region and to ameliorate living conditions on the farms and in the cities of the South were aimed primarily at white institutions and communities. With the disfranchisement of black men at the beginning of the twentieth century, black women were deprived of the political influence available to white women of the period.

White supremacy meant decreased public expenditures for black schools and municipalities, and black women had to overcome tremendous economic, social, and political obstacles to acquire a higher education. Yet, focusing on the shortcomings of public efforts for educational and social reform on behalf of African Americans ignores the extraordinary accomplishments of educated black women who creatively used racial and gender stereotypes to win support for measures to improve black schools and communities. As Glenda Gilmore has argued in her study of the politics of white supremacy in North Carolina, "[S]outhern black women initiated every progressive reform that southern white women initiated, a feat that they accomplished without financial resources, without the civic protection of their husbands, and without publicity." Rather than curtailing their activism, Jim Crow measures led to new roles for educated African American women, who became "the standard bearers for community improvement and liaisons with the white power structure."[4] To understand Southern progressivism and its impact on educational and social reform, one must acknowledge the "twoness" of Southern society.

Educational attainment was low for most Southerners in the late nineteenth century, but the plight of the Southern woman was particularly poignant.[5] Walter H. Page, in his famous "Forgotten Man" speech, delivered at the North Carolina Normal and Industrial Institute in Greensboro in 1897, deplored the cultural impoverishment of most of the region's women. Let the political and religious leaders who claimed they had provided for the education of the women of the South, Page declared, examine the life of the average rural family: they would "see women thin and wrinkled in youth from ill prepared food, clad without warmth or grace, living in untidy houses, working from daylight till bed time at the dull round of weary duties, the slaves of men of equal slovenliness, the mothers of joyless children—all uneducated if not illiterate." Educational institutions had been established for "the fortunately born and the religious well-to-do," but "all the other women," Page concluded, had been "forgotten."[6]

Page's "forgotten women" found it difficult to obtain even an elementary education in the late nineteenth century. Few localities had enough qualified teachers or adequately equipped schools to meet the basic educational needs of the population. Secondary education was often available only at private seminaries or academies. Vocational training was equally hard to procure. Private academies and colleges for white women seldom provided more than a "finishing" school education; public institutions of higher education rarely admitted white women or offered pedagogical or industrial courses. And at almost every level and in almost every place, the situation was worse for black women. Most of the colleges for blacks established by various philanthropic and denominational groups after the Civil War concentrated on precollegiate training. State-supported institutions of higher education for blacks were practically nonexistent before the 1890s.[7]

A number of factors hindered attempts at Southern educational reform. Extensive poverty, a sparse population, and white opposition to the education of blacks all thwarted the establishment of locally funded schools in the postbellum South. As late as 1900, no Southern state had compulsory school attendance legislation, and the South spent, on the average, one-third as much as the country as a whole on public school education.[8] Illiteracy rates in the region were more than double those in the United States as a whole. Figures were higher for blacks than for whites and for women than for men. The "backwardness of its educational provision" was one of the "unmistakable marks" of Southern distinctiveness in the postbellum period.[9]

Interest in economic reform spurred educational developments at the turn of the century. Southern progressives, like the New South proponents before them, believed that the region's poverty could be alleviated by the diversification of agriculture and the introduction of industry, and they looked to the public colleges and universities to convey this new agricultural and industrial knowledge to the rural masses. Education subsequently became the key to regional economic progress.[10]

Southern progressives saw education as a means of improving society, not just the individual. Focusing on the family as the unit of social change, progressive reformers argued that men, women, and children would have to be trained to meet the needs of the New South. Progressive education would prepare the rural population "for participation in a cooperative democracy by inculcating in each citizen a sense of responsibility and civic training."[11]

Most solutions to regional problems proposed by Progressives were contingent on educational reform. "Our institutions needed to be democratized; our thought to be nationalized; our life to be industrialized, and the whole process was one of education," Edwin Alderman wrote in 1907. Alderman, a North Carolinian who served successively as president of the University of North Carolina, Tulane University, and the University of Virginia, was certain that "the school was the heart of the South's problem."[12]

One of the leaders of the educational reform movement in North Carolina was Alderman's friend and colleague Charles Duncan McIver. McIver worked at a private school in Durham after graduating from the University of North Carolina, but he soon realized that private institutions could not meet the educational needs of the larger community. He supported efforts to create a public school system in Durham and became convinced that a statewide system of public schools would solve many of North Carolina's problems. Providing qualified teachers for such a school system would be difficult, however. Although plenty of women were interested in the teaching profession, there was no public provision for their higher education. As McIver's wife, herself a teacher, pointed out, the establishment of public elementary and secondary schools necessitated the establishment of public normal colleges that could train teachers. The couple's discussions led to McIver's first public speech on education at an 1885 teachers' institute in Winston. It was the beginning of a lifelong campaign for the higher education of white women in the state.[13]

"The greatest problem in the south," McIver told audience after audience of North Carolinians, "is not the negro problem." It is education. "For whites and blacks, rich and poor, cultured and illiterate the question of questions in the Southern states is 'How shall the great mass of people in that section be educated?' " For McIver, the educational deficiencies of the region were a disgrace that could be overcome only by the establishment of a universal system of public education. And because these new schools would need teachers, the state should provide normal training for those who were the "natural teacher[s] of the race"—the young women of North Carolina.[14]

McIver's speech touched on many of the political, economic, and social factors that affected the higher education of women in the South. The so-called negro problem was an important concern of white legislators in the late nineteenth-century South. Beginning with Mississippi, state after state rewrote its constitution in the years after 1890, adding poll taxes and literacy requirements for voting that effectively disfranchised the black citizens of the region. Concomitant with suffrage restrictions, legislatures also passed measures segregating schools and public accommodations.

Disfranchisement and segregation in turn affected public education. To maintain the support of the white masses, many of whom were uneducated themselves, Southern legislators incorporated "grandfather" and "understanding" clauses into their new constitutions that would make exceptions for illiterate whites. But in most states, including McIver's North Carolina, there were time limitations on such exceptions, and if the white masses were to retain suffrage, they had to be educated. As a consequence, a sudden interest in public education for whites developed in almost every Southern state in the 1890s.

McIver thought that new literacy requirements in the constitutions of the Southern states would only increase the educational disparity of the sexes (and, he might have added, of the races). He did not want illiterate women to be forgotten in the efforts to educate white boys and men. As he stumped the rural areas of North Carolina between 1889 and 1891, campaigning for universal public education and offering county institutes and special summer schools for teachers, he urged his listeners to remember the women of the state. The education of girls, he told them, was even more important than the education of boys, for the wives and mothers of the future would be the ones who would educate the next generation of North Carolinians. "If it were practicable," he argued, "an educational qualification for matrimony would be worth more to our citizenship than an educational qualification for suffrage."[15]

McIver could not understand those nearsighted individuals who opposed universal education because it might benefit black children as well as white. Why, he wondered, would a community "doom" all its citizens "to mental starvation because of the unwillingness to provide even a scant supply of intellectual food for the negro children dwelling among them"?[16] When it came to higher education, however, McIver believed it was the white woman, not the black woman, who had been treated unjustly by the philanthropist and the legislator. Although colleges and universities had been established throughout the South for "the education of white men, negro men, and negro women, there is not in all the South, with possibly one exception," he noted in 1901, "a liberally endowed college for women, and . . . until recently there have been no women's colleges receiving annual appropriations from the state." It was only fair, he concluded, to provide the same educational opportunities for white women as had been provided for white men and black men and women.[17]

Despite McIver's demands for the "same educational opportunities" for white women, McIver did not believe that they had to be educated in the same classrooms or to be offered the same subjects as men. By "same" he meant "the same rate of expense in securing such education as is needed for women." The lack of public subsidies and private endowments for women's colleges meant that it was much more expensive for parents to educate their daughters than their sons, and this was the inequity that McIver hoped to remedy.[18]

McIver played an integral part in the "educational awakening" of the South that occurred at the turn of the twentieth century. He was elected president of the North Carolina Teachers' Assembly in 1890 and chosen chair of the committee that lobbied the legislature for the establishment of a training school for teachers. Thanks to his efforts, a bill to establish the North Carolina Normal and Industrial School for white women was passed in 1891. Serving as the institution's president until his death in 1906, McIver urged young women to work to improve public education in their rural communities.

McIver's efforts for school reform caught the attention of Robert C. Ogden, a wealthy New York industrialist. Ogden brought together a number of Southern and Northern educators and philanthropists connected with the Conference for Education in the South to discuss the educational problems of the region; the result was the formation of the Southern Education Board (SEB) in 1901. The SEB was essentially a propaganda agency aimed at convincing localities to tax themselves to provide free schools for all the children of the community. Ogden was the board's first president, McIver its first secretary. The SEB's educational efforts soon aroused the interest of the Rockefeller family, and the General Education Board (GEB), supported by donations from John D. Rockefeller, Sr., and chartered by Congress in 1902 as a general educational agency, provided moneys for various Southern school projects.[19]

Many of the Northern philanthropists involved in the efforts of the

SEB and GEB were concerned about the educational problems facing African Americans in the region, but they concluded that the education of blacks was a "red flag" to many white Southerners. Poor whites feared that educated blacks would compete with them for jobs, and wealthy whites wanted to ensure an abundant supply of cheap labor. Whites in the "Black Belt" opposed the equal distribution of tax moneys for public schools because they thought that "white" taxes would pay for "black" schools.[20]

Even progressive educators such as McIver, who advocated the education of both races, argued that whites had to be educated first. "For fixed as fate," McIver asserted, "is the law that any other race living with the Caucasian race anywhere must follow it, not lead it." He cited Booker T. Washington's "belief that the negro's civilization cannot go in advance of that of his white neighbors, and that any very material progress of his race along educational lines must be preceded by educational progress among the white people in the rural districts of the south." McIver believed that the education of white women was the "quickest method" of elevating the entire Southern population.[21]

Many poor whites had suffered severely from the economic depression of the 1870s and 1880s, and they joined farmers' alliances and populist parties to demand justice from the planters and capitalists who exploited them. Their request for agricultural and normal programs that would benefit the "forgotten women" of the region led to the establishment of public colleges for white women throughout the South.

The first publicly supported institution of higher education for women was the Mississippi Industrial Institute and College for the Education of White Girls of the State of Mississippi in the Arts and Sciences (II & C), chartered by the legislature in 1884. The Mississippi Grange, a statewide organization of farmers, had endorsed practical education for both men and women in the 1870s and in 1871 had supported the establishment of the all-male Mississippi Agricultural and Mechanical College. In 1881 the Grange called for the creation of a state school to provide vocational training for women. Educators and legislators took up the call, and a bill was drafted for a college that would offer a liberal arts as well as a normal and industrial education to women. Not wishing to share its appropriations with a state woman's college, the University of Mississippi announced that it would admit women to its liberal arts programs in 1882.

But the university did not provide any vocational courses, and it barred women from preparatory courses and from campus housing. In arguing for a separate women's college, Representative Wiley Norris Nash explained that "the way our girls were raised in antebellum times will not suit the present" and that the creation of the college would give "the poor farmers of Mississippi" a place where they could "send their daughters" to "gain a good practical education." The bill passed, and II & C opened in October 1885 with 341 students. To ensure representation from every segment of the white community, the legislators mandated free tuition and established a county quota system.[22]

25

A similar combination of farm leaders, legislators, and educators joined forces in South Carolina to establish a state normal and industrial college for women. "Pitchfork Ben" Tillman, a reformist Democrat from Edgefield County, advocated agricultural and mechanical training for the common folk of the state in a speech at the Farmer's Convention of 1886. The need for teachers in the new public schools had earlier led to the founding of Winthrop Training School in the city of Columbia. In 1886 the superintendent of schools, D. B. Johnson, secured a grant from the Peabody Fund to establish a year-long normal course for teachers, and in 1887 he successfully petitioned the South Carolina General Assembly to appropriate funds to provide annual scholarships to the training school for one student from each county. When Tillman was elected governor in 1890, he brought his campaign for practical education to the legislature. A committee was established to study the feasibility of taking over Winthrop Training School and expanding it into a publicly supported industrial and normal college.[23]

The committee report revealed the ways in which issues of class, race, and gender entered into discussions of education. Tillman had already expressed his dislike of the upper-class "dudes" who populated The Citadel, the state military college. Winthrop Training School, he told the General Assembly, was doing more for South Carolina "with a one-year course and a $150 scholarship" than The Citadel with its four-year program and $300 subsidy. Further, whereas the normal-school students contributed to the general welfare by teaching in the public schools, Citadel cadets went into other careers or even left the state after graduation.[24]

Tillman believed that education should provide vocational training for the white masses, not cultural elitism for a privileged few. And this was true for women as well as men:

> Our system of education for women looks to training their minds and giving them accomplishments for the adornment of society. But reverses of fortune, or death, often bring the necessity of bread-winning; and the tender mother left a widow, or daughter left an orphan, finds how little worth in dollars and cents is the music, drawing and painting, etc., upon which money and time had been lavished in her so-called education.[25]

The commissioners agreed that a publicly supported college ought to prepare women "to earn their own livelihood," but they did not want women educated like men. Students should be taught "those domestic arts that lie at the foundation of all successful housekeeping and home-making" as well as vocations that were "suitable for women." Although the commissioners did not share Tillman's opposition to the liberal arts, they advocated "the higher branches of learning" because they believed they would have "an uplifting and refining influence on [the] family."[26] The commissioners also played on the racial prejudices of the legislators, noting that the state had already provided a college for "her colored men and women . . . at Claflin University." A state that cherished its womenfolk, the report concluded, ought "to make proper provision for her fair daughters in this respect."[27]

The Act "to establish a Normal and Industrial College in the State of South Carolina for the Education of White Girls" was passed in December 1891. The initial emphasis of the new South Carolina Industrial and Winthrop Normal College was on vocational training, and students could choose between one- and two-year courses resulting in diplomas or certificates of attainment. In addition to classes "in the higher branches of learning," students were offered vocational instruction in "[s]ewing, art, needlework, dressmaking, millinery, cooking, housekeeping, drawing . . . , design and architectural drawing, clay modeling, wood carving, engraving, stenography, typewriting, telegraphy, photography, book-keeping, typesetting and printing." The school soon outgrew its Columbia site and limited curriculum, however. In 1895 the college moved to a new campus in Rock Hill and expanded its offerings to include a four-year degree program for teachers.[28]

Mississippi and South Carolina were not the only Southern states to establish public women's colleges. By 1910, similar schools had been chartered in Georgia (1889), North Carolina (1891), Alabama (1893), Texas (1901), Florida (1905), and Oklahoma (1908). Because women who agreed to teach for two years after graduation received free tuition, most students who attended public women's colleges in the years before 1920 enrolled in teacher training programs.[29] Industrial courses usually focused on domestic skills. As one North Carolina legislator explained, it was important for young women to learn "how to stuff a chicken as well as the head of a dull boy."[30]

The industrial curriculum of the public women's colleges was related to the Progressive effort to promote scientific agriculture. The farm demonstration programs begun by Seaman Knapp in Texas in 1902 had been institutionalized by Congress in the Smith-Lever Act of 1914. Land-grant colleges throughout the country were given moneys to conduct farmers' institutes and to train home demonstration agents. When the Smith-Hughes Act of 1916 expanded the teaching of improved farming and homemaking practices to the lower schools, the demand for teachers trained in home economics soared. The establishment of home economics departments at the state and normal colleges of the South after World War I was a direct consequence of those acts. Graduates were expected to return to their communities and demonstrate the scientific techniques of food preparation and home management they had learned in college.[31]

Publicly supported women's colleges impressed on their students the necessity of community service. "State education is not charity," McIver told the women at the Normal and Industrial School. "North Carolina has simply invested in you . . . [and] has a right to a return for her investment." An alumna recalled that McIver often lectured students on their responsibilities as citizens: "He urged us not to be mere consumers, but to give back to the world all that we could—not like sponges absorb and give nothing."[32] Students in McIver's civics classes were exhorted to "[s]ee the real needs of the world and then do something about it." The school's professor of psychology and pedagogy, Philander Priestly Claxton, was equally inspirational. Emma Lewis Speight, a graduate of the class of 1900, recalled that "[h]e had us all so concerned over the number of adult illiterates that when I graduated I wanted to go to Buncombe County and teach the moonshiners. My mother was properly horrified at the prospect."[33]

Speight taught for two years after her graduation from the normal school—although not in Buncombe County—and then went back for another year of schooling to earn a bachelor's degree. She resigned her teaching post when she married in 1906, but she did not give up her interest in education. She helped establish the public library in Salisbury, North Carolina, and served on state and national committees formed to eradicate adult illiteracy.[34]

Many young women from the public colleges did become involved in educational reform in their communities at the turn of the century, but the greatest service provided by the public women's colleges was their training of teachers for the common schools of the South. Because of the pressing demand for teachers in the expanding public school system, Southern legislators often chartered normal schools in several regions of a state. According to the Report of the U.S. Commissioner for Education, there were six public normal schools in Alabama by 1907, two in Arkansas, one in Florida, four in Georgia, four in Kentucky, two in Louisiana, two in Mississippi, six in North Carolina, four in Oklahoma, two in South Carolina, one in Tennessee, three in Texas, and four in Virginia. Thirty of these institutions were for whites and eleven for African Americans.[35] The overwhelming majority of normal school students of both races were women.

It was difficult at first for normal and industrial schools to offer a four-year college program. Few Southern communities in the late nineteenth century provided the eight years of elementary education or the four years of high school courses that were common in the schools of the Northeast and Midwest. Consequently, most institutions accepted women who had completed the schooling available in their hometowns.

The entrance requirement for two of Virginia's normal colleges was two years of high school. Teacher training consisted of "two additional years of high school work, together with two years of professional study." There were so few public high schools in the counties surrounding the other two normal colleges, however, that students were allowed to matriculate when they had "exhausted all the public school facilities offered in the home town." This meant that many students entered after having completed only the seventh grade.[36]

Charles McIver found it equally hard to enforce entrance standards at the North Carolina State Normal and Industrial School. When the first class arrived in 1892, some students had already earned a baccalaureate degree, whereas others had received only an elementary education. One young woman from a poor family in the mountains had had less than a week of formal education.[37]

Attracting college-educated faculty was also a problem for many Southern women's institutions in the late nineteenth century. The only person with an advanced degree on the faculty of the North Carolina Normal and Industrial School in the 1892–1893 academic year was the "lady doctor." President McIver and three other faculty members had bachelor's degrees; the remaining seven had only the equivalent of a high school diploma. Eighty percent of the faculty were from the South, but only McIver and Alderman had degrees from a Southern school.[38]

Financial problems often made it hard to keep good faculty and to staff new academic programs. State appropriations proved insufficient, and it was impossible to raise additional moneys with student fees. Most of the students were from families of modest means and applied for county scholarships that paid their tuition. "For sometime [sic] I have anticipated being enabled to go to some Northern school to complete my education but my means are limited," one woman wrote President McIver in 1892. "I am delighted to know of a College in my own state with such moderate terms that I may avail myself of the advantages offered."[39]

McIver told the North Carolina legislature that 63 percent of the 391 women enrolled at the Normal and Industrial School (N & I) in the 1893–1894 academic year stated that they could not have afforded to attend any other institution. Even with their tuition paid, many women still had to work during the summers, the school year, or both to earn their room and board. "I am a poor girl and have to work my way in school," one prospective student wrote McIver. "I am willing to do anything just so it is honerable [sic] in order to get an education." She was not alone. Thirty-two percent of the N & I students defrayed their own expenses without any assistance from relatives or friends.[40]

Low fees, tuition grants, and vocational courses made publicly supported institutions of higher education for women immensely popular. Most schools could not accommodate all the women in the state who wished to attend. When the North Carolina N & I opened in 1892, McIver discovered that he had to find room for 176 instead of the expected 125 young women. Four students were put in rooms designed for three by pushing together the double and single beds in each room and having the women sleep across the beds.[41]

Because of the predominance of scholarship students and the provision of room and board at cost, public women's colleges were chronically short of funds, and requests for additional appropriations from the state legislature were often opposed by private and denominational colleges who resented giving state moneys to their competition. In North Carolina, Baptists and Methodists had opposed appropriations for the all-male University of North Carolina since the school reopened after the Civil War in 1875, and they equally resented the state-supported institution for women that began instruction in 1892. Religious leaders argued that the state should confine its educational efforts to the elementary schools and leave the responsibility for higher education to the denominations. In 1895 a bill was introduced into the North Carolina legislature to stop all appropriations for the University and for the N & I. Fortunately for public education in North Carolina, the measure was defeated. President McIver, among others, managed to convince opponents that the state schools were supplementing rather than supplanting the denominational colleges.[42]

Most Southern institutions of higher education, whether public or private, suffered from a chronic shortage of funds. Private endowments were generally low, and public institutions received inadequate state appropriations. Historian C. Vann Woodward calculated that in 1901 Harvard College alone had an annual income greater than that for "the sixty-six colleges and universities of Virginia, North Carolina, South Carolina, Georgia, Alabama, Mississippi, and Arkansas" combined.[43]

With no endowments, public colleges for women had to "make do" with what they could squeeze out of their legislatures. It was tempting, therefore, to admit as many fee-paying students as possible, regardless of their qualifications. Special courses in music and art were often added because they were popular among women from wealthier families who wanted a "finishing" school type of education.

There was only one Southern institution for women that possessed a large endowment at the turn of the century—the H. Sophie Newcomb Memorial College for Women in New Orleans. The school was neither a woman's college nor a coeducational one, but a combination of the two known as a coordinate college. In the pattern of Radcliffe and Harvard, Sophie Newcomb was established in 1886 as a department of Tulane University. The college had its own campus and awarded its own degrees, but Newcomb students used the Tulane library and gymnasium and participated in the university social life.[44]

Newcomb College was a private rather than a public institution, but its educational program resembled that of the state women's colleges in a number of ways. Josephine Louise Newcomb, who had liberally endowed the college in honor of her only daughter, requested "that the education given shall look to the practical side of life as well as to literary excellence." Courses were offered in classical, literary, scientific, and industrial subjects, and teachers of good standing in the public schools could enroll for a year free of charge. Classes in art and music were popular from the start. Of the 150 students who enrolled in 1887, sixty-six chose the art course. When the college was reorganized into schools in 1909, schools of both art and music were established.[45]

In the years before World War I, Newcomb "was both physically and spiritually separated from Tulane University. Newcomb was a college within the framework of the university, but that was all. Neither faculty nor students felt themselves to be part of the whole. They were Newcomb people." Besides the wish to maintain a distinct women's culture at the coordinate college, Newcomb administrators wished, for financial reasons, to separate themselves as much as possible from the larger university. Newcomb's endowment made the school the "wealthiest independent college for women in the *country*," and college officials feared that Tulane authorities might try to expropriate Newcomb moneys and use them for general university purposes.[46]

Being without the large endowment of Newcomb, most private colleges for women in the region shared the financial and curricular problems of the public colleges. Because they depended on tuition fees for much of their support, private colleges for women often accepted more students than they could accommodate on campus. An alumna of the class of 1902 of the Baptist Female University in North Carolina recalled that there were not enough beds for all the students who arrived in the fall of 1899 for classes. Dormitory rooms were lined with mattresses, and students "went to sleep one night in a room with two mattresses on the floor and woke up the next morning to find that three other mattresses and six other girls had been put in during the night."[47]

Money was a constant problem for most private institutions in the South. Parents and students were reminded to pay their bills on time and encouraged to remember the institution in their future financial plans. Randolph-Macon Woman's College in Virginia even included a plea "To the Wise Philanthropist" in its annual catalog. "Will not the friends of education in the South," college authorities asked plaintively, "build upon this foundation a worthy colleague of the colleges for women in the North, equaling them in faculties for culture, while preserving the Southern type of womanhood?"[48]

Students at private schools generally came from wealthier homes than students at public institutions, but their academic backgrounds were often equally poor. Institutions tried to "compensate" for these educational deficiencies by organizing preparatory schools or by diluting the requirements for the baccalaureate degree. Like the public colleges, private institutions relied on fees from preparatory departments and from special music and art students for income to support their collegiate programs. Few schools in the South, lacking the students, the faculties, and the facilities of their Northern counterparts, were able to maintain the rigorous standards of the women's colleges in the Northeast. As late as 1903, only two Southern women's colleges—Randolph-Macon and Goucher (then the Woman's College of Baltimore)—offered "four years of college work."[49]

The education provided by the other institutions varied tremendously. Some "colleges" were actually elementary and secondary schools; others were "finishing" schools; and still others were "vocational" schools of some sort. Most private women's colleges added special "women's subjects" to the traditional liberal arts curriculum of the men's colleges. Col-

32

legiate students at Converse College in South Carolina in the 1890s, for example, could choose between a classical *artium baccalaureatus* (A.B.) degree and a bachelor of English (B.E.) degree that substituted additional courses in English and modern languages for courses in a classical language and literature. In addition, the college provided "Special Schools of Music, Art, Expression, Physical Culture and Medicine," as well as "Full classes in Telegraphy, Stenography, Book-Keeping and Type-Writing."[50]

33

To compete with the vocational attractions of the state normal and industrial institutes, many private liberal arts colleges for women advertised the utilitarian nature of their course work. "The young woman who returns from a four years' course in college unfitted by her mental attainments for any useful work is a failure," one 1899 catalog from a private, denominational college proclaimed. "Only that education which impresses our women with the dignity of labor and makes them helpful in their homes and to their fellows should be recognized as Christian education." The catalog went on to assure prospective students that they could find a "practical" curriculum at a liberal arts institution: "Noble young women of North Carolina avail yourselves of this opportunity to be at least partially self-supporting and independent and to develop a love for domestic pursuits."[51]

The overwhelming majority of Southern women's "colleges" at the turn of the century were "colleges" in name only. When the Baptist convention in North Carolina voted to charter an institution for the higher education of women in the state in 1891, they decided to call their school "The Baptist Female University" to avoid the frivolous connotation associated with the title "college." "Our state and the South," the editor of the *Biblical Recorder* wrote, are "afflicted with a great number of institutions which their superintendents choose to call colleges that are hardly worthy of the name of academies."[52]

Southern "colleges" allowed young women to spend too much time on nonacademic, "ornamental" subjects, John McBryde, a professor at Sweet Briar Institute (later College), in Virginia, complained in 1907. "If the education given in the Northern colleges for women was inclined to be too severely intellectual," McBryde wrote, "that offered in our Southern . . . 'female' institutes and seminaries tended to become too superficial." Southern schools were so dependent on student fees from art and music courses for their survival, McBryde concluded, that they gave such subjects an unwarranted prominence in the curriculum.[53]

To many white parents at the turn of the century, college was a place to shelter young women until they came of age for marriage, not a place to encourage intellectual development. Most students did not stay at college long enough to earn a degree.[54] Parents' unwillingness to take their daughters' education seriously also confounded efforts to maintain academic standards at many women's colleges. Administrators at Meredith College in North Carolina, thought it necessary to remind parents "that so long as students are in this institution they must be under our direction, and not that of their parents."[55]

Similar problems existed in Southern coeducational and men's colleges in the late nineteenth century. Because of the economic backwardness of the region and the scholastic deficiencies of the public schools, Southern institutions lagged behind their Northern counterparts in almost every measure of academic achievement.[56] "The term 'college,'" Vanderbilt University's Chancellor James H. Kirkland noted, was "broad and vague" and like " 'charity' . . . cover[ed] a multitude of sins."[57] There was virtually no regulation of degree-granting institutions in the region before World War I, and most state legislatures issued college charters to any individual or group willing to pay the requisite fee. Matriculation and graduation requirements varied tremendously from institution to institution. Even the best Southern schools lacked sufficient libraries and laboratories to undertake original research.

In 1895, spurred on by the faculty of Vanderbilt University in Tennessee, eight Southern universities organized the Association of Colleges and Preparatory (later Secondary) Schools of the Southern States in order to "elevate the standard of scholarship and to effect uniformity of entrance requirements." The organization sought to improve secondary education in the region so that preparatory work could be "cut off" from the colleges. This would enable institutions of higher education to focus on collegiate instruction. The association developed a list of guidelines to evaluate schools and colleges and admitted only approved institutions to membership.[58]

One of the major achievements of the Association of Colleges in the years before 1920 was its definition of a college. To be ranked as a "standard college" by the organization's accrediting body, an institution had to meet seventeen specific criteria. Students had to present fourteen standard high school units for admission and complete four full years of liberal arts and science courses for graduation. At least 75 percent of all college students had to be enrolled in courses leading to a baccalaureate degree. Faculty had to hold a master's degree or a doctorate from a recognized college or university, and full professors had to be paid a minimum salary of $1,500. Students, faculty, and buildings of preparatory schools had to be separated from those of the college. Institutions had to employ at least one professor per college department and to maintain at least eight departments offering liberal arts subjects. Schools had to possess a productive endowment of at least $200,000. Additional regulations mandated a maximum class size and teaching load, a minimum level of equipment for classrooms and laboratories, and a minimum number of library books.[59]

Only five Southern women's colleges—Agnes Scott, Converse, Florida State, Goucher, and Randolph-Macon—and two coordinate colleges—H. Sophie Newcomb and Westhampton—were able to meet the criteria for accreditation established by the Association of Colleges in 1917. Most institutions of higher education for women had far more students enrolled in their preparatory departments and in special art and music courses than in their liberal arts programs. Generally speaking, women's colleges faced greater financial difficulties than men's colleges or coeducational institutions in the region. Because of low endowments, they found it impossible to provide adequate facilities for students or to pay for well-trained faculties. Thus a number of women's college alumnae decided to found their own organization, one that would focus on the special concerns of Southern women.

The Southern Association of College Women (SACW) was organized during a summer school session for white teachers held at the University of Tennessee in July 1903. The seventeen charter members who had gathered together to discuss "Southern educational problems" included women who had graduated from both Northern and Southern colleges but who were all living in the South. They were upset by the fact that many Southern colleges for women were nothing more than "finishing" schools, and they wanted to improve educational opportunities for young women in the region. Although an Association of Collegiate Alumnae (later the American Association of University Women) had been in existence since 1882, SACW wanted to concentrate on regional issues.[60]

The aims of the SACW paralleled those of the Association of Southern Colleges and Preparatory Schools. Whereas the latter talked of organizing Southern institutions "for cooperation and mutual assistance," the former wished "to unite college women in the South for the higher education of women." The Association of Colleges focused on raising the general standard at Southern schools, SACW on raising "the standard of education for women." Both organizations wanted to improve secondary education and to separate preparatory schools from the colleges.[61]

One of the first goals of SACW was to determine the type and quality of education available at Southern colleges for women. This unenviable task fell to Elizabeth Avery Colton, a professor of English at Meredith College, who was elected chair of the Committee on Standards in 1910. Between 1910 and 1917, Colton single-handedly investigated 142 institutions of higher education for white women in the region. She read catalogs and promotional materials, toured campuses, interviewed administrators, studied financial reports, compiled lists of faculties and students, and then evaluated schools according to the criteria established by the Association of Colleges. Her findings were published by SACW and distributed to prospective students.[62]

Colton believed that the attempt by "Southern colleges for women to be everything combined—preparatory school, finishing school, and college"—hindered the development of academic standards in the region. She found that many schools admitted students of all ages and abilities. Beaumont College in Kentucky, for example, employed only three faculty members to teach all the school's preparatory and collegiate courses. Such a task would have been overwhelming for even the best-trained professors, but these individuals possessed no degrees, Colton noted, only "a gracious personality, dignified bearing, and exquisite courtesy."[63]

The practice of calling "private secondary schools, 'special study' schools, and normal schools" colleges, Colton argued, led many students to "mistake nominal colleges for real colleges."[64] In a letter sent out to North Carolina high school students in 1915, Colton stressed the importance of attending a standard college and listed the approved institutions in the South that were open to women. North Carolina women who wanted to go to a standard college in the state had only one choice—Trinity (later Duke University)—because none of the women's colleges in North Carolina belonged to the Association of Colleges of the Southern States and the university at Chapel Hill did not accept women until their junior year.[65]

37

Unfortunately for prospective students, many institutions falsely claimed to be "standard colleges" or to "duplicate the work of the best Eastern colleges." The promotional catalogs from such schools, Colton warned, often looked more like photograph albums than academic bulletins. Instead of listing faculty credentials and describing the collegiate curriculum, they featured "pictures of class day exercises, of basket ball squads, of tennis teams, of glee clubs, of 'merriment' clubs, of 'al fresco scenes' from various plays," and similar attractions.[66]

Colton hoped that the publication of her findings would not only encourage colleges "to improve their standards" but would also "educate public opinion to such an extent that nominal colleges [would] be ridiculed out of existence."[67] To concentrate the region's resources where they would do the most good, Colton advocated reducing the total number of institutions of higher education and applying the name "college" only to four-year liberal arts institutions that met the standards of the Association of Colleges.[68]

The SACW established a Committee on College Clubs and College Days to publicize the findings of its Standards Committee. SACW branches organized annual programs known as "College Days" where prospective college students and their parents learned about the benefits of a college education, the nature of college life, and the advantages of a standard college. Special "College Clubs" composed of alumnae from a single institution provided similar information about their individual alma maters.[69] Committees on scholarships and on loan funds established special accounts that enabled Southern women of modest means to attend standard colleges. Individual branch clubs also granted their own scholarships. By 1915 some seventy scholarships, varying in amount from $75 to $300, were offered through SACW. Loan funds were introduced to supplement the organization's scholarships.[70]

Efforts by progressive educators such as McIver and Colton were successful in reducing illiteracy rates in the region. The percentage of illiterates in the Southern population dropped drastically between 1900 and 1920. In North Carolina, illiteracy rates dropped from 28.7 percent in 1900 to 18.5 percent in 1910 and to 13.1 percent in 1920. For women in the state, the improvement was even more dramatic. Whereas 29.9 percent of women in North Carolina were illiterate in 1900 and 18.7 percent in 1910, the figure had dropped to 12.5 percent in 1920. For the first time in census records, the illiteracy rate for women in the state was lower than that for men.[71]

Despite the many improvements in white women's higher education by 1920, education reform shared many of the shortcomings of other social programs in the progressive era. Educators did little to challenge chivalric images of Southern womanhood. Progressive reforms, as C. Vann Woodward has argued, involved "no basic alteration of social, racial, and economic arrangements." Historian Edward L. Ayers described most Southern colleges in the early twentieth century as "awkwardly pinned between the weight of the past and the pull of the future." Dewey Grantham similarly concluded that women—like blacks—were only "marginal beneficiaries of the movement to develop higher education."[72] Certainly more women were able to attend college than ever before, but the choice of programs open to them remained narrow. By arguing that women were the "natural teacher[s] of the race," McIver and other reformers both extended and circumscribed the professional horizons of educated Southern women. Maternal metaphors encouraged women to leave the home for the school and to contribute in a public way to the well-being of their communities.[73] But such language also perpetuated the social segregation of Southern society by suggesting that inherited rather than acquired characteristics determined an individual's suitability for employment. Assumptions about women's nature could and would be used to close as well as to open the doors of opportunity.

Education reform left the racial "settlement" of the turn of the century unchallenged at all educational levels. For blacks, Anne Firor Scott noted in her study of women's associations, "the progressive era" was a "nadir."[74] The gap between white and black schools widened in the years between 1890 and 1920. Black illiteracy rates declined after 1890, but they remained abysmally high. More than 25 percent of blacks living in the South were still illiterate in 1920.[75]

None of the reforms instituted by the Association of Southern Colleges and Secondary Schools or by SACW were aimed at black women or schools. Neither organization had black members or evaluated black institutions before 1920. African Americans were not admitted to the public normal and industrial institutes or to the state universities. In fact, the "educational awakening" of the turn of the century had a distinctly different impact on black Southerners.

At the elementary level, much of the money obtained in the early education campaigns of Northern philanthropists and Southern progressives was funneled into white, urban schools. Schools for rural blacks and whites remained poor throughout the region. Even the General Education Board "refrained from active involvement with black schools until 1910." Not until the Anna T. Jeanes Foundation directors encouraged African Americans to conduct their own campaign for school improvement did philanthropic funds find their way into the coffers of the black rural schools.[76]

Few black institutions of higher education offered an exclusively collegiate curriculum. A Bureau of Education study of black higher education conducted by Thomas Jesse Jones between 1912 and 1916 found that the overwhelming majority of black "colleges" in the South were, in effect, elementary and secondary schools. Jones concluded that even under a "liberal interpretation of college work, only 33 of the 653 private and State schools for colored people are teaching any subjects of college grade." Only Howard University in Washington and Fisk University and Meharry Medical College in Nashville had the "student body, teaching force, equipment, and income sufficient to warrant the characterization of 'college.' "[77]

One reason for the prevalence of precollegiate courses at black institutions of higher education was the low level of public assistance for black elementary and secondary schools in the region. In Mississippi, for example, blacks received 19 percent of the money allocated for public schools at the beginning of the twentieth century; yet they made up 60 percent of the school-age population. In Mississippi, as well as in several other Southern states, "black" money paid for "white" schools. African Americans who wanted their children educated often had to resort to private tuition. As late as 1916, there was no four-year public high school in the entire state of Mississippi. If it were not for the private education provided by the black colleges, many black children in the South would have gone uneducated.[78]

Modern equipment, qualified faculty, adequate facilities, and new programs all cost money, and most black colleges, like most women's colleges, were chronically short of funds. Offers of financial aid for black institutions often came with "strings attached." Most of the trusts established for black education—such as the Peabody Fund, the Slater Fund, the Anna T. Jeanes Foundation, and the Phelps-Stokes Fund—were administered by the General Education Board in conjunction with the advice and consent of the Southern Education Board, and the Northern industrialists and Southern educators on these boards overwhelmingly favored "the Hampton-Tuskegee program of industrial training."[79]

White Progressives argued that industrial education would promote "individual moral development" and inculcate the "habits of work and self-discipline which blacks as a race allegedly lacked." African American reformers saw such programs as a means to gain white support for black schools.[80] A desire to placate white philanthropists even led some black liberal arts colleges to emphasize practical subjects and public outreach. Schools that "showed the most vivid signs of following this pattern," one historian noted, "were given the greatest share of the money which had begun to flow South and into the Negro schools at the opening of our century."[81]

Not all educators who supported industrial education accepted white views of black inferiority, and reformers such as Lucy Craft Laney, Nannie Burroughs, and Mary McLeod Bethune were able to make industrial training serve a very different purpose than that envisioned by white racists. Often "called the most important female black educator of the progressive era," Lucy Craft Laney became a teacher after graduating from Atlanta University in 1873. With help from her family, friends, and church, she opened her own school, the Haines Normal and Industrial Institute in Augusta, Georgia, in 1896. Although she originally intended to admit only girls, she made the school coeducational when boys showed up for classes. Laney shared the belief of white Progressives such as McIver that the education of women was the best means of elevating the entire population, but she did not think it was only the white woman or child who had been "for-

gotten" by the educational system. In her opinion, it was the black community that most needed the elevating influence of educated women. As she
told an audience at the Hampton Negro Conference in 1899, educated
women "would prescribe: homes—better homes, clean homes, pure homes;
schools—better schools; more culture; more thrift; and work in large
doses." In Laney's view, schools were instruments of intellectual enrichment, economic growth, and social welfare. Her students, women such as
Mary McLeod Bethune and Charlotte Brown Hawkins, were inspired to
use their education to improve themselves and their race.[82]

41

Mary McLeod Bethune's school in Daytona, Florida, strongly encouraged students to become involved in community service. Bethune, a
native of Mayesville, South Carolina, and a graduate of Scotia Academy in
North Carolina, opened her Daytona Literary and Industrial Institute for
the Training of Negro Girls in October 1904 in a rented cottage furnished
with chairs and linen from the city dump. She raised the funds to buy a lot
for the campus by "selling ice cream and sweet potato pies to the workmen
on construction jobs." Money for tuition fees was used for teacher salaries
and facilities; Bethune "wore old clothes sent . . . by mission boards, recut
and redesigned . . . in . . . dress-making classes." As a result of Bethune's
efforts, the institute expanded to include high school, junior college, and
nursing courses, and a hospital and a normal school. In 1923 the women's
school merged with the all-male Cookman Institute in Jacksonville to become a four-year liberal arts institution, Bethune-Cookman College.
Looking back in 1941 at her creation, Bethune noted proudly that the college had "enriched the lives of 100,000 Negroes."[83]

Recognizing the need for a school to prepare young women for careers as "missionaries, Sunday school teachers, stenographers, bookkeepers, musicians, cooks, laundresses, [and] housemaids," Nannie Burroughs,
secretary of the Woman's Auxiliary of the National Baptist Convention,
was instrumental in establishing the National Training School for Women
and Girls (NTS), which began classes in Washington, D.C., in October
1909. Designed to prepare black women for "effective service in slum, social settlement, reformatory and missionary work," the NTS offered the
equivalent of a high school and junior college education and combined academic with religious and vocational education.[84]

Burroughs was criticized for confining women to traditional domestic vocations and for putting too much emphasis on the "Three B's" (Bible, bath, and broom), but her advocacy of racial pride and community solidarity was considerably in advance of the times. She worked tirelessly to raise funds for the school from the black community so that the institution would not be dependent on white charity. She required students to take a course in African American history so that they would be familiar with their own people and past. She wrote editorial after editorial on racial issues for the school newspaper, *The Worker.* When Woodrow Wilson's presidency led to the segregation of public accommodations in Washington, D.C., she told students to boycott the buses and come to class on bicycles or roller skates instead. Burroughs's NTS stressed the importance of working together as a group to improve racial relations in the community and in the nation.[85]

Philanthropic efforts such as Bethune's and Burroughs's were necessary because there were so few public schools above the elementary level for black women in the years before 1920. Southern states were slow to establish institutions of higher education for African Americans, and no state ever established a college solely for black women. Opportunities for a public education in a coeducational institution were also limited. The federal government had set up Howard University in 1867 "for the education of youth in the liberal arts and sciences," but only Mississippi, South Carolina, and Virginia took advantage of the first Morrill Act of 1862 to fund agricultural and mechanical schools for blacks.[86]

The majority of public colleges for African Americans were founded as a consequence of the second Morrill Act of 1890, which required states to use moneys from the sale of public lands to establish agricultural and mechanical schools for both races. Some states gave their black "share" of land-grant funds to existing institutions; others created new schools. Seventeen land-grant colleges were opened for African Americans by 1914. All were coeducational, and in these early years, there were more African American women attending land-grant institutions than African American men. The popularity of such schools among black women was due to their normal courses. Until the 1920s, the two-year teachers' programs offered by the land-grant colleges and the state normal schools were the highest level of public education provided for black women in the South.[87]

In addition to teacher training, land-grant institutions were supposed to provide agricultural and mechanical education for their students. But black students rarely received the "advanced college level technical and agricultural training" given to their counterparts in white schools. In fact, no black land-grant school offered baccalaureate programs before World War I. Students were trained instead "for an agricultural economy in which employment had begun to shrink even before the curricular programs were well under way."[88]

Alabama was the first state to charter a public normal school for African Americans when it appropriated funds for a private school at Marion in 1873 to provide teacher-training instruction. The school eventually became the Alabama State Teachers College. North Carolina also provided for the public education of black teachers. In 1877, the same year the state instituted a summer school for white teachers at the university at Chapel Hill, the legislature established a year-long normal school for African Americans in Fayetteville. Pupils promised to teach three years in the public schools of the state in return for their education.[89]

A number of states and counties established public normal schools for blacks at the turn of the twentieth century, but these teacher-training programs included few collegiate courses. Most normal institutions were essentially secondary schools, and county training schools often provided only an advanced elementary education. Students could enter the Virginia Normal and Industrial Institute, for example, after completing the sixth grade. Requirements for county training schools were even less rigid. After a few courses in educational methods and a general review of common school subjects, graduates were considered "qualified" to teach in the rural areas.[90]

Mississippi was one of the worst offenders when it came to the education of black youth and the preparation of black teachers. Governor James K. Vardaman closed the state's only black normal school in 1904, and from then until 1940 there was no publicly funded institution dedicated to the education of black teachers. There was some normal training available at Alcorn Agricultural and Mechanical College, but the school was inconveniently located for most black Mississippians. Private institutions tried to compensate for the shortcomings in public education. The "single greatest contribution" of Tougaloo College, Neil McMillen has argued in his study of Jim Crow Mississippi, "was the training of qualified black teachers." A liberal arts institution founded by the American Missionary Association in 1869, Tougaloo eventually became the first black institution in Mississippi to be accredited by the Southern Association of Colleges and Schools. Its graduates received a thorough classical education along with their teacher training. But Tougaloo could not meet the needs of all the black Mississippians who wanted to become teachers. The lack of a publicly supported normal college meant that the majority of black teachers in Mississippi did not have access to a college education.[91]

Because of the great demand for teachers, most black industrial schools were also teacher training institutions. A department of education official described Hampton Institute in 1914 as a "vocational school of secondary grade, preparing teachers of academic, industrial, and agricultural subjects and supervisors of county industrial-school work." Women in advanced courses at Hampton were offered two programs: an academic-normal course for those wishing to teach in the public schools and a home economics course "for those desiring special training as teachers of girls' industries."[92]

The academic component of Hampton's teacher training program was gradually strengthened in the first decades of the century, and in 1922 the institution offered its first B.S. degree in education. Most alumnae of Hampton became teachers—and social activists. Students were encouraged to use their education for racial uplift. A questionnaire sent to graduates in 1922 asked, "What are you doing in addition to your regular employment to help your community?" Janie Porter Barrett, a Hampton graduate and the first president of the Virginia Federation of Colored Women's Clubs, recalled that she did not always appreciate Hampton's emphasis on racial responsibility: "At the Institute [Hampton], we were always hearing about our duty to our race, and I got so tired of that! Why, on Sundays I used to wake up and say to myself, 'Today I don't have to do a single thing for my race.' "[93] Hampton graduates such as Barrett contributed immensely to Southern progressivism even though their alma maters were not recognized as standard colleges in the years before 1920.

Southern black women had fewer opportunities to obtain a liberal arts education in the Progressive Era than Southern white women. There were no private colleges for black women before World War I. The first "female seminary" for blacks was Scotia, founded in Concord, North

Carolina, in 1867 and directed by the Presbyterian Board of Missions for Freedmen. Although Scotia was known for "the high grade of its work," its only advanced courses were in teacher training. Bennett, a coeducational institution in Greensboro, North Carolina, which would become a women's college in 1926, had no college students before 1920.[94]

The Atlanta Baptist Female Seminary (later Spelman Seminary and College) was established in 1881 by Sophia Packard and Harriet Giles, two New England Baptists who came South after the war "to provide training for teachers, missionaries, and church workers." From the beginning, Spelman instructed young women in both literary subjects and practical skills—the former to "build teachers and leaders of the race" and the latter to "make black women good homemakers and mothers." Spelman did not offer the traditional, classical curriculum of the white women's colleges in the years before 1920, although it did share their interest in the fine arts and in general "culture."[95] Most Spelman graduates became teachers, and Spelman's teacher training program was one of the first in the South to require applicants to be high school graduates.[96]

The majority of African American women seeking a higher education in the South attended a coeducational school rather than a women's college, received vocational or normal training rather than a liberal arts education, and enrolled in a private and denominational college rather than a public and nondenominational school. As late as 1916, 80 percent of the secondary schools and colleges for African Americans were "owned by church boards and private boards of trustees." Few black women earned bachelor's degrees. In 1900, for instance, there were 606 women enrolled as college students in black institutions of higher education but only 22 college graduates.[97]

The predominance of private, denominational schools had both positive and negative effects on the educational experience of black women in the years before 1920. The strict moral codes and rigid discipline of the denominational colleges seldom encouraged independent thought or action. Yet educators' belief in spiritual equality often led them to support social equality as well, and racial and gender attitudes at black denominational colleges were far ahead of those at white institutions. The first woman to be promoted to full professor at a coeducational institution, for example, was Helen C. Morgan, a professor of Latin at Fisk University, an AMA college in Nashville. Fisk also boasted the first women to receive bachelor of arts degrees from a Southern liberal arts college.[98]

Black denominational colleges were the first schools in the nation to hire black faculty and the first in the South to be integrated. Berea College, founded by the AMA before the Civil War, was open to black and white students alike until the Kentucky legislature passed a law in 1904 "forbidding the mingling of the races in the same department of any institution of learning."[99] Children of white faculty attended Fisk University in the late nineteenth century. Mary Spence, a white woman who received her bachelor and master of arts degrees from Fisk at the turn of the twentieth century, served the school for many years as professor of Greek. Her father, Adam Spence, was a well-known advocate of civil rights, and Mary Spence followed proudly in his footsteps. She was one of the few older faculty to side with the students when they revolted against the repressive social policies of President McKenzie in 1924.[100]

Missionary teachers imparted a "strong sense of service" to their students. Mamie Garvin Fields, a normal student at Methodist Claflin College in South Carolina in the early twentieth century, recalled that her professors always told student teachers to consider the "condition" of the children they would be teaching and to help those who were in need. African American students at denominational colleges such as Claflin were encouraged to do the Lord's work wherever they found themselves. When Garvin's parents refused to give her permission to go to Africa as a missionary, she "decided to be that missionary right in South Carolina" and set off to teach in a one-room schoolhouse on rural John's Island.[101]

Segregation of educational facilities separated blacks from whites, but it also united blacks in a common effort to improve their own schools and communities. African American educators from all over the South joined together in the years before World War I to discuss their mutual problems and to raise academic standards at black colleges. In 1909 a number of schools organized the Association of Colleges for Negro Youth to assess teacher-training programs for African Americans. In 1913 administrators at Atlanta, Fisk, Howard, and Virginia Union universities and at Knoxville, Morehouse, and Talladega colleges agreed on uniform requirements for their institutions. College women also came together to share their mutual concerns. In 1910 African American women founded the

College Alumnae Club of Washington, D.C., to encourage young women in the city to seek a college education. After World War I the group expanded into the National Association of College Women (NACW), an African American equivalent of the American Association of University Women. "Raising the status of women's education was the raison d'etre of the NACW," one woman wrote.[102]

African American women founded numerous organizations aimed at improving black schools in the region in the years before World War I, but, as Jacqueline Rouse discovered in her study of the Women's Civic and Social Improvement Committee in Atlanta, they often received little support from white women. In fact, Rouse concluded that progressivism, instead of uniting various segments of the Atlanta community in an all-out effort to better life in the city, "became a major component in promoting white supremacy and solidarity and in maintaining African American subordination and intimidation."[103] White supremacy did serve, however, to unite various segments of the black community. In her biography of Lugenia Burns Hope, Rouse described how the Atlanta race riots of 1906 prompted educated, middle-class blacks to join with the city's masses in an attempt to provide educational, medical, recreational, and municipal services for blacks in the city. The Neighborhood Union, organized by Hope and other college women in 1908, had as its motto "Thy Neighbor as Thyself."[104]

In other communities throughout the South, educated black and white women did come together to work for temperance, to clean up the town, to improve public health, and to support the war effort. Although the first attempts at racial cooperation for social reform were often marred by white women's patronizing treatment of black women, repeated contact between educated women of both races led to increased respect for and recognition of black women's abilities and accomplishments. As Glenda Gilmore has shown in her examination of progressive reforms in various North Carolina towns, "Contacts between white and black women with progressive agendas set the groundwork for inclusion of African Americans in formal social service structures" and laid the foundation for the interracial movement of the post–World War I period.[105]

World War I was in many ways a turning point for Southern blacks. African Americans had helped make the world "safe for democracy," but no one seemed concerned that America was not "safe for black Americans."[106] In a 1922 speech at a home missions conference, Charlotte Hawkins Brown, principal of the Alice Freeman Palmer School for Negro Girls in North Carolina, complained that there was "a deeper chasm between the educated black women and the white women of today than between the black and white women of the Old South." Although black women had joined enthusiastically in the volunteer efforts of the war years, white women did not want anything to do with them when the war was over. "The Negro woman does not seek to push herself into the society of the whites," Brown explained, "but she does feel a right to demand the enjoyments to which she is entitled by high education. The Negro woman wants everything a white woman wants, except a white husband."[107] As Brown's speech indicated, racism continued to limit the personal and professional horizons of African American women, regardless of their education.

Progressive educators did little to ameliorate racial inequalities. To the contrary, college preparatory courses for blacks in Georgia were "denounced . . . in the name of 'democracy.' " The acceptance of "woman's higher education, itself a liberal reform," Lynn Gordon noted in her study of women's education in the Progressive Era, likewise "did not lead to a reexamination of racial ideology."[108] The seeds of interracial cooperation sown by educated Southern women in the years before 1920 would take many years to bear fruit.

The reforms that were implemented in the white colleges of the South between 1890 and 1920 would be begun in the black colleges of the region in the 1920s. Whereas public school reform and college standardization had practically eliminated elementary and secondary students from white institutions by 1920, 85 percent of the students in black colleges were still enrolled in precollegiate programs in 1922. One reason for the slower pace of collegiate reform at black institutions of higher education was, of course, the inadequate provision of public moneys for black elementary and secondary schools. It was not until after World War I that the philanthropic agencies and Southern state legislators began "to give serious attention to plans for the systematic and rational improvement of Negro education all along the line." The Southern Association of Colleges had established criteria for defining and accrediting standard colleges in 1917, but it did not begin rating black colleges in the region until 1930.[109] The efforts of educated black women helped make these reforms possible.

White progressives advocated social reform but not social equality. Educational improvements often reflected the middle-class biases of reformers. Most members of the North Carolina Woman's Association for the Betterment of Public School Houses, for instance, were more concerned "with aesthetics and environmental purity and . . . outward appearances of poverty . . . than [with] the inequities from which it grew."[110] Poverty was blamed on poor land management, lazy housekeeping, and low ambitions rather than on a regressive social, economic, and political structure. The public agricultural and industrial colleges that had originally been conceived as "farm-life schools where poor young men might acquire the rudiments of agriculture and some mechanical craft" and where poor farmers' daughters could gain a good practical education soon developed into "technical schools of professional pretensions if not rank" or liberal arts institutions much more attuned to the vocational interests of the upper than the lower classes.[111]

It is difficult to calculate the impact of Progressive Era reform on the faculty, staff, and student body of "nominal" colleges. Although those schools did not meet the certification criteria of the Association of Colleges, they were often the only educational institutions accessible to lower- and middle-class white women in the South. Colton hoped that standardization would eliminate inferior establishments, but she did not consider the plight of the individuals affected by those changes. How many faculty who did not possess the advanced degrees required by the association lost their jobs when their schools raised standards or closed? How many young women were unable to pursue a higher education because they could not meet the entrance requirements of the standard colleges?

Ironically, racism lessened the gender and class divisions among black progressives. As Jacqueline Rouse has noted, "[C]aste disabilities were color-blind." Rouse described Lugenia Burns Hope as typical of the middle-class black women "who were members of a privileged class, yet who used their time, influence, prestige, and contacts to advance their race." Racism made these elite black women sensitive to discrimination in all its forms—racial, sexual, and social. Rouse concluded that "Black female reformers became national spokespersons for societal changes by challenging factors that limited them as women and especially as Blacks. . . . They emerged not only as Progressives but even more as race people."[112]

Progressive educational developments reflected the "double consciousness" of Southern culture. State universities and professional schools continued to discriminate against women and blacks; yet these were the institutions that were transforming the nature of American education in the years before 1920.[113] Educational standards meant different things for men and women, whites and blacks, rich and poor. Southern women, regardless of their economic or racial background, were trained primarily as teachers or housewives. Regardless of their sex or economic background, blacks were expected to serve the needs of white and black America. Poorer women of both races were steered into industrial and normal programs.

Charles McIver had justified the higher education of women by arguing that such training benefited society, not just the individual. Progressive educators had built on this traditional view of women's education. Women were to be educated for their families, not for themselves. They were to become better mothers, better housekeepers, better public-school teachers. Few proponents of higher education suggested that education might make them better professionals or leaders.[114] Yet some Southern women employed these very same cultural prescriptions to justify their social activism. As an examination of the curricula offered women at Southern colleges and universities in the early twentieth century will reveal, the "double consciousness" of Southern culture continued to affect the educational experiences of Southern women well into the twentieth century.

2

A Lady, a Scholar, and a Citizen

The Impact of Nineteenth-Century Plantation
Ideology on the Curricula of Twentieth-Century
Southern Colleges[1]

Concepts of race, gender, and class associated with the antebellum
plantation permeated educational philosophies and practices in
the South in the first half of the twentieth century. Progressive reforms
had created new educational opportunities for both black and white women
but had done little to challenge traditional notions of womanhood. The di-
chotomy between the progressive ideology of the New South and the regressive imagery of the Old posed problems for students, educators, and
institutions. Should schools factor different societal expectations for men
and women, blacks and whites, rich and poor into their educational programs? What courses should be taught to whom at what type of institution
and to what purpose? Could higher education relieve women of the burdens of the plantation past and prepare them for the challenges of the present and the future? The double consciousness of Southern culture pre-
cluded simple answers to these questions and complicated curricular
discussions at the normal schools, colleges, and universities of the region in
the years between 1900 and 1960.

The debate over what constituted a proper education for women and
for blacks was not confined to the South. Throughout the United States,
economic, political, and social developments in the years after World War
I raised questions about the efficacy of higher education in preparing youth
for the realities of American life. The passage of the nineteenth amendment in 1920 led to a demand that women be educated for their new political roles. At the same time, sociological studies of alumnae from women's

colleges criticized these institutions for breeding spinsters, contributing to "race suicide," and neglecting the family. The Harlem Renaissance of the twenties challenged many of the racial stereotypes on which the curriculum of black colleges and universities was predicated. The agricultural crises of the twenties and the Great Depression of the thirties brought to light another weakness in women's education—it did not prepare them for the harsh realities of economic life. In response to these changing conditions, educational institutions sought to design a pedagogy that would provide for the "new women" who participated in the economic and political as well as the social life of the country.

For much of the twentieth century, the South was more rural and less affluent than the rest of the United States, and Southern educators had to consider these economic factors in fashioning their institutional missions and setting their educational priorities. Political conditions were also different in the South. The enfranchisement of women in the twenties came on the heels of the vast disenfranchisement of black persons. Thus it was much more difficult for black women than for white women to use legislative pressure to effect changes in their communities. Segregation effectively barred black women from regional branches of national reform organizations and programs. It also meant insufficient funds and inferior facilities for black schools and communities. As a consequence, African Americans had to create and finance their own social welfare systems. Educated black women were expected not only to improve themselves but also to elevate the race.[2]

African Americans seeking a higher education had to contend with insults to their character and capabilities from pseudoscientific studies that claimed to document the intellectual and moral deficiencies of the race. Even white "friends," such as General S. C. Armstrong, the creator of Hampton Institute, "regarded Blacks as childlike, lazy, slothful, and in need of the most rigid and civilizing discipline."[3] African American women had to refute both racial and sexual slurs: a white writer in the woman's magazine *The Independent*, for example, claimed that she could not "conceive of such a creation as a virtuous black woman."[4]

For Southern white women, the disagreement over educational means and ends was complicated by the plantation ideal of a lady. The concept of an educated woman, North Carolina journalist Nell Battle Lewis explained in 1925, was "inconsistent with the chivalric ideal." It was more than mere coincidence, Lewis argued, that the higher education of women "was slower in gaining a foothold in this section than in the North." She also saw a connection between the elevation of white women and the debasement of black women: "In Southern chivalry, the queen and the concubine were inseparably connected. The same system produced them both." The heritage of slavery kept women of both races from achieving their full potential as human beings.[5]

53

What role should higher education play in enabling women to achieve their full potential as human beings? There was no consensus on the best curriculum to accomplish this task. Educational philosophy in the years between 1900 and 1960 seemed divided into two antithetical schools. The first, which I will label the traditionalist, had its roots in the determination of the founders of women's colleges to give women an education that was every bit as good as that provided for their brothers. This was the view of M. Carey Thomas, president of Bryn Mawr in the early years of the twentieth century and an inveterate champion of a rigorous and comprehensive liberal arts curriculum. Thomas insisted that women needed "the same intellectual training and the same scholarly and moral ideas" as men—there was "but one best education."[6] Traditionalists believed that the goal of education was the cultivation of the mind, and they expressed "no fear about womanly charm, no compunction about physical weakness, no anxiety about what might happen to puddings and pies when women became scholars."[7] To these advocates of the liberal arts, nothing was worse than an education that confined students to subjects or vocations based on gender stereotypes. As Dean Thompson of Vassar commented in a speech at the twenty-fifth anniversary of the founding of Georgia State Woman's College in 1938: "Man does not live by bread alone . . . nor does woman . . . by the baking of bread alone."[8]

The best known African American advocate of this traditionalist view was W. E. B. Du Bois, an Atlanta University sociologist with a doctorate from Harvard University. Du Bois argued that "the first step toward lifting the submerged mass of black people in the South is through the higher training of the talented few." The most intelligent youth (or those he called the "talented tenth") needed an education that would prepare them to become the future leaders of their communities. And this meant the study of the liberal arts, "that part of human training which is devoted specifically and peculiarly into bringing the man into the fullest and roundest development of his powers as a human being."[9]

The traditional liberal arts curriculum at the beginning of the twentieth century emphasized classical studies and languages. For most A.B. degrees, students were required to take four years of Latin or Greek, two years of a modern language, four years of English, two years of history, and a year or more of math and science.[10] Because the degree programs at men's colleges had centered on classical subjects ever since the founding of the first European universities in the Middle Ages, many institutions for women and black persons were hesitant to depart from what had been accepted as the standard college curriculum.

The second school of thought had nothing against intellectual rigor or cultural enrichment; its advocates simply preferred an education that was useful, one that prepared women for life outside the cloister of the college. Inspired by John Dewey's efforts to unite education and experience, utilitarians wanted the curriculum to reflect women's peculiar life experiences. As President Charles Eliot of Harvard explained, "[T]he prime motive of the higher education of women should be . . . the development in women of the capacities and powers which will fit them to make family life and social life more intelligent, more enjoyable, happier, and more productive."[11]

Proponents of a utilitarian curriculum wanted women to be taught the art of motherhood, the science of homemaking, the psychology of child care, and the sociology of the family as well as Renaissance culture, Latin grammar, and Shakespearean sonnets. In case they should have to support themselves, women should be offered normal and industrial courses that prepared them for "female" professions. Utilitarians accused traditionalists of elitism, of forgetting that most graduates had to raise a family, earn a living, or both, and that a liberal arts education offered little preparation for either.

Booker T. Washington, a graduate of Hampton Institute and the founder of Tuskegee Institute, argued that industrial education was eminently practical for African Americans who had just come out of slavery. In a speech at the Atlanta Exposition of 1895, Washington told blacks to "cast down your bucket where you are" and advised them to improve their knowledge of the agricultural and mechanical trades that had been their province on the plantation. The best education for African Americans, he argued, was one that enabled them to meet the economic demands of the times.[12]

Some educators advocated a curriculum that combined traditional humanities courses and contemporary vocational offerings. In a commencement address at Hampton, Dr. Alain Locke insisted that African Americans needed knowledge of both the liberal and practical arts if black communities in the segregated South were to be self-sustaining: "[T]he education of the Negro is not a conflict between two theories of education, or two kinds of education, but is a mutually supplementary program of the collegiate professional and collegiate economic, technical and vocational with the important field of teacher training and social service training harmoniously balanced and divided between them."[13]

Southern institutions of higher education were very much part of the national debate over curriculum, and no one pedagogical view was dominant. The extent to which colleges adopted a traditionalist or utilitarian curriculum depended largely—but not entirely—on the social and racial composition of the student body. Moreover, all schools, regardless of the overall emphasis of their curriculum, added special courses and programs that satisfied regional conceptions of a woman's nature and of a college's purpose. The "double consciousness" of Southern culture was apparent in the curricular offerings of every type of educational institution.

White private and church-affiliated women's colleges seldom offered any professional or vocational courses at all, preferring to emphasize instead a general education that provided "an enriching heritage for life."[14] At the same time, however, these schools were careful to complement their "masculine" liberal arts curriculum with a "feminine" atmosphere conducive to ladylike deportment and cultured elegance. Statements of purpose from college catalogs of the twenties and thirties reflected these dual concerns. For instance, the Queens-Chicora College Bulletin of 1930 noted that its curriculum contained "the substantial features of a broad, liberal education . . . especially adapted to the needs and desires of cultured womanhood."[15] Randolph-Macon Woman's College began every catalog in the interwar years with a statement from its nineteenth-century founders:

> We wish to establish in Virginia a college where our young women may obtain an education equal to that given in our best colleges for young men, and under environments in harmony with the highest ideals of womanhood; where the dignity and strength of fully-developed faculties and the charm of the highest literary culture may be acquired by our daughters without loss to woman's crowning glory—her gentleness and grace.[16]

Many of the adaptations made by liberal arts institutions to the demands of cultured womanhood were extracurricular. Colleges established regulations to ensure that student life resembled that in "the best homes of the State."[17] Parental permission was required for women to leave campus, to date, or to smoke. Hours were set for study and "lights out." Activities were designed to teach etiquette and ethics. Teas and formal dances provided practice in the social graces, while chapel services and convocations encouraged the development of spiritual and moral character.

Some aspects of the liberal arts curriculum meshed nicely with traditional concepts of womanhood. The Southern lady was noted for her piety, and courses in religion and ethics were an integral part of the curriculum at liberal arts colleges throughout the South. Judson, a Baptist college for women in Alabama, prescribed courses in the Bible and religion and required students "to attend chapel services every morning, and also Sunday School and the church of their parents' choice every Sunday." In addition, the college held daily morning watch and vesper services that students were encouraged to attend. Christian influences were fundamental, Judson's faculty argued, to preparing "young women for intelligent, cultured, and competent living."[18] Clarissa Kennedy Towell, who graduated from the College of Charleston in 1933, remembered compulsory chapel services during which students would "turn around and face the South" for prayers.[19]

The major curricular concessions to womanly graces occurred in the fine arts. Art, music, and expression, three favorite female subjects in the nineteenth century, survived the twentieth-century transformation of seminary into college. In 1908 Converse College in South Carolina became the first liberal arts college to allow courses in music and art to count toward an A.B. degree, and other schools in the South soon followed suit. The College of Industrial Arts became the first school in Texas to create a department of music, and in 1913 college officials declared that "there is probably no institution in this section of the country that can boast of a stronger department of fine arts."[20]

Few men's or coeducational institutions in the South or women's colleges in the North offered the musical opportunities of the Southern women's colleges. Elizabeth Avery Colton, chair of the standards committee of the Southern Association of College Women in the second decade of the twentieth century, complained that Southern women's colleges seemed determined to "compete with conservatories." Whereas one-tenth of the students at New York's Vassar College were studying music in 1911, three-fourths of the students at North Carolina's Greensboro Female College were. And although most Northern students of music were working on academic degrees, most Southern students were not.[21]

Art history was also a common elective among students at Southern women's colleges, and studio art courses were popular at land grant institutions with industrial arts programs. H. Sophie Newcomb, the women's coordinate college of Tulane University, and Florida State College for Women, a public college, both established separate schools of art in the first decades of the twentieth century. The art department of Newcomb, which had won third prize at the Paris exhibition of 1900 for several ceramic projects, was renowned for its pottery, and numerous Newcomb students sought a bachelor of design degree in the twenties and thirties—an unusual choice for liberal arts students elsewhere in the country.[22]

Most private women's colleges in the tens and twenties offered courses in expression to help the "shy, diffident girl," as Georgia's Cox College catalog explained, to develop personal charm and "a voice 'ever soft, gentle, and low.' "[23] Judson College reminded students that "[t]rue culture in women is more readily shown by their use of conversational English than in any form of vocal expression."[24] By the thirties, lessons in elocution were incorporated into standard English offerings, and dramatic presentations were limited to courses in theater and participation in May Day festivals. The art of expression nonetheless remained an integral component of the liberal arts curriculum. English was the most common subject pre-scribed for an A.B. degree and the most popular elective chosen by women in A.B. programs.[25]

58

The concession most often made by the liberal arts college to the utilitarian demand for educational relevance was an occasional course in home economics, education, or commerce. Converse College offered home economics as early as 1914 and in 1915 introduced a major in "Chemistry and Home Economics," which required four courses in the latter. In 1927, however, all home economics courses were discontinued. "Converse students," the school's historian remarked, "had shown no great interest in the practical arts."[26] Home economics suffered a similar fate at Agnes Scott in Georgia. In 1934 J. R. McCain, the college's president, proposed the estab-lishment of a department of the home where students could take courses in child psychology, nutrition, and household budgeting.[27] Neither faculty nor students at Agnes Scott seemed overly enthusiastic about McCain's plans, however, and the school continued to offer only a traditional bache-lor's degree.

Liberal arts institutions tended to view vocational training as pe-ripheral to the "real" work of the school. Salem College in North Carolina, for instance, offered business courses only to students who were not en-rolled in its baccalaureate programs. Judson College never considered its commerce courses as part of its academic curriculum, either, and in 1918 eliminated its business department completely. Wesleyan College in Georgia would not allow courses in education to count toward fulfillment of its major or minor requirements.[28]

Often students resented the introduction of vocational subjects, be-lieving that they distracted their peers from the finer things in life. An editorial in the Queen's College student newspaper criticizing the institu-tion's commercial course is indicative: "[I]t makes us fear that the colleges are going into the business of training our women for the business world rather than to make lasting contributions to society in the form of literary works or art treatises."[29]

The Queen's College editors need not have feared; in the years be-fore World War II, few liberal arts colleges considered courses in business, education, or home economics as central to their programs. In fact, many of these electives were added grudgingly in response to student requests, as evidenced from the comment in a Mary Baldwin catalog of the thirties: "Mary Baldwin is in no sense a vocational school but, recognizing the present day demand includes in the curriculum a number of vocational and pre-vocational courses for the benefit of those students who may desire them."[30] The student who desired too many courses in bookkeeping, cooking, or teaching was, the catalog implied, better off elsewhere.

Liberal arts majors often did go elsewhere to obtain their professional training. Kathleen ("Kay") White Schad, who majored in French at Judson, dreamed of a career as a librarian: "I can't help believing that I might be able to help a lot of people's lives by introducing books into them," she wrote in 1939. "I like to visualize myself bumping around the country in a book truck. These farmers spend hours inside in the winter when they would gladly accept any reading material. . . . [I]t should be rather easy to develop in them a real love for it. It requires professional training and the pay is pitifully meager, but I want to just the same." Because Judson did not offer any library courses, Kay spent her summers at Louisiana State University, working on a library degree. Eventually, she became Judson's head librarian.[31]

There were few utilitarian courses at coeducational liberal arts colleges, either. Carlotta Petersen Patton, a 1928 graduate of the College of Charleston and a mathematics major, could recall only one class that was even remotely vocational: "We were allowed to take a course in education which the city required for teaching, but we didn't get any credit on our degree for it." When asked whether she would have taken vocational courses if they were offered, she replied, "No, I never cared especially for that." She would have liked to take more advanced mathematics courses, however. After completing her liberal arts degree, Patton did graduate work at the University of North Carolina and taught mathematics at North Carolina State.[32]

As President Emilie McVea, of Sweet Briar College in Virginia, told the members of the Association of Colleges and Secondary Schools of the Southern States in 1922, most women's colleges did not plan curricula "with reference to professional requirements. . . . In a day when utility has too often been the test of a college course, the devotion to culture as such is commendable."[33] Despite high attrition rates, often attributed to the lack of vocational courses, private women's colleges maintained a traditional liberal arts curriculum into the 1960s.[34]

Was the traditional liberal arts curriculum of the private woman's college relevant to the needs of the white women who attended these institutions in the first half of the twentieth century? Students at such schools tended to come from the upper echelons of American society, where women were "traditionally free from economic responsibilities," and they were expected to "restrict themselves to work in the home and to the rearing of a normal family."[35] Many alumnae of Southern liberal arts colleges did exactly that. Sweet Briar College bragged that its entire class of 1945 was married within eight years of graduation and had an average of two children each in 1954. The members of the senior class of 1920 at Columbia College, when asked whether they would "sacrifice marriage for a career," emphatically answered no. Nor were these examples unique. A national survey of alumnae from the Seven Sisters found that 82 percent of the class of 1934 had married, and for most graduates "a job was only a stop gap before marriage."[36] For these middle-class, white women, anyway, a vocational education did not seem necessary.

Even wealthy Southern women played other roles besides housewife in the years before World War II, however. Women of both races and all classes were involved as individuals and as women's club members in various and sundry volunteer activities in their communities. They taught Sunday School, supported missionary societies, organized school improvement leagues, joined temperance groups, and served on assorted cultural and social welfare boards. Did liberal arts colleges provide the practical organizational and administrative skills needed for later volunteer work?

The involvement of large numbers of alumnae in clubs and voluntary organizations suggests that the curricular offerings, and even more the extracurricular offerings, of the liberal arts colleges proved relevant to women's later lives. Often membership in a college organization led directly to participation in related community associations. Methodist colleges, such as Wesleyan and Randolph-Macon Woman's, had student Volunteer Bands for women interested in missionary work. Baptist colleges had similar organizations that encouraged missionary activity at home and abroad. Many graduates of these denominational colleges became leaders in church-related societies, and some even served as foreign missionaries.[37]

A study by Gail Apperson Kilman of students who attended Wesleyan and Randolph-Macon women's colleges between 1893 and 1907 found that alumnae "continued to be involved in the types of volunteer associations which their colleges had fostered." Almost all the women whom Kilman surveyed taught in the Sunday school or sang in the choir of their local churches, participated in voluntary activities in their communities, and joined the local women's club.[38]

Reports of alumnae in various school publications reveal that college-educated "housewives" were anything but idle. Correspondents consistently noted their church and club work. The comments of one graduate from the class of 1915 of Meredith College in North Carolina were typical: "Besides keeping house, I do some church work, am interested in things musical, play bridge, and have a weakness for taking classes in music appreciation, Bible study, interior decorating, even cooking—and for forums for the discussion of varied subjects." Two of her classmates at the Baptist institution were engaged in missionary work: one in China and the other in Nigeria.[39] The November 1927 issue of the Meredith College Quarterly Bulletin noted that the school had nineteen alumnae serving as missionaries in seven different countries.[40]

The Young Women's Christian Association—typically the largest student organization on Southern college campuses in the early twentieth century—provided practical training in the social gospel for women at both denominational and nondenominational institutions. Student groups at Methodist colleges were also encouraged to help the poor in their communities, and this often involved interracial work. Dorothy Rogers Tilly, a 1901 graduate of Wesleyan College, became active in efforts for interracial cooperation sponsored by the women's group in her local Methodist church. In 1946 she was chosen by President Harry Truman as one of two Southern members on his Committee on Civil Rights.[41] As these examples suggest, women at liberal arts colleges often acquired "useful" knowledge and skills without the presence of vocational courses.

The utilitarian approach to women's education, which was largely rejected by private white women's colleges, was enthusiastically adopted by the black private and public colleges and the white, state-supported institutions of the region. White normal and state schools drew a larger proportion of their student body from the lower-middle class of the small towns and the farms than did white private colleges. These women often went to college for the sole purpose of getting an education that would qualify them to teach. When President Taft visited the Mississippi Industrial Institute and College in 1909, he praised the students for their utilitarian approach to the future. "A girl has the right to demand such training that she can win her own way to independence, thereby making marriage not a necessity, but a choice," he told them.[42]

As Stephanie Shaw has shown in her study of black professional women in the early twentieth century, the jobs women found themselves filling—especially in the rural South—required a wide range of knowledge and abilities. Teachers were often required to be nurses and settlement workers as well as educators. "It was quite common," Shaw observed, "for teachers to be sent or called to work at a place where a school did not yet exist, and in those cases, they had to begin by raising the money for, and organizing, the school." Shaw discovered instances where teachers actually helped to build their schools, and noting that a number of institutions "taught carpentry to female students during the late nineteenth and early twentieth centuries," she wondered whether "the construction role was more typical than our ability to document it can show."[43]

Shaw argued that black institutions of higher education in the Jim Crow South, regardless of their curricula, shared a common mission. All "were designed to cultivate or further develop a Christian (communal) spirit in the students; to instill leadership qualities in them; and to prepare them to use their training—moral, mental, and manual—to go into any community and establish themselves as useful members."[44] Whether this community service was inspired by the social gospel or by a sense of noblesse oblige was unimportant. What was clear was that students needed "moral, mental, and manual" training to fulfill the diverse tasks that awaited them in the black communities of the region. A teacher's work was not limited to the classroom. She was expected to address the social and economic as well as the intellectual needs of the community.

In *Gender and Jim Crow*, Glenda Gilmore found that the Jeanes teachers supported by the Negro Rural School Fund often "combined public health work with their visits to schools and homes." The Fund was established by the Quaker Anna Jeanes in 1907 to improve conditions in the black rural schools of the South. Virginia Randolph, the first Jeanes Supervising Industrial Teacher, taught her students both academic and practical skills and then took her lessons to the students' families and communities. As Gilmore concludes, the Jeanes teachers "had no counterpart in the North" and help account for the distinctiveness of Southern progressivism: "To locate the progressive South, one must not just visit New South booster Henry Grady in Atlanta but find as well a schoolroom full of cleanly scrubbed Modern Health Crusaders, lined up for hot cereal cooked by the older girls in Rosenwald kitchens, each Crusader clutching the jelly jar that served as his or her very own glass."[45]

White teachers in poor rural areas also were expected to carry out a variety of tasks inside and outside the classroom. When "Mrs. Nannie Carson" became a Works Progress Administration (WPA) teacher in the thirties, she was sent to "Hackletown," an isolated mountain community in North Carolina, to teach reading. Because it was a difficult trip over rough terrain to the county school, school attendance was irregular, and most families were illiterate. The clannish nature of the community and its association with bootlegging had prompted other teachers to turn down the position. During her first year in Hackletown, Carson walked fifteen miles once a week to reach her students. Because the walking took too much time from her teaching, she hired a local farm boy to drive her on her rounds, but the location of many of the families' cabins still required a considerable amount of daily hiking. She taught reading and mathematics to children and adults in their homes, persuaded parents to send their children to school, provided medical treatment to several burned children, and encouraged the women to serve balanced meals, to mend and wash their clothes, and to keep their houses clean. Poor nutrition was a real problem. "The people in Hackletown plant nothin' but corn," she told an interviewer, "so I'm tryin' to get the women interested in makin' vegetable gardens. . . . I'm givin' all the women packages of seeds, and I'm plannin' to teach them how to can their surplus. . . . I asked Sheriff Davis to save me all the fruit jars he takes up on his raids on 'stills.' " Concerned about the moral standards of the community, Carson taught the women Bible stories and hymns so that they could pass them on to their children. Carson was proud of what she had accomplished as a "teacher" for the WPA: "The most important thing in the work I do . . . seems to me to raise the standard of livin' and to break up the isolation in which the women live."[46]

64

What type of education prepared Carson and others like her for their eclectic duties? Carson began teaching after she finished tenth grade: "The superintendent came to me and begged me to take a one-room county school." After two years, Carson left teaching, took a business course, earned her high school diploma, studied practical nursing, and then returned to the classroom. For eight summers she took classes at the Asheville Normal and Teachers' College, completing the equivalent of two years of college work. Despite her demanding job with the WPA, Carson took the bus once a week into Asheville for classes: "We study textiles and how to dress neatly and suitably on small incomes. Last quarter we studied community hygiene. These courses, two hours a week, will help me raise the grade of my teacher's certificate. I take a music lesson every Monday to help me play accompaniments and teach community singin' better. And I'm takin' a correspondence course in Education with a state teachers' college."[47] For women such as Carson, as for the black professional women studied by Shaw, a broad education that combined the academic knowledge of the liberal arts college with the practical training of the normal and industrial school best met the demands of their professional and personal lives.

What Carson's story also illustrates is that many women's education did not end with the acquisition of a certificate, diploma, or degree. The rising standards demanded by professional and state boards for teachers and other professionals required them to take additional courses and training to remain competitive. Stephanie Shaw contends that these additional requirements were especially problematic for black women: "By the 1930s, membership in the national occupational organizations was required for full credentialing, but the national organizations generally had no room for African Americans." This meant that black women often had to found their own professional organizations as well as attend the workshops and take the courses that they needed to maintain their professional status. What is striking about the life histories of professional Southern women— black and white—recorded for the Federal Writers' Project of the 1930s is the frequency with which these women had returned to school to enroll in classes or programs that would improve their vocational opportunities. For the majority of Southern women, work was not a luxury but a necessity.

A 1939 report on enrollment at the Georgia State College for Women predicted a "trend toward careers for women." In five years the enrollment in education programs at the woman's college had increased 40 percent, "indicating that more attention [was] being given toward specific preparation for teaching jobs rather than using school teaching as a backlog against ill-fated romances." The report concluded that even though 96 percent of the student body expected to marry someday, the "trend to consider school teaching as a full time profession [was] greatly on the increase."[48]

Similarly, women at black colleges, regardless of their marital status or socioeconomic background, were expected to pursue and did pursue a vocation after graduation. A 1942 survey of 172 African American alumnae who were graduated between 1892 and 1941 found that 81.3 percent were employed outside the home. The study noted that "twice as many Negro women as white women are gainfully employed."[49] Cultivated leisure might be the ideal of the Southern lady, but in the real world of the segregated South the African American woman would have to use her education to get a job. Thus, for economic and social reasons, black public and private colleges and white state-supported schools tended to focus on utilitarian courses.

The majority of private black institutions had originated as missionary schools, and their belief in Christian service partially explains the importance they placed on practical subjects and public outreach. Lucy Hale Tapley, who became president of Spelman Seminary in Georgia in 1910, wanted "all the school activities . . . to give instruction in housewifely arts" and refused to include "any course of study which fail[ed] to cultivate a taste and fitness for practical and efficient work."[50] Tapley believed that graduates should use their education to enrich the communities from whence they came, and she found it hard to see how classical studies could be much use to poor, rural Southerners.

Not all twentieth-century educators shared Du Bois's faith in the liberating qualities of the liberal arts. A U.S. Department of Education study of African American education undertaken in 1916 criticized black private colleges for clinging to the classical curriculum of the white schools. It questioned the relevance to African American youth of subjects "introduced in the middle ages" to meet the needs of a European aristocracy. The race could hardly afford the luxury of individuals simply acquiring "culture." As Mary Church Terrell explained in a report on the accomplishments of African American women in the field of education, "It is a great thing to want to acquire knowledge for its own sake, but it is a better and nobler thing to use it to benefit one's fellow man. And that is precisely what colored women have done."[51]

Many philanthropists seemed more interested in the service African American women would render to the white community, however. A 1923 publication of the Phelps-Stokes Fellowship Papers of the University of Virginia favored "increased agricultural and industrial education" for blacks. For black women the report recommended more courses in home economics. The author, a white man, described the advantages that would accrue from such a change: "Domestic service will no longer be held in contempt, but will be placed once more on the high plane which it occupied in slavery days when only the most intelligent Negroes were favored by being given a position in the 'Big House.' " He opposed giving blacks "an extensive literary training, for there . . . [was] only a small demand for the service which they would be prepared to render." In fact, he feared that a liberal arts education could turn African Americans into "Bolshevists, murderers or thieves."[52]

The Klein Survey, issued by the U.S. Bureau of Education in 1928, similarly "recommended teacher, agricultural, and industrial training for all black colleges" and encouraged "land-grant colleges . . . to strengthen their agricultural and mechanical departments."[53] Given the segregation of Southern society, professional opportunities for African American graduates were certainly limited, but the vocational orientation of black colleges often reflected white prejudices rather than black interests. Whites wanted literate and hardworking employees, not independent professionals. The education offered African American students at Hampton Institute and similar industrial schools seemed designed "to make the negroes of service to themselves, their people, and the white race."[54]

Because black colleges relied heavily on the good will (and monetary distributions) of white legislators and philanthropists, they were forced to amend or at least pretend to amend their curricula accordingly.[55] Promotional materials stressed vocational offerings and practical training. A 1930 advertisement for Tuskegee Normal and Industrial School in Alabama, for instance, ignored its teaching preparation to boast that its "Woman's Industries included Home Economics—Courses in Foods, Clothing, Millinery, Applied Art, Laundering, Household Management in addition to Home Crafts and Ladies' Tailoring."[56]

Glenda Gilmore believed that this emphasis on industrial education for blacks hurt women more than men. "It reinforced differences in men's and women's curricula after black women had battled for years for equal consideration in coeducation, and it drew money away from women's teacher-training programs . . . [by reallocating] scarce funds from teacher preparation to male students' manual training." Gilmore cited the example of North Carolina's Agricultural and Mechanical College, which was transformed from a coeducational to an all-male institution in 1900 "to open up dormitory space for men."[57]

Black colleges with high aspirations sometimes felt the wrath of the white community, as the fate of the Virginia Normal and Industrial Institute exemplified. Although the Institute had awarded the A.B. degree since 1889, the Virginia State Legislature revised the school's charter in 1902 and forced it to substitute industrial for collegiate work. Student interest in liberal arts courses was apparently not considered. In Tennessee, Fisk's commitment to a liberal arts curriculum made it difficult for the university to get grants in the years before World War I. Often, foundation gifts were tied to special vocational programs. The Slater Fund, for instance, gave Fisk $5,000 in 1905 but earmarked the money for use in the Department of Applied Sciences.[58]

The changes in American economics, politics, and society that occurred in the first half of the twentieth century were seldom reflected in the curricular offerings of Southern black colleges. Despite the prominence of black sociologists such as George Haynes and Charles Johnson, most African American students had little exposure to the social sciences. Despite the promulgation of the Nineteenth Amendment and the expansion of employment opportunities for women, colleges did little to prepare students for the complexities of modern life. A 1933 survey of women students at forty-four black colleges, by Howard University dean Lucy Slowe, revealed that only 4 percent of women were enrolled in economics and political science courses, only 7 percent in sociology courses, and only 8 percent in psychology courses. Extracurricular activities did not provide many opportunities for student self-development, either. Only twelve of the forty-four colleges had a student council, only three had dormitory self-government, and only three had a women's league. To Slowe, it seemed clear that college curricula were not designed "to meet the needs of women who must live in and make their contribution to a changed economic, industrial, and political order."[59]

Slowe focused on the shortcomings of the curricula of black liberal arts colleges; other educators found similar problems with the curricula of black vocational colleges. Buell Gallagher, the president of Talladega College in Alabama, criticized those who argued that "the *only* kind of education which should be given to Negroes is training in the crafts and trades." The best education for African Americans, Gallagher believed, was one that combined cultural enrichment with vocational training. He agreed with Slowe that curricular offerings must reflect the changes occurring in the world outside of academe. Vocational education that substituted "a kind of dilettante hand-craft training" for a "genuine, rigorous, modern training in trade and profession" was hardly utilitarian, Gallagher pointed out, if all it did was "to steer the Negro into the fast-declining and poorly paid trades."[60]

Even at black liberal arts colleges, the curriculum tended to emphasize women's traditional duties and responsibilities. Officials of the Methodist Episcopal Church, explaining why they decided to convert Bennett College in North Carolina into a single-sex institution in 1926, "recognized that studies especially adapted to the needs of women should be included in the curriculum, and that attention should be given to matters relating to the refinements of family and community life."[61] Bennett established a B.S. degree in home economics and nutrition and shifted the focus of many traditional courses toward domestic applications. The third physics course in the science sequence was, for instance, entitled "Household Physics."[62] Spelman College in Georgia also offered a B.S. degree in home economics and required all freshmen to take a personal service course. Additional courses were available on personal problems in foods, personal problems in clothing, home equipment and furnishings, meal planning and serving, and home management. For the latter course, a "practice apartment" was available for "managerial practice and experience."[63]

Practical training usually involved putting students to work around the campus. At Hampton Institute in Virginia, women students took turns "cooking in two kitchens, waiting on table in the dining rooms, [taking] care of bedrooms, . . . halls and baths, [and] work[ing] in the school laundry . . . [and] industrial sewing room."[64] At Benedict College in South Carolina, the cooking and serving of dormitory meals was done by the women students, and Allen, Claflin, and Clark universities and the North Carolina State Normal and Industrial School for the Colored Race all expected their students to labor for free when asked.[65] Until 1929, Spelman students "had to get up at 4:45 one morning each week to do their washing!" Although this service was subsequently contracted out by the college, students still had to "demonstrate at the end of the year that they knew *how* to wash and iron properly."[66]

Colleges stressed the character-building function of such labor, but economic exigencies also explain the deployment of students at manual tasks in the halls and on the grounds of black institutions. Chronically short of endowments, black colleges seldom had any other type of financial aid to offer students. Significantly, the adoption of vocational courses or programs often brought in donations to the college coffers. In 1921 Howard University in Washington, D.C., received $210,000 from the federal government for a building to house the School of Home Economics.[67]

The acquisition of "womanly charm" was another domestic value seen as useful to black women. In an article entitled "The Place of the Women's College," President Tapley of Spelman argued that "women are in a special sense the keepers of social standards, the guardians of spiritual values. Unless the women of any race have high standards of personal and family and community life, those standards will slump and social life will decline." This was the reason, Read explained, for the emphasis on "manners" and "character" at women's colleges.[68]

A perusal of campus publications at Spelman in the years before World War II suggests that the acquisition of "manners" and "culture" often became an end in itself and that some black students held a stereotype of the ideal woman remarkably similar to that of the white Southern belle. "A true Spelman Girl," the *Spelman Messenger* of 1927 noted, "is quiet, gentle, and ladylike."[69] A national survey of black alumnae noted that Southern graduates found courses in "grooming and social poise" particularly relevant; they wanted to "learn how to pour tea with gloves on."[70]

The concern with "cultured womanhood" at black colleges was more than simply elitism, however. Given contemporary white stereotypes of African American women, lessons in behavior and demeanor assumed a racial as well as a personal significance. Jeanne Noble, in *Negro Woman's Education*, published in 1956, wondered whether the emphasis on moral character at black colleges was not so much a desire to promote the purity of Southern womanhood as it was to negate the image of the promiscuous slave. "Overnight she was to so live that by her ideal behavior the sins of her foremothers might be blotted out. Her education," Noble argued, seemed "to have been based on a philosophy which implied that she was weak and immoral and that at best she should be made fit to rear her children and keep house for her husband."[71] Yet the emphasis on women's morality was more than a historical albatross. In the competitive job market of the Jim Crow South, administrators "would not employ a person of questionable character. And equally important, if the women were not morally upright, self-controlled, and community oriented, the black community they were to serve would also reject them . . . for being unacceptable role models for the children of the community." Thus moral training was anything but antiquarian.

Religious courses were an important part of the curricula at all black colleges. Dean Lucy Slowe, of Howard University, thought that the religious philosophy of these institutions discouraged women from "developing their talents to the fullest extent." Religion led them to accept "what [was] taught without much question," and it fostered "the psychology of inaction rather than that of active curiosity."[72] Yet, as Eugene Genovese has demonstrated in his study of antebellum slave communities, religion could be a double-edged sword. The same faith that taught submission and service also spoke of a God who saw neither Jew nor Gentile, male nor female. "Afro-Americans," Genovese concluded, "accepted Christianity's celebration of the individual soul and turned it into a weapon of personal and community survival."[73] It was not an accident that the Civil Rights Movement of the 1950s and 1960s drew its personnel and strength from the black churches and that many of these activists were women.

Despite African Americans' turning of such stereotypes to their own educational advantage, the curricula of African American colleges too often reflected the religious, social, and economic values of white, not black, America. Under pressure from white philanthropists and legislators, administrators at black colleges provided black students with the type of education whites wanted them to have. As a Bureau of Education bulletin explained, "In the conduct and management of colored schools, it is to be expected that the South should stress conformity to the community standards of white people."[74] Although some educators criticized the black colleges for refusing to challenge the status quo, others believed that their training enabled graduates to survive in a hostile environment. In a 1941 article "About Negro Education," in *Phylon*, Alfonso Elder asked how the black schools could "in the light of existing circumstances . . . promote a socially significant educational program which would not meet with active opposition from those in control?" African American students had to learn to make choices based on much more than their individual abilities and preferences; they had to consider "the immediate as well as the desirable environmental conditions" and to find "group ways of acting which [would] promote the welfare of all."[75]

For an African American woman living in the early twentieth-century South, an education that stressed individualism and personal achievement was a luxury the race could not afford. The encouragement of utilitarian knowledge at the expense of the liberal arts may have circumscribed the curricular choices of the South's brightest women, but it imparted a very positive message as well: those who had the privilege of education had the responsibility of sharing their knowledge with less fortunate members of the community. The emphasis that colleges put on domesticity, piety, and conformity may have stifled the creativity and limited the opportunities of African American women, but at the same time it prepared them for a world in which the observance of codes of racial etiquette could be a matter of life and death. In this sense, courses in "culture" were eminently utilitarian.

Gender and racial biases in collegiate vocational programs tended to

71

restrict African American women to careers in teaching and social work. Of the sixty liberal arts graduates from Howard in 1920, for example, seventeen of the twenty-six women mentioned teaching as their intended vocation, whereas only six of the thirty-four men made such a choice. Eleven men and no women planned to study medicine, eight men and no women to read law, and three women and no men to pursue social work. The one woman who did choose a nontraditional career hoped to enter Howard's pharmacy program.[76]

The vocational preferences of Howard students mirrored the pattern throughout the South. A 1938 study of black college graduates found that "[t]he male graduates . . . engaged in 206 different occupations, and the female graduates in 102, including those of housewife and student." Women were conspicuously absent from the ranks of doctors and lawyers while noticeably dominant in the professions of social work and teaching. A 1947 survey of Bennett College alumnae found that 68 percent were "employed in teaching, social service, home demonstration work, government service, medicine, and dietetics."[77]

The curricular programs provided by black colleges may have limited the individual options of African American women, but they also stressed societal needs over self-aggrandizement, a factor that had important repercussions for the black communities of the South. Jeanne Noble, in her study of African American alumnae, found that more than half were active in "civic organizations, social organizations, and church organizations" in their communities and also in national organizations such as the Young Women's Christian Association and the National Association for the Advancement of Colored People. Whereas black alumni sought their fortunes in the large cities, black alumnae tended to return to the rural areas, where their skills and leadership were most needed.[78]

The utilitarian philosophy of education that dominated the curriculum of black schools also predominated in the white, state-supported institutions of the region. Most public colleges for women were founded "to serve the cultural *and vocational* needs of women." In fact, the majority originated as normal and industrial training schools and became four-year collegiate institutions only after World War I.[79] These institutions for women remained dedicated to providing professional and vocational training for the "fairer" sex.

The catalog of Georgia State College for Women frankly proclaimed its woman-centered and utilitarian pedagogy:

> The Georgia State College for Women is distinctly a woman's college. It does not seek to imitate the educational practices that have prevailed in colleges for men. It does not seek to conform to tradition. . . . It believes that women have interests and ambitions and spheres of usefulness peculiarly their own. . . . It believes that all sciences and arts should be made to contribute to the improvement of the home, the school, the farm, the child, and of society in general. Following these new ideals in education, the College asks not only what has been taught, but also what ought to be taught to women.[80]

On the top of Georgia State College for Women's list of what ought to be taught to women was home economics. The institution was the first white college in Georgia to teach home economics and the first white school in the South to require it for a degree.[81]

Home economics soon spread from Georgia to the other state schools and even to some of the private colleges of the South. Home economics and many of the other vocational courses adopted by Southern colleges in the early twentieth century were intended to meet the region's unique economic needs. The South was still overwhelmingly rural and agricultural, and most Southern families were eking out a subsistence living from the land. The utilitarian curriculum of the public colleges and universities of the South was connected to the efforts of the farm extension movement to promote scientific agriculture. The farm demonstration programs begun by Seaman Knapp in Texas in 1902 had been institutionalized by Congress in the Smith-Lever Act of 1914. Land-grant colleges throughout the country were given grants to conduct farmers' institutes and to train home demonstration agents. The Smith-Hughes Act of 1916 expanded the teaching of improved farming and homemaking practices to the lower schools.[82]

The establishment of home economics departments at Southern colleges in the years after World War I was a consequence of the demand for teachers created by the Smith-Hughes Act. As high schools throughout the country introduced home economics courses to prepare girls for homemaking, additional trained teachers were needed to conduct these courses.

Most Southern teachers were educated in state-supported colleges or normal schools, and their desire for degrees in home economics was primarily vocational.[83]

The number of courses offered under the rubric of home economics proliferated in white and black Southern schools in the interwar years. Besides the standard offerings in child care, nutrition, cooking, sewing, and home management, students could get college credit for such unconventional courses as personal service, courtship and marriage, cosmetic hygiene, dinner work, the school lunch, household engineering and equipment, "mothercraft," poultry raising, household physics, chafing dish and fancy cooking, and table service. These courses were designed to combine "French Art" and "Southern Hospitality" and "to fit woman for a sphere which [was] pre-eminently her own, a sphere which includes both the science and the art of homemaking."[84] Certainly Southern fathers could not complain that professional training of this sort was unfeminine.

Classes in child care were also extremely practical in a region with a high rate of infant mortality and a low percentage of trained physicians. Mississippi II & C made a course on "mothercraft" a required part of its hygiene curriculum. It was important, Professor Martha Eckford believed, that future mothers know "how to save babies."[85]

Almost all the public women's colleges in the South created extension programs to spread "the gospel of good housekeeping" to rural families in the state. Special summer schools were organized to familiarize teachers with the latest techniques in home economics, and various "extension demonstrators" were trained to assist rural women with their domestic problems. Texas College of Industrial Arts (CIA) equipped a railway car with educational exhibits prepared by the students who traveled throughout the state, bringing home economics lessons to the remotest families. To meet the demand for home demonstration agents, CIA introduced a bachelor's degree in home demonstration in 1922.[86]

The public women's colleges also contributed to the growing volume of self-help literature issued by the nation's land-grant colleges in the Progressive Era. The CIA prepared a series of informational bulletins that were distributed free of charge to the women of Texas on topics such as "practical sewing, cookery, canning and preserving, laundering, gardening, poultry-keeping and dairying, and rural social problems." One of the most popular bulletins was the *Home Makers Course*, which "offered information on virtually all aspects of the home from house planning and decoration to household sanitation, personal hygiene, and home care of the sick." With the advent of women's suffrage in 1920, CIA bulletins provided political information as well. Texas women were given a history of the Nineteenth Amendment and were encouraged to work for legislation that would benefit the family and the local community.[87]

As such projects and publications suggest, home economics majors often saw themselves as crusaders, eager to proselytize other women regarding the virtues of a proper diet and good hygiene. They often began with their classmates. "You can't know what it is to eat meals in the company of girls majoring in Home Economics," one Judson senior complained in 1939. "[T]hey count every vitamin I eat, watch me with hawk-like eyes, warn me when I refuse something, praise me when I tackle the carrots. They recite with knowing looks every word that was said in their Nutrition class that day. Today they unanimously decided that I ought to start taking Brewers' Yeast before nightfall."[88]

Besides taking courses in child care, nutrition, and household management, students at Southern colleges could also gain experience at homemaking by living in special "practice homes" located on the campus but furnished and operated like a family residence. These practice homes, home management cottages, or homemaking institutes, as they were variously labeled, were, like the practice schools that inspired them, usually associated with colleges with a strong teacher-training orientation. For example, Asheville Normal and Teachers College, East Carolina Teachers College, Georgia State College for Women, Georgia State Teachers College, Mississippi State College for Women, Texas College of Industrial Arts, and Winthrop College all had variants of the practice home and required students to spend anywhere from a few weeks to an entire year cooking, cleaning, and running such establishments. The aim of practice home courses, East Carolina's catalog explained, was "to develop ideals and standards of good living."[89]

Home economics courses and practice homes were equally popular at black colleges. Clark University in Atlanta had its Thayer Home, Shaw University in Raleigh a practice home, and Bennett College in Greensboro a homemaking institute. Because "women exert the principal influence in home and family life," the Bennett bulletin of 1935 noted, "a college devoted to the education of young women may be expected to emphasize home-making as a career. To meet this responsibility, Bennett emphasizes the study and the teaching of scientific home economics and the art of home-making."[90] Hampton Institute in Virginia also stressed the relevancy of its home economics course. Women who majored in this field were told that they could find jobs as "teachers in elementary and secondary schools and colleges, supervisors of home economics for public school systems, state and district leaders in extension work, dieticians for institutional work, leaders to help solve home and family problems, [and] efficient homemakers."[91]

As well as practice homes, a number of normal and state institutions established demonstration schools where student teachers could observe "the latest and best instructional technique[s]." The model school at Mississippi II & C began in 1907 as a kindergarten and first grade that were squeezed into one room of the industrial hall and expanded by 1929 to include a modern school building and six grades of classes. A number of public colleges also offered special summer sessions where older teachers could hone their skills while providing extra instruction for the children of the area.[92]

Neither the utilitarian nor the traditionalist curriculum prepared women to challenge the political or economic status quo, however. After conducting a survey of seven Southern women's colleges in the late twenties, one critic concluded that "there is nothing in the published outlines of study of the Southern colleges to show that the extension of universal suffrage to women in 1918 had any immediate effect on their programs of formal instruction."[93] President Emilie McVea, of Sweet Briar, agreed: "Most of the women's colleges," she told the Association of Colleges and Secondary Schools of the Southern States in 1922, "have been calmly unaware of industrial, rural, or educational problems at their very doors."[94]

Political science courses were slow to reflect the change in women's political status. How many political science departments at women's colleges had "shifted their point of view so that they [were] clearly teaching possible future participants in the political game, not just observers?" President Katherine Blunt, of Connecticut College, wondered. Textbooks seldom included the political accomplishments of women, and professors often taught their courses as if the Nineteenth Amendment had not been ratified. "Women have had the suffrage for ten years," Blunt wrote, "but I do not believe that colleges as a whole have quite grasped that fact."[95]

President Bessie Carter Randolph, of Hollins, blamed students rather than faculty for women's political apathy. Randolph believed that women were not taking their college educations seriously, and graduates who could provide solutions to contemporary problems preferred to devote their time to "useless and frivolous pursuits." Randolph reminded parents that education for women was utilitarian not simply in the literal sense of preparing for a career or a family but also in the philosophical sense of preparing citizens for democracy.[96]

77

Controversial political topics rarely penetrated the classrooms of Southern colleges. Despite the prominence of racial issues in the region, white professors generally ignored race when discussing contemporary Southern history, politics, or economics. The State College for Women in North Carolina was alone, it seems, in offering a three-credit course analyzing the political, social, cultural, and economic role of African Americans.[97]

Generally speaking, the teaching of African American history was left to the black colleges. One of the consequences of the Negro Renaissance of the early twentieth century had been a growing interest in black history. Carter Woodson, a Harvard Ph.D., had founded the Association for the Study of Negro Life in History in 1915 "in a dedicated attempt to focus the Negro American's cultural tradition before the world and . . . [to] extol the image of the race." *The Journal of Negro History*, created as a mouthpiece of the organization, helped educate African Americans about their past culture and present plight. Courses on African American history and culture proliferated at black colleges in the years after World War I, exposing generations of students to the contributions of great "race" men and women. But even at black institutions, educators were often adverse to or afraid of recognizing some of the "unpleasant features" of what was called the "Negro problem." In an address at Fisk University in Tennessee in 1933, W. E. B. Du Bois criticized his contemporaries for refusing to face up to the fact that "the American Negro problem is and must be the center of the Negro American University." Faculty were teaching students who were "the subjects of a caste system" and whose "life problem [was] primarily this problem of caste." Although Du Bois reaffirmed his faith in the liberal arts curriculum, he believed that the teaching of these subjects had to include references to the present conditions of African Americans in the United States. In other words, the liberal arts curriculum had to be made utilitarian.[98]

Despite Du Bois's criticism of contemporary courses on the black experience, most students appreciated the opportunity to learn more about the "twoness" of their history and culture. And for the thousands of black women who went on to be parents, teachers, social workers, and community activists in the first half of the twentieth century, such courses were eminently practical. Cynthia Neverdon-Morton, in her study "Issues in Afro-American Higher Education," found a correlation between "the increased emphasis on Afro-American culture and history" and "the development of social service courses and programs to deal with the problems of the masses."[99]

Neither white nor black women had much opportunity to examine the peculiar history of their gender. Chicora College for Women in South Carolina was one of the few institutions to offer a course on the social and economic status of women."[100] Most college courses that purported to look at contemporary issues of significance to the student concentrated on great men and on other subjects of interest to men.

When courses were offered dealing with contemporary political issues, they were often superficial. Coker College's "Current Thought," for instance, covered recent scientific development, contemporary literature, religious problems, studies in South Carolina citizenship, international relations, and appreciation of art, all in one semester.[101] Sweet Briar College in Virginia tried a new approach in 1929—an interdepartmental major in American problems. As it turned out, students and faculty were more intrigued by the interdisciplinary approach than by the problems of contemporary America. In the next eight years, nine other interdepartmental majors were created, centering on such distinctly noncurrent topics as the quadrivium, classical civilization, and revolution and romanticism.[102]

The political climate at Southern colleges was generally not conducive to the development of courses in controversial issues. Most boards of trustees and the administrators they chose were conservative businessmen and politicians with no desire to rock the boat of white male supremacy. As

late as 1960, a South Carolina historian commented that "academic freedom is altogether absent or greatly restricted in South Carolina institutions of higher learning." Despite the greater academic freedom elsewhere
in the nation, disinterest in public affairs was not confined to Southern colleges, either. Helen Horowitz, in her study of the women's colleges of the
Northeast, found the following opinion of one Seven Sisters' student all
too common in the twenties: "We're not out to benefit society. . . . We're
not going to suffer over how the other half lives."[103]

The Great Depression did lead a number of women's colleges to
add courses in economics, and some educators hoped that such classes
would "inspire undergraduates to an enlarged social consciousness." But
even when economics was offered, the course was structured to emphasize
woman's role as a consumer rather than a creator of wealth: "[W]omen
students, since they are members of a class that has been shown to control
such a large proportion of the world's money and goods, are instructed in
wise spending and intelligent saving."[104]

From our perspective in the nineties, the curriculum of Southern
colleges in the first half of the twentieth century did not seem to prepare
women students for the commercial and industrial world of the modern
South. Utilitarianism consisted of courses in teacher training and homemaking, not in contemporary politics and economics. Traditionalism involved the creation of a cultured mind and a "womanly" woman.

From the perspective of women who were educated at Southern colleges in these years, the distinctions between the traditional and utilitarian
curricula were not always as clear in practice as in theory. Many alumnae
found their liberal arts training practical and their utilitarian course work
liberating. The educational experiences of Dr. Pat Carter are illustrative. A
native of Charleston, South Carolina, Carter graduated from the College
of Charleston in 1937 with an A.B. degree in Latin, received her M.D. degree from the Medical College (now University) of South Carolina in
1941, and completed her residency in obstetrics at Margaret Hague Mater-
nity Hospital in New Jersey in 1944.[105]

When Carter's father died of an obscure illness during her high
school years, Carter decided to become a physician "so this would not happen to anyone else." She had been awarded a scholarship to a private college, but her father's death made it imperative that she live at home and

attend the municipal College of Charleston. The College offered a three-year premedical course (B.S. degree in medicine) that prepared students for the nearby Medical College of South Carolina. During Carter's freshman year, she went over to the Medical College to get advice on her undergraduate course work. The dean called her into his office. "Young lady," he said, "let's face it. The practice of medicine is very unladylike. There is no place for women [in medicine] here in the South." He went on to tell her that she "would be taking a place from a man" who would practice the profession.

Carter replied that, ladylike or not, she wanted to attend medical school. The dean cautioned her that the Medical College would not accept a woman with a B.S. degree in medicine. "You get an A.B. degree in Latin and complete your premedical courses," and then you will be considered seriously. "But," he added, "you can't do that at the College of Charleston." When Carter returned to talk to her adviser at the college, she discovered that the dean was right. If she completed the four years of Latin, the three years of German, and the two years of English required for the A.B. degree, she could not take the premedical courses offered at the same time. "How did the men do it?" she was asked. "They did B.S. in medicine. But he told me I couldn't get in without an A.B. and a B.S. degree." Carter circumvented this roadblock by taking her A.B. courses at the College of Charleston and commuting every summer to the University of South Carolina in Columbia to complete her premedical courses.

Instead of being bitter, Dr. Carter was thankful for the extra requirements. "I got the greatest education in the world by being forced into an A.B. program." She believed that her grounding in the classics made her a more humane practitioner. "There is no substitute for the wisdom, knowledge you get from a solid curriculum." Carter derided the "practical" subjects for women offered by many public colleges during her youth: topics such as "hair curling," she quipped, should be noncredit courses.

Despite Carter's high class rank, she was the last of her College of Charleston classmates to be notified of her acceptance to the Medical College. As one of only two women in her medical class, she was warned by the dean that the rules were different for men and women: "Unless you are thirty-three and one-third percent above any male in that class, you'll be gone by Christmas." Many of the men clearly resented her presence. When she was asked to present the arm of a cadaver which she had spent many days dissecting to her professor for examination, she found that her specimen was "missing." She requested a delay in her examination, went back to the laboratory at night, and discovered "my arm" in a male classmate's box. She confronted the student the next day, declaring that she had five older brothers and was a very "good pugilist." The male students never bothered her again.

Carter had a difficult time getting an internship. The local Charleston hospitals were not interested in a woman, no matter how good. "A woman? We have no place for that." Fortunately for Carter, a woman doctor in clinical pathology had contacts in Philadelphia, and Carter went north to do her twenty-seven months of residency in obstetrics. By this time, Carter recalled, "It was war, and they needed people." In 1944 she came back to Charleston to begin her practice, returning to the North in the fifties to be certified in gynecology. Although Carter's patients were all women, she resented the implication that certain fields of medicine were gender linked. "I hate when people ask, 'What is the best speciality for women?' A woman can be anything she wants to be in this day and age." This was certainly true for Carter, who went on to become the first woman to be given full obstetrics-gynecology privileges at a Charleston hospital, the first woman chief of staff of a major hospital in Charleston, and the first woman M.D. on the Board of Trustees of St. Francis Xavier Hospital.

For Pat Carter, the traditional classical curriculum turned out to be practical. It gave her the oral and written skills to communicate effectively, it imparted a humanism that was lacking in the medical training of her male contemporaries, and it encouraged her to "do her homework." The obstacles she faced in pursuing a medical career were not curricular but societal, and different courses would not have made her professional progress easier.

Neither traditional nor utilitarian curricula served to destroy the pedestal on which Southern white women had been placed, but both educational programs supplied the steps by which, if they wished, women could work in their churches, clubs, and communities to bring about change. The path on which women walked was still prescribed by images of a woman's place, but college had given them the building material to change its direction. College women had shown that ladylike demeanor was not incongruent with scholarly achievement or community activism.

At first glance, the college curriculum at black colleges offered little to challenge plantation stereotypes, either. Yet an education that seemed to reinforce the economic, political, and social order of the Old South also nourished "womanly" behaviors vital to the sustenance of the African American community—what Stephanie Shaw has called "socially responsible individualism."[106] Black colleges taught young women to be proud of their race and heritage and encouraged them to work in their clubs, churches, and communities for social, economic, and political reform. The "double consciousness" of Southern culture shaped the higher education of women, enabling them to use the traditions of the past to create a new and better tomorrow. In the years between 1900 and 1960, Southern colleges had produced women who were ladies, scholars, and citizens.

Maintaining the Spirit and Tone of Robust Manliness

The Opposition to Coeducation at Southern
Public Universities[1]

*A*n awareness of difference—between men and women, blacks and whites, rich and poor—pervaded discussions on the nature of women's higher education in the twentieth-century South. This "twoness" was apparent in debates of standards, funding, and curriculum. But nowhere was the double consciousness of Southern culture more obvious than in the controversies surrounding coeducation at the state-supported institutions of the region. From the attempts to bar women from the public universities of the Southeast in the 1890s to the efforts to exclude women from the corps of cadets at Virginia Military Institute (VMI) and The Citadel in the 1990s, Southern educators have been concerned about the impact that coeducation would have on traditional gender, racial, and class relationships.

Southern public universities were primarily single-gender institutions at the beginning of the twentieth century. The U.S. Bureau of Education recorded no women students at the universities of Virginia, Georgia, and Louisiana in the 1902–1903 academic year and only three at the University of North Carolina.[2] Although all Southern state universities except Florida enrolled women by 1925, the majority of white public institutions in the South were only nominally coeducational (public institutions for African Americans, on the other hand, were all coeducational). Some admitted women solely to graduate programs, others restricted admission to upperclassmen, and still others accepted only women residents of the town. Schools were unwilling to provide campus facilities and supervisory personnel for women students, and yet they cited the absence of deans of women and women's dormitories as reasons to limit the number of women admitted. Men students often resented women's presence on campus and barred them from clubs, activities, and buildings. There were attempts throughout the first half of the twentieth century to restore coeducational institutions to male exclusivity by establishing coordinate colleges for women students on sites removed from the main campus. Until educational equity was required by law, few Southern states provided women with academic opportunities comparable to those offered to men.

The first coeducational colleges were in the American Midwest. Oberlin College, founded in 1833, admitted women in 1837 and Antioch College in 1852. The State University of Iowa (later the University of Iowa) became the first public, coeducational institution of higher education when it opened its doors in 1865.[3] By the turn of the century, schools as diverse as Cornell, Wesleyan (Connecticut), Boston, and Stanford universities and the state universities of California, Michigan, and Wisconsin had all admitted women. In 1900 more than 71 percent of the institutions of higher education in the United States were coeducational. West of the Mississippi, every state university except Louisiana accepted women.[4]

The picture was different in the segregated schools of the South. At the beginning of the twentieth century, 66 percent of the nation's women's colleges were in the South, and only six of the white state universities in the region were coeducational.[5] The prevalence of single-gender schools in the Southeast was, in part, historical. Because the coastal regions were the first to be colonized by the English, their colleges had been established at a time when higher education was designed to prepare white men for the professions; the education of women was confined to domestic accomplishments. Accustomed to single-gender institutions for white men, Southern educators preferred to establish separate schools for white women, just as they later would for African Americans, rather than admitting them to existing colleges or universities. The first state college for women was established in Mississippi in 1884, and by 1914, North Carolina, South Carolina, Georgia, Florida, Alabama, Texas, and Oklahoma all funded separate normal or industrial schools for white women.[6]

Educational policies in the postwar South reflected planter and populist political philosophies. Southern planters hoped to use the votes of their former slaves to restore their prewar political hegemony. They believed that the university should serve the needs of the white, aristocratic male, who was the state's natural ruler. They favored the education of blacks and women but not at the university. Populist politicians resented the planters' use of black votes to reestablish the antebellum class system and wanted a political and educational system that would consider the needs of common whites. Believing that black rights hindered white democracy, these politicians rewrote the state constitutions of the region, disfranchising blacks and segregating schools and public accommodations. They advocated agricultural and mechanical colleges for men, advocated normal and industrial institutes for women, and opposed the idea of an elitist university.[7] The separate education of women was intricately interwoven with the politics of race.

Educational policies in the South were also shaped by regional gender stereotypes. Pedestal imagery was employed by students, faculty, administrators, and legislators alike to forestall attempts at coeducation. When Governor Ben Tillman of South Carolina suggested making the state college at Columbia coeducational in 1893, the Charleston *News and Courier* protested: "Our people still believe in manly men and womanly women," the editors explained, "and whether right or wrong the impression prevails that co-education after a certain age tends to modify those distinctive qualities which should be the pride of each sex."[8] Women, it was feared, would corrupt and be corrupted by the masculine atmosphere of the university. The *Courier*'s attitude was shared by young men at the municipal College of Charleston. In June 1903 the students unanimously approved a petition opposing "the introduction of co-education in the College of Charleston." The admission of women, the petition explained, "would inevitably tend to alter the spirit and tone of robust manliness of the student body which we believe to be of even greater importance than scholarship."[9]

Class, too, was an issue to many of the Populists in the state legislatures of the 1890s. The university, with its classical education, prepared the region's ruling elite for careers in government and law; it did not provide the type of utilitarian education that would benefit the average working man and woman. In the so-called Shell Manifesto of 1890, which was written by Tillman although attributed to the President of the Farmers' Association, George Washington Shell, Tillman associated the University of South Carolina in Columbia and The Citadel in Charleston with the "aristocratic oligarchy," or "ring," which had dominated South Carolina politics since the colonial period. Such institutions benefited the "lordly planters" at the expense of the "poor farmers."[10]

The introduction of coeducation at South Carolina College (later the University of South Carolina) illustrates the ways in which politicians used gender, race, and class to carry out personal political agendas. Governor Tillman was not about to let his enemies in Charleston or Columbia undermine his plans for the state college. John Gary Evans, Tillman's right-hand man and successor as governor, told legislators the story of two South Carolina teens who drowned on "their way to attend a northern college." Evans concluded: "[I]f this institution had been opened to the women of the state, two of the state's fairest and noblest daughters would not now be lying cold in death in the frigid waters of a northern state."[11]

The Tillmanites were not consistent supporters of coeducation, however. In 1891 Tillman had established South Carolina Industrial and Winthrop Normal College to provide a vocational education for white women who might have to support themselves. The College offered training in traditional female pursuits. Winthrop students were prepared to be teachers, dressmakers, secretaries, and farmers' wives, whereas men who wanted training in agricultural or industrial subjects prepared to be engineers, mechanics, or farmers at Clemson College, also established by Tillman and opened to the men of the state in 1893. There was no mention of coeducation for either of these institutions. Only the Colored Normal, Industrial, Agricultural and Mechanical College, located in Orangeburg, was coeducational. One wonders whether Tillman's enthusiasm for coeducation at Carolina was not part of his efforts to humiliate the graduates of a school that he had already reduced from a university to a liberal arts college—and that he associated with his planter enemies.[12]

Under the Tillman plan, admission to the state college was limited to white women who had completed two years of college elsewhere. As one politician quipped, "[I]f girls were admitted before maturity, the girls of South Carolina being so pretty and the boys so attractive, time would be lost in flirting."[13] Even this modest proposal was an anathema to South Carolina faculty and trustees; they agreed to the plan only because it was a condition of their appropriations' moneys. Much to the relief of the professors, no women matriculated in 1894. Tillmanites would not be rebuffed so easily; the following year the legislature amended the bill to admit all qualified women, and in the fall of 1895, thirteen women registered.[14]

Neither the male students nor the faculty suffered coeducation gladly. The college's prestigious literary societies immediately amended their constitutions to keep women from joining. Although a woman was elected president of the freshman class in 1897, disapproving upperclassmen forced her to resign.[15] No attempts were made to procure housing for out-of-town students, and many of the men were downright hostile. Administrators also hoped that coeducation would be abandoned. President Mitchell told the trustees that "co-education does not accord altogether with the instincts and ideals of the Atlantic states, and particularly in this institution."[16] Nell Crawford Flinn, a 1905 alumna of the college, advised women to stay away: "[A] college for men where women are permitted to take degrees, where the number who take advantage of this privilege is small, where there are no provisions made for them, where the whole atmosphere is one which makes them feel that they are intruders—in such a situation a woman is out of place." Flinn conceded that coeducation might work in the West, but her own experience suggested that it was "not compatible with Southern traditions."[17]

In 1913 South Carolina's administrators joined the nearby Presbyterian College for Women in a plan to establish a coordinate college for women. The university would purchase the land and buildings of the Presbyterian college, which was experiencing severe financial troubles, and transfer all women students to the new site. As one member of the board of trustees from the College for Women explained: "[T]his plan does not contemplate co-education in any sense. The social life of the College will be entirely distinct from the University, and there will be no women on the campus. The two institutions may unite in a common auditorium when one can be provided and the women students will be given the use of the library, museums, and laboratories, but otherwise there will be no commingling [*sic*] of students."[18]

Because the university was a state institution, the merger had to be approved by the legislature. The first reading of the bill went smoothly, and public opinion seemed to favor the action. Ironically, opposition came from another institution in the city, the Columbia Theological Seminary.

One of the faculty of the seminary maintained that state purchase of the property violated the original terms of the endowment that had been given by the Presbyterian Church "to provide to the higher education of women under distinctly Christian influence." As a result of these objections, the plan fell through, and the University of South Carolina remained, albeit unenthusiastically, coeducational.[19]

Gradually, the administration and faculty were coming to the realization that women were on campus to stay and that something ought to be done to integrate them into the university community. In 1916 President Melton complained to the trustees that the legislature had placed the school "in the anomalous position of offering these advantages to the women of the State without providing adequate equipment for their accommodation." As a result, the university had been "forced to discourage at least passively the enrollment of young women." Melton believed that this was a shame because "they are amongst our most excellent students." Without a dormitory or meeting place, "they are denied all of the advantages of college life, which accrue from association with their own sex in the institution."[20]

With the entrance of the United States into World War I, women became more prominent on the University of South Carolina campus. In 1918, with the men's dormitories only half full, the university suggested converting one of the buildings into a women's dormitory. The trustees refused to approve the plan, arguing that "the presence of women in a campus dormitory is undesirable." The board believed that college facilities were the responsibility of the legislature: "Until adequate provision by the General Assembly is made for women students," they told the president, "it does not seem expedient to encourage them to enroll at all."[21]

Encouraged or not, however, women enrolled in increasing numbers in the postwar years, so that by the mid-twenties more than 350 women, approximately one-fourth of the total student population, were registered for classes. Despite the wishes of conservative trustees and alumni, benign neglect had not eliminated women from the campus. Finally, in 1923, construction was begun on a women's dormitory, and in 1924 a dean of women (who would also be the first woman faculty member) was hired.[22]

When the Great Depression of the thirties decreased the appropriations to the university, women students were the first to suffer. Freshmen and sophomore women were denied access to dormitory facilities, an action that severely limited the enrollment of out-of-town women below the junior class. Nor were nonresidents the only women affected. Women day students had to pay a surcharge of $10 per semester, a significant amount at a time when the university faculty itself was paid in scrip. These restrictions remained in effect until 1936.[23]

Clemson College (later Clemson University), the land-grant college in South Carolina, did not become coeducational until 1955. State authorities argued that women could receive a vocational and professional education suited for their sex at Winthrop, the State College for Women, and had no need to attend Clemson. The first women on the Clemson campus were three faculty members who were hired in the fall of 1918 because of the manpower shortage occasioned by World War I. The board of trustees discussed admitting women to the graduate programs in 1923 and again in 1929, but nothing was done until 1950, when the graduate school was opened to white women with bachelor's degrees. Seven undergraduate women were trained by the engineering department for factory production jobs in 1942, but they were not considered regular students. Finally, the board voted to admit undergraduate women to the college beginning in January 1955. Women students had to find their own housing, however, and their numbers remained low until a dormitory was provided for them in 1963. As at the University of South Carolina, women were initially barred from working on school publications and from participating in social clubs. In response, they formed their own student government organization and planned separate social activities.[24]

Women at the University of North Carolina were similarly thwarted in their efforts to obtain educational equity. The first "ladies of the hill" attended classes informally, but, one alumna recalled, they "were required to sit behind screens in classes in order that the boys might keep their minds and eyes on their work." At the request of President Alderman, women were officially admitted to graduate courses at the University in 1897 and to classes at the junior and senior level the following year. Students and faculty were far less hospitable. The names of women students did not appear in the school annual until 1900, nor their pictures until 1907. After World War I, women were allowed to enter the professional schools, and residents of Chapel Hill could enter in their freshman year, but the "official attitude of the University," one woman wrote in 1921, "seems to be that women are admitted but not encouraged to come."[25]

In Chapel Hill as in Columbia, no provisions were made for housing women students until the mid-twenties. When the subject of a dormitory for women was raised in the campus newspaper in the spring of 1923, it was overwhelmingly opposed by the student body. The president of the athletic association saw the dormitory as an affront to university tradition: "This is a man's school and was founded as such," he asserted. "Once co-education is permanently rooted here there will be a substantial increase in the number of male applicants denied entrance. Co-education means inadequate provisions for the advantages which men should enjoy." The president of the YMCA was even less generous. "If a co-ed dormitory is built," he concluded, "it will simply mean the beginning of a flow of co-eds and other female species into the walls of our campus that will never stop until we are all flapperized." The majority of the undergraduates saw no need for a women's dormitory at Chapel Hill as long as there was a women's college in Greensboro.[26] Fortunately, the legislature proved more progressive than the student body, and a dormitory for women was opened in 1925, but admission continued to be limited to junior and senior transfers.

In 1931, as part of an attempt to rationalize and economize the administration of institutions of higher education in the state, the University of North Carolina at Chapel Hill, the North Carolina State College of Agriculture and Engineering at Raleigh, and the North Carolina College for Women at Greensboro were "consolidated and merged" into the University of North Carolina. The women's college at Greensboro lost all programs of "professional and specialized training" except those for teachers and secretaries. Critics of the merger noted that there was not enough space at Chapel Hill "to handle all the students above junior-college level" who wanted to take advantage of its exclusive graduate offerings.[27] Although never specifically stated, one object of the consolidation plan was the transfer of all undergraduate women to Greensboro. "Women," some trustees were said to have remarked, "had no place on a men's campus." Undergraduate women remained in Chapel Hill but in limited numbers.[28]

In 1951 freshmen women were admitted to a new four-year program in nursing at the university, and in 1962 freshmen women were also admitted to the four-year degree program in fine arts. But the absence of

adequate dormitory facilities continued to limit the undergraduate enrollment of women at Chapel Hill. Admission quotas were tied to dormitory
and program spaces, resulting in much higher entrance requirements for
women than for men. Not until 1972 were single admission requirements
adopted for all students.[29]

The University of Georgia did not admit women to its College of
Arts and Sciences until the twenties. A women's normal and industrial
school had been established in Milledgeville in 1889 and a coeducational
normal school in Athens in the same year, but there were no public liberal arts institutions for women in the state before World War I. Women
gained access to the summer school of the University of Georgia in 1903,
to its graduate school in 1916, and to its undergraduate curriculum in 1918,
but they were initially confined to "programs in education and home economics." As in North and South Carolina, a shortage of dormitory rooms
limited the number of women students on the main campus. As late as
1926, the university had just one women's dormitory, which housed only 70
of the 260 women enrolled. Many parents preferred to send their daughters
to one of the state teachers' colleges, where campus accommodations were
readily available. The Georgia State College for Women enrolled 1,051
women in 1921, and the University of Georgia, 132.[30]

More than a decade after women were admitted to the University of
Georgia, there were still those unhappy with their presence in the College
of Arts and Sciences. One legislator even voted against university appropriations in 1919 because a dean of women had been appointed for the entire university rather than for just the School of Education.[31]

As in South Carolina, coordination was proposed as a way to remove
women from the main campus, and in 1933 a coordinate college was organized for freshmen and sophomore women. Women took their first two
years of courses on a separate campus and then joined the men for classes
during their junior and senior years. The dean of the coordinate college
did not believe that this plan went far enough, however, and in June 1934
he wrote to the president, recommending that all four classes of women be
kept together. "The double-header organization," he complained, "has deprived the younger and less experienced girls very largely of the natural guidance and leadership of the older and more experienced girls. It has
also deprived to a large extent the older and more experienced girls of an

opportunity to use and exercise their potential leadership (a serious educational loss to them)." The best solution, he thought, would be to establish a coordinate college for all the women students.[32]

The executive committee of the faculty of the University of Georgia also favored the separation of undergraduate male and female students. In 1938 they adopted a resolution requesting the trustees to establish a four-year college for its women students "along the plan of Tulane–Sophie Newcomb, Harvard-Radcliffe, Duke and other outstanding institutions."[33] Only the advent of World War II prevented the implementation of the plan.

The opposition to coeducation was strongest in Virginia. In 1892 a local woman, Caroline Davis, had petitioned the faculty of the University "for permission to take the regular examinations required of candidates for the A.B. [degree] in the School of Mathematics." Ms. Davis's petition was granted, and after a year of private tuition with an instructor in mathematics, she passed the graduating examinations with distinction. A special committee was created to establish a uniform policy on such requests. The faculty voted in favor of such examinations, but it also told the board of visitors that they were "not prepared to undertake for young ladies the duties of instruction." Although the admission of women to the university was subsequently discussed by the faculty, the overwhelming majority opposed coeducation.[34]

By the turn of the century, Virginia supported four state colleges for men: the University at Charlottesville, Virginia Polytechnic Institute in Blacksburg, William and Mary College in Williamsburg, and VMI in Lexington. It supported no four-year colleges for women. The two-year normal colleges provided preparation for elementary teachers but did not offer the academic subjects needed for secondary teaching. Yet, 70 percent of Virginia's secondary teachers were women. Because the private women's colleges in the state were beyond the financial reach of most Virginians, the provision of a liberal arts education by the state seemed the best solution to this inequity.[35]

Thus began a ten-year campaign, spearheaded by Mary Munford of Richmond, to establish a coordinate college for women at the University of Virginia. Coordination was said to combine the best features of the coeducational and women's college at the least cost to the state. Because women students would be able to use "the library, the laboratories, [and] also to a large extent the teaching staff" that already existed in Charlottesville, a coordinate college would be less expensive to create than a separate woman's college. On the other hand, "[s]ince young men and young women [were] not to be taught in the same classes or rooms, there [could] be no possible lowering of the high standards of classes maintained only for boys."[36] To those who feared that coordination was but the first step toward coeducation, proponents of the plan claimed that only coordination could prevent coeducation at the University of Virginia. As Mary Munford explained in a 1917 pamphlet, "Co-education is too alien to the spirit and customs of the University, with a hundred years of masculine tradition behind it, to be the wisest method of development there. But co-education will be inevitable, unless Virginia women are given opportunities absolutely equal to those afforded Virginia men."[37]

This appeal to anti-coeducation sentiment was probably not politic. Most alumni could see no difference between women on a nearby campus and women on *the* campus. Every biennium from 1910 until 1920, a bill was introduced into the legislature to establish a coordinate college at Charlottesville, and every biennium a powerful lobby of university men defeated it.[38] Arguments against coordination were those often employed against coeducation. Women would lower the standards and ruin the traditions of the university. They would distract men from their studies. They would be corrupted by the masculine nature of campus life. One professor predicted that women would become "familiar, boisterous, bold in manners, . . . rudely aggressive, and ambitiously competitive with men." A coordinate college might work at Columbia or Harvard, opponents conceded, but these were private and urban colleges, and there was "no proof that one would succeed as a State-supported institution in such a community as Charlottesville." Besides, if Mr. Jefferson had wanted women at his school, he would have provided for them in his plan.[39]

There were some victories for advocates of equal education for women. In 1918 William and Mary College was made coeducational; in 1920 the University of Virginia opened its graduate and professional programs to women; in 1921 Virginia Polytechnic Institute (VPI) admitted women to "all courses except [the] military"; and in 1925 the University of Virginia allowed women to enroll in undergraduate courses during the summer.[40] But none of these concessions was adequate to meet the educational needs of the women of the state. Ten years after Mrs. Munford launched her campaign for a coordinate college, Virginia remained the only Southern state without a publicly supported liberal arts college for women.

Women who entered the professional and graduate programs of the University of Virginia in the twenties and thirties often found themselves to be unwanted guests. Men students stomped their feet when "coeds" came into a class, and one professor even refused to allow a woman to register for his course. Another faculty member remarked that "[w]omen are lovely creatures, but they should not be educated." As a student explained, the admission of undergraduate women would turn "the lure and lilt of the Lawn" into the "love-making atmosphere of the mid-Western campus," and he would rather see the University burned to the ground first. A poll of students and faculty by the student newspaper indicated that most men were still vehemently opposed to unrestricted coeducation.[41]

Inequities also remained in the coeducational public colleges of the state. At William and Mary, women could not exceed 45 percent of the student body, and tuition fees for women were forty dollars higher than those for men. At VPI, women could not write for campus publications, belong to certain clubs, or walk in specific areas of the campus. Cadets claimed that women would ruin "school spirit, athletics, academic standards, and school traditions." The admission of women did change academic standards at VPI—they rose—but women's success in the classroom hardly converted the cadets to coeducation.[42]

In 1928 the Virginia legislature again looked into the creation of a state liberal arts institution for women, this time at a site removed from Charlottesville.[43] After several years of investigation, a special legislative committee recommended that the State Teachers' College at Fredericksburg be turned into a liberal arts college for women, coordinate with the University of Virginia.[44] The Great Depression and then World War II intervened, and not until February 1944 did the Virginia General Assembly finally approve the bill that converted Mary Washington College at Fredericksburg into a liberal arts college for women, coordinate with the University of Virginia.[45]

The educational opportunities available to women at Mary Washington were not equal to those available to men at the University of Virginia. Because the coordination plan involved converting an existing women's college into a liberal arts college modeled after the liberal arts program at Charlottesville, Mary Washington had to discontinue many of its specialized courses and degrees. Students could no longer receive credit for work in home economics, library science, and stenography, and the college could no longer offer bachelor's degrees in education, music, home economics, commerce, or physical education. Technical courses developed for the preparation of teachers were also eliminated. It was highly unlikely that students at Mary Washington would have access to the libraries or faculty of the University of Virginia—the coordinate college was almost seventy miles from Charlottesville. The men's and women's branches shared little except a formal administrative structure.[46]

A 1965 report of the Virginia Higher Education Study Commission revealed that Mary Washington College profited little from its affiliation with the University of Virginia. Mary Washington programs received no university endowment funds, the students were given no preference when they transferred to the university, and the alumnae were not named to the university board of visitors. "There is suspicion in some quarters," the commission concluded, "that the main interest of the university in maintaining Mary Washington College as a branch with enrollment limited to women students is to prevent pressure for a coeducational program in undergraduate arts and sciences at Charlottesville." The introduction of equal admission standards at the university in 1970 ended the need for a coordinate college, and in 1972 the ties between the two schools were formally severed.[47]

Mary Washington College admitted its first male students in 1970, although it remained overwhelmingly female until the 1980s. In the mid-1980s the trustees entertained a proposal to rename the institution Washington-Monroe College because some were concerned that the name "Mary Washington" was discouraging male applications. Of course, there was no similar discussion about changing the names of James Madison or George Mason in order to attract more female applicants. Alumnae protested vehemently against the change, and the board dropped its proposal in January 1986.[48]

The establishment of full coeducation at the University of Virginia was a consequence of both internal and external pressures. In 1967 a seven-member committee headed by Professor T. Braxton Woody was appointed to study the issue. Committee surveys revealed that faculty and graduate students generally favored coeducation, whereas alumni and undergraduate students generally opposed it. The Woody Committee itself voted six to one in favor of admitting women to the undergraduate arts and science programs. The board of visitors concurred and announced that the college would begin opening its doors to the daughters and wives of students and faculty in the fall of 1969.[49] A legal challenge brought by the American Civil Liberties Union on behalf of four women who were not student or faculty relatives forced the university to change its plans. Instead of a gradual transition to coeducation, the university was required to achieve equal representation of the sexes within two years.[50]

In Florida the consolidation of state-supported institutions of higher education in 1905 ended decades of coeducation in the white public colleges of the state. Public higher education in Florida dated from 1851, when the new state legislature proposed to establish two seminaries, one on the east and one on the west side of the Suwannee River, to instruct "persons both male and female in the art of teaching, . . . in the mechanic arts, in husbandry and agricultural chemistry, . . . in the fundamental laws, . . . [and in the] arts which ennoble man." The East Florida Seminary opened in Ocala in 1853, moving to Gainesville in 1866; the West Florida Seminary opened in Tallahassee in 1857. The West Florida Seminary initially taught only male students, but pressure from the community led to the creation of a "female department" in 1858. Coeducation in the classrooms dated from 1882, when financial exigencies induced administrators to combine the separate departments of the male "college" and the female "academy." Some parents complained and withdrew their children from the school, but coeducation "saved so much money that it was continued." By the turn of the century, the State of Florida was subsidizing eight institutions of higher education in the state, and all but the South Florida Military College in Bartow were coeducational.[51]

By 1905 Florida was finding it difficult to fund so many institutions of higher education, and legislators acknowledged the need to consolidate educational efforts and to create "a real state university." Henry H. Buckman, a representative from Jacksonville, introduced a bill that would abolish all existing white institutions of higher education and replace them with a university for men and a college for women. The Buckman proposal became law on 5 June 1905, and Florida State College in Tallahassee, the original site of West Florida Seminary, was chosen for the location of the Florida Female College, and East Florida Seminary in Gainesville was chosen for the men-only University of Florida.[52]

The Buckman Act did not claim to establish equal opportunities for the sexes. Legislators intended the university for men "to be the major institution in the state" and envisioned the female college as primarily a normal and industrial school. Fortunately for the women's college, the newly created single-gender institutions kept their old coeducational presidents, and President Albert Murphree, of the Female College (later Florida State College for Women), used his political influence to make Florida Female College "a university in fact, if not in name."[53]

Thanks to Murphree's efforts and those of other presidents, the women's college held its own. In 1915 it became the first publicly supported college for women to be accredited by the Southern Association of Colleges and Universities. In March 1935 it was awarded Florida's Alpha chapter of Phi Beta Kappa—the University of Florida also sought the honor, but the women's college was chosen "because of its scholastic strength, particularly in the classics."[54]

Students could get around the single-sex provisions of the Buckman Act by attending summer sessions. In 1923, for example, a woman was awarded a master of arts degree in English from the university, a degree she had earned over numerous summers. The first male graduate of Florida State College for Women received his bachelor's degree in 1934 and his master's degree in 1946, also having completed all the requirements for both degrees during the summer sessions. Because the university offered many more professional programs than the college, the legislature amended the Buckman Act in 1925 to allow junior and senior women twenty-one years of age and older to enroll in University of Florida courses that were not available to them in other public institutions.[55]

With the end of World War II and the introduction of the GI Bill, the University of Florida found itself with several thousand more qualified applicants than it could handle. The governor, not wishing to turn away deserving veterans, asked the women's college whether it could provide for a thousand men on its campus. In May 1947 the legislature voted to make both the Gainesville and Tallahassee institutions coeducational.[56]

The name of the women's college was changed to Florida State University, and a new alma mater, written by a man, was adopted. The literary magazine and yearbook were also given new, more masculine names. A new school mascot, the Seminole, was chosen, and the old school songs, based on class rivalries and traditions, were replaced by new Florida State University songs and cheers. A football team was added to the athletic program, along with intercollegiate competition for men in basketball, swimming, volleyball, and golf. Women's sports remained intramural. Family-style meals in the dining hall were replaced by less formal and less intimate meals in four cafeterias. Men took over the student government organizations. Between 1947 and 1982, only one woman was elected student body president.[57]

The same concessions were not made to women at the University of Florida. Aside from the construction of new dormitories and the addition of women's restrooms to the classroom buildings, few special accommodations were made for women students in Gainesville. Women were banned from Florida Blue Key, the "most prestigious campus organization," until 1974, and they were offered no intercollegiate athletic programs until 1972. A woman who dared to enter the law library would be "shuffled" by male students, who would rub their feet against the tiled floors until she left. The custom died out only in the late sixties, when carpeting in the new library made shuffling impossible. There were few women in leadership positions on the University of Florida campus. A woman was not elected president of the student body until 1983, and the only woman dean before 1972 was the dean of nursing.[58]

Newly established Southern states tended to be more amenable to coeducational public universities in the nineteenth century than their colonial neighbors farther east, but even in the south-central region, the academic offerings and educational facilities provided by the state for women were seldom equal to those provided for men. In Alabama the General Assembly appropriated $100,000 for three women's "branches" of the University in 1822, but administrative and financial difficulties with the men's university led legislators to forget about the higher education of women.

Only the tireless campaigns of Julia Strudwick Tutwiler, the daughter of a university professor and the president of Livingston Normal College, succeeded in opening the University of Alabama to women in 1893.[59]

Alabama legislators legally limited university admission to women "able to pass the necessary examinations to enter the sophomore or any higher class," and the absence of dormitory facilities practically limited enrollment to residents of or boarders in Tuscaloosa. Although a men's dormitory was converted into a women's residence in 1898, the first housing facility constructed especially for women was not built until 1914. In the twenties, President George Denny set out to create a women's campus, which would eventually include several dormitories, a home economics and fine arts building, a gymnasium, and numerous sorority houses—one hundred years after the first facilities at the University of Alabama were constructed for men.[60]

Women were admitted to Alabama Polytechnic Institute (later Auburn University), the state land-grant institution, in 1892. The first three "coeds" included the daughter of the president of the college, the daughter of the mayor of the town, and the niece of a professor at the college. Many men students hoped that the admission of these three women was an aberration because "no publicity was given to their entrance." Although women attended classes with the men, they were confined to a special study room between classes and were warned to look "neither to the right nor to the left" while on the campus. By the first decade of the twentieth century, coeducation was clearly established, however, and a separate women's dormitory was constructed and special women's courses in home economics, secretarial training, and nursing science were introduced.[61]

The 1871 act establishing the "Arkansas Industrial University with a normal department therein" was passed during Reconstruction, and as a consequence of radical politics the school was open to all qualified youth "without regard to race, sex, or sect." The creation of a separate branch of the university in 1873 "for the benefit of the colored population" prevented the racial integration of the university, but one woman was among the seven students who matriculated in January 1872. Relationships between the sexes were strictly regulated. Women were "prohibited from receiving the attentions of young men . . . and all associations between male and female students, such as visiting, riding, driving or walking, [were] forbidden." The shortage of dormitories for women kept enrollments low into the twentieth century. In 1903 school administrators estimated that more than three hundred women left the state to attend college elsewhere because there were no dormitory accommodations for them at the University of Arkansas.[62]

The predecessor of the University of Tennessee, Blount College, was one of the first Southern institutions to admit women. Five women—including the daughter of the territorial governor—enrolled at Blount in 1804, but others did not follow in their footsteps. By the last decade of the nineteenth century, women were increasingly seeking teacher education training, and the faculty and trustees of the University of Tennessee endorsed coeducation as a means of boosting the school's sinking enrollments. The first women enrolled in the fall of 1893, and the first bachelor's degrees were awarded to two of these students in 1895. Women did well academically, winning scholarship awards for the freshman, sophomore, and junior classes in 1894. Professors were also pleased with the "civilizing" influence that the women had on the men students, and the faculty defended coeducation when the General Assembly tried to limit the admission of women in 1895. Legislators argued that university funds should be spent primarily for education in agricultural and mechanical arts, that is, for "men's subjects." University officials responded by creating practical courses for women. In 1897 courses in domestic science and domestic art were added to the curriculum of the College of Liberal Arts. As elsewhere, the absence of campus housing kept women's enrollment low. As late as 1940, women made up less than 30 percent of the student body.[63]

As these examples illustrate, few schools in the South offered the same opportunities to women as to men in the first half of the twentieth century. Most opened their doors to women only out of fiscal pressures or legislative demands. Even then, administrators, faculty, and students tried to discourage women from taking advantage of these opportunities. Women were denied facilities for housing and socializing and then advised to stay away because these facilities were lacking. They were told they could not compete with men in the classroom and then were blamed for taking a man's place at the university. If women persevered despite these impediments, they were subject to admissions quotas and residence restrictions. Coeducational institutions tended to view men students as the primary recipients of their educational largesse. As one woman writer concluded in 1936, "[W]omen have been accepted into men's institutions as stepsisters for whom life is rendered as intolerable as possible, or there have been made arrangements that hark back to the day when the wife legally relinquished not only name but property rights as well."[64]

The white women who first attended the public universities of the South in the 1890s encountered much the same initial resentment as the African Americans would when they integrated the white universities of the region in the 1950s and 1960s. Although students and faculty were eventually reconciled to their presence, the newcomers needed considerable stamina to stay the course. The determination of the first woman to enroll at South Carolina College, Frances Gibbs, was probably typical. Gibbs decided to attend college because "I wanted to be a writer, and I knew that to be a successful writer I would need an education." South Carolina College was close to her home, and when the General Assembly voted to admit women to all classes in the fall of 1895, she applied for admission. President James Woodrow, shortly thereafter, wrote to her father, advising him to withdraw his daughter's application: "Your daughter is the only woman who has registered for classes here. As feeling is strong both among professors and students against women entering college it would be most unpleasant for a girl reared as she has been reared." Gibbs's father urged her to comply, but she held firm and "entered school, much to the dissatisfaction of all concerned except myself." Although she initially "crept into the backmost seats of the class rooms and blushed very painfully whenever spoken to," she eventually discovered that "no one held any real animosity toward me. They were all gentlemen despite the fact that they all avoided me."[65]

Frances Gibbs's independence extended to her choice of classes. She refused to enroll in the mathematics and chemistry courses required for a degree, remarking that "mathematics had not helped Milton to write 'Lycidas,' or Keats to write 'The Nightingale.'" She stayed four years at South Carolina College, studying "what I liked" and becoming "one of the foremost writers in South Carolina." She subsequently married the head of the language department at the university and established a close friendship with President Woodrow. She never completed the requirements for the A.B. degree.[66]

Another of the first women students at Carolina, Beulah Calvo, wrote an article on coeducation for the school literary magazine in 1897. Describing the progress of coeducation in the United States, she scoffed at the assumption that "[d]own South, the girls do not care to go to college with men." Such statements only showed "what little they know about us." When Southern women witnessed the success of Northern women in breaking down the barriers to coeducation, they also "became restless, aggressive, iconoclastic, and the doors of the South Carolina College opened to us." And, Calvo concluded, "we propose to stay."[67]

Why did Southern women persevere in their efforts to obtain educational equity at the state universities when so many obstacles confronted them? In most cases the decision to attend a public institution of higher education was based on practical and pecuniary considerations, not philosophical ones. A convenient location meant that students could live at home rather than board elsewhere. The tuition at public universities was extremely low and was often waived for students who promised to remain in the state and teach after graduation. Public normal and industrial schools were equally inexpensive but seldom offered the academic subjects needed for secondary teaching. Thomas Dyer, in his history of the University of Georgia, noted that "no public institution in Georgia offered a four-year course leading to a degree for women" before World War I. Private women's colleges did have good liberal arts programs, but their tuitions were high. Few women's colleges had graduate or professional programs, and fewer still, the physical plant or national recognition of a large public university. As late as 1916, there were only "seven standard colleges for women" in the entire South.[68]

The University of South Carolina Board of Trustees, in a 1919 discussion of coeducation, admitted that the university possessed "facilities for special training along a number of lines which are not offered by any other institution in the State. Many young women are leaving the State who would come here for their education if adequate provision were made for them in comfortable dormitories under proper supervision." An 1898 graduate of the school and the first woman to earn an A.B. degree explained that she had enrolled in South Carolina College because she "needed a better education than the one provided by Southern female colleges."[69]

Most women who enrolled in the public colleges and universities of the South when they became coeducational did so because of their low tuitions, convenient locations, and unique academic programs. Few women saw their entrance as a symbolic statement of sexual equality. Indeed, the coeducational environment of the university was often incidental to their choice.[70] Philosophical arguments about the relative abilities of the sexes were more likely to come from men students, who claimed that the admission of women would destroy the "spirit and tone" of the university.

This resentment of women on the campus was not peculiar to the early twentieth-century South. The first women students at the University of Michigan and Cornell, Helen Horowitz noted, "were as unwelcome as any uninvited guest." Men students excluded them from "student government, the newspaper, honor societies, athletics," and any other activities that might serve as unpleasant reminders that "Cornell was not Yale."[71] Lynn Gordon documented similar discrimination at the University of California, where women made up 46 percent of the student body by 1900. Women were denied representation on the executive committee of the Associated Students of the University of California, passed over for scholastic honors, and barred from intercollegiate competition. When men shifted their majors from the liberal arts to technical fields such as engineering, agriculture, and mining, women were blamed for driving men out of the humanities and feminizing the university.[72]

Barbara Solomon, in her history of women's higher education, found that the very success of women at coeducational schools such as Stanford, Chicago, and Wisconsin led to a fear among men students, faculty, administrators, and alumni that women would "take over" their institutions. Stanford first limited the enrollment of women to 500 students and then in 1904 adopted an admissions ratio of "three males to each female student." The University of Chicago established a separate junior college for freshmen and sophomore women in 1902. Critics of coeducation at Wisconsin talked about "the feminine equivalent to the yellow peril in education," and only the support of progressive Senator Robert La Follette kept women from being barred from the College of Liberal Arts. Women, Solomon concluded, "could not win. They either drove men out of the classroom, or they attracted them into it and then distracted them too much. The best solution was to have women attend their own schools."[73]

As Solomon's statement suggests, the South was not alone in viewing coordination as a means of preventing or ending coeducation. In the years before World War I, a number of Northern schools—Brown, Columbia, Western Reserve, Tufts, and Rochester, for example—had established coordinate colleges that educated women students separately from men. Radcliffe, one historian of the college wrote, "was perhaps the most exaggerated example of a college created solely on the basis of sex discrimination. . . . The fundamental purpose behind the establishment of Radcliffe College, from the vantage of Harvard, was to guarantee the segregation of women from men."[74]

The successful establishment of coordinate colleges in the Northeast was often cited as evidence of the superior nature of this hybrid institution, which provided women with both the resources of a big university and the intimacy of a women's college, but even at the most prestigious schools, separate was never equal. Women were seldom given the same access to the faculty, the libraries, or classroom facilities, and the women's division was always perceived as a subsidiary of the "real" university. As one member of the Harvard board of visitors commented in 1931, "Radcliffe students should come distinctly second in the use of libraries and laboratories, and . . . there should be no compulsion of any kind, either sentimental or moral, to repeat [professors'] courses at Radcliffe."[75] The dean of women at Pembroke, the coordinate college of Brown University, observed that some men students objected to "the presence of women students on the campus. . . . I suppose that this is a very natural feeling," she conceded, "since the men like to think of their campus as isolated and belonging to themselves." As one woman at Barnard College concluded, "[I]t is practically impossible to graft co-education upon an established college for men without great antagonism."[76]

Northern and Southern men expressed similar resentment at the integration of traditionally male institutions, but there were some important differences. Women in the affiliated colleges of such private schools as Harvard, Brown, and Columbia may have been treated as poor relations, but they did have the option of attending one of the public universities of the region. Many Southern women had no other alternative if the state universities, with their subsidized tuitions, were closed to them. Private liberal arts colleges were beyond the financial reach of most Southern parents.

Generally speaking, opposition to coeducation ended sooner in the West and North. Men at state universities such as Michigan and Wisconsin initially resented the arrival of women students on the campus, but they quickly adjusted to their presence. Even at the private University of Chicago, the segregation of the sexes, introduced in 1902 to prevent the "feminization" of the university, was discontinued within the decade. Women simply refused to stay away from the main campus, and college bureaucrats found the dual system too complicated to administrate.[77]

By the beginning of the twentieth century, the majority of public universities and denominational colleges in the United States saw single-sex schools as prohibitively expensive and philosophically objectionable. As Thomas Woody explained in his 1929 history of women's education, coeducation was most successful in the Western states that were "too poor to support two high grade educational institutions" and that at the same time saw the justice of "women's demand that they have equal opportunity with men." Sectarian colleges, too, tended to justify "coeducation in ethical and religious terms of the equality of souls, male and female."[78]

If financial hardship were the primary reason colleges adopted coeducation, the South should have been in the forefront of the movement. As the poorest region in the United States, it certainly could not afford separate colleges for its white men and women, especially since it already had committed its meager resources to maintain separate schools for blacks and whites. Despite the expense, the South, it seems, did not find segregation by race or sex "philosophically objectionable."

The South's opposition to coeducation paralleled rather closely its opposition to integration. Women demanding the vote or attending a historically male college conjured up fears of similar demands by Southern blacks. In South Carolina the first women to study with men at a public college were the African American women who enrolled in the normal school on the campus of the university during Reconstruction. When Carolina's dean of women, Irene Dillard Elliot, sought information on these black "coeds" in the university archives in the twenties, she was told "that the subject was taboo on campus and should continue as it had before—buried, untouched, and forgotten."[79] After all, it was Governor Tillman who had opened the South Carolina College to women, established Winthrop Industrial and Normal School, *and* reduced black Carolinians to second-class citizenship.

In Virginia, women seeking educational equity were quick to assure opponents that their "ambition to be educated" had nothing to do "with some women's ambition to be politicated." In Georgia, white women used arguments of racial superiority to justify their admission to the state university: "[N]egro men and women in the State are being given the opportunity for higher education," they told the trustees, "which, so far, the white women of Georgia have pleaded for in vain." Similarly, the president of the University of Virginia, hoping to shame the legislature into voting additional appropriations in 1925, remarked that North Carolina was "expending more money on an institution for the education of her colored youth than Virginia is expending on her State University."[80]

The similarities between the educational disadvantages of white women and African Americans in the twentieth-century South were all too apparent. Women's colleges, like black colleges, had poorer facilities, fewer degree programs, and inferior resources. By conceding that single-gender schools were not comparable to the coeducational university, legislators raised issues of educational equity that the courts would eventually use against racial segregation. Henri Monteith, the black woman who integrated the University of South Carolina in 1963, wanted to attend the school because "it was close to my home, it offered the courses that I wanted to take . . . and it would be cheaper than having to board somewhere at the college."[81] Her reasons were identical to those given by the white women who challenged the all-male admissions policy of the 1890s.

The civil rights legislation of the 1960s and 1970s attacked both racial and gender discrimination, and the integration of Southern colleges and universities resulted in increased educational opportunities for both blacks and women. As the Fourteenth Amendment's guarantee of equal protection was used to challenge the constitutionality of publicly supported single-gender as well as single-race institutions, Southern states found themselves embroiled in legal disputes over educational access. In every case the main issue was whether "separate but equal" was acceptable with respect to gender.

Although the Civil Rights Act of 1964 prohibits gender as well as racial discrimination, these two categories have been treated somewhat differently by the courts, and it is these differences between racial and gender discrimination that have been at the forefront of debates over the legality of single-gender education in a public setting. Title IX of the Education Act Amendments of 1972, which prohibited discriminatory admissions policies at schools receiving federal funds, included several significant exclusions: "certain religious institutions, elementary and secondary schools, military institutions, and undergraduate institutions that have been traditionally and continually single-sex from their inception."[82]

Generally speaking, the courts have applied strict scrutiny to cases of racial discrimination while using the less rigorous intermediate-level scrutiny test with gender. To pass the mid-level test, a state that wanted to support a single-gender school must "first prove the existence of important governmental interests that are advanced by the exclusionary admissions policy" and then show that this policy is "based on real differences between the sexes rather then [*sic*] stereotypic notions about the proper roles of men and women."[83]

In July 1982 the United States Supreme Court ruled in *Mississippi University et al. v. Hogan* that the single-gender admissions policy of the women's college's School of Nursing violated the Equal Protection Clause of the Fourteenth Amendment. The plaintiff, Joe Hogan, was a registered nurse working in a medical center in Columbus, Mississippi, when he applied for admission to the School of Nursing baccalaureate program at Mississippi University for Women (MUW). The women's school was located in Columbus, whereas the state's coeducational nursing programs were a considerable distance from his work. When MUW denied Hogan admission because of his sex, he sued.[84]

The district court denied Hogan preliminary injunctive relief, arguing that the "maintenance of MUW as a single-sex school [bore] a rational relationship to the State's legitimate interest 'in providing the greatest practical range of educational opportunities for its female student population'" and that single-gender education was "consistent with a respected, though by no means universally accepted educational theory that single-sex education affords unique benefits to students." The Court of Appeals for the Fifth Circuit reversed the district court's ruling: "Recognizing that the State has a significant interest in providing educational opportunities for all its citizens, the court . . . found that the State had failed to show that providing a unique educational opportunity for females, but not for males, bears a substantial relationship to that interest."[85]

Mississippi contended that Congress had exempted schools that had historically been single-sex institutions from its gender discrimination prohibition of Title IX, but the court of appeals rejected this argument, stating that under the terms of the Fourteenth Amendment, Congress could not grant states the right to violate the amendment. The court would not accept MUW's claim that its admissions policy compensated for earlier discrimination against women, either. "Rather than compensate for discriminatory barriers faced by women, MUW's policy of excluding males from admission to the School of Nursing tends to perpetuate the stereotyped view of nursing as an exclusively woman's job."[86]

The United States Supreme Court affirmed the judgment of the court of appeals and ruled that males should be admitted to MUW's School of Nursing. Although Justice Sandra O'Connor, in delivering the opinion of the Court, interpreted the case narrowly, insisting that the ruling applied only to MUW's School of Nursing, Justice Powell, in his dissent, raised questions about the breadth of the Court's decision. "It seems to me," Powell wrote, "that in fact the issue properly before us is the single-sex policy of the University. . . . The Court of Appeals so viewed this case, and unambiguously held that a single-sex institution of higher education no longer is permitted by the Constitution."[87] Not wishing to face additional lawsuits, MUW decided to open all of its programs to men. By 1994, men constituted 20 percent of the student body.[88]

Texas Woman's University (TWU), another publicly supported institution for women, had voluntarily opened its undergraduate and graduate programs in nursing and public health to men in 1973. But men continued to be barred from other majors and programs at the university. This policy presented a problem for Steven Serling, a man accepted into the nursing program at TWU in the fall of 1994. Serling was thinking of changing his major to business, only to discover that business courses were closed to men.[89] When Serling threatened to sue for sex discrimination, TWU's Board of Regents voted in December 1994 to admit men to all undergraduate degree programs.[90]

The admission of men to MUW and TWU left only two publicly supported, single-gender institutions in the nation—The Citadel in Charleston, South Carolina, and Virginia Military Institute (VMI) in Lexington, Virginia. Both were subsequently the focus of lawsuits aiming to integrate their all-male corps of cadets. In a 1990 letter the U.S. Justice Department claimed that VMI's all-male admissions policy violated the Equal Protection Clause of the Fourteenth Amendment and the Civil Rights Act of 1964. In response, the Virginia Attorney General filed a lawsuit in the federal district court, maintaining that state-supported, single-gender institutions were legal under Title IX of the Education Amendments Act of 1972.[91]

A series of appeals and countersuits between the state and the Justice Department soon followed. When U.S. District Judge Jackson L. Kiser ruled in 1991 that VMI's admissions policy was constitutional, the U.S. Court of Appeals for the Fourth Circuit overturned his ruling. VMI, in response, appealed to the United States Supreme Court, but the Court refused to hear the appeal. This left Virginia with three options presented by the court of appeals: make VMI a private institution, provide a parallel experience for women, or admit women to the corps of cadets at VMI.[92]

In February 1994 VMI presented its proposal for a Virginia Women's Institute for Leadership (VWIL), to operate at Mary Baldwin College, a private women's college located approximately 30 miles from VMI. The women would be subject to the same military training as the VMI cadets, although first-year students would not be required to have their heads shaved as do VMI's "rats." Judge Kiser ruled that the VWIL program met the requirements of the appeals court.[93] The Justice Department appealed Kiser's ruling, insisting that the women's leadership institute was not a parallel program as required by the court but, rather, "a marriage of convenience among an institution that irrationally fears women, an institution that justifiably fears red ink, and a state government that defines diversity by abdication."[94]

Virginia's decision to create a separate leadership institute for women at Mary Baldwin was compared to earlier attempts to maintain racial segregation. "Separate-but-equal," a *New York Times* editorial proclaimed, "is a doctrine long discredited for addressing racial inequality. There should be the same presumption against using it when the discrimination is against women." The editorial found Virginia's actions "unworthy of a state that has survived its own widespread resistance to racial integration to offer its moral, political, legal and financial support to this new form of resistance to equality." The *Times* believed that the best solution was the simplest: admit women to the corps of cadets at VMI.[95]

At The Citadel in South Carolina, where officials were fighting their own battle against coeducation, Judge Kiser's ruling was applauded. "The court's decision affirms the validity of single-gender education for males and females," Citadel president Lt. Gen. Claudius E. Watts stated, "and we obviously support the preservation of that freedom of choice for both sexes. I think it is very gratifying that the court has ruled that single-gender programs in public schools are constitutional."[96]

The U.S. Justice Department suit against VMI in 1990 brought the question of The Citadel's admissions policies to the public's attention. Citadel officials, as those at VMI, argued that the rigorous military training and barracks life of a cadet was not suitable for women. The admission of women, it was argued, would destroy the male bonding that arose from the single-sex experience. "There's a feeling of brotherhood," one Citadel student explained. "Women would drive a wedge of division between us."[97]

The participation of women in the Gulf War in 1991 led South Carolina Representative Sarah Manly to introduce a bill into the General Assembly that would withhold state funds from any public institution that discriminated against individuals because of their sex. Manly, wearing a button that said, "Women are in the gulf war; why aren't they in the Citadel?" led the fight for what was dubbed The Citadel bill. The measure was quickly tabled in committee.[98]

In June 1992 navy veterans Patricia Johnson and Elizabeth Lacey sued for the right to attend day classes at The Citadel. Neither woman wanted to live in the barracks or drill with the cadets; they simply wanted to have the same options for classes as the male veterans. Only three degree programs were available in the evening program; seventeen, in the mornings and afternoons. Worried about a sex-discrimination lawsuit,

The Citadel responded by eliminating its day program for veterans altogether.[99]

The Citadel's battle to keep women out of its day classes soon intensified. In December 1992 a South Carolina high school senior, Shannon Faulkner, became involved in a class debate over a *Sports Illustrated* article on hazing at The Citadel. One thing led to another, and the students ended up discussing the school's all-male admissions policy. On a whim, Faulkner went down to the guidance office and picked up an application. She asked the counselor to delete references to her gender on her transcripts and sent off her application. Shortly thereafter, she was offered a place in the corps.[100]

The Citadel discovered its mistake and rescinded Faulkner's acceptance. In March 1993 Faulkner sued, arguing that the admissions policy of The Citadel denied her equal protection under the law as guaranteed by the Fourteenth Amendment and asking to be admitted to the corps of cadets as a "knob" in the fall of 1993. In June 1993 the U.S. Government joined her suit, expanding the case to demand the admission of all qualified women.[101]

In August 1993 U.S. District Judge C. Weston Houck ruled that Faulkner should be allowed to attend day classes at The Citadel while the court reviewed her request to be admitted to the corps of cadets. When The Citadel gained a stay by the court to keep her from enrolling in the fall, Faulkner appealed, and a panel of the U.S. Court of Appeals for the Fourth Circuit voted two to one to allow Faulkner to attend The Citadel as a day student until the court decided whether or not she could become a member of the corps of cadets. Judge Kenneth K. Hall wondered "whether, under the Equal Protection Clause, a state can ever have a sufficiently important interest to justify expending public funds to maintain an institution that not only practices inequality, but celebrates it."[102]

Faulkner's lawsuit was set for 16 May 1994, and Judge Houck told The Citadel and the state that they needed to propose an acceptable remedy that he could consider during the trial. Hoping to prove that the school's admissions policy was constitutional, The Citadel's lawyers saw no need for a "remedial plan." They believed their claims were bolstered by Concurrent Resolution 4170, passed by the South Carolina General Assembly on

20 May 1993, which set forth "a policy of diversity in education which include[d] single-sex institutions where there [was] sufficient demand to support the same.[103]

Both the lawyers for Faulkner and those for The Citadel referred to the Fourth Circuit Court of Appeals' rulings in the VMI case, in particular its conclusion that "the Commonwealth of Virginia, despite its announced policy of diversity, has failed to articulate an important policy that substantially supports offering the unique benefits of a VMI-type education to men and not to women." Faulkner's lawyers interpreted this ruling to mean that Faulkner's constitutional rights would be infringed if she were not admitted to the corps of cadets. The Citadel's lawyers disagreed, arguing that the cases were not parallel because South Carolina, unlike Virginia, had a policy, established in Concurrent Resolution 4170, justifying the exclusion of women from the corps.[104]

At the end of the May trial, Judge Houck gave The Citadel two weeks to prepare a contingency plan in case he found its admissions policies unconstitutional. The Citadel's plan provided for Faulkner only and would delay her admission to the corps until the fall of 1995. She would then have to get the traditional shaved haircut required of knobs, wear a Citadel uniform, meet the Army's physical requirements for women, board in an unlocked, single room in the school's infirmary, and be admitted to the barracks only for company formations and activities.[105]

Because Faulkner was already in her second year of college, Judge Houck decided to separate her case from that of subsequent female applicants. He ordered The Citadel to admit Faulkner to the corps of cadets. In addition, the school was to "pursue their proposed remedial plan without delay and formulate, adopt, and implement a plan that conforms with the Equal Protection Clause of the Fourteenth Amendment of the Constitution . . . by the beginning of the school year, 1995–1996."[106]

The committee established by the Concurrent Resolution had posited several alternatives to coeducation, including "a new public institution for women in South Carolina, a 'women's college' within a larger university, a compact arrangement with Mary Baldwin College in Virginia or with Converse College or Columbia College in South Carolina, and an increase in the tuition grants program to provide more money for women to attend single-gender private institutions." Houck noted that in the case of

Missouri ex rel. Gaines v. Canada (1938), the Supreme Court rejected Missouri's claim that it did not have to provide equal law facilities for blacks because there was not sufficient demand for them. He believed that this decision also made a compact arrangement with Mary Baldwin unconstitutional.[107]

When the Fourth U.S. Circuit Court of Appeals ruled two to one to grant The Citadel's request, dissenting judge Kenneth Hall exploded: "South Carolina stubbornly maintains that a system, proved by the nation's service academies to work, is unworkable. . . . That such a situation could be tolerated in the 19th century is not surprising, but we're about to embark on the 21st." African Americans in the region were quick to note the parallels between the treatment of women by officials at VMI and The Citadel and the treatment of blacks by educators of an earlier generation. In September 1994 Faulkner was awarded the National Association for the Advancement of Colored People Trailblazer Award at the Charleston branch's annual Freedom Fund banquet. The chapter president explained that Faulkner was given the award "because of her action to open the door to education for women of all colors."[108]

The Citadel in the meantime filed an appeal asking the Fourth Circuit Court of Appeals "to throw out Houck's order or, failing that, reverse the part allowing Miss Faulkner to become a cadet." Instead of admitting women to the corps, the state proposed a women's leadership program similar to the one put forward by VMI. The Citadel argued that this option would give women the same benefits that men received in the corps of cadets. Faulkner's lawyers disagreed. Women in the leadership program would not have the living experiences of cadets and would not have the prestige of a Citadel degree.[109]

Faulkner's court-ordered admission to the corps of cadets on 12 August 1995 ended a week later with her voluntary withdrawal from the school. Her departure was accompanied by accusations of foul play from both sides. That same fall, young women enrolled in the parallel programs established by VMI at Mary Baldwin and by The Citadel at Converse, and a new plaintiff, Nancy Mellette, announced her intention to seek admission to the corps of cadets at The Citadel. An attractive and athletic young woman who had excelled in the physically and academically demanding environment of Oak Ridge Military Academy in North Carolina, Mellette was a formidable plaintiff. The daughter and sister of Citadel alumni, she had attended numerous functions on The Citadel campus and had voiced a wish to attend The Citadel since she was a small child. The Women's Leadership Program at Converse did not offer the courses in electrical engineering that she wanted to take.[110]

As the debate over the admission of women to VMI and The Citadel indicated, traditional views of woman's nature and place continued to influence discussions on higher education in the nineties. Supporters of the all-male corps of cadets quoted studies which showed that "some males thrive best in an educational setting entirely suffused with a confrontational and disciplinary focus" and contended that experiences at the national service academies have shown that such programs cannot survive coeducation.[111] Supporters of coeducation insisted that they were not against single-gender education but against segregation funded by taxpayer money. Others argued that the benefits of single-gender education for men were not as clear as they were for women. As a professor at Tulane explained, "[C]o-educational institutions reflect the values, perspectives and the practices of the dominant male culture. . . . Therefore, men do not necessarily get anything different by going to a single-sex institution." One of Faulkner's lawyers went even further, contending that all-male schools produced "men who feel that they are superior to women" and encouraged "racist and homophobic attitudes."[112]

In the spring of 1996, the Supreme Court agreed to rule on the constitutionality of VMI's admissions policy. Although The Citadel was not a party to the suit, lawyers for both sides acknowledged that the ruling would affect the single-gender status of the South Carolina school as well. In a seven-to-one decision, handed down on 29 June 1996, the Supreme Court ruled that "the Constitution's equal protection guarantee precludes Virginia from reserving exclusively to men the unique educational opportunities VMI affords." Significantly, the Court concluded that neither VMI's "goal of producing citizen-soldiers" nor its "adversative method of training" was "inherently unsuitable to women." It also disagreed with the Fourth Circuit's ruling that a parallel program for women at Mary Baldwin provided an opportunity for women equal to that provided for men at VMI. The Court compared the VWIL program with ones established fifty years earlier to keep blacks out of the flagship universities of the region. Separate was not equal when it came to gender or to race.[113]

VMI's initial response was disappointment, and many alumni suggested privatization to avoid coeducation. The Citadel acquiesced more quickly to the Court's decision. On 28 June its board of visitors voted to "eliminate gender as a restriction to admission, effective immediately." The institution would, the board chairman announced, "enthusiastically accept qualified female applicants into the Corps of Cadets." Val Vojdik, the lawyer who had first represented Shannon Faulkner and later Nancy Mellette, remarked, "I knew they would admit women, but the speed and graciousness with which they did it was really impressive."[114]

The Citadel's decision to admit women in the fall of 1996 did not bring an end to the controversy, however. Two of the four women "knobs" withdrew from the military college after only one semester, alleging that they had been physically and mentally harassed. Kim Messer, of Clover, South Carolina, and Jeanie Mentavlos, of Charlotte, North Carolina, subsequently went public with their complaints. Cadets had pushed Messer's face against a wall with a rifle, forced her to drink tea until she vomited, rubbed up against Mentavlos while she stood in formation, barged into her room wearing only boxer shorts, refused to allow her to obtain physical therapy for pelvic stress fractures, and set both women's uniforms on fire with Cutex nail polish remover.[115] Messer later brought suit in state court and Mentavlos in federal court for violations of their civil rights.

Administrators at The Citadel initially denied the allegations, claiming that the women had fabricated the charges to justify their own poor academic performance. Although they later acknowledged that the incidents had occurred and eventually disciplined fourteen cadets as a consequence, Citadel officials claimed that the hazing was not "gender based" but rather related to endemic problems in the Fourth Class System. The commandant of cadets told an ad hoc committee reviewing the coeducation plan that "he was convinced that the women were so well accepted that male cadets treated them like any other first-year students. He noted that two male cadets also had their shirts set afire after being doused with nail polish remover."[116]

The media seemed unconvinced that the mistreatment of Messer and Mentavlos had nothing to do with gender. "Coming after the Citadel's years-long struggle to keep women out," a *New York Times* reporter wrote, "the accusations of abuse by the two cadets have once again focused a national spotlight on this pocket of fierce resistance, long backed by the state, to the national norm of coeducation."[117] To many who had followed developments at the military school over the years, this latest incident was only part of a pattern of institutionalized intimidation designed to scare women away from the campus: "The Citadel's hazing tradition teaches young men that brutalizing others and denigrating women is what it takes to be a military officer. . . . Unless they take steps to change an institutional culture so at odds with American society, Citadel graduates will find they are unprepared for the real world after playing sadistic games for four years."[118]

Faced with a public relations crisis, officials at the military institution decided to cancel classes in order to hold a day-long session of sensitivity training. Brigadier General Emory Mace, a Citadel graduate and father of Nancy Mace, one of the two remaining female cadets, was hired as new commandant of cadets, and school officials pledged to purge the Fourth Class System of its abuses. Thus, when the second class of women entered in August 1997, they found not only two upper-class women on campus but two adults in each barracks to oversee cadets at night, a new female assistant commandant, and revised regulations for the treatment of knobs.[119]

The first class of women at VMI arrived on campus in August 1997. VMI had been less willing than The Citadel to concede defeat when the Supreme Court ruled against the school in June 1996. Postponing a decision on whether to admit women until September, the governing board studied the feasibility of buying the school from the state and becoming a private institution.[120] Although the board eventually voted nine to eight in favor of coeducation, officials refused to make any exceptions to the VMI fitness test administered to each "rat" on admission. Women would also receive the same close-cropped haircuts and the same uniform items as male cadets. As VMI Superintendent, Major General Josiah Bunting III, declared, "It is my fixed intention to preserve and sustain those principles and features of a VMI education that have proved their worth for a century and a half. One of them is that all cadets be treated the same, and their achievements be measured by common standards. The egalitarian ethos of VMI does not know gender."[121]

In the eleven months between its decision to admit women and the arrival of the first female rats, VMI developed a detailed assimilation plan that addressed such issues as fraternization, jewelry and cosmetics, visitation, cadet privacy, billeting, cadet terminology, physical education, recruiting, and orientation. Women exchange students were brought in from Texas A&M and from Norwich University in Vermont to serve as role models for the new women cadets, a woman gynecologist was employed to provide health care services, and a woman admissions officer was hired to develop coeducational marketing and recruitment strategies. VMI's web page added information for female high school students, high school coaches, high school guidance counselors, and alumni recruiters. A letter to the latter significantly noted: "Representing the Institute, you must treat all prospects, male and female, with equal enthusiasm. If, for some reason, you no longer feel comfortable in this role, please give me a call so that we can discuss your reservations so other alumni willing to participate can be identified from your part of the country."[122]

The admission of women to VMI in the fall of 1997 marked the end of publicly funded, single-gender education in the region. Nonetheless, opponents of coeducation remained defiant. When Citadel alumni announced plans to change the name of their organization from the Association of Citadel Men to the Association of Citadel Graduates, a 1973 graduate of the school placed advertisements in newspapers throughout South Carolina asking alumni to vote against the provision. "There is no reason women can't create a new parallel association," claimed the author, obviously unaware that the Justices had ruled that "parallel" was not equal. To their credit, most alumni had no desire to continue the gender wars and voted overwhelmingly to approve the change.[123]

Other opponents of coeducation proposed the establishment of a new private, all-male military school, to be known as the Southern Military Institute (SMI). The brainchild of a 1977 VMI graduate, Michael Guthrie, the proposal soon gained the support of a secessionist organization, the League of the South, which hoped to make the new college "a bastion for the dignity of Southern culture." The school would celebrate

Confederate Memorial Day, glorify Confederate heroes such as Robert E. Lee and Stonewall Jackson, and teach Christian values. According to league spokesman Michael Hill, "SMI students will be gentlemen, 'not imbued with the virus of political correctness—who are real men, who will not be wimps . . . and who will not kowtow to the feminists." For entertainment, there would be formal military dances "with girls wearing their pretty dresses."[124]

The SMI proposal resulted in a media debate on what was meant by "Southern culture." Larry Evans, in an editorial for the Fredericksburg, Virginia, *Free Lance-Star,* quipped that the SMI "might as well offer a major in secession science." Evans warned that such a school would "not only attract VMI alums who want to sit around sipping Virginia Gentleman whiskey and pining for the Old South. No, when the Confederate flag starts flapping in the breeze it will also attract a rag-tag army of racists, misogynists and angry young men with an assortment of twisted agendas." He questioned whether "American ideals [would] be taught at . . . a college where 'admission preference' will be 'given to young men from Dixie.' " Northern commentators were even less kind. *The Philadelphia Daily News* labeled its column on SMI "Losers Academy" and suggested that "before the gentlemen tell Mammy to dust off Captain Butler's saber," they need to be reminded that "[t]he Confederacy lost its war." In an Internet chat column, "Where the Boys Are," author Cody Ann Michaels similarly wondered about the "traditions" that the Southern League wished to defend: "[A]s far as I know from school, the military traditions of the Confederacy were a. losing the war and b. defending slavery. . . . I'm also curious to know how graduates of a boys school dedicated to defending slavery and being misogynistic can be expected to fit into society of the 21st century."[125] Most critics argued that an all-male military college was simply not appropriate given the coeducational nature of today's army.

United States v. Virginia et al. reopened the century-long debate over the relative merits of single-gender and coeducational schools. Opponents of coeducation at The Citadel and VMI repeated the arguments used against the admission of women to the flagship universities of the Southern states decades earlier: "Cadets say that coeducation will destroy tradition, force longtime habits to change, dilute the alumni network, diminish the stature of the Citadel [and VMI] man, lower standards, remove privacy and the special bonding experience Citadel [and VMI] men enjoy, and change the ethical, intellectual makeup of the Citadel [and VMI] man." Bumper stickers pleaded, "Save the Males," and T-shirts proclaimed, "Better Dead Than Coed." Most officials at previously all-male institutions believed that such fears were unfounded. The head of physical education programs at West Point claimed that "[t]he standards are as high [as] or higher than they were." The former associate dean at Washington and Lee University (whose campus is contiguous to VMI's "post") claimed that the advent of coeducation in 1985 "propelled the school from a good school of Southern reputation to an excellent school of national reputation." Similarly, Yale alumni discovered that the presence of alumnae did not lessen the power of the "Yale club." As one graduate put it, "Power is expanded by its use—not diluted." He stressed the changes that have occurred nationwide in the student population: "Today almost every single student who would enter The Citadel or Yale comes from a coeducational background, contrary to 20 years ago. . . . Going to school with the other sex is . . . no big deal."[126]

Many who favored the admission of women to The Citadel and VMI also favored the continued existence of women's colleges and girls' schools. As Judith Shapiro explained in an article, "What Women Can Teach Men," all-male and all-female colleges fostered very different cultures: "In a society that favors men over women, men's institutions operate to preserve privilege; women's institutions challenge privilege and attempt to expand access to the good things of life." To Shapiro, the issue was one of nurture, not nature: "Women's colleges . . . exist to address inequality between the sexes and to serve the interests of women—not as places where women can think differently, or learn differently, or speak differently, but as the proverbial room of one's own."[127] Similar arguments have been used, of course, to justify the continued existence of historically black colleges and universities.

Twentieth-century discussions of coeducation at public colleges and universities revealed the ways in which the "twoness" of Southern culture affected educational philosophy and practice. Opponents of coeducation argued that individual difference—between white and black, men and women, rich and poor—justified education in separate and dissimilar institutions. The university was, in many ways, the ultimate symbol of male dominance, white supremacy, and class privilege, and the men who ran the state legislatures of the region were no more willing to grant sexual equality than they were to acknowledge racial or social equality. For many institutions, maintaining the "spirit and tone of robust manliness" was more important than promoting academic excellence or educational equity.

~4~

Peerless Standards of Unsullied Honor

Women's Social Life on the Southern College Campus[1]

Southern women possessed a distinctive college culture during much of the twentieth century, a culture that reflected the "twoness" of Southern society. Social regulations, physical education programs, extracurricular activities, student government, and even college architecture created a campus climate that both reinforced and challenged regional gender, class, and racial stereotypes. Prescriptions for dress and behavior; membership criteria for clubs, sororities, and other organizations; the nature of residential life; and the conservatism of Southern institutions—all made it difficult for Southern women to question tradition and to assert their individuality. Yet these same factors created bonds of sisterhood that encouraged women to unite with other like-minded women to work for community improvement and social change.

Certain regional peculiarities made the Southern woman's educational experience different from that of other American college women, especially in the first half of the twentieth century. In her study of white, middle-class college youth, Paula Fass remarked on "the increased size and heterogeneity of school populations" in the years after World War I, which made it harder for college administrators to maintain the degree of control over students that they had held earlier. Fass believed that "the democratization of family relations" associated with the small, middle-class families of the nation's cities began to affect higher education in the twenties. Students resented the paternalistic rules and regulations of the colleges of the era and demanded from educational institutions the same sort of independence and trust they received from their families.[2]

The liberalization of college restrictions that Fass documented was, however, associated with particular demographic developments that were less pronounced in the South. Fass found that the most "plastic" youth—those who "knew that they lived in a changing world that demanded new understanding, new conventions, and constant readjustments"—came from small, urban families and attended large, coeducational universities.[3] Until the forties, however, Southern families remained large, the Southern economy rural, and Southern educational institutions small (and, for white women, predominantly single-sex). The student bodies of the segregated colleges of the South were also far less heterogeneous than those in the schools of the North. The white population was largely Western European, the black population was largely West African, and both were overwhelmingly Protestant.[4] Thus Southern women were far less likely than their Northern counterparts to encounter classmates from different cultures.

Southern perceptions of women also differed from those in the North. Anne Firor Scott, in her study of the Southern woman from 1830 to 1930, found that even the suffrage campaign, which "more than any other aspect of the feminist movement became the symbol of women's emancipation, . . . had certain strongly marked regional characteristics" associated with antebellum views of woman's nature and sphere.[5] Belief in biologically determined attributes or roles was, of course, not confined to the antebellum South, but regional variations in "celebrations of women" were clearly apparent by the early nineteenth century.[6] Scott found a "more rigid definition of the role of women" in the antebellum South than in the North; in fact, the image of the "beautiful, gentle, efficient, morally superior" lady who was graciously willing to "accept without question the doctrine of male supremacy" was elevated in the South "to the position of a myth."[7] Likewise, Catherine Clinton concluded that Northerners and Southerners defined a good woman differently: "[I]n the North, virtue was synonymous with industriousness. . . . In the South, . . . chastity."[8]

Both Scott and Clinton saw the antebellum image of the lady as limiting Southern women's freedom into the twentieth century. Although Scott believed that the association of the image with the rural life of the plantation meant that it was doomed as "people began to move to town," she conceded that "the image lived on as habit or useful protective coloration" even among the urban women who led the fight for progressive reforms in the twenties. Clinton explained the longevity of the pedestal ideology by its connections with white racial supremacy.[9] The myth of the benevolent patriarch who lovingly protected and cared for his black and white family seemed to justify the sexual and racial segregation of the Old and New South. Indeed, Patricia Stringer and Irene Thompson's 1982 study of academic women in the South concluded that traditional conceptions of the lady restricted opportunities for college women into the mid-sixties.[10]

African American women had to deal with antebellum racial as well as sexual stereotypes of their nature and abilities. The "good" black woman was the plantation "Mammy," docile and domestic, a motherly figure who looked after the white children and the big house. The "bad" black woman was "Jezebel," passionate and wild, a sexual temptress who led black and white men astray. African American women faced with such stereotypes were forced to prove to the world that they could be moral, rational, and responsible individuals.[11]

The fundamentalist religious orientation of the region also contributed to differences in the educational experience of Southern women. Scott found that the "image of the submissive woman was reinforced by evangelical theology," which took literally the advice of St. Paul that "women submit unto their husbands." Although Fass noted that religion was becoming less important among college youth nationally in the twenties, historian George Tindall described the interwar South as "a bastion of evangelical Protestantism. It outranked other regions in its proportion of church membership, in denominational colleges, in the general position and influence of the church."[12]

Purity was one of the most cherished qualities of the Southern woman. The strict regulation of heterosexual contacts by institutions of higher education reflected this concern for virtuous behavior. Rules prescribing social interactions of every variety were common to all the early colleges. At nineteenth-century Vassar, for instance, "rules regarding etiquette and dress were as important as those establishing religious practices."[13] But the post–World War I rejection of Victorian values forced Northern and Midwestern institutions to liberalize and often eliminate restrictions on social life. Barbara Solomon's history of American women's colleges described the decade before World War I as a time of student challenges to restrictions on heterosexual activities. Fass noted that women's protests led to the abolition of chaperon requirements at the University of Wisconsin in 1923, the lifting of the nonsmoking ban at Bryn Mawr in 1925, and the ignoring of curfew regulations at coeducational institutions throughout the country in the twenties.[14] Elaine Kendall found that the advent of the automobile and, ironically, Prohibition "effectively finished off the last vestiges of Victorian social customs at the seven sister colleges." The car gave students unprecedented mobility and increased opportunities for unchaperoned sexual contact. Prohibition brought the speakeasies, where young people could smoke, drink, and dance freely—"[i]nstead of amusing themselves at well-lighted and adequately chaperoned college proms." Rules limiting automobile excursions were dropped because college authorities found no way they "could be enforced," and students simply ignored remaining restrictions on coeducational socialization.[15]

Similar changes in social life occurred much later at Southern schools. For example, chaperonage, which had all but disappeared from Northern women's colleges in the twenties and thirties, was very much in evidence at Southern women's colleges into the forties.[16] At Coker College in South Carolina, gentlemen callers were allowed "only on certain Saturday nights," and dating involved a ritual that must have discouraged all but the most ardent couples. "Properly dressed in formal attire, the student [had first to] introduce her date to the dean of women. If the dean approved of the young man, then the couple would be escorted to a . . . parlor where . . . they would visit for two hours while monitors paced the hall, observing them from glass panes placed in doors for this purpose."[17]

Converse College in South Carolina required faculty chaperonage "for automobiling at night, dinner at hotels, public entertainments in the evening, ball games, etc." Mary Baldwin College in Virginia forbade students "to attend dances in Staunton or the vicinity during the scholastic session, except . . . with [their] parents," and Wesleyan College in Georgia would not allow boarding students "to attend theaters, circuses, or other questionable places of amusement in the city."[18] Asheville Normal, Chicora College for Women, Columbia College, Georgia State College for Women, Hollins College, and Judson College all required written permission from parents for students to date; Coker, Converse, Cox, and Queens colleges and the North Carolina College for Women required approval from college administrators as well. Such rules provided little opportunity for unsupervised contact with the opposite sex.[19]

Public and private coeducational institutions also regulated the behavior of women students. At Alabama Polytechnic Institute (later Auburn University) a woman student was "expected to conduct herself as a lady at all times." She should dress properly for class and meals, sign an "in-and-out card" when she left the dormitory, and refrain from attending unchaperoned fraternity parties. Image was important; Auburn ladies were forbidden to talk to men from their windows or from the sundecks. At Mississippi Normal College, students caught kissing were suspended, and "anything more daring was likely to be a 'shipping offense.' "[20]

When the College of Charleston in South Carolina admitted its first women students in the fall of 1918, administrators hired a matron, Miss Emma Gibbes, to look after the "girls." Pierrine Smith Byrd, the only one of the "original thirteen" women to persevere and graduate from the college, described Gibbes as "the very living example of an old-fashioned school teacher—a very stern attitude and a tiny little figure. . . . We couldn't go anywhere without her." Separated from the men outside of class, the women formed their own societies and organizations. "We were just little sheep gone astray," Byrd recalled.[21]

Black colleges were especially strict about student associations with the opposite sex. W. E. B. Du Bois, whose daughter was enrolled at Fisk University in Nashville in the mid-twenties, complained that the students were treated as though they were attending a "reform school." Men and women could not walk together on the campus, and women students were allowed "to receive [only] one caller each week between 4:30 and 5:30." Writer Langston Hughes, who visited Fisk and numerous other black colleges in the thirties, thought black campuses resembled "mid-Victorian England or Massachusetts in the days of witch-burning Puritans." Colleges such as Morris Brown in Georgia and Claflin and Benedict in South Carolina forbade contact between men and women students without parental or administrative permission. At Howard University in Washington, D.C., "all social functions at which young men and women [were] present [had] to be chaperoned." Spelman College in Atlanta reserved a special room in Rockefeller Hall for male visitors. Men "could call on a particular

Spelman student for only twenty minutes once a month . . . and the length of the call was clocked." In 1927 these rules were liberalized to allow for an "open house for two hours each Saturday afternoon . . . in the various dormitory reception rooms." The presence of house matrons preserved propriety.[22]

Black colleges regulated the behavior of students of both sexes, but they were especially solicitous of the behavior of women students. Almost every coeducational institution added to its list of rules and regulations special injunctions for women students, and women's colleges were even more restrictive than coeducational schools. Benedict College had a provision that allowed parents to prevent their daughters from receiving "calls" from young men but no similar provision that kept sons from receiving visits from young women. Fisk University eliminated its "lights out at 10:00 P.M." policy for the men's dormitories in 1926 but kept the restrictions for the women's dormitories. Howard University required women students whose parents did not live in the city "to reside and board in the University dormitories." First-year women who lived in the city with their parents or guardians could "not remain out after half-past seven o'clock on any evening, without special permission from the head of the house." No women students were allowed to attend coeducational social functions or take trips outside the city without a chaperon. A chaperon or special permission of the matron or house mother was required for "motoring or driving."[23]

Dr. Marlene O'Bryant Seabrook, who graduated from South Carolina State College in 1955, met her future husband on the campus. "I looked out the window and said, 'Now, there's someone I'd like to know.'" It just so happened he was a friend of her roommate's cousin, and the necessary introductions were made. When asked whether they dated much as students, Seabrook laughed. Women had to be in their dormitories or in the library by 6:00 P.M., and at no time could they ride in an automobile driven by a male student. There were dances on campus, but they were always chaperoned, and the dean of women escorted the women back to the residence halls when the dance was over.[24]

Historically black colleges were among the last schools in the nation to liberalize their visitation policies. South Carolina State College did not allow coeducational visits in dormitory rooms until January 1995. Even then, the visits were part of a pilot program that allowed weekend visitations only for juniors and seniors. The change made the college more progressive than other historically black institutions in South Carolina. Allen University, Benedict College, Claflin College, Morris College, and Voorhees College limited their coeducational visitation to the "lobby area only with restricted hours." Other black schools in the South also retained many of their restrictions on heterosexual contacts into the nineties. At Hampton University, "freshmen have curfews, and they don't have visitation privileges until after homecoming." Florida A & M and Tougaloo College in Mississippi both confined male-female visits to dormitory lobbies. Russell Adams, Chair of Afro American Studies at Howard University, explained that these restrictions were associated with the middle-class conservatism of educated African Americans: "Middle-class blacks are extremely conservative on every point except racism. . . . Black schools have a dash of Southern and New England attitude. . . . They have circumspection and decorum in matters of gender beyond speculation."[25]

As Stephanie Shaw has shown in her study of black professional women workers in the Jim Crow era, the promotion of "circumspection and decorum" by administrators of black denominational colleges cannot be "attributed solely to puritanical values among the many white missionary teachers." Black parents shared these values and wanted schools to demand the same strict standards of morality that they demanded in their homes. Such "puritanism" had a practical as well as a philosophical foundation. In a segregated society, where professional jobs were at a premium, the possession of a good character was equally as important as the acquisition of a higher education. Women who "were not morally upright, self-controlled, and community oriented" would simply not be hired.[26]

Regardless of their race or college, Southern women were expected to behave as "ladies" on and off the campus. Rules and regulations mandating such ladylike conduct were not conducive to developing intellectual independence or critical thought, unfortunately. The code of behavior at Judson College in Alabama, for example, included a "Principle of Conformity," which asked students to "conform to the conventions of cultured society and the traditions of Judson." Students were to learn what others expected of them, not to challenge existing customs or mores.[27]

Regulations against smoking, drinking, cardplaying, and dancing with men remained in force longer at Southern colleges. Helen Horowitz found that smoking as "the outward sign of acknowledged female sensuality" was "the most highly charged issue" on Northeastern college campuses in the twenties. "Its lure for the female collegian was that it announced her sexual maturity and her interest in men even when she remained in the weekday company of women."[28]

Given the Southern definition of womanly virtue and the fundamentalist religious origin of many private colleges in the South, it should not be surprising that smoking was taboo at almost every Southern institution in the twenties. In 1930, at Winthrop College in South Carolina, seniors caught smoking were suspended for the term.[29] At Sweet Briar College in Virginia, students often left the campus to indulge, leading a faculty member to lament that "the most animated conversations among our students" were occurring elsewhere. Bowing to reality, Sweet Briar allowed smoking in 1929, as did neighboring Randolph-Macon the following year. On many coeducational campuses, smoking restrictions remained in force longer for women students. Fisk allowed men to smoke at the Chocolate Shop on campus in 1926; women were not permitted to smoke until 1935.[30]

Even when rules against smoking were eliminated, new regulations often limited the time and place where smoking was allowed. When Converse College in South Carolina lifted the ban on cigarettes in 1933, it specified four discreet locations where students could smoke. Mississippi State College for Women finally allowed smoking on campus in 1937 but only if students provided written consent from their parents and limited their indulgences to special rooms in the dormitories. Florida State College for Women allowed women to smoke in the "rec rooms" in 1936 but forbade them to smoke in front of men.[31] Women smoking in public was still considered unladylike in the fifties.

Some Southern college administrators frowned on dancing in the early years of the twentieth century. Sweet Briar College, which admitted its first students in 1906, shocked the sensibilities of collegiate neighbors by allowing dancing among the students and by inviting gentlemen to dances on weekends. But even such indulgences as Sweet Briar permitted had their limitations. When the students petitioned the faculty in 1914 for the right "to dance the once step and the hesitation waltz at the May Day ball," the faculty agreed only on the condition that "the Floor Committee would see to it that dancing was not objectionable."[32] Some schools allowed women to dance with each other but not with men. The junior prom at Florida State College for Women was a major social event for many years before men were invited for the first time in 1927. Randolph-Macon Woman's College permitted the students to dance among themselves in 1925 but maintained the rule against heterosexual dancing until 1932. Converse College did not hold its first formal dance until 1933.[33]

Church-supported colleges were often the last to allow dancing on campus. Mildred McEwen, Queens College's historian, recorded her surprise when, while reading student newspapers from her Presbyterian alma mater in the twenties, she saw a reference to "a 'tea dance' given by students. My reaction was, 'This *can't be!*' Then I discovered the date on that paper was April 1. In another paper," she recalled, "I came across a notice that there would be a 'movement' in the gym Saturday night (for girls only, of course) and *that* was the Queens I remember during those days. The word *dance* was not even used."[34] A similar ban existed at Methodist Wesleyan College. As an alumna of the class of 1938 explained, "proms" meant "promenades": "[E]ven at formal proms with an orchestra, male students from Mercer, and special boyfriends from home, we did *not* dance at Wesleyan."[35]

Students often did not share the attitude toward dancing held by church authorities. Between 1939 and 1945, Centenary College, a Methodist institution in Louisiana, was embroiled in a debate with the Louisiana Methodist Annual Conference over whether to allow social dancing on campus. Succumbing to student pressures, the administration introduced a motion to the board of trustees that would allow the president and faculty "to control and regulate all social affairs on the campus." Dancing would be permitted but only "under strict faculty supervision." The Reverend W. L. Duren, editor of the *New Orleans Christian Advocate* and a member of the board of trustees, was outraged by the other trustees' approval of a motion that condoned "worldliness and worldly amusement" on a Methodist campus. In editorial after editorial in the *Advocate*, he lambasted the college's decision to allow student dancing and was able to convince the Louisiana Annual Conference of the Methodist Church to overturn the motion. College administrators, faculty, and students were in turn angered over what they saw as unwarranted interference in campus affairs.

The Centenary trustees reminded church authorities that the charter of the college "clearly authorized the Board of Trustees as the governing authority of the College." The trustees subsequently voted to give control over student life to the faculty. Fortunately for the students, the faculty were willing to allow properly chaperoned social dancing.[36]

Kathleen (Kay) White (later Schad), a 1939 alumna of Judson who worked in the college's library first as a student and then as its librarian until 1943, justified the school's liberal social policies against the criticisms of Baptist trustees and ministers. Judson's president, she explained in a letter to her future husband, Ted Schad, "believes that girls in college ought to lead normal lives. They smoke when they come here—why should they do it in secret and burn up these old buildings? Of course they smoke only in their rooms. The dances here are lovely—very simple—8–12 affairs—and no boy would ever dream of taking a drink before or at a Judson dance." Kay thought that the Baptist harping on smoking and drinking was just an "excuse" to withhold needed moneys from the school. "This year," she wrote Ted in March 1940, "things got to the point financially where [the president] couldn't be responsible for saying No—any longer. So he broke down and said—'We'll stop dances. You give us $35,000 before the year's over.' " Although she knew the Baptist Convention would have to act quickly to save Judson from bankruptcy, Kay dreaded the arrival of the delegates on campus: "They'll probably hunt up a cigarette butt, offer it as evidence that the college is a den of iniquity, and decide to abandon us to go to the hell [to which] we're doomed." Judson's financial crisis was eventually resolved by the Baptist Convention, and Judson students continued to dance and smoke—discreetly.[37]

Denominational influences also limited social dancing on the campuses of black colleges and universities. Atlanta University, a black coeducational college founded by the Congregationalists after the Civil War, did not allow dances for the first fifty years of its existence. Students had to be content to march "side by side to the accompaniment of music." Officials at Fisk University, which was founded by the American Missionary Association, considered dancing "a trap of the devil" and would not even allow students to attend off-campus dances.[38]

The attitude of Southern parents and administrators toward social dancing was different from the national view. Paula Fass noted that youth in the twenties generally "danced whenever the opportunity presented it-self" and considered dancing "the least disreputable" of heterosexual social activities. Yet dancing remained suspect at Southern schools for decades. The predominance of single-sex institutions in the South partially explains the difference. Barbara Solomon found that women's colleges were the last to join "the dance vogue," although she conceded that "by 1913 college men and women everywhere danced together regularly."[39] The antipathy to dancing at Southern schools in the early twentieth century was largely a consequence of the region's religious conservatism. Fundamental Protestant churches were among the most vocal and steadfast opponents of ballroom dancing, and these very churches, of course, dominated the Southern scene.

Both academic and religious considerations inspired prohibitions against cardplaying. At Converse College, the faculty turned down student requests to repeal the law against playing cards as late as 1932, arguing that students who spent hours at cards would lose valuable study time and might be tempted to bet or gamble.[40] Randolph-Macon removed its prohibitions against bridge playing in 1928, but other schools, like Winthrop, Georgia State College for Women, and Chicora, which had large contingents of Methodist, Baptist, and Presbyterian students, kept their regulations into the thirties.[41]

No Southern college for women allowed alcoholic drinks on campus in the years before World War II. Administrators at Wesleyan, Salem, and Queens colleges considered drinking and smoking "shipping offenses."[42] In the large coeducational universities of the North, however, women's drinking "became an issue" in the mid-twenties.[43] Prohibition meant that consumption of alcohol was illegal for most of the period, but in the Northeast, speakeasies ensured a bountiful supply of liquor for college parties nonetheless. There is little evidence, however, that Southern college women had the same access to illegal drink as their Northern sisters. A Coker College editorial on the school's "drinking problem" chastised students who ordered Cokes to be delivered to the dorm for failing to meet the delivery boy.[44] The reminiscence of one Hollins student seems typical: "*Nobody* drank. It was never an issue, and would never have been permitted."[45]

Even at coeducational institutions where alcohol flowed freely, women students were forbidden to imbibe. As late as 1963, the student handbook of Auburn University proclaimed that "women are not allowed to drink INTOXICATING BEVERAGES in Auburn or when attending college activities off the campus, which include football weekends and fraternity houseparties." The justification for this prohibition was the same as that for other regulations: "An Auburn woman is expected to conduct herself as a lady at all times."[46]

The Southern college woman also dressed differently from the "typical eastern college girl" described by the editors of *Fortune* in June 1936. The Northern woman may have presented "a casual, even an untidy appearance while on the campus," but the Southern woman was expected to maintain a proper, ladylike demeanor.[47] Rules and regulations moderated student dress and deportment at all Southern colleges.

Many state-supported schools mandated uniforms for their students "to promote economy, simplicity, and good taste in dress." Teachers' or public colleges such as Asheville Normal, Georgia State College for Women, Georgia State Teachers College, Mississippi State College for Women, and Winthrop College prescribed specific colors and styles of clothing for academic and extracurricular occasions.[48] At Mississippi State College, for instance, women were to wear "dark navy blue one-piece dresses, dark navy blue blouses and skirts, or dark navy blue coat suits." There was also a dress uniform (design and fabric varied with the season), which had to be worn "to town, to church, and to all public gatherings on the campus." Hose and heels were required with the dress uniform and hats for trips to church and town.[49] Most Southern colleges had more general prescriptions on dress, however. The Coker College catalog of the 1932–1933 academic year warned that "extravagance and freakishness in dress [is] not approved by students or officials of the college; [rather] neatness and simplicity [are] the rule."[50] Although some colleges such as Cox, Columbia, and Judson required a coat-suit for public occasions, most schools had statements similar to that of Hollins: "No uniform is prescribed for ordinary or public occasions. Students are expected to observe simplicity, good taste and neatness in everyday life."[51] Women, one alumna of Wesleyan noted, "seemed to automatically wear what [they] were supposed to wear." Her classmate concurred: "A dress code was not necessary—everyone dressed properly at all times."[52]

At black coeducational colleges, dress codes applied almost exclusively to women students. At Clark University, skirts could "not be too short or too narrow and necks must be high enough to avoid the appearance of immodesty." Morris Brown University mandated "plain white shirt waists" for its women students and limited their jewelry to a "wrist watch, plain ring, plain beads or necklace." One's character, the college catalog declared, was reflected "in the manner in which each girl dresses and conducts herself." The Claflin College bulletin for the 1929–1930 academic year listed the "dress problem [as] one of the most serious problems in connection with the adolescent girl." To deal with this scourge, the administration required "every girl [to] be neatly and becomingly dressed."[53]

Black women's colleges also regulated the dress of their students. Women at Bennett were informed that "elaborate and expensive wardrobes" were "not appropriate for school nor in keeping with the ideals of the college." Spelman students learned that it was "an indisputable fact that the well-dressed woman is one whose clothing is selected with care and thought as to its style and material" and that too much jewelry and too fancy clothing were to be "avoided by the cultured and virtuous."[54]

Dress codes had their advantages as well as their disadvantages. By mandating certain simple styles, schools removed the temptation (and cost) of competitive dressing and eliminated a visible form of class distinction. Uniform clothing gave students a sense of community and purpose and implied that there were other things more important than expensive outfits and accessories. But dress prescriptions also rewarded conformity and encouraged dependence on the standards and opinions of others.

The Southern college woman was expected to act as well as dress respectably. Rules governing deportment emphasized "good taste and judgment." Coker College authorities told prospective students that "[e]mphasis [was] . . . placed on culture and refinement of taste, courtesy in conversation, gentleness and propriety of manners, and appreciation of simple elegance characteristic of our best homes." Hollins College's regulations required every student to "be decorous and upright in her conduct," and Agnes Scott College "sought to cultivate true womanliness, a womanliness which combine[d] strength with gentleness and refinement."[55] Historians who characterized the twenties as "the watershed in the history of American morals" and personified the contemporary woman as the flapper who drank, smoked, danced with men, petted, and wore revealing clothing and makeup had clearly not drawn their conclusions from observations of the Southern college scene.[56]

Religious practices, too, remained far more traditional at Southern colleges in the first half of the twentieth century. At Mt. Holyoke, "chapel talks tended to deal with current social problems," priests and rabbis appeared as guest speakers, and "the college YWCA chapter was quietly replaced by a Fellowship of Faiths." Vassar abolished compulsory chapel attendance in 1926, and Barnard "abandoned the idea that a 'Christian spirit' was essential to the well-rounded woman."[57] Such innovations were not to be found at Southern colleges for women, where attendance at chapel services and Sunday church continued to be required into the fifties and where religious activities were believed "to promote the highest type of Christian womanhood and to develop the spirit of Christian service."[58]

Southern denominational colleges usually advocated religion courses and Bible study as well as church attendance and chapel programs. Mary Baldwin College, a Presbyterian school in Virginia, required nine credit hours of Bible study for graduation and encouraged students and faculty to "meet together each morning of the school week except Saturday, for a half-hour chapel program in which correlation [was] made between religion and all the activities of the college."[59] Methodist Columbia College requested that "[e]ach young lady . . . be furnished with a Bible, a Hymn Book, and a Webster's Academic Dictionary," and Queens, Cox, and Flora Macdonald colleges all used the Bible as a textbook.[60] Queens College closed the campus to all visitors on Sundays, putting a chain with the sign "Sabbath Day. No Admittance" across the entrance—that is, until "one Sunday some irreverent Davidson boys . . . painted out the Sab."[61]

When Kathleen (Kay) White (Shad) attended Judson in the late thirties, there was "a prayer service before breakfast, chapel at noon (everybody goes), vespers after dinner—every day in the week—in addition to 4 dozen other things like that." Kay seemed to find chapel tedious. In fact, she confessed that her favorite senior privilege was getting to leave chapel first. But she considered the vesper services, which were held outdoors in good weather, "impressive beyond words." Students "who never voluntarily go to any other type of worship service are irresistibly drawn out there. The last rays of the sun, the moon's first appearance, the gentle breeze, somehow there is the most wonderful sense of peace. Everybody has just bathed and is wearing fresh, crisply starched summery clothes. . . . The program is simple and brief—usually a song like 'Day is dying in the west' and a short but thoughtful talk. You never feel that it lasts long enough, you rise reluctantly." Kay found her religion classes equally stimulating, especially a course in comparative religion, which she took in her senior year: "When I'm at home and we discuss anything in the world which might have more than one aspect, the family always asks me what Dr. Jones [her religion professor] thinks about it."[62]

Religion was an integral part of campus life at black colleges, too. President Tapley, of Spelman, told students that from its founding, "Spelman Seminary has stood first of all for moral and religious training." Its alumnae were to be "cultured, Christian women imbued with a zeal for service."[63] Students at Spelman were expected to attend chapel and church services regularly.

Although the national trend was away from sectarian education, the majority of private colleges in the South were affiliated with religious bodies. Of the schools in South Carolina, for instance, only Converse College claimed to be nondenominational; Benedict, Coker, Furman, Limestone, and Morris were owned and controlled by the Baptists; and Columbia and Wofford, by the Methodists. Newberry was Lutheran; Presbyterian and Erskine were Presbyterian; and Claflin and Allen were supported primarily by the Methodist Episcopal Church.

Religion was an important part of women's campus life at all Southern colleges. Even nonsectarian, state schools boasted that their "principles and influences" were distinctly Christian. As the Georgia State Woman's College Catalog explained, "[T]he state institutions of a religious people are naturally religious institutions. While the College is non-sectarian, a sincerely spiritual atmosphere is cultivated in all the relations of the institution." Mississippi Normal College held morning prayer services daily in the dormitories, midday devotionals in the chapel, and additional prayer services in the chapel every Wednesday evening. Faculty taught Bible classes on Sunday morning, and students were expected to attend Sunday evening services and periodic revival meetings. Georgia State's Young Women's Christian Association sponsored a Sunday school, which was taught by members of the faculty and attended by most of the student body.

Winthrop, the South Carolina College for Women, sponsored similar activities.[64]

Domesticity was another antebellum virtue that schools claimed their campus life would promote. Familial imagery was repeatedly employed to assure parents that daughters would find a home-away-from-home at college. Judson's catalog proclaimed that "college life ought to approximate that of the cultured home." Students at Randolph-Macon Woman's College were told that they would all "be treated as daughters of equal maturity in a well-regulated Christian family."[65] Wesleyan College described its president as "head of the College household"; Judson's dean of women maintained a "motherly oversight"; Queens College received its students "as members of one large family." Chicora College for Women had "only such rules as [were] needed for the orderly government of a large family," and Columbia College tried "to make the life at the College as much like that of a well-regulated Christian family circle as possible."[66]

Dining accommodations—especially at women's colleges but also at many smaller coeducational schools—reinforced the familial atmosphere. Students ate together with administrators and faculty at small tables where they were served "family style." At Mississippi Normal College, a faculty member "presided at each meal, making announcements and offering thanks for the food."[67] Schools prided themselves on their "home cooking" and warned that students would gain weight from the good fare. Winthrop freshmen, for example, gained an average of eight pounds each the first semester of college.[68]

Kay White raved about Judson's good food in her letters to her future husband: "Our meals would be noteworthy anywhere—but in an institution! They are varied, artistic, and every dish is served at exactly the right temperature. No matter how fierce the tests are, the food will usually restore our spirits." It is hard to imagine a contemporary college student giving such glowing recommendations of her cafeteria fare. "One nice thing about getting back," Kay wrote, "is getting to have a reunion with some of your favorite dishes as well as friends: the eggplant souffle, carrot souffle and fritters, spoon bread, pecan rolls, Pleee-zing bran flakes (unique), chicken cutlets, cheese sauce and bacon strips on rye—and a good two dozen more." In addition to regular meals, the Judson cooks also prepared special snacks for the students: "One thing I will say for old

Mother Judson is this: When you get weary and hungry from studying, she serves you hot chocolate and angel food cake." On the other hand, Kay had little good to say about the food at Louisiana State University, which she attended in the summers for her library courses. After her third summer there, she told Ted that if he ever had a "fat wife, all you have to do is send her to the LSU skulehouse [*sic*]. . . . It is almost immodest to get as thin as you do at that place."[69]

There were limits to the domestic analogies. "Homey" did not mean sloppy, for instance. Students were expected to dress properly for all meals. At Alabama Polytechnic Institute, women were reminded to "come to breakfast fully dressed and with hair presentable." Regardless of the day of the week or the occasion, "[n]o shorts, slacks, or riding breeches [were] allowed to be worn in the dining rooms at any meal." Most women's colleges required church clothing (nice dress, hose, heels) for Sunday dinner. At Mississippi State College for Women, students had to wear their dress uniforms all day on Sundays.[70]

Domestic analogies were carried over into the architectural design of buildings. A 1940 booklet for prospective students, *Life at Converse*, described the school as "Our Converse College Home" and listed the ways in which the college authorities had tried "to make the College as much like home as possible." There were lovely "parlors provided for the reception of . . . dates, and for informal gatherings in the evenings." The offices of student personnel were conveniently located. The dean was "accessible" to all, and the college doctor had "no other practice" and devoted "her entire time" to the students. Salem College put out a similar brochure that told of its "Room Company System, . . . the nearest approach to home life that has ever been devised, and [that was] largely responsible for the Salem type of happy, healthy, adaptable young women."[71]

At black colleges and universities, considerable effort was made to accentuate the domestic qualities of living arrangements for women students. The Howard University bulletin for the 1920–1921 academic year simply described the dimensions of its men's dormitory, whereas it waxed poetic on the familial qualities of its women's dormitory: "It is three stories in height above a basement story which contains the dining rooms and kitchen with an outside entrance for young men. The building has a reception parlor, music and sewing rooms, and no effort is spared to give it a home-like atmosphere." Livingstone College was similarly uneven in its description of men's and women's dormitories. The catalog noted that Dodge Hall provided rooms for young men but explained that Goler Hall, the women's dormitory, contained "music rooms, reception rooms, a large and commodious dining hall, all of which are steam heated, lighted with electricity, and provided with modern conveniences. Every room has an outside exposure."[72]

To administrators of many Southern colleges, a wholesome social environment was as important as a stimulating intellectual atmosphere. Judson College told students and parents that "[s]ocial training is a definite part of any modern college program for young women," and Columbia College explained that "no education can be true or complete which does not provide culture of heart, sentiment, and emotions, as well as mind. . . . [We try] to make every possible provision for the development of the well-rounded, full-orbed life."[73]

The Limestone College catalog of 1932 made explicit what was elsewhere implicit: "Limestone College strives to preserve as a precious elixir of life all that was finest in the civilization of the Old South—its exalted ideals of manhood and womanhood, its liberal culture at its best, its peerless standards of unsullied honor, the delicate charm of its manners, and the ineffable beauty of its social life."[74]

College customs and rituals also seemed to reinforce traditional conceptions of womanhood. Founder's Day, school songfests, senior investiture, May Day, Class Day, and Senior Recognition Day all emphasized the importance of past values and family expectations. Although Fass remarked on the "loss of class spirit" and the disappearance of "academic class rituals" from the colleges of the twenties, intracampus activities remained an integral component of Southern social life into the sixties.[75] Women dressed in white danced around a Maypole in a seemingly incongruous celebration of the fertility of nature and the virginity of students. They sang of the "goodness" and "purity" of their institutions. Seniors marched in academic robes to the chapel, where in a ceremony reminiscent of Sir Walter Scott, they knelt and were "knighted" with their caps.[76]

As late as the sixties, Westhampton College held its honor code ceremony in the chapel. There, new freshmen, wearing white dresses and black shoes, recited the honor pledge, walked across the stage with a lighted candle, and signed their names in the honor-code book. Once they had completed the ceremony, students were not required to write the honor pledge on their tests or assignments. As one graduate of the class of 1971 recalled, "[O]ur signatures as Westhampton ladies were indicative of our honor."[77]

The small size of most women's colleges in the South allowed such schools to perpetuate an intimate campus life, which was increasingly difficult to maintain in the larger institutions of the Northeast and Midwest. But size was not the only factor facilitating social traditions at Southern schools. Students at large public women's colleges and coeducational institutions organized similar social activities. Mississippi State College for Women, which enrolled some one thousand students in the years before 1950, had a number of interclass activities, including a junior-freshman wedding: a formal ceremony was held during which the "bride" of the freshman class was "wed" to the "groom" of the junior class, "uniting forever the classes . . . that together they may carry the ideals of our Southern womanhood, and in turn bequeath them to their successors."[78]

Not all commentators on the Southern college scene thought class rivalries were always such a good thing. As a student at Judson, Kay White had written enthusiastically about the senior play, the senior theme song ("Do not study; do not study; / always shirk; always shirk. / It will do you no good; it will do you no good; / if you work; if you work"), the May Day pageant, and other class activities. When she became a faculty member, however, she began to question the value of many of these traditions. Kay was upset when she was chosen freshman class sponsor in 1941: "[I]n a college this size everything depends on class sponsorship, rivalry, etc. . . . [H]ow can I possibly entertain them? The classes always have a Christmas party and one in the spring." She wondered how she could afford to fete 90 students on a librarian's salary. In addition, Kay worried about the exclusivity and materialism that class identifications fostered. After observing the junior-freshman wedding, she observed, "It knocks you down for them spend hundreds and hundreds and hundreds of dollars on that ceremony and end up with nobody married." In an October 1942 letter to Ted, Kay explained why she refused to serve as class sponsor again: "They want somebody who can whack down $50 in one evening to entertain them. They want somebody who has a car to use as a dray-cart for them. . . . They don't want any ideas or originality. They want to do everything exactly as it was done the year before. . . . Thirty years after this war is over[,] Judson will still have a Defense Council." Kay was also concerned about the impact of her sponsorship on her student assistants: "[M]y staff is composed of girls from all the classes. And in this school class rivalry is as far out of bounds as tradition. For me to be sponsor of any one class is just deadly as far as the staff is concerned. . . . Maybe they shouldn't resent it, but they did."[79]

Kay preferred college customs that required acts of kindness rather than wads of cash. She wrote excitedly about Peanut Week: "Everybody in school drew a Peanut with someone else's name in it. All week you do nice little things for them. And Saturday night at dinner, you sit at their customary place so they'll know. Everybody just breaks her neck seeing who can think up the cutest things to do." She enjoyed spontaneous "jam sessions" and songfests. She reminisced about one such session, which began with student bantering at the dinner table. Everyone ended up gathering around the piano, and "we didn't leave the dining room 'til 10 o'clock." Kay also liked it when students used their imagination to create inexpensive costumes and decorations for school performances. She bragged about the "gillion [sic] cute things" the seniors did for the sophomore banquet: "Cost—0. Effect—: no money could have made them cuter." Her letters had little to say about the formal campus organizations that proliferated at most Southern colleges and universities.[80]

Such campus organizations ranged from prestigious literary clubs and honor societies to social groups based on common interests and backgrounds. Many colleges had "state" clubs composed of all the residents from that state attending the school. Large public institutions such as Texas College of Industrial Arts even had "county" and "city" clubs; by 1914 the college's campus boasted some twenty-seven different regional organizations. Almost every college had departmental clubs consisting of majors in particular fields and special interest clubs focusing on specific campus activities. Thirteen seniors and thirteen juniors from Mississippi State College for Women formed a group called the Black List to plan Halloween "Hell Week" functions. Some organizations were rather quixotic, such as "The Cistern Sisters," founded at the College of Charleston in 1922. The club's motto was "Seize every passing 'opportunity,' " and its objective was an "M.R.S. degree."[81]

Women's organizations included national academic and social fraternities as well as collegiate and class clubs. Many of the nation's first sororities originated on Southern college campuses. The "two oldest, continuous college fraternal organizations for women"—Alpha Delta Pi and Phi Mu— were founded at Wesleyan Female College in Georgia in 1852 as the Adelphean Literary Society and the Philomathean Society. Both were incorporated as national organizations in 1904 and adopted their Greek letter designations several years later. Phi Mu's constitution stated the object of the fraternity as "the social, mental, and moral improvement of its members," and its official creed, adopted in 1916, pledged members "[t]o lend to those less fortunate a helping hand. . . . To walk in the Way of Honor, guarding the purity of our thoughts and deeds . . . [and] to reverence God as our Maker, striving to serve him in all things." Almost all of Phi Mu's first collegiate chapters were founded in the South: Beta at Hollins College in Virginia in October 1904, Gamma at Salem College in North Carolina in March 1906, Delta at H. Sophie Newcomb College in Louisiana in October 1906, and Upsilon Delta at St. Mary's Seminary in North Carolina in November 1906.[82]

The first black sorority, Alpha Kappa Alpha (AKA), was established in 1908 at Howard University in Washington, D.C. Delta Sigma Theta, founded in 1913, and Zeta Phi Beta, founded in 1920, also had their beginnings at Howard. Only one black sorority, Sigma Gamma Rho, founded in 1922 at Butler University in Indianapolis, had its origins outside the South.[83] Although a number of the first chapters of these black sororities were located on predominantly white campuses in the North and Midwest, the majority of the chapters created in the thirties and forties were at historically black colleges in the South. As in the case of the white sororities, the founders of black sororities had more in mind than a simple social gathering of friends. The constitution of AKA announced the fraternity's intention to "cultivate and encourage high scholastic and ethical standards, improve living conditions among Black people and promote unity and friendship among college women."[84] Delta's oath was written by black social reformer Mary Church Terrell in 1914 and reflected the organization's commitment to racial uplift as well as individual achievement: "I will strive to reach the highest educational, moral, and spiritual efficiency which I can possibly obtain. . . . I will take an active interest in the welfare of my country, using my influence toward the enactment of laws for the protection of the unfortunate and weak, and for the repeal of those depriving human beings of their privileges and rights."[85]

Despite the idealism expressed in sorority mottos, constitutions, and oaths, these organizations were often viewed suspiciously by the uninitiated. In the early decades of the twentieth century, many public colleges in the South opposed the introduction of exclusive organizations of any sort. Southern populists saw fraternities and sororities as elitist, and conservative Protestants disliked their oaths and rituals. The Mississippi legislature went as far as to ban secret societies at its public colleges in 1912 and did not revoke the law until 1926. Greek letter fraternities were not allowed at state-supported institutions in South Carolina until 1927.[86]

Antifraternity feeling also led to the banning of sororities at private institutions. When Wesleyan College decided to abolish sororities in 1914, it eliminated the Alpha chapters of both Alpha Delta Pi and Phi Mu. These two organizations had already lost early chapters when Salem College outlawed fraternities in 1909.[87] Administrators at private women's colleges often thought that social clubs and sororities interfered with their efforts to "knit the student body into one cohesive family." When secret clubs began to spring up on the Sweet Briar College campus, the president told students that such organizations "could destroy the unity and friendliness of a group as small as ours." After a discussion by the Student Government Association on "democracy" at Sweet Briar, students passed a resolution banning all secret societies. At Hollins College, one of the few women's colleges in the South to have established national sororities in the years before World War II, students voted to abolish all social sororities in 1929.[88]

Similar opposition to social sororities and fraternities existed at black institutions. Fisk University officials banned "fraternities and other secret or oath-bound societies" until 1927, noting that such organizations "did not accord with the type of democracy the school was trying to teach." Spelman College authorities wanted extracurricular activities to encourage "getting together on the basis of common interests, not . . . on . . . snobbishness."[89]

Students often viewed social clubs and sororities differently, however. Especially at larger schools, such organizations promoted a sense of sisterhood and recalled the family life that students had left behind. Fisk University women had been active members of national sororities in the town of Nashville for years when the college trustees reluctantly allowed the organizations on campus. Sororities proved so attractive to women at the University of Mississippi in the thirties and forties that the president of Mississippi Southern College sought to establish chapters of national sororities on his campus so that the school would be "socially acceptable" to "a great number of fine girls."[90]

The debate over sororities illustrates the difficulty in determining the impact of college social life on Southern women. There is no question that sororities had restrictive membership clauses that discriminated against applicants not only because of their academic records and affiliations but also because of their gender, religion, race, ethnicity, and class. Until 1950, for example, Phi Mu's constitution required women to be "of the white race and Christian religion."[91] As Paula Giddings has shown in her history of Delta, "Racism, sexism, and the sense of racial obligation were also forces that helped shape the Black Greek-letter groups."[92] Generally speaking, black fraternities were founded to help African Americans grapple with the prejudices of American society, but such organizations could be discriminatory themselves. AKA was associated in many women's minds with light-skinned women from elite backgrounds.[93] Most early chapters of black sororities were established at four-year liberal arts institutions, and yet these schools educated only a small proportion of black women. During the thirties, there was considerable debate at Delta's national convention about whether to establish chapters at black land-grant institutions, because students from these "lesser-rated schools could affect the *social* prestige of the sorority as a whole." A compromise "gave the 'B' schools seven years to become 'A' institutions, or lose their right to initiate."[94]

Despite the exclusion of certain individuals, Southern sororities— black and white alike—had impressive records of community service, and their members often became political and social activists. One of the earliest public actions of Howard's Delta sisterhood was to participate in the 1913 suffrage parade in the capital. AKA's first president, Lucy Slowe, became Howard University's first Dean of Women and later president of the National Association of College Women. Grace Lumpkin, a South

Carolinian who had joined Phi Mu while a student at Brenau College in Georgia, was sent by the sorority to France in 1919 as the country's first "War Worker." Charlayne Hunter-Gault pledged Delta at Wayne State University while she was waiting for the resolution of her suit to integrate the University of Georgia. Significantly, she was attracted to Delta for the stands it had taken against racism. Patricia Roberts Harris, Secretary of Housing and Urban Development, and Barbara Jordan, U.S. Senator from Texas, were both also Deltas.[95]

Sororities took on major welfare projects that focused on Southern problems. AKA's Mississippi Health Project grew out of the 1933 Summer School for Rural Teachers, which revealed the lack of medical provision for blacks in the Mississippi Delta. The sorority established inoculation programs, nutritional lectures, and personal hygiene sessions, and provided general health services until the advent of World War II. AKA, along with other African American fraternities, lobbied the government on behalf of minorities, and these efforts eventually culminated in the creation of the American Council on Human Rights. Phi Mu, in conjunction with the Georgia Board of Health, funded a "healthmobile," which provided medical services to whites and blacks in rural Georgia from 1922 to 1939; supported the Buffalo School Library, established by Alpha Delta Theta in rural Kentucky in the thirties; invested in war bonds during World War II; placed Phi Mu toy carts in children's hospitals and rehabilitation centers in the forties; and helped support the S.S. *Hope* hospital ship, which provided medical services to underdeveloped countries throughout the world in the sixties and seventies.[96] These "privileged" women, because they were women, because they were black, or because they were both, had a heightened sense of responsibility for those less fortunate. As the Delta Oath poignantly declared: "I will not shrink from undertaking what seems wise and good because I labor under the double handicap of race and sex."[97]

Sororities were not, of course, the sole discriminators on the Southern campus. Class, race, gender, and religion were all often barriers to women's full participation in the social life of Southern institutions. Dr. Pat Carter, a 1937 graduate of the College of Charleston, believed that she had three strikes against her as a student: "I was a woman; I was a Catholic; I was a Charlestonian. None of these things gave me any kudos." When asked why being a Charlestonian was a disadvantage in Charleston, she replied: "Charleston was divisible into a lot of layers. . . . [I was from] the other side of the drain. I lived on Calhoun Street [not in the elite, south-of-Broad area of town]." Certain ethnic groups were looked on as being less desirable. Nicky Pappas, who attended the College of Charleston in the thirties, recalled ironically that Greeks could not be "Greek." Race, too, was a significant divider. The only African Americans on the College of Charleston campus before 1968 were the maids, porters, and grounds-people.[98] Even in Charleston, which had a larger proportion of Jews and Catholics than the rest of South Carolina, non-Protestants were some-times ostracized. Esther Finger Addlestone, a 1925 graduate of the college, met her husband during registration for classes for her freshman year: "He was the only Jewish boy in the room." Her husband was a member of one of the school's "Jewish" fraternities.[99]

Not surprisingly, religious and ethnic minorities often stuck to-gether. Carter was president of the Newman Club. She remembered having fights with a history professor who was vehemently anti-Catholic. "I was not going to let him say all those scurrilous things about my church." Al-though Carter herself was a member of a sorority, she believed that a num-ber of Catholic male students were not invited to join a fraternity because of their religion.

Carter's gender also made her "ineligible" for certain clubs: "I wanted to go on the Debating Team but no dice. There were no women on the team." Similarly, women were not allowed to be members of the pre-medical club. In many ways, this discrimination on campus reflected atti-tudes in the larger world outside the college gates. African Americans and women were barred from numerous civic clubs and boards. Carter noted that she was only asked to join the Medical History Club of the Medical University of South Carolina in 1980. Their constitution read "white males. . . . "

College provided women with many opportunities not available to them elsewhere in American life. An integral feature of the extracurricu-lar program at all women's colleges was student government.[100] In 1899 Randolph-Macon Woman's College and Limestone College became the first women's colleges in the South to set up systems of student govern-ment. Converse College was next, in 1905.[101] Although it may seem ironic that self-government was instituted at these schools during a period when women had few political rights at all, most student government associations were designed for social rather than political purposes. As one Coker College catalog put it, "[S]elf-government freed the faculty from minor regulation enforcement duties . . . [like] checking under doors [at night] to determine whether students' lights were out after study hours."[102]

146

Associations were concerned with "maintaining order," "promoting good conduct," cultivating "self-control," elevating "honor," instilling "self-discipline," and developing "self restraint, consideration for the majority, and the true cooperative spirit."[103] As the bulletin of Mississippi State College for Women explained, "Student government does not mean that students may conduct themselves according to their own inclinations." Student government, like other women's activities, stressed group rather than individual interests, and social rather than academic matters.[104] Coeducational colleges and universities sometimes had separate student government associations for men and women. Alabama Polytechnic Institute, for example, had a Women's Student Government Association "to further a spirit of unity among women students." The Women's Association published a handbook for women students called *Co-Etiquette*, which focused on "the problems which naturally arise in dormitory life."[105] Even when there was only one organization, however, student governments in coeducational institutions tended to reinforce traditional gender relationships. The Student Self-Government Association of Mississippi Normal College, for example, had the following motto: "Every Man a Gentleman and Every Woman a Lady."[106] Student government was a way for college authorities "to make the life at the college as much like that of a well-regulated Christian family circle as possible." Thus there were "regulations which encourage[d] orderliness, which protect[ed] the hours of work, which foster[ed] lady-like demeanour under all circumstances."[107] Student government associations, regardless of the intent of their promoters, also provided women with significant leadership experience and fostered interpersonal skills that they could later use in their clubs and communities.

Sports programs similarly illustrate the dual impact of college life on Southern college women. Physical education had been introduced into college curricula in the late nineteenth century to promote the physical and emotional well-being of students. But by the twenties, physicians began to worry that the aggressive nature of athletic events might pose a threat to the feminine physique and psyche. Some argued that intense athletic activity would cause amenorrhea or even infertility; others noted that competitive sports created belligerent behaviors.[108] The Women's Division of the National Amateur Athletic Federation was formed in 1923 to deal with these perceived problems in women's physical education programs.[109] The Women's Division was determined to remove from women's athletics the commercialism, cutthroat competition, and exclusivity that characterized intercollegiate activities for men. Women's programs were discouraged from seeking publicity, going on road trips, and rewarding talented individuals at the expense of less athletic participants. Instead, physical education departments were encouraged to develop a new form of athletic endeavor known as "play day." A play day was an opportunity for women from different schools to get together and "play *with* rather than *against* each other." Teams were mixed, and everyone, regardless of her athletic ability, would play every game.[110]

Southern schools made a number of modifications in their athletic programs to conform to the recommendations of the Women's Division of the Federation. Varsity competition was replaced with interclass games and intercollegiate "play days." As the University of North Carolina *Daily Tar Heel* quipped in 1934, "Charles I had his Cromwell, Caesar his Brutus, Sweet Briar its May Day, and now Carolina co-eds have their Play Day." The play day was a "gathering of women of North Carolina colleges for the enjoyment of sport." Specific accomplishments were less important than team efforts: "Only in tennis and archery contests [would] the winners be officially recognized by the group."[111]

Members of the Flora Macdonald College varsity basketball team, for example, were selected on the basis of their scholarship and "loyalty to college ideas," as well as because of their athletic ability, and the team ceased playing intercollegiate matches. Queens College awarded letters and college sweaters to members of its interclass baseball and basketball teams. Spelman College awarded "varsity" letters and numbers on the basis of a point system—500 points won a letter; 250 points, a numeral. Hikers were awarded 50 points; basketball and soccer players, 5 points; archery, baseball, and tennis participants, 3 points; and volleyball and officiating, 2 points. As the Spelman *Campus Mirror* explained, the purpose of such varsity programs was to emphasize "the development of attitudes and habits that make for fine living rather than competitive spirit."[112]

Play days and other group activities were popular in the South because they provided women with "wholesome" exercise and inculcated valuable social lessons. Sportsmanship, Judson College's athletic board explained, meant "playing the game for the game's sake and not merely for the sake of winning."[113] Sports were credited with teaching honor, cooperation, practical hygiene, fair play, grace, and poise. No athletic program for women claimed that it would make students stronger individuals or better leaders; none suggested that team sports could prepare participants for the competitive and aggressive world of business or politics. In sports as in other social activities, women were to be ladies.[114] But, as ladies, they also learned to be good team players.

Not all Southern women in the first half of the twentieth century meekly followed the prescribed path to ladyhood offered by their alma mater. Some students indulged in forbidden beverages despite national and campus prohibition. Sweet Briar's historian, Martha Lou Stohlman, related how a Sweet Briar student caused a Virginia gentleman to lose not only his illusions of female propriety but also seven bottles of whiskey. The gentleman, it seems, was a passenger on a train traveling through central Virginia in the mid-twenties with an illegal cache of whiskey. When an inspector appeared, he quickly hid his bottles "under the mattress of the berth of a Sweet Briar girl who was chatting in another car," figuring that if she discovered the liquor, "it would not be valued." His expectations proved wrong, however. "When the train stopped at Sweet Briar in the early morning seven bottles were lugged off in a bulging suitcase and," Stohlman notes, "were properly appreciated in a series of eggnog parties, judiciously distributed so that no conspicuous effects were noted."[115]

Students challenged other social restrictions as well. A Salem student managed many "sneak smokes" in her dormitory room, and one Wesleyan woman "argued with the dean of women about playing tennis with a date in the day time on campus." The freshman class at Hollins successfully petitioned the dean of students in 1934 for permission "to wear bobby sox (instead of stockings) to class."[116] As a result of student complaints, bans on smoking were lifted at a number of schools. At

Wesleyan and Hollins, upperclassmen were allowed to chaperon freshmen when they went into towns.[117]

The most significant student revolt of the interwar years occurred at Fisk University in Nashville in 1925. In October 1924 a group of students at the African American school complained about the authoritarian atmosphere on the campus in a statement of grievances given to the board of trustees. The following month, students appeared before the board in person to petition for a liberalization of social regulations and the establishment of a student council and a student newspaper. Although a few minor reforms were made in dress regulations and a student council was promised in the future, the president refused to modify "regulations affecting conduct, especially the prohibition against young men and women fraternizing on campus." Tensions mounted, and on the night of 4 February 1925 about a hundred students went on a rampage. Windows were broken in the administration building, and furniture was overturned in the chapel. When the president called in the all-white city police and a number of students were arrested, expelled, or both, protest expanded to the rest of the student body. Classes were boycotted, and university affairs came to a halt. Only the resignation of the president in April 1925 restored order to the campus.[118]

As a consequence of the student protests, social regulations at Fisk were liberalized, chaperoned dances were allowed on campus, the prohibition against fraternities and sororities was lifted, and smoking was permitted for men. The new student council was given "charge of student decorum on and off campus." Rules and regulations did not disappear from the Fisk campus, but they were modified considerably.[119]

In some ways, the Fisk experience was an anomaly. Demographic factors made Fisk more "radical" and less "Southern" than its collegiate neighbors, white and black. The school was a big university in an urban setting, and it enrolled a large number of students from outside the region, giving it a much more cosmopolitan atmosphere than most Southern institutions of higher education. In addition, Fisk students had the support of powerful and outspoken alumnae and alumni, such as W. E. B. Du Bois, who had attacked many of the president's racial policies in national periodicals such as the *American Mercury* and *Crisis*. The New York Fisk Club had even contacted other alumni and alumnae organizations to agitate for the president's removal. Joe Richardson, the university's historian, believed that pressures from these organizations helped bring about the changes on the Fisk campus.[120]

Many "friends" of Fisk, on the other hand, opposed the campus re-forms that occurred as a consequence of the protests. The president, fac-ulty, trustees, and most parents "viewed student revolt as a part of the revo-lution in morals and manners . . . which was distasteful to them." One father thanked the president for calling in the police and halting the "riot" before it reached his daughter's dormitory. He was distressed that so many "boys" had forgotten "to act as gentlemen." The strike also had serious financial repercussions for the institution. Contributions fell off, and Fisk officials had to work hard to assure potential donors of the school's future stability.[121]

Generally speaking, incidents of student protest at Southern colleges were few and far between, and those which did occur were, on the sur-face at least, resolved in favor of college authorities. The settlement of the week-long disturbances that broke out at the State Teachers College of Fredericksburg (later Mary Washington College) in 1934 is illustrative. When the head of the school's Student Government Association presented the student body with a new set of rules restricting automobile visits to town, her audience was outraged. A committee was elected to appeal to the president for a modification of the restrictions, but instead of modify-ing the restrictions, the administration put five students on probation for "leading the agitation against college authority." When one of the five was subsequently "expelled for her part in the protest, the campus was thrown into an uproar." Details of the unrest were leaked to the press, and the *Washington Post* ran a front-page story on the expelled woman. Groups of angry students gathered outside administration offices and in the dor-mitory parlors. The president called a meeting of the student body "to explain how the new rules had come into being," insisting that such regulations were necessary for "orderly procedure" and "student self-government." But then he proceeded to modify the new regulations by limiting them "to pick-up rides and not to other forms of riding." Students were appeased, and the protests halted.[122]

The explanation of the outcome provided by the school's historian, Edward Alvey, is revealing: "In reaching this resolution of the week's events, the students, no doubt, had come to realize that [the rules] were not so unreasonable as they had first seemed, and that the publicity given the disturbances was unfavorable to the college. Many students had also been advised by parents not to participate in any uprising against those in authority at the college."[123] The president was more concerned with the image of his institution than with the literal enforcement of its restrictions, for the "new" interpretation of the rules was more lenient than that given initially by the head of the student government. Most parents were more interested in the maintenance of *in loco parentis*. As long as their daughters conceded the major issue—obedience to authority—the minor subject of the parameters of that authority could be determined however the college wished. Although the new regulations remained in effect, the protests had resulted in their modification. And students had learned the lesson their mothers had learned in their own campaigns for social reform: "maintaining the ladylike image was still considered to be good politics."[124]

The protests at Fisk and Fredericksburg also illustrate the willingness of Southern college authorities to punish recalcitrant students. Women were "campused," put on probation, and expelled for violations of social regulations. One Wesleyan alumna believed that she was not elected to Phi Beta Kappa in her junior year because of her "attitude about dating rules." At Salem, social violators had a "little chat" with the president's wife. Students who found the restrictions intolerable often transferred to other institutions; those who remained grumbled to themselves or kept quiet.[125] When parents supported restrictions on social life, there was no one to whom college women could appeal. "My family was very strict and so was Wesleyan," wrote one alumna. "I had to have most of my social life after graduation." Other women made a virtue of necessity: "We expected and did not mind (though being human we always complained) the various disciplines and restrictions—and, we are better people because of them."[126]

In some respects the continued advocacy of antebellum views of woman's sphere and nature at Southern colleges was only a reflection of the many obstacles to women's liberation that survived the promulgation of the Nineteenth Amendment and the upheaval of the First World War. David Levine omitted women from his analysis of the impact of higher education on American society and culture from 1915 to 1940 because "they were excluded from the occupational opportunities that stimulated the rise of

American higher education after World War I." Although more and more Americans were seeking a college education in the twenties and thirties, Levine explained, "WASP [white Anglo-Saxon Protestant] upper-middle-class male prerogatives were still preserved."[127]

Estelle Freedman, in the article "The New Woman," argued that despite the tendency of historians to describe the twenties as a period of "revolution in manners and morals," traditional views of woman's place (in the home) remained strong and impeded efforts at economic and social reform.[128] Similarly, Barbara Solomon conceded that everywhere in the thirties "[s]erving society as educated wives and mothers remained the educators' ideal" for women, and colleges were expected "to transmit the traditional values of genteel ladyhood." By advocating the development of the "whole woman" and "well-rounded personality," colleges could cultivate the social and moral behaviors that were associated with traditional feminine virtues.[129]

The resurgence of domestic ideology in the twenties and thirties was often directly connected to fears of depopulation. A statistical analysis of women in *Who's Who in America* carried out by the sociologist Persis Cope revealed that college alumnae married at a later age and produced fewer children than noncollege women of the same social status. "If this highly superior group fails to leave descendants, while the less desirable elements of the population continue to multiply rapidly," Cope warned, "race suicide will be the inevitable result."[130] A 1941 study by Time, Inc., supported Cope's findings: "[A] college degree [was] very likely to lead women to spinsterhood," they concluded, because "the College Bloc [was] falling far short of reproducing itself numerically."[131] Accusations of race suicide had been leveled against college women in the 1890s; the population losses of World War I, combined with the decreased family size of the postwar period, revived such fears in the twenties and thirties.[132]

The renewed emphasis on marriage and motherhood in the thirties was also a consequence of the Great Depression. Women in the marketplace competed with men for jobs, and the result was a nationwide effort to keep married women at home. A survey of some 8,000 members of the American Association of University Women by the *Monthly Labor Review* found that in 1934 "married women had more unemployment and part-time work than single women."[133] State and national laws were passed limiting and often forbidding the employment of married women. Women found it difficult to get jobs even in the traditional "pink collar" occupations. African American women—married or unmarried—had higher rates of unemployment than white women.[134]

The intellectual atmosphere of the twenties and thirties was not particularly conducive to the advancement of women. The postwar popularization of Freud may have removed the taboo against female sexuality and lessened the proscriptions against premarital intercourse, but it also reinforced traditional views of "womanliness." Freudian theory seemed to provide scientific proof of woman's "inferiority and passivity."[135]

The literature of the interwar period also tended to be antifeminist. In the study "Literary Men, Literary Women, and the Great War," Sandra Gilbert found that the works of D. H. Lawrence and Ernest Hemingway and even those of Radclyffe Hall and Gertrude Atherton seemed to condemn women for prospering from a war that had caused so much suffering for men. Women were made to feel guilty for the economic, social, and political benefits they had reaped over the dead bodies of their brothers and husbands.[136]

Analyses of interwar demographics, psychology, economics, and literature may account for the reappearance of antifeminist attitudes in the twenties and thirties, but they do not explain why restrictions on social life were so much greater at Southern than Northern schools as late as the sixties. They also do not explain the apparent willingness of Southern college women to abide by such rules and regulations. These differences appear to be related to peculiar economic, social, and political conditions in the South.

The agrarian lifestyle and white supremacy that had made the South a distinctive region were threatened by events of the twenties.[137] The South was particularly hard hit by the postwar agricultural depression. Cotton prices fell from 40 cents per pound in 1920 to 10 cents per pound the following year. Black tenant farmers, no longer able to eke out a living from the patch of ground they rented from the white landowner, migrated in large numbers to the cities, depriving wealthy white Southerners of "a large work force of domestic servants and field hands."[138] World War I had exposed black Southerners to the world beyond the farm, and subsequent social and economic upheavals gave them hopes of a better future. Unfortunately, the rising expectations of black Southerners collided with the desire of poor whites to keep blacks in their place (one rung below themselves in the social ladder). Race relations worsened; Ku Klux Klan membership grew to one million by 1921, and race riots broke out throughout the South in 1919.[139]

The postwar era also saw the rise of an African American intelligentsia, a second generation of educated, rebellious, and defiant blacks. The "New Negro" no longer exhibited "attitudes of servility and dependence" in the presence of whites and rejected the "values of the dominant [Anglo-Saxon] culture."[140] In 1930 the National Association for the Advancement of Colored People began a campaign against the educational inequities in Southern schools, and in 1936, federal rulings forced the University of Maryland to admit a black student to its law school.[141]

The passage of the Nineteenth Amendment was doubly threatening to a region that had long associated women's liberation with racial equality. Paternalism justified Southern proscriptions for women and blacks; if male supremacy fell, could white supremacy be far behind? Significantly, only three states of the former confederacy—Arkansas, Tennessee, and Texas—ratified the Nineteenth Amendment.

Southern religious views based on a literal reading of scripture were challenged by the promulgation of Darwinian theories of evolution in the schools of the twenties. Southern fundamentalists resented the new science textbooks, which undermined the faith of their fathers. In 1924 Tennessee responded with the Butler Act, making it a crime to teach evolution or any other nonbiblical account of creation. The result was the famous Scopes Trial of 1925, which brought national attention (and scorn) to the religious beliefs of the region. But the premises of Darwinian evolutionary theory undermined more than just religion. By destroying "the changeless Newtonian universe, operating according to immutable laws, including immutable moral laws," Darwinism questioned all traditional beliefs, not just those about creation.[142]

Colleges and universities throughout the South were attacked for proselytizing new and "godless" ideas. From 1926 to 1929, clergymen in Tallahassee tried to have two professors at Florida State College for Women fired because they assigned textbooks that taught "young women evolution and Freudian sex theories." The professors remained, but the offending books were removed from the list of required readings—and from the open stacks in the library. The attempt at censorship backfired, however. Once the books were banned, everyone wanted to know what had made them so controversial, and students with copies of texts "rent[ed] them out to other girls at 25 cents an hour."[143]

155

Southern beliefs were also particularly vulnerable to the "Red Scare" of the twenties and thirties. Socialism, with its emphasis on communal responsibilities and central control, was inimical to a South that espoused individualism and states' rights. The growth of "leftist" unions and farm-labor political parties in the years after 1918 was upsetting to a people who believed that "well-being is ultimately a man's own lookout, and he ought to be able to work it out without the help of institutions like government, unions, and the like."[144]

The thirties were hardly a time to rock the boat, either. The Great Depression only further darkened the already bleak economic picture in the South. State colleges were particularly hard hit by the economic recession. The University of South Carolina, for instance, was forced to pay its faculty in scrip in 1932. In July 1938 Roosevelt labeled the South the "Nation's Number One Economic Problem," and his pronouncements came after considerable New Deal aid had been funneled into the region. Southern politicians, although they welcomed federal moneys, resented federal efforts to change traditional Southern social patterns: "For them the New Deal jeopardized a power that rested on the control of property, labor, credit and local government. Relief projects reduced dependency; labor standards raised wages; the farm program upset landlord-tenant relationships."[145] It seemed as though Southern civilization were under attack once more.

How could the Southern establishment maintain its economic, political, and social supremacy in a world increasingly characterized by industrialization, modernization, and change? Historian William Taylor, in his study of the Southern past, argued that threats of social, economic, and political decline led Southern conservatives to grasp "for symbols of stability and order to stem their feelings of drift and uncertainty and to quiet their uneasiness about the inequities within Southern society."[146] And the foremost symbol of that Southern aristocratic tradition was the lady on the pedestal. The Southern belle—pious, virtuous, and docile—was the dutiful daughter and nurturing mother who learned the Southern way of life at school and imbued the home with its virtues and values. Similarly, the white view of the ideal black woman was that of the nurturing caregiver and faithful domestic.

Preserving traditional views of sex and race was thus vital to preserving the twentieth-century hegemony of the white, upper-class man. Campus rules and regulations, college activities and traditions, and domestic imagery and architecture assured legislators and parents, fearful of the social effects on women and blacks of an education that had once been the exclusive preserve of white men, that students would "use what they [had] learned in the particular sphere to which God had appointed them."[147] Social restrictions assured Southern conservatives that the next generation would help preserve the stability and order they held so dear. Nell Battle Lewis, a North Carolina journalist, expressed these sentiments in a 1936 speech to the alumnae of St. Mary's School in Raleigh: "And in standing for what it does—for propriety, for decorum, for a certain ordered standard of behavior, for what we may call the old-fashioned virtues—St. Mary's stands for something good, something which is of definite social value, and especially at the present time when the general trend of life is toward the left."[148]

Why didn't more Southern students strike out at a stereotype that denied their individuality and limited their options for self-development? For many women, it seems, the benefits of an exclusive womanly culture and the ability to use traditional concepts of womanhood to effect change far outweighed the costs to individual self-determination. When asked about their fondest memories of college life, alumnae from Southern colleges inevitably mentioned close friendships with fellow students and personal relationships with faculty and staff.[149] A Hollins graduate of the class of 1938 explained: "[W]e were privileged to be 'Hollins Girls' and no longer 'individuals.' There was a camaraderie and esprit de corps that made for conformity but did not stifle inventiveness. I enjoyed maturing in the refined, protective, cultured environment."[150] In *Womenfolks: Growing Up Down South*, Shirley Abbott described this feeling of sisterhood as a distinctive feature of Southern women's lives: "Next to motherhood, sisterhood is what they value most, taking an endless pleasure in the daily, commonplace society of one another that they never experience in male company."[151]

Stephanie Shaw, in her work on black professional women, referred to this "sense of mutual obligation among [black] women, their families, and the larger black community" as "socially responsible individualism" and argued that black women's education in the Jim Crow era helped them link "individual success to community development." Such group socialization was not limiting but empowering. It could lift an entire race.[152]

Bonds of sisterhood were far less important elsewhere. Intimate contact among women students and between women students and faculty was discouraged in the women's colleges of the North and the coeducational universities of the nation.[153] Influenced by Freudian psychological theories, administrators of Northern women's colleges tended to promote heterosexual activities and to view "female intimacy . . . as 'abnormal.' " At coeducational universities, the large size of the student body limited "contact with professors . . . to formalized classroom instruction that lasted for no more than a semester."[154]

The predominance of segregated institutions and the influence of a traditional, rural culture made campus life distinctly different for college women in the South. Southern colleges, with their restrictions on heterosexual contacts, encouragement of social traditions, promotion of communal activities, and use of domestic analogies reinforced the bonds of sisterhood already existing in Southern society. Campus life at Southern colleges in the first half of the twentieth century was different because Southern life was different.

The "twoness" of Southern society both enriched and impoverished the lives of college women. On the one hand, it preserved a climate in which decorum and obedience were more important than independent thought and action, femininity more valuable than scholarship, and the past more salient than the future. By employing the analogy of the Christian home and by promoting traditional views of woman's nature and sphere, college authorities hoped to keep young women in a state of perpetual adolescence and to reinforce the paternalism inherent in Southern society. On the other hand, the creation of a distinctive female culture provided a sense of sisterhood and security. It prepared women for working together in single-gender clubs and organizations and for dealing with the prejudices of a segregated society. Many Southern women were able to use the skills they had acquired as students and the respect they inspired as educated "ladies" to challenge the status quo.

Avery Normal Institute, class of 1908. The Institute, established by the American Missionary Association, served as a collegiate preparatory school and normal college for African Americans in Charleston, South Carolina, from 1865 to 1954. (Courtesy Avery Research Center for African American History and Culture, College of Charleston)

Lillian Kiber in the home economics laboratory at the College of Industrial Arts (CIA), 1912. CIA was the original name of Texas Woman's College, now Texas Woman's University. At CIA, as at other women's industrial colleges, the home economics curriculum included course work on the chemical analysis of foods. (Courtesy the Woman's Collection, Blagg-Huey Library, Texas Woman's University)

Student Body, Agnes Scott College, 1912–1913 (Courtesy Agnes Scott College Archives)

Madeleine Longcope in horticulture class at the College of Industrial Arts (CIA), 1912. The female counterparts of the male A & M, early-twentieth-century women's industrial colleges often included courses in horticulture and animal husbandry to help rural women become good "farmers' wives." (Courtesy the Woman's Collection, Blagg-Huey Library, Texas Woman's University)

Students tending bees at the College of Industrial Arts (CIA), c. 1900 (Courtesy the Woman's Collection, Blagg-Huey Library, Texas Woman's University)

Students in a summer school course in woodworking at the University of Alabama, 1915. This course was offered by the University's Department of Manual Training as part of its teacher-training program. (Courtesy W. S. Hoole Special Collections Library, University of Alabama)

Cast of "Song of Hiawatha," Avery Normal Institute, Charleston, South Carolina, 1916 (Courtesy Avery Research Center for African American History and Culture, College of Charleston)

Farmerettes, World War I, North Carolina Normal and Industrial College (Courtesy University Archives, Walter Clinton Jackson Library, University of North Carolina–Greensboro)

First African American faculty, Avery Normal Institute, Charleston, South Carolina, 1916 (Courtesy Avery Research Center for African American History and Culture, College of Charleston)

Support for Women's Suffrage, North Carolina Normal and Industrial College, 1919 (Courtesy University Archives, Walter Clinton Jackson Library, University of North Carolina–Greensboro)

First women's basketball team, College of Charleston, 1921. Women were not admitted to the college until 1918. This team included Pierrine Smith Byrd, class of 1922, the college's first woman graduate. (Courtesy College of Charleston Archives, Photograph Collection)

Girls glee club, Avery Normal Institute, Charleston, South Carolina, 1925 (Courtesy Avery Research Center for African American History and Culture, College of Charleston)

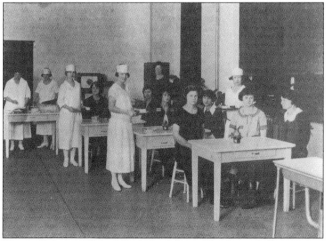

Home Science Club, Mississippi State Teachers College, 1925 (Courtesy McCain Library and Archives, University Archives, University of Southern Mississippi)

Girls' band at M.E.A., Mississippi State Teachers College, 1924 (Courtesy McCain Library and Archives, University Archives, University of Southern Mississippi)

Cheerleaders, University of South Carolina, 1933 (Courtesy University Archives, South Caroliniana Library, University of South Carolina)

Decagynian Club, Fisk University, 1930. Organized in February 1899, the Decagynian was the oldest literary club of young women at Fisk. (Courtesy Special Collections, Fisk University Library)

Class of 1939 field hockey team, Westhampton College, 1939 (Courtesy University Archives, University of Richmond)

Girls' basketball team, Avery Normal Institute, Charleston, South Carolina, 1939 (Courtesy Avery Research Center for African American History and Culture, College of Charleston)

Radio class, Texas Woman's College, 1941. Even before the United States formally entered World War II in December 1941, college women were being prepared to assist in the war effort. (Courtesy University Archives, Blagg-Huey Library, Texas Woman's University)

Debs, Alpha Kappa Alpha Sorority, Inc., Columbia, South Carolina, 1948 (Courtesy Septima Poinsett Clark Collection, Special Collections, Robert Scott Small Library, College of Charleston)

Red Cross work, University of South Carolina, 1944. Classes in first aid were offered both as part of the formal curriculum at women's colleges and as one of the various ways collegiate clubs contributed to the war effort. Sororities throughout the South commonly offered such courses for their members. (Courtesy University Archives, South Caroliniana Library, University of South Carolina)

Graduating class, Hampton Institute, 1946. Septima Clark is fourth from the left on the front row. (Courtesy Septima Poinsett Clark Collection, Special Collections, Robert Scott Small Library, College of Charleston)

Nursing class, Texas Woman's College, c. 1950 (Courtesy University Archives, Blagg-Huey Library, Texas Woman's University)

Business machines class, Texas Woman's College, c. 1950 (Courtesy University Archives, Blagg-Huey Library, Texas Woman's University)

Journalism students and a pressman setting type in print shop, Texas Woman's College, 1950s (Courtesy University Archives, Blagg-Huey Library, Texas Woman's University)

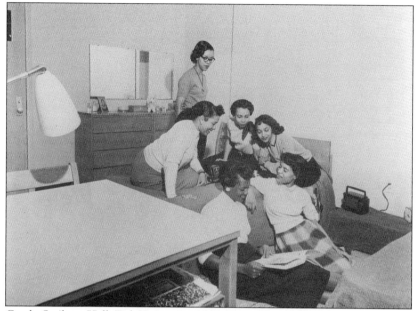

Coeds, Scribner Hall, Fisk University, 1954. Regardless of the type of institution a Southern woman attended, dormitory life was an important part of her college experience. Through involvement in official dormitory functions and in extemporaneous get-togethers, she acquired important social and political skills. (Courtesy Special Collections, Fisk University Library)

The female half of the 1959–1960 University of Alabama cheerleaders. Left to right: Vanessa Cox, Judy Justice, Sharon Russman, and Barbara Edwards. (Courtesy W. S. Hoole Special Collections Library, University of Alabama)

Fisk University Sweethearts, 1955. The caption that accompanied this photograph in the Fisk yearbook— "We believe in the high ideals of womanhood and that personable character and comely grace should be rewarded; therefore we present our Sweethearts"—suggests stereotypes of the Southern lady survived into the post–World War II period. (Courtesy Special Collections, Fisk University Library)

Vivian Malone (*far left*) in her first day of class, June 12, 1963. In 1965 Malone became the first African American student to graduate from the University of Alabama. (Courtesy W. S. Hoole Special Collections Library, University of Alabama)

174

May Day, University of South Carolina, 1968 (Courtesy University Archives, South Caroliniana Library, University of South Carolina)

Arrest of a female student at the University of Alabama on May 13, 1970. Nearly sixty students were arrested on this evening after a week of protests and general student unrest escalated into a shouting match between pro-administration and anti-administration student groups. (Courtesy W. S. Hoole Special Collections Library, University of Alabama)

Student in botany lab at the University of Alabama, c. 1970 (Courtesy W. S. Hoole Special Collections Library, University of Alabama)

Sweet Briar College, class of 1987. Kelly Reed (*left*) and Teresa Pike (*right*) are facing the camera. (Courtesy Office of Public Relations, Sweet Briar College)

Petra Loventinska stands guard at the front gate of The Citadel. Loventinska was one of four women admitted in the fall of 1996 when The Citadel went coeducational. She is scheduled to graduate in 2001. (Photograph by Russell K. Pace, courtesy Office of Public Affairs, The Citadel)

~5~

Tomorrow and Yesterday
College Women, Economic Depression,
and World War

*A*cademic standards, administrative policies, curricular offerings, and extracurricular activities at single-gender and coeducational colleges in the region were all significantly affected by the economic and political crises of the thirties and forties. The Great Depression and World War II brought both despair and hope to the South and its people. Southerners were attracted to and repulsed by the radical solutions to their regional problems offered by the federal government. Some welcomed innovation, especially when it promised prosperity; others were afraid that externally imposed changes would create even more problems. Because the higher education of women was closely connected to economic, social, and political developments, the ideologies and measures employed to combat first economic and then political disaster not only challenged the traditional culture of the region but also influenced education at all levels. Southern colleges shared the regional ambivalence toward federal intervention. Educational philosophies and practices in the years between 1930 and 1950 reflected the South's Janus-like propensity for looking forward and backward at the same time. Whereas one side of the regional psyche looked hopefully to a promising future where ability—not sex, race, or class—would determine one's inclusion in public life, the other side looked nostalgically to an idealized past where women, blacks, and the poor remained contentedly in the background and where the economic, social, and political life of the region retained its familiar patterns. The crises of the thirties and forties accentuated the "twoness" of Southern society and of Southern women's education.

The Great Depression and the Second World War contributed considerably to the "Americanization of Dixie." As the South grew more urban, industrial, and cosmopolitan, customs and mores associated with the region's agrarian and rural past became increasingly anachronistic. The South had been identified by President Roosevelt as the nation's number one economic problem, and federal measures of radical proportions were needed to deal with the widespread unemployment and poverty in the region.[1] The Great Depression forced Southerners to reexamine traditional economic arrangements, and New Deal programs enabled thousands to leave the farm for new jobs in industry and new homes in town. Federal intervention in the economic problems of the region led many Southerners to believe that the government could ameliorate their social and political problems as well.[2] Wartime programs similarly increased the flow of outside money and people to the region. The contributions of women and men, whites and blacks, rich and poor to the war effort raised questions about regional stereotypes of race, class, and gender. It seemed as if the long-heralded "New South" had come at last. The prodigal region was returning to the American fold.

Yet, the more things changed, the more things stayed the same. Local administration of relief measures often meant that financial aid was manipulated by the white, wealthy men who controlled the county political machines. Discrimination—against women, against blacks, against the poor—was everywhere apparent, even in the civil service and in the military. Not everyone welcomed the challenge to the "Old South" brought by depression and war. As regional values and practices were replaced by national ones, many conservatives sought to protect what they saw as the "Southern way of life" by opposing attempts by "outsiders" to change traditional gender, race, and class relationships. They feared that the South would lose its distinctiveness and independence if it conformed to national patterns. The fifties seemed to mark a return to the status quo antebellum. Historian David Goldfield described the late forties as "a false spring. The Americanization of Dixie could occur on one level," Goldfield wrote, "while regional traditions prevailed on another. Southerners were comfortable living in tomorrow and yesterday because for so many years time had been immaterial and undefined."[3]

Southern college women in the thirties and forties also found themselves living in "tomorrow and yesterday." The economic dislocation brought by the Great Depression forced many institutions of higher education to reduce financial assistance and pare academic programs, and institutions that catered to those segments of Southern society that had the least power—women, blacks, the poor—were often the first to suffer and the last to recover. The Southern economy was "depressed" before the Wall Street Crash of 1929. Agricultural prices dropped sharply in the years after World War I, and the twenties were characterized by agricultural surpluses and penniless farmers.[4] Most state governments in the region tightened their belts and cut back on already meager educational budgets. Private philanthropic agencies also had less money to spend in the postwar period.

Colleges for African Americans were under considerable financial strain by the early twenties. As public education became the wave of the future, privately endowed missionary colleges were pressed to provide the facilities and programs needed to compete in the market place. Fisk University in Nashville, for instance, had to turn away 300 women in 1919 because of lack of housing facilities. Black women, like white women, were increasingly enrolling in the publicly supported land-grant colleges. Philanthropic sponsors and educational agencies pressured private black colleges to combine with neighboring schools to create more economic and efficient programs. In 1927 both the Bureau of Education (U.S. Department of the Interior) and the General Education Board (a private philanthropic organization) "urged greater cooperation between schools located in the same city." Philanthropic organizations concentrated their efforts on a few select institutions. The Julius Rosenwald Fund contributed more than a million dollars in the twenties and thirties to develop "university centers" at Atlanta, Nashville, New Orleans, and Washington, D.C., for the "education of professional personnel and other Negro leaders."[5]

The first consolidation plan was drawn up in Atlanta. Spurred on by the promise of philanthropic funds for a new citywide library, representatives from Spelman and Morehouse colleges and Atlanta University met in February 1929 to discuss how they could combine forces to form a "University college." The result of their meetings was the creation of an Atlanta University Affiliation, with Spelman providing undergraduate education for women and Morehouse for men and Atlanta University offering graduate and professional work for students of both sexes.[6]

The Great Depression accelerated the movement to cooperate in the cause of "increased economy and efficiency." In New Orleans, Straight College, an American Missionary Association institution, combined with New Orleans University, a Methodist Episcopal Church college, to form Dillard University in 1935. The schools had been promised grants from the General Education Board and the Rosenwald Fund if they would "unite in the creation of a single strong university."[7] In Nashville, Fisk University and Meharry Medical College agreed to consolidate their educational efforts in the city. In Washington, D.C., Howard University was voted "regular status in the federal budget," providing African American youth with "a university at public expense comparable in plant, support and general range of activity to a state university." One African American educator predicted that the financial crisis would benefit black colleges in the long run because it served "to remove the obstacles to consolidation that vested interests and denominational differences [had] set up."[8]

The movement toward consolidation resulted in the demise of the oldest institution for the higher education of black women. Barber-Scotia College in Concord, North Carolina, a Presbyterian school that traced its origins to the first seminary ever established in the South for black girls, merged with the all-male Johnson C. Smith University in Charlotte in 1932. Although the Concord campus was retained as a "junior college for female students," upper-level women were consigned to coeducational classes in Charlotte.[9]

Black students and colleges were particularly hard hit by the Great Depression. A study of the socioeconomic status of students at Howard University during the school years 1929–1930 and 1930–1931 found that "ninety per cent of the out-of-town students . . . are living at a level which, if it is not actually inimical to health, is certainly not conducive to the best interests of scholastic success." The study revealed that the average family income of Howard students was half that of the average white college student. In comparison with black students living in the Deep South, Howard students were well off. "It is impossible to explain," the study concluded, "how homes with such meager incomes can afford to expend such disproportionate amounts for education, except in terms of a sacrifice that is hardly credible."[10]

Black colleges, because they seldom had much in the way of an endowment, found it almost impossible to reduce tuition fees or to increase scholarship moneys. Instead, African American women earned their way through college by doing work around the campus. A 1933 study of black colleges noted that "[t]wo schools report[ed] that they accepted farm products in place of fees. One reduced the rates for board. Another permitted students to cook for themselves to save expenses. Only one college reported any reduction in student fees."[11]

Even before the Great Depression, African American women had worked to help pay for their college costs. The Howard study revealed that 28 percent of the women students were employed during the 1929–1930 academic year. Almost 10 percent of the out-of-town women supported themselves entirely from their own earnings; corresponding figures for white women were less than 1 percent in women's colleges, 7 percent in state universities, and 6 percent in private coeducational colleges.[12]

Barred from most jobs in offices and department stores, African American students were often forced to engage in backbreaking labor to earn their keep. One Spelman woman did the laundry for a family of eight for $1.50 a week and "picked 150–200 pounds of cotton daily so that [her] father wouldn't have to hire someone else to do the picking." She was able to obtain a scholarship covering her tuition, and neighbors chipped in and provided her with "towels, soap, and undies."[13]

Many black colleges depended on philanthropy to keep their heads above water. Tillotson, a women's college in Texas, reported in 1932 that "[m]any students found it difficult to meet their bills to the College and many would have been dropped but for loans from The American Missionary Association." The following year, Tillotson authorities were even more despondent. "Collections have been poor," the president wrote, "and we have been hampered by lack of funds. We dismissed our cook and laundress and put girls to work in their places, allowing room and board to five girls. We were forced to give work aid to more than ninety percent of our students, and even at that, their accounts are far in arrears and we closed the year with a small deficit." To increase enrollment, Tillotson became coeducational in the fall of 1935. The admission of men to Tillotson and the merger of Barber-Scotia with Johnson C. Smith University left only two single-sex colleges for black women in existence—Bennett in North Carolina and Spelman in Georgia.[14]

As the Great Depression worsened, many of the philanthropic

groups that had funded black colleges were unable to meet their financial commitments. The American Missionary Association, the American Baptist Home Mission Society, the Friends Freemen's Association, the Board of Education of the Methodist Episcopal Church, and the Board of National Missions of the Presbyterian Church were all forced to cut positions and salaries in their denominational schools in 1933. The John F. Slater Fund halted contributions to "the more well-to-do colleges and tried to concentrate on those most in need of assistance."[15]

Black colleges were not the only Southern institutions to be threatened by the Great Depression. The financial crises of the twenties and thirties also brought many white women's colleges to the verge of bankruptcy and led to a spate of mergers and consolidations. In 1928 the Presbyterian Synod of South Carolina, realizing that Chicora College for Women in Columbia did not have an adequate endowment for accreditation, recommended that the institution be merged with Queens College in Charlotte, another Presbyterian women's college. Although Chicora students had to move seventy-five miles to the Queens campus in 1930, the union of academic and social programs took place smoothly. A new seal was produced, combining the crests and mottos of both schools, and the new institution was given a hyphenated name, Queens-Chicora College.[16]

Hard times also speeded up the coordination plans of Greenville Woman's College (GWC) and Furman University. Both institutions belonged to the South Carolina Baptist Convention and had shared a common board of trustees from 1854 until 1908. GWC students attended Furman athletic events, and students from both colleges often cooperated on extracurricular projects and organized joint social functions. GWC was the poor sister, however. Whereas Furman had embarked on a multimillion-dollar fund-raising campaign in the postwar period, GWC "had no endowment and no hope for endowment." A temporary plan of affiliation between the two schools had been suggested in 1929, whereby Furman would take over half of the instruction of the senior class of women, but it was soon apparent that this would not solve the GWC's financial difficulties. A joint committee of both boards of trustees subsequently recommended a more extensive plan of coordination. There would be one board of trustees, one president, and one set of academic standards, but two campuses. Although students would continue to live on the GWC campus, "junior and senior women would do most of their [academic] work at Furman."[17]

The Great Depression also led some states to reorganize their publicly supported colleges in the interests of efficiency and economy. In Georgia and Mississippi, state institutions of higher education were put under the control of a single board. In North Carolina, the State College of Agriculture and Engineering, the North Carolina College for Women, and the University of North Carolina were merged into the Consolidated University of North Carolina in 1931 "to save money and to prevent overlapping educational functions."[18]

Consolidating boards and institutions alleviated some financial problems, but most Southern colleges operated in the red, at least in the early years of the Great Depression. Although private schools with small or no endowments were hard pressed to survive, public colleges reliant on state appropriations for most of their support often experienced similar difficulties. Winthrop, the South Carolina College for Women, had more than $74,000 cut from its budget in 1931, forcing it to lay off faculty and staff and to reduce by 10 to 15 percent the salaries of those who remained. Additional funds were saved by dropping the graduate programs. In 1933 the College literally ran out of money, and employees went without pay for several months. To make things worse, the legislature also eliminated the county scholarships, which provided free tuition and $100 in cash for 124 students. Raising tuition fees was not a viable alternative; students would simply be unable to attend. In fact, Winthrop tried to cut student costs as much as possible to encourage continued enrollment. The college uniform, which had cost $72.50 in 1931, for instance, could be purchased for $30.30 in 1933. Despite these efforts, enrollment dropped 19 percent in 1934.[19]

In North Carolina the legislative appropriations to the Woman's College of North Carolina dropped drastically between 1929 and 1934. In the 1929–1930 academic year, the original allocation of $470,000 was reduced by the budget commission to $419,927.91, and in 1930–1931, to $312,291. By 1934 the initial allocation was down to $182,420, and even this paltry amount was cut by the budget commission to $182,000. At a hearing before the appropriations committee in January 1933, the president of the Woman's College noted that Southern faculty carried a 30 percent larger teaching load than Northern faculty and received salaries that were 30 percent lower.[20]

At Mississippi State College for Women (MSCW), the educational crisis caused by the Great Depression was aggravated by the political machinations of Governor Bilbo. When Bilbo fired ten faculty members and four support personnel and replaced them with his cronies, MSCW lost its accreditation and was censured by the American Association of University Professors. The number of students dropped by almost a third, and the college did not regain its 1930 enrollment level for twenty-five years.[21]

The financial crisis worsened MSCW's plight. In 1931 professors were paid with warrants, "good for any amount from 40 to 90 cents on the dollar, depending on the ability or the willingness of the local businessmen to accept [them]." Some teachers actually moved into the classrooms to live in order to have enough money for food. By 1932, Mississippi was bankrupt, and state employees, including the faculty and staff of the public colleges, received no salaries for six months.[22]

At Florida State College for Women (FSCW), students sometimes bartered farm produce for expenses. One father delivered three truckloads of oranges to the school in exchange for his daughter's tuition and board. Another student paid her bills with sweet potatoes. Such creative financing allowed many students without cash reserves to remain in school. Students also sought all sorts of ways to earn and save money. So many women used vinegar to rinse their hair that one date complained that "all the boys hate to come to FSCW because all the girls smell like vinegar." Nonetheless, Florida State was one of the few public colleges that were able to maintain enrollment levels throughout the thirties. But even at FSCW, faculty and staff did not escape budget paring. Sixteen professors lost their jobs, and retained employees all suffered salary cuts. The president's salary was reduced 18 percent and the faculty's, 11 percent, in 1933 alone.[23]

At Texas College of Industrial Arts, there were four applicants for every one of the 160 paid positions on campus in 1930. Concerned with shrinking enrollments, the school began building cooperative houses where students could live for less than ten dollars a month by preparing their own meals, doing their own housework, and splitting their expenses.

By 1936, almost 300 students were living in eight cooperative houses scattered throughout the campus. Without such inexpensive accommodations, most of these women would have been unable to stay in college.[24]

Private women's colleges also found it difficult to sustain student enrollments, to pay faculty salaries, and to fund academic programs in the early thirties. Queens-Chicora College cut expenses in the 1931–1932 academic year by reducing salaries by 20 percent. The school maintained its enrollment by keeping fees low. The total cost for tuition and board remained at $440 until 1937. The only increase in expenses at all between 1928 and 1937 was a $15 laboratory fee introduced in 1937.[25] Some families were still unable to meet college costs. Converse College in South Carolina lost students every year from 1927 until 1934 despite its reductions in salaries and procurement of loans.[26]

Columbia College in South Carolina tried to keep its enrollment high by cutting annual fees for tuition and board from $445 to $305. The president told the trustees that the "college, true to her traditions of service, is anxious to contribute in a peculiar and practical way to meeting the present situation, making it possible for hundreds of young women who desire to attend College to do so." The plan worked. In the 1931–1932 academic year, Columbia College was the only women's college in South Carolina "to show an increase in student body."[27]

Some women's colleges became temporarily coeducational. Limestone College in South Carolina admitted "boys" as day students in the fall of 1930 to keep from closing.[28] The Woman's College of the University of North Carolina also admitted men students during the Great Depression. In 1932 seventy-five young men from Greensboro who otherwise would be unable to afford college were allowed to attend classes on the women's campus.[29]

As these examples indicate, women's colleges that had small endowments and relied on tuition fees or state appropriations to fund their programs were particularly hard hit by the Great Depression. A 1932 study of enrollment at thirty-one women's colleges throughout the nation revealed a large drop in enrollment in every region of the country except the Middle Atlantic states. The enrollment at women's colleges in the South declined 7.8 percent between 1930 and 1932.[30]

Federal aid in the form of student loans, work programs, and building grants helped alleviate the financial problems of Southern colleges and universities after 1934. South Carolina's State Agricultural and Mechanical College, a black land-grant school, obtained several thousand dollars in the spring of 1934 from the Federal Emergency Relief Administration (FERA) "for the aid of worthy students." Students earned money by working as "janitors and helpers" around the campus. The funds enabled women and men "who would have been compelled to leave, because of lack of funds, to remain in school."[31] Winthrop, the public college for white women, used money from the Works Progress Administration (WPA) to purchase new boilers and to pave the streets around the campus. The University of South Carolina received grants from several New Deal agencies to repair its physical plant and establish work scholarships. Converse, a private woman's college in the state, used moneys from the Reconstruction Finance Corporation for campus beautification projects. [32]

These South Carolina examples were not atypical. In 1933 alone, some 1,500 college campuses were participating in the FERA student aid program. Between 1935 and 1943, American students received almost $100 million in emergency assistance from the federal government.[33] The New Deal also benefited college building projects. At the University of Alabama, the Public Works Administration (PWA) aided in the construction of fourteen buildings, including two women's dormitories. At the University of North Carolina, PWA funds were used to construct a physical education building and four women's dormitories, while FERA and WPA moneys were used to remodel the Fine Arts Gallery. Texas State College for Women constructed three new dormitories, three classroom buildings, and a hospital with the $1.25 million in grants it secured from the PWA.[34]

The financial exigencies of the Great Depression and the cooperative aspects of New Deal programs often involved students in community projects and encouraged closer relationships between white and black campuses. In Nashville, all-black Fisk University and the all-white Young Men's Christian Association Graduate School carried out a joint fundraising campaign to increase Fisk's endowment so that the university could be placed on the approved list of the Association of American Universities.[35] Talladega College, a black school in Alabama, invited students from all over the state to an interracial conference in 1934. The administration believed that this was "the first time that students of both races have lived together on the same campus in [Alabama]." Not all administrators approved of collegiate efforts for interracial cooperation, however. A professor of social ethics at Vanderbilt University in Nashville almost lost his job in the 1930s because he taught a class at Fisk and brought students from both universities together in a seminar on current affairs.[36]

Fisk University's sociology department, under the chairmanship of Charles Johnson, was recognized as "a center for research in the South, especially upon problems involving race relations." Johnson's students were instrumental in establishing the Fisk University Social Settlement in 1937, an organization that provided educational and recreational programs for the African American community of Nashville. Fisk students were also involved in a number of "state-wide PWA projects; a survey project of the social, economic and health conditions of rural Negroes in [Tennessee]; [and] an urban study, sponsored by the Department of Interior . . . [on the] training of 'white-collar' and 'skilled Negro workers.' "[37]

The results of such student surveys, combined with the general financial lessons of the Great Depression, led many educators to raise questions about the nature of existing vocational programs at black colleges. Many "mechanical" and "industrial" courses were clearly outdated; they prepared students for jobs and technologies that no longer existed. Colleges would need to update their curricula to meet the demands of the new technology, but this in itself would not solve the problem. Even when blacks were qualified for new positions, "they were not employed if white persons were available." Efforts would have to be made to improve interracial relationships so that qualified graduates would be hired regardless of their color or sex.[38]

The Great Depression also revealed the need for improved career counseling. In some states such as North Carolina, black public and private colleges were producing far more teachers than there were jobs available. In 1938, for instance, 347 black students—mostly women—received certificates to teach in high school, but only 100 positions were open in black high schools throughout the state. Some graduates sought jobs in elementary schools even though they received a pay reduction for teaching "out of their fields of training"; others found themselves unemployed. In Mississippi, on the other hand, the demand for teachers far outstripped the supply. As late as 1941, only 10 percent of the state's teachers had college degrees, and 50 percent had never attended college at all. Clearly, black colleges in Mississippi needed to be directing students into education programs. Since most African American women attended college to prepare for a profession, colleges that did not consider job opportunities were doing them a disservice.[39]

Educators at white women's colleges came to similar conclusions about their curricular offerings and vocational preparation. The financial crises of the twenties and thirties increased the demand for "practical" courses that would help women to understand and improve the world around them. One author, after examining the curricula of Southern schools, bemoaned the fact that "it has been and still is possible for a student to go through course after course, presumably to prepare . . . to live in some Southern Middletown, without ever having dealt with such important matters as industrial and agricultural problems, or the problems of race relationships."[40]

The Great Depression served to popularize the educational ideas of John Dewey. His call for educational relevancy and sensitivity to individual differences made sense in a world that had become disillusioned with traditional economic, social, and political developments. Private women's colleges were among the first educational institutions to apply Dewey's ideas to their curricula. *The Journal of Higher Education* noted four ways in which women's colleges in the mid-thirties were trying to make their education more relevant. These included the "adjustment of the curriculum to the individual so that her powers may be developed to the fullest; cultivation of the student's independence and initiative; education of the student as a social being by making the residence life a part of the curricular life; [and] construction of courses that prepare for modern living." Although many of these changes were begun in the women's colleges of the Northeast, Southern women's colleges were not far behind. Goucher College in Maryland assigned a faculty member to work with each entering student, and together they planned a unique four-year program. Sweet Briar College in Virginia established a special honors program that allowed students to work on independent projects. Courses "in preparation for civic and political understanding" were added to the curriculum of colleges throughout the South. More than ever before, college women in the thirties saw education as "a key to life problems."[41]

Women began to study themselves. The American Association of University Women, assisted by private donations, established the Institute of Women's Professional Relations on the campus of the North Carolina College for Women in 1929. The purpose of the institute was to investigate the business and professional opportunities that existed or would exist in the future for women, to determine the skills and training necessary to secure these jobs, and to encourage educational institutions to provide students with a more functional education.[42]

One of the most interesting studies of Southern women was that undertaken by Margaret Jarman Hagood in the mid-thirties. Born in 1907 in Newton County, Georgia, Margaret Jarman had an interest in the disadvantaged of her community that stretched back to her childhood, when she taught Sunday school to the local mill children. On finishing high school, she entered Agnes Scott College but dropped out in 1926 to marry Middleton Hagood. Although she had given birth to her only child, a daughter, in 1927, she returned to college, this time enrolling at Queens in Charlotte, North Carolina, where her father was president. After receiving her undergraduate degree from Queens in 1929, Hagood continued her studies at Emory University in Atlanta, where her husband was a dental student. She earned a master's degree in mathematics from Emory in 1930. In 1935 Howard Odum, director of the Institute for Research in Social Science at the University of North Carolina and a family friend, invited her to come to Chapel Hill to work on her Ph.D. degree in sociology. Her dissertation, a statistical analysis of the fertility patterns of white tenant farm women in the Southeast, was later expanded into a book, *Mothers of the South*, published in 1939. An "effort to get at the daily reality behind the statistics of the Depression," the work was based on interviews with 254 families in the Carolinas, Georgia, and Alabama.[43] Hagood saw her study "as a microcosmic examination of the wider regional scene; for Southern tenant farm mothers compose a group who epitomize, as much as any, the results of the wastes and lags of the Region." Economically, socially, and culturally, these women represented the past, present, and future of the South. "They suffer the direct consequences of a long-continued cash crop economy, they undergo extreme social impoverishment from the lack and unequal distribution of institutional services; and they bear the brunt of a regional tradition—compounded of elements from religion, patriarchy, and aristocracy—which subjects them to class and sex discrimination." And, of course, they were the mothers of the next generation of Southerners, children who were "simultaneously the Region's greatest asset and most crucial problem."[44]

In the interviews, Hagood asked the women about their own and their children's education. Educational levels were generally low. Only three of the women had completed high school, and eighteen (approximately 14 percent) were illiterate. Few of the homes contained reading materials of any sort: "Only one mother had a sizable collection of books, which included, in addition to novels, semiscientific treatises on child psychology. This mother had attended during the past year several 'literary' lectures at a nearby university and was the only mother visited who had ever utilized any of the services other than hospital offered by the several centers of higher education in the area."[45] Many parents resented compulsory education laws because they needed their children's assistance with the crops. Only three of the children in the study were receiving any form of higher education: "one girl was taking a business course by correspondence, another was at a state college for women, and a boy was at a junior college." Nor did there seem to be much family support for education: "A girl who had graduated . . . with the highest record ever made at the village school had wanted to go to the same junior college, which costs only $200 a session. The preacher tried to persuade her father to send her and pointed out that the $600 he paid that year for a truck would have kept her in school for three years, but the father said there was no use in it—as sure as they spent money on her education, she would go get married and then what use would it be?"[46]

Other studies from the thirties found Southerners with more positive attitudes toward education than Hagood's farm tenant women. The importance of education—and especially of an education that could prepare a woman for a profession—was a theme in many of the "American Life Histories" collected for the Federal Writers' Project between 1936 and 1940. Henrietta Pendleton, of Newton, North Carolina, told an interviewer that although she had quit school at fifteen to get married, she planned to give her daughters a "good education. Then if they marry a man who won't provide for them, they can leave him and make their own way."

Pendleton added that she was trying to remedy her own educational deficiencies "by reading good literature" obtained from her local library. Eugenia Martin, a WPA housekeeping aide from Atlanta, reflected on the importance of education to black families. Although her father had been a slave, he "knew the value of an education for any people regardless of color and to this end he worked and sent four of his children to college." A Florida respondent, "Mary Taylor," explained how she "was so careful to give each [daughter] a good education with some special work or profession in view." The words of Charles Robinson, a Georgia native who had moved to Florida to find work, captured the sentiments of many Southerners in the thirties: "I believe mother wit is good, but give me education."[47]

The Southern women interviewed for the Federal Writers' Project also indicated their willingness to return to the classroom to acquire the knowledge and skills that would qualify them for new employment opportunities created by the various New Deal programs. F. Hodge, who had completed the four-year normal course and two years of college at Atlanta University, lost her job as a bank cashier in 1937. After fruitless attempts to find employment in the private sector, she applied for WPA work. Hodge was assigned first to a sewing project and then to a library located in her neighborhood. She liked the work as a librarian so much that she "decided to take a course in library work so that should there be changes wherein WPA will have to withdraw its help I shall be able to take over." Eugenia Martin also turned to the WPA when she could not get work in private industry. While engaged in a "Survey of White Collar and Skilled Negroes" for the WPA, Martin "went to school at night where I took a two-year commercial course . . . as prescribed by the Board of Education, City of Atlanta." Another "Mrs. Martin," this one from Charleston, South Carolina, was able to use her nursing experience with the WPA to obtain a permanent position in the city and county health department. She told her interviewer: "Often at night I attend classes, either teachers classes or first aid. . . . [L]ast September . . . I decided that I would like to take a post graduate course in Public Health Nursing at the Peabody College for Nurses in Nashville, Tennessee, so I asked for and was given a three months leave of absence." Martin found her education useful at home as well as at work: "I find the problem of four grown daughters in this modern world is a real one. That is why I am attending these night classes and studying psychology, hoping to find the answers to the many questions and problems which arise daily."[48]

Southern college women in the thirties and forties also looked beyond themselves to wider social issues. Hollins College in Virginia founded the International Relations Club in 1932, and in 1934 the organization "sponsored the first southern regional conference of the Women's League for Peace and Freedom." African American women from Dillard University in New Orleans were part of a debating team that toured the South "in the interests of the Emergency Peace Campaign." As the threat of totalitarianism grew in Europe, progressive educators "began to call for education for the reconstruction of social values."[49]

One of the most radical educational institutions of the Great Depression era was Black Mountain College in North Carolina. Established in 1933 by a group of dissident students and faculty from Rollins College in Florida, Black Mountain was conceived as an experimental community where young and old would live and learn and create together. Because the founders believed that each person should be free to develop her or his own talents, there were "no required courses, no system of frequent examinations, no formal grading." Fees were low, and most students earned their keep by working on the college farm, in its cooperative store, or at its "cottage school" for children. Unlike other colleges in the region, Black Mountain had no established social restrictions. Students would agree among themselves "not to leave for vacation before a stated time, not (for girls) to hitchhike, not to enter the bedrooms of the opposite sex." The lack of such rules and regulations led the townspeople to describe the school as "a haven for free love and Communism." Because Black Mountain drew most of its student body from the North and had little interaction with other educational institutions in the region, its curricular offerings and extracurricular activities seemed to have had no impact on the higher education of Southern women in the era.[50]

Developments at Black Mountain, although not indicative of the Southern college scene generally, did, however, reflect a trend among educators to question the value and purpose of a college education. Because obtaining a higher education in the thirties often required considerable personal and familial sacrifices, the Great Depression caused women to take their education more seriously. "The background of the average college girl of 1933–34," one educator wrote, "is less snug and the future more uncertain." Parents did not want to waste their money, and students did not want to end up on the dole. Consequently, women were working harder at their studies and looking for jobs as well as husbands after college.[51] Employment opportunities became an important consideration in the choice of a major. Administrators at the Woman's College of Duke University noted a decline in the number of students interested in teaching careers and a rise in the number of those pursuing degrees in medicine, law, business, and social service.

193

Sororities responded to the crisis by cutting back on their social activities and increasing their community service programs. As Hilda Davis, the dean of women at Shaw University in North Carolina, warned, the Great Depression demanded "that sororities justify their existence or give way to more beneficial activities."[52] Growing unemployment among blacks prompted Delta's national organization to petition the federal government for increased aid to black land-grant colleges and to ask the secretary of labor to create an extensive public works program. Financial hardships reduced the number of new members in sororities throughout the country. Phi Mu lowered its collegiate dues and initiation fees, but invitations were almost 20 percent lower in 1930–1931 than in 1929–1930. Despite their scarce resources, sororities acknowledged the severity of the economic depression in the South by establishing national projects that focused on regional problems. Alpha Kappa Alpha (AKA) began its Mississippi Health Project in the summer of 1934; Delta, its Southern "traveling library" in 1937.[53]

Stephanie Shaw, in her study of black professional women in the post–World War I period, found that college-educated women became increasingly involved in race relations work designed "to relieve, mask, or eliminate the stress generated by tension-filled interracial public encounters." White public officials were terrified of the appeal that left-wing agitators might have to blacks in the region, and they hoped that the employment of "educated, articulate, and relatively conservative professional women" for community development work would dampen the flames of revolution in the black community. The women thus employed soon realized, however, that it was not enough to address the symptoms of underdevelopment but that they also needed to attack its cause—"institutionalized racism." They often used their educational connections and professional associations for such race relations work. The efforts of Norma Boyd, an AKA from Washington, D.C., to establish an antilynching campaign were not atypical. Boyd contacted the sorority's national president, Dorothy Ferebbe, about using AKA networks to organize the campaign, and as a result, AKA members "designed and distributed Christmas cards to promote the antilynching law; they sold antilynching buttons; and they printed and distributed special newsletters about the . . . bill."[54]

The Great Depression led many of the agencies and organizations involved in Southern education to review their various programs. Officials of the General Education Board decided to focus on professional and graduate opportunities in the region and introduced fellowships "in fields especially related to Southern economic and social development." The Association of Colleges and Secondary Schools of the Southern States also turned its attention to postbaccalaureate education, and its subcommittee on graduate programs eventually developed into a new organization, the Southern University Conference. Although the initial beneficiaries of these new graduate and professional opportunities were men, the war led to "a sudden wealth of fellowships for women."[55]

New opportunities for graduate and professional training also appeared for black women in the thirties, partly because of the success of several suits brought by the National Association for the Advancement of Colored People (NAACP). Charles H. Houston, a professor at the Howard University Law School, orchestrated the NAACP plan to sue for equal educational opportunities at the postbaccalaureate level. In *University of Maryland v. Murray*, the Maryland Court of Appeals concluded "that an out-of-state scholarship failed to meet the requirement of equal protection." Two years later the U.S. Supreme Court ruled that the University of Missouri Law School had to admit a young black man, Lloyd Gaines, because the state had no separate law school for blacks and out-of-state grants were not equivalent alternatives.[56]

In an attempt to avoid the integration of white state universities, Southern legislatures rushed to add graduate and professional curricula to their black state colleges. A number of states, hoping to satisfy the equal protection clause, also increased the number and size of their out-of-state tuition grants available to African American students. Such efforts would continue throughout World War II and into the late forties and early fifties.[57]

The Great Depression brought temporary hardships to college women throughout the South, but by the late thirties, most schools appeared on the road to recovery and students were enrolling once more in record numbers. A 1938 study of enrollment trends in Southeastern colleges and universities found that in the years between 1933 and 1938 the percentage of women in liberal arts courses rose 21.6 percent whereas the percentage of men in these programs increased only 18.4 percent. The study also noted that the greatest gain in numbers of women students occurred in the public universities.[58] The enrollment of African American women increased phenomenally in the interwar years. By 1940, women constituted 58 percent of the student body of black colleges. The women were increasingly attracted to state colleges and universities. In 1940, for the first time in history, there were more black graduates from public than from private institutions.[59]

Southern higher education benefited considerably from federal intervention designed to remedy regional economic problems, and white and black college women were affected in a number of ways by this intervention. Facilities had been improved, curricula revised, and students encouraged to work together to solve regional problems.

The outbreak of World War II also had a profound effect on Southern college women. A number of historians have described the war as "a more important turning point in southern history than even the Civil War."[60] Women's historians have similarly characterized the conflict as a "milestone for women in America." William H. Chafe, in his study of American women in the twentieth century, noted that "[d]espite the persistence of traditional ideas on woman's place, . . . the decade of the 1940s—paradoxically—marked a turning point in the history of American women." Chafe believed that the employment opportunities of the war, although they did not bring economic equality for white or black women of any class, still had long-term social and psychological impacts: "[T]he content of women's lives had changed, and an important new area of potential activity had opened up to them, with side effects that could not yet be measured."[61]

It was apparent by the early forties that the Second World War would be a war of ideologies as well as of technologies, and colleges would have to prepare students to fight the ideas as well as the armies of the enemy. In a speech to the South Carolina Association of Colleges, the president of Coker College, a women's college in Hartsville, South Carolina, told his colleagues that institutions of higher education must prepare women as well as men for the conflicts that lay ahead. Colleges for women must "put new emphasis on social sciences and develop intelligent and practical individuals who understand the issues that are shaping their lives." Education should help women "to evaluate the ideals of democracy, in order to save what is worth saving" and to "develop non-military techniques for defense of democracy."[62]

As in World War I, educators called for practical training—especially in scientific and professional subjects—which would enable women to fill the positions vacated by men who went off to war. The Subcommittee on Women in College and Defense, established in 1942, suggested that colleges also encourage women to volunteer for "part-time work in fields useful for defense."[63] Black sororities publicized the new employment opportunities for African American women. Deltas in Baltimore organized the Occupational Conference for Women in Industry in May 1941, and the national organization developed a project "to win job opportunities and improved working conditions for Black women in all kinds and levels of employment."[64]

At Hollins College in Virginia, students and faculty picked apples at a nearby orchard, "helping the war effort by contributing their pay plus bonuses." Students at Mississippi State College for Women worked in the local Gulf Ordinance Plant. Furman University women made bandages, knit sox and sweaters, and volunteered as "junior hostesses" at a nearby air base. Throughout the South, college women took Red Cross classes, contributed "Bundles for Britain," bought war bonds and stamps, planted victory gardens, and volunteered their time for all sorts of patriotic projects. Fisk's Jubilee Singers traveled to army bases throughout the country to entertain the troops before they went overseas.[65] At the University of Alabama, women even organized special war-related social events such as the 1942 "scrap dance." An announcement for the dance proclaimed: "Slap the Jap With Scrap. Bring That Old Junk to the Scrap Dance." Admission was ten pounds of scrap and twenty-five cents. More than twenty tons of metal was collected.[66]

College women also enlisted in the armed forces. More than 400 students and alumnae of Florida State College for Women served their country during World War II. A woman from Fisk was one of the first officers to graduate from the Women's Army Corps training center in Iowa. An alumna of Texas State College for Women was the first woman from Texas to become an ensign in the WAVES (Women Accepted for Volunteer Emergency Service). Black sororities joined the effort to equalize the terms under which black women were admitted to the military.[67]

The U.S. Office of Peace Administration labeled Texas State College for Women (TSCW) "the nation's model wartime educational institution" for its contributions to the war effort. TSCW students formed their own war council, which appointed air-raid wardens for the dormitories and classrooms, sponsored scrap metal drives, and organized contests for the "best victory song, slogan, and cartoon." A student finance council sold war stamps and bonds in the dorm, and the student body held countywide rallies to encourage residents to buy stamps and bonds. TSCW was the first college in Texas honored with a "Schools at War Flag," an award bestowed on institutions when 90 percent or more of the student body purchased at least one war stamp per week.[68]

Thousands of TSCW students enrolled in knitting courses or worked in the Red Cross Knitting Room and Red Cross Surgical Dressing Room on campus. Hundreds joined the Women's Motor Corps and signed up for college defense courses. Students collected waste paper, hose, and canceled postage stamps to be recycled for the war effort. They adopted a clean-plate policy in the dining halls and a "lights out at 11:15" policy in the dormitories.[69]

New courses were introduced at TSCW on such war-related topics as the geography of the war, meteorology and navigation, bandage rolling, radio, and group discussion and leadership. The college developed a new major in child development and nursery education in response to the increasing demand for trained nursery school teachers. An occupational therapy major was created in anticipation of postwar rehabilitation needs. Courses were added for foods and nutrition majors who wished to become army dietitians. Special summer sessions were offered to help high school teachers meet the wartime needs of their schools. TSCW students increasingly switched their majors from education and the humanities to mathematics and the sciences. Economics and business replaced home economics as the largest department in the college.[70]

The war changed the extracurricular life of TSCW students considerably. Students no longer had to wear hose after six o'clock at night: silk was needed for military uses. All campus activities were tied in some way to the war. Some students spent their spare time picking cotton in Denton County to help local farmers deal with the labor shortage. One year sixty-four student clubs chipped in to buy a wedding gown for use by British brides in the armed forces who could not obtain special clothing because of rationing. The student government established a "date bureau" to arrange dates between students and soldiers on nearby military bases. In 1945 the student body even voted to cancel spring vacation so as not to overtax the already overcrowded public transportation system.[71]

The war led a number of educational institutions in the South to offer accelerated programs so that men could complete their education before they entered the service. Furman University increased the duration of its summer school so that students should graduate in three years. Women were also encouraged to take advantage of these opportunities to finish their degrees in a shorter time. At Alabama Polytechnic Institute (later Auburn University), the quarter system was introduced to enable students to complete a four-year course in three years. Women were "urged to enter in June instead of in September" and were told that it was important for them "to secure as much training as possible in as short a time as possible" because "women will have to take up many kinds of work for which men will not be available."[72]

Because the departure of male students from the colleges and universities was often followed by the arrival of military training units, women seldom had the campus all to themselves. At the University of South Carolina, most of the approximately 1,000 civilian students on campus were women, but there were 1,400 men enrolled as students in three naval training programs. At the University of Georgia, there were 1,538 civilian students and 3,116 military students in 1943. The U.S. War Department established an army administrative school on the campus of Mississippi Southern College in 1942, providing 165 new men students every eight weeks. At Alabama Polytechnic Institute, women gave up their dormitories to soldiers enrolled in the Army Specialized Training Program. Mississippi State College for Women did not have any military units on campus, but visitors from nearby Columbus Air Base were so common that the college president warned students that "[f]or a young man to wear a uniform doesn't make him a gentleman."[73]

The war increased the proportion, but not the absolute number, of women on the campus. The number of American women in college declined by 25,000 between 1940 and 1944 as students left school to join the service, to take jobs in defense industries, or to get married.[74] A Randolph-Macon Woman's College student commented that "[t]he most noticeable effect of the war on our campus . . . is the number of girls leaving to marry their soldier boys before they leave to fight for Uncle Sam." At Winthrop College in South Carolina, enrollment declined so much that a number of tenured faculty had to be let go, and the college found itself being investigated by the American Association of University Women.[75] Private women's colleges in the region generally experienced a drop in enrollment as women enrolled in the less expensive public colleges and universities or found work in defense industries.

The employment of college women in industry also marked a sharp break with the past. Poor white and black women had, of course, always worked outside the home, but the ideal "lady" was dependent on a man for her economic support. The entrance of married, middle-class white women into the labor force, albeit temporary, had important economic and psychological consequences. Women's "sphere" widened considerably: "activities once viewed as inappropriate for women suddenly became patriotic duties for which women were perfectly suited." And although women still found themselves steered into less skilled and lower-paid positions than men, most women noted a marked improvement in their paychecks.[76]

Changes in employment patterns were of great concern to educators. At Hollins College in Virginia, only about one-third of the entering students persisted until graduation, leading some trustees to question the viability of the college's traditional curriculum. President Bessie Randolph resisted any suggestions that the college change course, reaffirming her faith in the liberal arts: "To the immediate winning of the war all higher institutions must dedicate all their resources, but they must not fail to prepare their students for the gigantic task of shaping a better world after the struggle ceases." She reminded the trustees that the "very existence of the liberal arts is one great objective for which this war is being waged throughout the earth."[77]

Alice Mary Baldwin, dean of the Woman's College of Duke University, shared Randolph's concerns. Baldwin believed that the liberal arts curriculum could prepare women for long-term employment opportunities far better than specific vocational training, and she feared that women would be lured away from degree programs by high wages in "temporary subprofessional jobs" that held no future for them after the war. The dean encouraged students at the Woman's College "to participate in war activities in addition to rather than as a replacement for their regular academic programs."[78]

Randolph's and Baldwin's fears seemed groundless in the early forties. At coeducational institutions the drastic drop in enrollment for men often created opportunities for the women students who remained. At Mississippi Southern College (earlier, Mississippi State Teachers College) the virtual disappearance of men allowed women to become active in such male preserves as the debate club and student government association. One debater who came to the fore in the war years, Evelyn Gandy, would later become Mississippi's first woman lieutenant governor. At the University of Alabama, 241 women received degrees in 1944, compared with only 152 men. Women at Furman University outnumbered men three to one during the war years, and classrooms on the men's campus were turned into women's dormitories.[79]

In Virginia the college enrollment of white women exceeded that of white men for the first time in history in 1943. In the 1944–1945 academic year, white women outnumbered white men two to one in the colleges of the state. Although the enrollment of black women in Virginia colleges was considerably lower than that of white women, black women's enrollment climbed steadily throughout the forties. In the 1944–1945 academic year, black women outnumbered black men in Virginia colleges almost three to one.[80]

Wartime propaganda had a significant impact on traditional concepts of womanhood. "We are fighting a stupendous war," Mildred H. McAfee, director of the Naval Reserve and president of Wellesley College, told students at the Woman's College of North Carolina in October 1942, "partly to attack a social philosophy which treats individuals as nothing but representatives of their group." McAfee hoped that women's contributions to the war effort would "be sufficient evidence to shatter some of the myths about feminine inadequacy." Women, too, were individuals. "We are concerned with the education and effective participation in society of *a* woman—this one, that one, every woman, with the strength of her own uniqueness and her own utility," she told students.[81]

Wartime ideologies and experiences had a considerable impact on traditional racial relationships. "Southern blacks emerged from World War II with reasonable expectations that life would be better," historian David Goldfield concluded. In a 1944 book entitled *What the Negro Wants*, a number of prominent African Americans demanded the right to participate equally in American political, economic, and social life.[82] And it was clear to most African Americans that separate schools were not equal.

The war made educators look more closely at the type of education they were offering African American women. The curriculum of black colleges was criticized for its "lack of emphasis upon technical training" and for its failure to prepare "students for wholesome community participation and leadership." One study noted that black women would have to assume leadership roles in black communities when black men left for the front and consequently needed to be taught the administrative and personnel skills required for such jobs. Most important, however, women needed to be able to apply the concepts of democratic action to themselves and their race. "Our women," the study concluded, "ought to understand what democracy means, what the implications of democracy are for a home, for a community, for a state and for a nation; and they should be given some simple techniques on how to attain the satisfactions of democracy, which up to this time have been denied." Such an education would prepare women not only for the present but also for the future. Significantly, prospective teachers were told that they should encourage students to defy "the social order imposed by racial segregation" and to develop courage "to withstand the rebuffs of intolerance."[83]

The war created immediate opportunities for African American women in the workforce. Educated black women found more professional and technical positions open to them than ever before. The number of African American women in government service, for example, increased from 60,000 in 1940 to 200,000 in 1944. Black women were hired for defense work in the factories; some even found employment as engineers. Others became nurses. The Cadet Nurse Corps, established by the Bolton Act of 1943, provided federal funds for women to complete nurse training programs. A number of segregated schools opened their doors to minority students for the first time during the war years in order to meet the nursing shortage.[84]

The letters of Mary Kathleen White (later Schad), a Mississippi woman who attended Judson College in Marion, Alabama, in the thirties and who served her alma mater as a librarian into the forties, help give a human face to the educational experiences of Southern women during economic depression and world war. Between 1938 and 1943, Kay, as she preferred to be called, sent almost 400 letters and cards to Theodore (Ted) MacNeeve Schad, which described her life first as an undergraduate and then as a faculty member at Judson and as a summer-school student in library science at Louisiana State University. Kay and Ted "met" through an entry in the 1938 *Who's Who Among Students in American Colleges and Universities.* Ted, a senior at Johns Hopkins University in Baltimore, had been browsing the volume when he noticed that Kay, a senior at Judson, shared his hobby of map collecting. On a whim, he wrote her a letter, introducing himself and asking about the sources and types of maps in her collection. Kay responded in kind, and for the next five years the two recorded their daily activities; described their families, friends, and communities; and shared their view of politics, culture, and society.[85]

Kay, who came from a large family and attended Judson on a full scholarship, often did not have enough money to purchase schoolbooks, buy clothing, or indulge in map collecting. In February 1939 she confessed to Ted, "I am supposed to buy a whole stack of new books, but since I can't afford to buy them all I'm just not buying any, because I don't want to be accused of showing partiality toward any of my courses." Nor was her penury an isolated case: "nobody can afford 'em." Kay's French professors tried to help out by lending departmental copies, but other faculty resorted to more labor-intensive alternatives: "When Dr. Norton told us that we would take up a unit of German poetry we sighed in anticipation. But those sighs soon became puffs and pants. We couldn't afford to buy any of those anthologies, so she said we pore [*sic*] ones would have to copy the poems."[86]

Without any money for store-bought clothes, Kay and her friends were often forced to improvise the best they could. Fortunately for Kay, she and her mother could sew. Kay was ecstatic when a dress her mother had "whacked . . . out" without a pattern for under two dollars was described by a professor of clothes designing as "the most stunning thing she'd seen this season, exquisitely made, every detail perfect, the design a dream." In another letter, Kay bragged to Ted about one of her own creations made from "an old black satin dress" a friend had given her and some inexpensive "chiffony-mousseline" fabric found in a local Marion store. The "whole dress cost $1.50 and it looks like Elsa Schiaparelli. . . . The Lord couldn't have been more amazed when he whittled Eve out of a rib." Purchasing new clothing was out of the question, however, even when Kay became a faculty member. She was amused when the new art teacher told her "that all my clothes look just like me. Small wonder," she wrote Ted. "They say that if you stay around anybody long enough you'll get to look like 'em, and gracious knows all of mine have been associatin' with me enough years."[87]

Kay regretted the fact that her family could not afford to send her younger sister "Rinky" to college. During her senior year, she wrote Ted: "Graduate school for me is definitely out. Why, the sister next to me who gets out of high school this year [Rinky] isn't going to even get to start college. The tragedy of it is that she has got what it takes and a surplus of it, too. . . . It's not fair." The materialism of wealthier classmates who were "already waving checks for handsome sums and zooming around in new cars: graduation presents" offended Kay. "[W]hen your family works to get you through, they ought to be congratulated instead of having to top the struggle with a gift, it seems to me. The only thing I hope is that they'll go on and give Rinky generous gifts . . . and not divide them with me. I had my day."[88]

Kay's financial problems were insignificant compared with those facing her beloved Judson. Many of her letters focused on the hard times threatening the college. In March 1940 she wrote Ted: "There have been ups and downs always, but never a down like now. The endowment of the school has always been modest, of course, but by having the students pay a comparatively high rate of tuition and board, all was well." But, Kay went on to explain, "[d]uring the depression few girls could go to a school that cost $700–750 flat a year. . . . Some way the Baptists borrowed . . . from the endowment—and now it is tied up—not one cent does the school get from it. On the other hand the denomination hasn't given the college $1000 in 40 years." It was clear the institution needed additional funding, but the Baptists in the state were dragging their feet, using reports of the "sinful" social activities that occurred at the college as an excuse. Kay was furious: "Ted, they are so overcome by the idea of dancing and smoking, that they forget the good things about the school. Where else . . . do they have a prayer service before breakfast, chapel at noon (everybody goes), vespers after dinner—every day in the week. . . . Judson, to people who know it, is a strong-hold of an ideal. . . . And, kid, it's in real danger of collapsing!"[89]

After defending Judson vigorously, Kay nonchalantly noted that she and the other faculty members had received only three checks between September and March. Her room and board were provided by the college, but there was no money for clothes or entertainment, and Kay wondered how she was going to pay her note from the previous summer's schooling. "Ye gods," she told Ted. "You feel so helpless. Why, I'd marry any lout on earth on the condition that he'd rescue Judson." Yet, despite their desperate straights, Kay and her colleagues managed to keep their sense of humor: "There are as many faculty jokes about our being broke as there are about the W.P.A. Mr. Parker says he's going to go out and sit in his car, turn on all the gadgets, sputter with his lips, and pretend he's takin' a trip. We all chant, 'We toil but we do not spend.' "[90]

When the Baptist Convention met in May 1940 to discuss the college's future, town and gown came together to pledge their support: students filled the balcony in the hall where the convention met ("those men could hardly read their resolutions for looking up there"), and local merchants closed their businesses to attend as well. "Ted, never in your life have you seen anything like the way the town of Marion has supported this college. The people have given, given, given, given. . . . They printed appeals to the convention. They filled the auditorium and applauded like mad." Although Kay was unsure what, exactly, was accomplished—"it was just a muddle of bonds, interest, notes"—the meeting resulted in "two more months salary, and . . . a possibility of two additional months."[91]

Judson was not yet out of deep water, though. The college had been put on probation by the Southern Association, and another Baptist convention was scheduled for the fall to deal with the long-term financial problems facing the school. At this meeting a committee was formed to investigate the feasibility of "coordinating" Judson with Howard, a coeducational Baptist college in Birmingham. Kay wrote, "Over my dead body. . . . The students are in arms. The faculty is furioso [*sic*]. Marion is feverish. . . . Ted, pray for the Judson."[92]

Judson's president resigned, hoping that this would appease those who opposed his liberal social policies; a trustee loaned enough money to pay back salaries; Baptist ministers stumped the state, requesting donations; and a special session of the convention was called "to liquidate a big hunk of the endowment in order to pay all the debts." Once Kay realized the college was saved, she quipped, "The whole affair has been more exciting than a Mississippi political campaign."[93] Judson was fortunate. Many Southern schools did not survive the depression unscathed.

The policies of the Southern Association remained a "problem" even after Judson's financial difficulties were resolved. First as an assistant librarian and then as librarian, Kay worried about meeting the requirements for accreditation. "I would love to tear the Southern Association of Schools and Colleges to smithereens," she informed Ted. "They are so silly. . . . [Y]ou ought to just see the list of periodicals they make you subscribe to . . . 'n' you can imagine how much the girls in a small liberal arts college use them." Although Kay dreaded the association's visit, she was pleased that "Mr. Huntley, the Southern Ass'n boss . . . told me to disregard completely every S.A. ruling and go on and run the place intelligently—not only not to add $200 more periodicals—but even to cut down on those we take! I could've kissed 'em." And, best of all, the Association did not drop Judson from its list of accredited institutions.[94]

Kay kept Ted abreast of developments in her hometown of Canton, Mississippi, as well as at Judson, and the two often discussed the worsening international situation. The threat of war depressed Kay: "Isn't it distressing the way they won't let you listen to anything on the radio but war?" she wrote Ted in August 1939. "Sometimes . . . I fear they won't leave us 39 [cents] worth of Europe to look at." And Mississippi politics did nothing to inspire her faith in government generally: "The final election was held yesterday, and we are hoping the state will be normal again by the weekend. (The governor the hillbillies elected . . . is such a crook that I am going to disown Miss. and start voting in Al.) Ted, the radio may drive us batty, but the newspapers simply carried no war news. In the eyes of the Jackson papers, a Universal War couldn't compare with a Mississippi Election."[95]

Contemporary political issues were an integral part of class discussions in Kay's ethics class her senior year, and she continued to debate current events with Ted in her letters. She told Ted of the time her ethics class ranked "a list of 50 offenses in order of seriousness." The "very worst: 'A nation oppressing another nation over which it has power'—thinking of the Jews, of course." Kay's letters commented on government policies in Germany, Japan, Britain, and the United States. Initially, she opposed American intervention: "T. Mc, what do you think of building up the army and navy—for peace's sake? I don't care what they say—how logical it sounds—and how much I respect the people who believe in it—the idea leaves me cold. Those European nations worked like the mischief to build up theirs and look at 'em." She and Ted agreed that it would be wrong to declare war "purely because we love England" and thought that "we ought not to listen to F.D.R., but to the very senators who are opposing him."[96]

Kay was shocked by the Japanese invasion of China and the German defeat of Western Europe. After receiving a 1940 calendar decorated with Japanese prints, Kay remarked bitterly, "It burns me up for them to be sending soldiers to China and fragile, lovely prints to us." She found it equally hard to believe that France had succumbed so quickly to the Nazis: "[T]he Martian scare fall before last wasn't one bit more far-fetched than the present situation. Kid, can you make it soak in on yourself? Swastikas on the Eiffel tower—and tanks rumbling past the Place de la Concorde. It can't be." But the reality soon hit home. Three men from her hometown were killed at Pearl Harbor—more than were lost from the entire county in World War I. Even Judson's least politically conscious students were "stirred to utterance."[97]

War affected the social as well as the political life of the Judson campus. Parties were fewer and less extravagant, and women no longer had to wear silk hose for dressy affairs. The latter was not a sacrifice for Kay, who was delighted to trade her uncomfortable and expensive stockings for bare legs: "Kid, one thing I love this war for is leg make-up! It will save us enough on stockings to pay the additional income tax—and feel better—and look better." Even student performances reflected current events. Kay told Ted about a chapel skit that parodied the wartime leaders: "Mussolini & Hirohito played second fiddle to Hitler—; Churchill got overheated and started unbuttoning his coat, saying he guessed he'd open a second front, etc. The theme song: 'There'll be buzzards over—Berchtesgaden's clover.' "[98]

Most discussions of the postwar world were more serious. In April 1942 Dr. Hallie Farmer gave a talk to the American Association of University Women that predicted the end of white supremacy and British imperialism and the advent of desperate poverty. "She told the Seniors who were our guests that they could all expect to be old maids—or divorced because their husbands would emerge as strangers. . . . And . . . their teacher's certificates wouldn't mean much. . . . [Y]ou couldn't be too sure there'd be any children to teach anyway." Although most of Farmer's predictions did not materialize, her speech was indicative of the revolutionary nature of the wartime experience.[99]

The war did seem to spur interracial cooperation at Judson and in the Marion community. Kay had often complained to Ted about local whites' antagonism toward the white and black faculty of nearby Lincoln Normal School. She believed it was hypocritical to treat those Northern Congregationalists as "social pariahs" while collecting funds to send missionaries to Africa. Kay had been to a holiday concert at Lincoln as early as December 1941, but there were no mixed-race functions at Judson until February 1943: "I want you to know history was made last night," Kay informed Ted. "The negroes came to a program in the Judson auditorium. . . . [I]t's the first time they've ever had a 2-race audience in this town." Later that spring, Kay was asked to join an interracial group working to establish a library for African Americans in Marion. She regretted that she would not be staying in Alabama to see the plan to fruition and feared that "the next Judson librarian 99-0 will be too prejudiced to help. You would think nobody on a college faculty would be so prejudiced—but almost nobody isn't."[100]

As Kay's comments indicated, no one was sure what the future would bring. Depression and world war had brought considerable change to the region as to the nation, and the implications of these changes were not immediately clear. Would the restoration of peace mean the return of the status quo *ante bellum?* Or would the victory of the democratic forces be accompanied by a political and social revolution? What places would the postwar architects delegate for women?

Many of the doors opened to women during the war years were closed again in the postwar period. Despite the contributions of women to the war effort, women's educational and professional needs were set aside in favor of those of returning veterans. With the end of the war and the passage of the GI Bill, men flocked to the campuses of the nation's colleges and universities, and their presence was reflected in admission quotas and curricular offerings. By 1947, two-thirds of all college students and half of all black college students were men. Thousands of qualified women were rejected by schools that, five years before, had gladly taken the money of women with the same qualifications. Women who had been enticed into technical and professional programs by the promise of high salaries found themselves unemployed.[101]

The South was no exception to this national pattern. Only 32 percent of students enrolled in Southern institutions in the fall of 1949 were women. Although more than 34 percent of all college students and 27 percent of all black college students in the region were veterans, fewer than 2 percent of the veterans at Southern schools were women.[102] At Mississippi Southern College, the influx of veterans resulted in the largest proportion of male students in the school's history, and the administration set out to change the curriculum to provide courses that were popular with veterans. Thus a college that had originated as a normal institute redirected its emphasis from programs in teaching to courses in business.[103]

Furman University in South Carolina also experienced a shift in curricular emphasis as men returned to the campus. Whereas the class of 1946, "composed largely of women, majored in English, education, sociology, and history," successive classes, composed largely of veterans, preferred courses in accounting, economics, biology, and chemistry. Although the faculty reaffirmed its commitment to the liberal arts, veterans wanted the college to train them "for useful careers in engineering, business administration, the ministry, [and] medicine."[104]

No school was immune from the demands of veterans. Many women's colleges admitted men for the first time in the postwar period.

Columbia College in South Carolina enrolled sixteen veterans in 1947 and graduated its first male student in 1948. Queens College in North Carolina had as many as fifty men in classes in the late forties.[105]

The large number of veterans seeking admission to the University of Florida led to the restitution of coeducation at both the state university in Gainesville and the state college in Tallahassee. The Buckman Act of 1905 had turned coeducational schools in the two cities into the all-male University of Florida and the all-female Florida State College for Women, and although both institutions ran coeducational summer schools, regular undergraduate programs were segregated by sex. When two thousand more men than the University of Florida could enroll applied for admission in the fall of 1946, the governor asked the women's college to provide for a thousand men on its campus. To circumvent the Buckman Act, the state established the Tallahassee Branch of the University of Florida (TBUF) at the Florida State College for Women. Nomenclature notwithstanding, the women's college became coeducational. Men joined the women's clubs, sang in their choir, played in their orchestra, and participated in their social functions. At the University of Florida, wives of veterans pressured school authorities for admission to classes with their husbands. Bowing to reality, the Florida legislature voted in 1947 to make both institutions coeducational. The name of the women's college was changed to Florida State University, and the short-lived TBUF was dissolved.[106]

World War II also produced a large number of war widows. A study of public higher education in South Carolina conducted by the George Peabody College for Teachers in 1946 recommended that colleges plan for the educational needs of those women whose lives were "touched so tragically by the war." Because many of these women had small children, colleges would have to make special housing and child-care arrangements to accommodate them, the study concluded. Eager for the extra funds brought in by the GI Bill, most institutions accommodated the veterans but did little for the war widows.[107]

Some of the returning veterans were women, but their relative numbers were insignificant. Whereas 49.5 percent of all male college students in the region were veterans in 1949, only 1.5 percent of women students were.[108] The needs of women veterans and war widows, like the needs of

209

college women generally, were lost in the rush to reward the "men" who had won the war. Women were allowed to fill vacancies in college classrooms during the war, just as they were allowed to fill positions in defense industries created by the departure of men for the front, but as soon as the war ended and the men came back, women were expected to return to their "sphere." As historian Barbara Solomon noted, the late forties witnessed a "backlash" against the higher education of American women: "Fearful of the continuing changes in work patterns and in expectations of women trained during and after the war, educators, relying on studies in psychology from a Freudian perspective, again succumbed to circular arguments for a feminine education."[109]

The parallels with blacks were obvious. African American men and women were welcome to serve their country in wartime, but when peace returned, they were to go back to their segregated neighborhoods, schools, and workplaces. Ironically, the advent of "good" times meant the return of sexual and racial discrimination in higher education as in society in general, discrimination that had decreased during the "bad" times brought by depression and world war. The "twoness" of Southern society was only too apparent.

Probably no consequence of the depression and the war better illustrates the hopes and fears of the postwar South than the movement for racial equality. A number of intellectual, economic, and political developments undermined traditional racial stereotypes in the years between 1930 and 1950. Anthropological and sociological research on race and the rise of a black intelligentsia challenged nineteenth-century notions of racial inferiority, while the fight against fascism in Germany provided parallels to the struggle against racism in the United States. From the American perspective, the war was very much a war of principle—of democracy versus dictatorship, of justice versus injustice, of right versus wrong. For Southerners who took their religion seriously, the moral shortcomings of their own segregated society were obvious. But perhaps the most important factor influencing American leaders of the era was the political changes that resulted from the migration of large numbers of black Southerners to the cities of the North. The black vote suddenly became a pivotal factor in many urban elections. Politicians could not continue to ignore racial concerns and be sure of victory.[110]

Black intellectuals were well aware of the changing social and political climate and were determined to share in the fruits of victory. In 1944 a number of African American leaders—including educators Rayford Logan, Mary McLeod Bethune, and W. E. B. Du Bois—published a series of essays entitled *What the Negro Wants*. In the introduction, Logan explained that black Americans believed that "democracy, like charity, should begin at home." African Americans wanted "an equal share not only in the performance of responsibilities and obligations but also in the enjoyment of rights and opportunities." It was only just, Logan argued, that blacks have the "same racial equality at the ballot-box that we have at the income-tax window; the same equality before a court of law that we have before an enemy's bullet; the same equality for getting a job, education, decent housing, and social security that American kinsmen of our nation's enemies possess."[111]

By the mid-forties, Southern racial relations were beginning to attract national attention once more. In December 1946 President Truman established a Committee on Civil Rights to investigate the nation's racial problems. The committee included two white Southerners, Dorothy Tilly, a Randolph-Macon Woman's College alumna and Methodist activist, and Frank Graham, President of the University of North Carolina. Together the committee members produced a document entitled *To Secure These Rights*, which called for an antilynching bill, the integration of the U.S. Armed Forces, the elimination of poll taxes, the end of segregation in interstate public transportation, and the end of federal funding for segregated educational institutions.[112]

Truman's civil rights plank split the Democratic Party in the South. Many white Southerners were unwilling to give up their segregated society without a fight. Black and white proponents of racial integration were labeled troublemakers and "communists." Tilly was described by one Southern journalist as "a parasite who while living upon funds furnished by the Methodist Church has rendered much of her service to the cause of Socialism and Communism."[113]

Once again the South wavered between tomorrow and yesterday. Southerners had joined other Americans in the fight against fascism. They had defeated dictatorship and defended democracy. In the realm of foreign affairs, historian George Tindall wrote, "they had advanced boldly toward new horizons." But white Southerners were less future oriented when it came to democracy at home: many "had retreated within the parapets of the embattled South, where they stood fast against the incursions of social change. The inconsistency could not long endure," Tindall argued, "and a critical question for the postwar South, facing eventful issues of economic and racial adjustment, was which would prevail, the broader vision or the defensive reaction."[114]

Southern women had made many educational gains in the thirties and forties. The number of institutions that admitted white women had increased tremendously; black colleges and universities had developed their academic programs and improved their physical plants and offered women more educational opportunities than ever before. The expansion of the publicly supported universities meant that increasing numbers of white and black women could afford a college education.

The Great Depression may have brought the plight of black Southerners to the attention of the nation and encouraged interracial cooperation at some Southern institutions, and the Second World War may have inspired women to seek new majors and new professions, but racism, sexism, and elitism continued to flourish on most college campuses in the forties and fifties, and many of the traditional views of woman's nature and role remained entrenched in pedagogical theory and practice. After World War II, educational developments seemed to indicate that "yesterday's" stereotypes of gender, race, and class still shaped the Southern college scene. Men determined the college curriculum; men dominated the college campus; and men received the college degrees. Blacks remained segregated in "unequal" institutions, barred from most professional and graduate schools and excluded from positions of political and economic leadership. Women from the upper and middle classes predominated in the student bodies of all institutions, large and small, public and private, white and black. But Southern women were used to fighting lost causes. And tomorrow was another day.

6

The Voices of the Future

Social Protest on the Southern Campus

After two decades of economic depression and war, the American South seemed once more to be at a crossroads. The years of sacrifice and valor had weakened traditional stereotypes of race, gender, and class and buttressed individuals' faith in the promise of American democracy. Postwar youth were eager to apply the lessons of the classroom to the world outside, and their involvement in the civil rights struggles of the fifties and early sixties and the student demonstrations of the sixties and early seventies would transform the region, its residents, and its institutions. Blacks demanded full citizenship, students participatory democracy, and feminists equal opportunity.[1] College women throughout the nation wanted to be treated as adults, not little girls: to study where and what they pleased, to go and come when they wished, and to eat and wear what they wanted. As participants in and witnesses to these events, Southern colleges and college women were profoundly affected by the postwar protests against racism, sexism, and war.

Joan Gladden Mack was one of the many Southerners whose lives were transformed by the campus protests of the post–World War II period.[2] Born on James Island in rural South Carolina in 1943, Joan was the fourth of six children in a working-class family and the first of her family to go to college. Although Cut Bridge Elementary and W. Gresham Meggett High, which she had attended, were considered "country" schools and inferior to those in urban areas, her parents and teachers made sure that Joan had the same opportunities for academic development and scholastic achievement as students in the City of Charleston.

Segregation meant separate and unequal facilities for black and white South Carolinians. African American schools had inadequate and outdated buildings, equipment, and supplies. As a young girl, Joan would volunteer to clean the marked and damaged books that were sent over from the white schools. Gender perceptions also reflected antebellum concepts of place. Women—white and black—had fewer rights and opportunities than men. South Carolina did not allow women to become jurors until 1967 and did not ratify the Nineteenth Amendment until 1969.[3] Despite these obstacles, Joan excelled academically, and she and her friends eagerly competed for the "top place."

Mack was fortunate to have a number of wise and compassionate mentors. Her parents constantly encouraged their children to do their best, and when Joan's mother died when Joan was fourteen years of age, her older sister assumed the maternal mantle. She still remembers fondly teachers such as Mrs. Edith Henry, Mrs. Alice Jowers, and Mrs. Gwendolyn Manigault and principals such as Mrs. Albertha Murray and Dr. Leroy Anderson. These women and men did not want their students to settle for anything less than the best. Later, as a young broadcaster, Joan was mentored by the civil rights activist Septima Poinsett Clark. Joan admired Clark's "cool and calm" demeanor under fire and her resolute determination to fight injustice wherever and whenever she found it. Clark, in turn, made sure that Joan was the first of the local reporters to hear of her activities and accomplishments. In fact, when Joan's daughter Dandria had to do an interview for her African American Studies class at the University of South Carolina in the eighties, Clark invited the women to her Charleston home for the interview.

Higher education opened many doors for Mack. Aided by a county scholarship, student loans, and family savings, Joan entered South Carolina State College (SCSC) in 1960. None of the colleges and universities in the state were integrated despite various legal challenges to "separate and equal" in the forties and fifties. In fact, SCSC had been "given" graduate, law, and medical schools by the state general assembly in 1945 to avoid the integration of the state's all-white graduate and professional institutions.[4] Thus all the students and the vast majority of the faculty and administrators at State were black in 1960. Although student sit-ins had begun at North Carolina Agricultural and Technical College in January 1960, the atmosphere at SCSC was fairly quiet until Joan's senior year. Students and faculty were involved in civil rights demonstrations but primarily as individuals and not as representatives of the college.

Joan decided to major in professional biology—the choice of those who preferred the biology profession to biology teaching—and to minor in chemistry. She hoped to go on for an advanced degree, either in medicine or in biology. She was a conscientious student; extracurricular activities were not as important as academic achievements.

When civil rights protests escalated during Joan's senior year at State, her family warned her not to "get involved." They were afraid of what might happen to her and to her college credits. This was not an idle fear: Governor Russell had threatened to close the school and send the students home without their degrees. So, although many students left campus daily to march against segregation in the town of Orangeburg, Joan went to class. One spring day, she and six of her friends found themselves the only ones in biology class. Their professor chastised them: "What are you doing here? You should be supporting the cause." The friends returned to the dormitory to discuss the situation and decided to join the evening protest. Fearing their families' reprobation if they were arrested, they consoled themselves that the jails were full and that no one had been arrested during the morning march. The students met at Trinity Methodist Church after supper and marched peacefully through the streets of Orangeburg, singing "We Shall Overcome." No one was arrested, although Joan narrowly escaped injury when an elderly white man swung his cane at her.

Mack's second protest march did not end as well. The marchers were stopped by state troopers, forced to sit on the ground for several hours, and threatened with water hoses. And then came the worst news—the students would be imprisoned in the Pink Castle, a jail that had been condemned years before as uninhabitable. Joan, her friends, and two other young women ended up together in the same cell. There were only two beds in the room—which was not a problem because none of the eight wanted to touch either of the loathsome mattresses—and a filthy toilet that did not flush. The students comforted one another by singing "We Shall Overcome." The song "took on a whole new meaning for me that night," Joan recalled.

The protestors were forced to spend two days in the Pink Castle because the defense fund of the local chapter of the National Association for the Advancement of Colored People (NAACP) had been depleted by the mass arrests, and it took a while for supporters to come up with bail money. The women were warned not to eat the "grits and gravy" offered to the prisoners, but they did not go hungry. The black community of Orangeburg brought them sandwiches and beverages. When released, Joan called her father and sister. They were extremely supportive. Later, Mack would participate in other civil rights protests, including the Mother's Day March for the Charleston Hospital Workers in 1969.

After graduation Mack went to New York City to look for work. She had gone to New York every summer during high school. By living with her brother and his family, she had saved a considerable amount for college expenses. When she first arrived in New York as a young teen, she was teased about her "geechee" accent, and Joan soon concluded that as a professional woman she had to "learn to speak the way I read the language." She copied the speech patterns of educated New Yorkers and later enrolled in a public speaking class at State. "I still speak gullah when I get angry," she confessed.

With her degree from State in hand, Mack went right to the professional employment bureau at 444 Madison Avenue. Here she had a "really good counselor, a young white woman," who encouraged her to apply for jobs outside biology. Joan was at first disappointed that she could not find a position employing her major. She feared that a degree from a black Southern college was not taken seriously in the North. Despite her concerns about working outside her field of expertise, she loved her first job as a community organizer for the New York City Youth Board. When she returned to Charleston in 1968, her New York experience helped her to get a job as a caseworker for the Department of Social Services, where she helped establish the very first food stamp program in the state.

In New York, Joan not only worked full time but also attended classes at the City College of New York, where she earned a teaching certificate in the Intensive Teachers Training Program, sponsored jointly by the New York State Board of Education and the college. Through the years, Joan would often use the communication skills that had she acquired in her education courses but, ironically, never in a traditional classroom setting. In 1972 Joan was told by black community leaders in Charleston that Channel 5 was looking for a black woman to co-host a talk show, and they urged her to apply for the position. She was working at Manpower at the time and enjoying her job, but she agreed to fill out an application in order to satisfy her friends. Much to her surprise, she was hired on the spot. "You don't have an accent," the general manager of the station told her. In the following week, Joan went "on air," co-hosting a daytime talk show called *Kaleidoscope*. Here her research skills, developed in the biology laboratory at State, and her people skills, fostered at the Department of Social Services, were put to the test. The new job also forced her to get involved in the community—she had to choose appropriate speakers and topics for the various shows. She was one of the first to interview Septima Clark on television and to recount her civil rights activities. In fact, when South Carolina public television decided to do a special on Clark for its civil rights series, Joan was asked to give the highlights of the older woman's amazing career. Joan later interviewed other prominent South Carolinians, such as Mamie Fields. She was so successful as a television personality that when she left the network for the College of Charleston, the station executives concluded that only another black woman could succeed her.

Mack sees education as the key to mobility for today's young Southerners, black and white. All three of her children went to college, although none attended a historically black institution. As students at Bishop England, a Catholic high school in Charleston, her children had "always been in integrated situations," and they elected to attend historically white institutions of higher education. "South Carolina State was good for me then and is still good for many blacks today," Mack concludes, but she is glad that her children "could freely choose" from a wide variety of schools.

Coming of age in the sixties, Mack felt the burden of being successful—"for myself, for blacks, for women." She fought for racial justice: "I paraded and marched in the 1960s because I had to." She saw herself as a trailblazer for women and for blacks: "[I]n every position I had in journalism another black woman followed." Today, she believes that she is more conscious of gender than race. In the South, traditions about women's place seem even more entrenched than those about blacks. Yet she concedes that "[w]hat I accomplish gender wise, I accomplish for my race." Joan Mack's story illustrates the "twoness" of Southern culture and the "multiconsciousness" of black women in the region. Her educational experiences were shaped by the fact that she was black, working class, Southern, and female.

Indeed, it was the tension between different elements of the Southern heritage that inspired the social activism of the postwar period. On 9 March 1960 students from the Atlanta University Center, a consortium of six educational institutions for African Americans in the city, issued a manifesto proclaiming their rights as human beings and American citizens. "Today's youth," their Appeal for Human Rights declared, "will not sit by submissively, while being denied all of the rights, privileges, and joys of life. We want to state clearly and unequivocally that we cannot tolerate, in a nation professing democracy and among people professing Christianity, the discriminatory conditions under which the Negro is living."[5] The Atlanta students were not the first or the last to point to the inconsistencies of an American creed that professed liberty and justice for all while denying equal rights to some because of their race, ethnicity, religion, or gender. But their manifesto demonstrated a "consciousness of the past in the present" that was characteristic of student protests in the post–World War II South. As Charlayne Hunter-Gault recalled in her autobiography, "We could see that . . . past for what it was: a system designed to keep us in our place and convince us . . . that it was our fault, as well as our destiny. Now, without either ambivalence or shame, we saw ourselves as the heirs to a legacy of struggle . . . that was ennobling, . . . that was enabling us to take control of our destiny."[6]

It is difficult for youth today to comprehend the restrictive nature of campus life in the fifties. "Yesterday's" images of gender, race, and class remained remarkably resilient—in politics, in economics, and in education. On college campuses throughout the South, the races and sexes were still largely segregated. White women were far more likely to attend a coeducational, public institution than their predecessors, but most women—even at the large state universities—still had their own student governments, their own social clubs, and often their own campuses. Even less progress had been made in racial relations. Except in a few border states, students attended all-white or all-black institutions. And black and white women of all classes were expected to behave as ladies.

At white institutions, nostalgia for the "Lost Cause" filled the pages of college publications, influenced the nature of campus social functions, and infiltrated the sancta of the classroom and laboratory. College annuals, newspapers, and literary magazines; May Day festivities, holiday cotillions, and sorority and fraternity functions; dress codes, gender-specific curfews, and student handbooks generally portrayed the woman student as a white, upper-class lady who was worshiped and protected by an attractive and rich Southern gentleman who sought her for his wife. The ideal woman possessed a childlike innocence and dependence; she was not likely to challenge the status quo. Female students who were not rich or white were encouraged to attain the ideal by acting like ladies.

Class prejudices were everywhere apparent, especially in the students' choice of extracurricular activities. The cotillion clubs at most Southern colleges and universities were as exclusive as regional debutante balls, and membership was often by invitation only. Certain sororities and fraternities also took pride in their selectivity. Poorer students were seldom given invitation bids and could not have afforded active membership if invited.

Academic programs did little to change traditional expectations of women after graduation. One alumna from the Woman's College of North Carolina complained that the institution was "mostly interested in creating uncritical brood-sows and finding suckers to fill underpaid teachers' positions." A 1954 survey of Woman's College graduates supported her contention: most alumnae got married, had children, and became full-time homemakers. Those who worked outside the home inevitably became teachers.[7] The ideal woman was still a wife and mother.

Racial stereotypes also survived the economic and social changes of the Great Depression and the war. Crude racial jokes permeated the pages of college publications and the chatter of student gatherings on white campuses. Segregation increased perceptions of racial differences. The only African Americans allowed to step foot on most white campuses in the Deep South before the 1960s were maids and janitors. Regardless of age, black college employees were always addressed by their first names—reinforcing their inferior status. Black and white students seldom interacted academically or even athletically. Intercollegiate competitions were as segregated as the colleges themselves.

Racial differences also existed on black campuses, where light-skinned women with "European" features and hair were often preferred to their darker and more "African looking" sisters. Certain clubs, sororities, and even schools were associated with students of specific skin tones. When Charlayne Hunter (later, Hunter-Gault) returned to Wayne State University in the fall of 1960 to begin her sophomore year, she found that the other African American students assumed that she would pledge Alpha Kappa Alpha with most of the other light-skinned women. Hunter was shocked to discover that "the Deltas, who ranged in color from jet black to light brown, were so convinced that I would follow the traditional color pattern of pledging that they did not invite me to their rush party." After assuring the sisters of her genuine interest, she joined Delta because she "resented the whole color issue."[8]

The campus climate in the postwar South was not conducive to social or political change, and it took a brave woman (or man) to challenge the status quo. When the United States Supreme Court ruled in 1954 that separate educational facilities for the races were inherently unequal, Alabama, Georgia, Florida, Mississippi, and South Carolina had state laws mandating segregation in their public and private colleges.[9] Even after *Brown*, opposition to integration remained strong, particularly in the Deep South. A special 1960 issue of *School and Society* on racial segregation in education characterized Alabama, Georgia, Mississippi, and South Carolina as "hard core" states.[10]

Administrators of most Southern colleges and universities opposed the integration of their institutions, and individuals who favored improvements in racial relations were often ostracized and harassed. The dean of the University of South Carolina School of Education was fired in 1955 for exhorting the state to abide by the Supreme Court decision.[11] A few years earlier, a Winthrop College student had barely escaped expulsion for dancing with a black student who had "cut in" on her during a dance at the Congress of the National Student Foundation. Winthrop's board of trustees subsequently forbade students from attending any "conventions where there were mixed races" and insisted that they "be properly chaperoned" at all off-campus meetings.[12]

Anyone who favored change was suspect. Katharine Lumpkin, whose 1946 autobiography detailed her rejection of "my old heritage of racial beliefs and racial practices," was subsequently called before the

House Un-American Activities Committee for her "communist" ideas. Lumpkin's biographer, Jacqueline Dowd Hall, has no doubt that the investigation was the result of her antisegregationist stand.[13] Southern legislators were particularly suspicious of academics. The state of Florida created a special senate committee in the fifties "to root out communists, homosexuals, and other allegedly subversive and un-American elements from the state universities." A number of University of Florida faculty were investigated by the committee and forced to resign. Florida State University added a new rule in 1959 that threatened to punish students who engaged "in an unauthorized mass demonstration."[14]

The majority of white students at institutions in the Deep South seemed to be staunch segregationists. Mississippi State College for Women had disbanded its Young Women's Christian Association (YWCA) in 1945 "after sixty years of continuous leadership activity" because it "disagreed with the national headquarters on matters of integration policy."[15] Students at the white public colleges in South Carolina withdrew from the U.S. National Student Association in 1960 because of its advocacy of integration.[16] Violent protests erupted at the University of Alabama in 1956 when a young black woman by the name of Autherine Lucy was enrolled. At the University of Mississippi, a white woman who sat next to James Meredith in class was so harassed by a group of students called the Rebel Underground that she left the campus and moved with her parents out of state.[17]

Even in the border states, which integrated first, racial progress was slow. The University of Tennessee had been chartered in 1869 as the state agricultural college by a legislature dominated by unionists from the Eastern part of the state and was prohibited from excluding students on the basis of race. Although the Tennessee constitution of 1870 subsequently forbade integration in the public schools of the state, the legislature continued to nominate African Americans as university cadets and to subsidize their education at neighboring black colleges. Black students began to apply for admission to the university's professional schools in the thirties, and in 1941 the legislature voted to establish comparable facilities for professional training at black institutions in the state. In 1951 a Federal district judge ruled that equal facilities were not being provided and ordered qualified black candidates to be admitted to the university's graduate and law schools. The first African American graduate, a woman, received her master's degree from Tennessee in 1954. Black undergraduate students were not admitted until 1961.[18]

Texas was the first state in the former Confederacy to integrate the professional schools of its state university. But as University of Texas historian Joe Frantz noted, college administrators "had to be ordered into the twentieth century." Although the United States Supreme Court ruled in June 1950 that the University of Texas had to admit Herman Marion Sweatt into its law school, the school's undergraduate programs remained segregated until 1956 and its residential facilities until 1964. Most of the opposition to integration on the state university campus came from administrators and legislators rather than from students and faculty. When a petition decrying integration was circulated on the campus in the mid-fifties, only 4 percent of the student body signed it. One could get this number of signatures, Frantz quipped, on "a petition suggesting that . . . the faculty teach in the nude, or . . . that football be discontinued, to suggest the utmost sacrilege."[19]

State legislators and college authorities opposed the integration of social organizations on the campus of the University of Texas. When an African American woman, Barbara Smith, was chosen to share the lead with a white man in an annual student production of Purcell's opera, *Dido and Aeneas*, in 1956, legislators demanded that the university president eliminate Smith from the opera "for the betterment of Texas." The president, claiming concern for Smith's safety, yielded to legislative pressures and removed her from the cast. His action made Smith "America's student celebrity of the week," and eight embarrassed legislators wrote her a letter of apology, explaining that their colleagues had forgotten "Christian principles of right and wrong."[20]

Legislative and administrative opposition limited social progress on many Southern campuses in the fifties. Constance Curry, an Agnes Scott student involved in interracial work, recalled having "to get written permission from my parents to attend interracial meetings in Atlanta."[21] Conservative executives at historically black colleges even discouraged African American students from working for their own civil rights. A South Carolina State College alumna of 1955 described the college administration as "hostile" to student concerns and indifferent to the racial problems of the community. The college, she wrote, "was set apart" and saw itself as a "sort of elite." There was no interaction between the college and the town; in fact, "student off-campus contacts [were] restricted."[22]

Women students had to contend not only with conservative attitudes toward racial relationships but also with traditional views of gender roles. Special curfews, dress regulations, social organizations, and campus activities all made sure that Southern women remained ladies. And ladies, of course, were docile and dependent; they did not challenge authority by engaging in campus protests. Those who ventured from the pedestal were warned that they would lose the protection it inspired.[23]

Feminine purity was still idealized. A sociology professor at the University of Florida was investigated in the mid-fifties because his book *Premarital Dating Behavior* included examples provided by University of Florida students. A woman student at Howard University was expelled in 1964 because she violated curfew regulations by spending the night outside the dormitory.[24]

College authorities served *in loco parentis* on most Southern campuses into the sixties. Marlene Linton O'Bryant Seabrook, an African American who attended South Carolina State from 1951 to 1955, recalled that women had to be in their dormitory or in the library by 6:00 P.M., and they had to "sign out" to go to the library. Female students were not allowed to have an automobile on campus or to ride in an automobile driven by a male student or faculty member, and students needed permission to visit someone off campus. College dances were chaperoned by faculty and the dean of women. There was, of course, no drinking on campus, and attendance at chapel was compulsory.[25] As late as 1964, women at Auburn University had to make their beds daily by 10:00 A.M., had to observe curfews and quiet hours, and had to attend college convocations. They were provided a list of "What to Wear When." Blue jeans were not allowed "at any time," dresses or skirts were required for class, and dresses and high-heeled shoes were expected for Sunday dinner. The suggested dress for Auburn football games was a nice dress or suit, heels, and gloves. "Girls" were expected to behave as "ladies." They were not to talk to "boys" while sunbathing, not to chew gum in public, not to play cards in the lobby on Sunday, and not to drink intoxicating beverages.[26]

Auburn ladies were not to participate in campus demonstrations, either. Students were given specific procedures to follow in case of a "demonstration" or "panty raid" in the vicinity of their dormitories. They were to close the blinds on their windows, shut the doors to their rooms, and "sit quietly in the hall until the demonstration [was] over." Offenders would be referred to the judiciary council for disciplinary action.[27]

But conservatives were not the only Southerners to employ traditional concepts of womanhood in their social programs. Regional reformers also took gender stereotypes into consideration. Perhaps one reason for the large numbers of black women involved in early integration efforts at Southern colleges and universities was the belief that black women were less threatening than black men to white culture and that white women were less likely than white men to react violently to the integration of their institutions.

Joanne Smart Drane, an African American woman from Raleigh, North Carolina, was the first black to attend the Woman's College of the University of North Carolina. As she prepared to drive to the campus in September 1956, she remembered being "optimistic that there would be no violence associated with my enrollment." Although she worried that "parents and other adults outside the college" might protest her arrival, she was confident "that young ladies simply did not behave in a violent manner."[28]

Bennett College, a black women's college in Greensboro, North Carolina, personified the strange blend of social conservatism and political radicalism that characterized student activists of the postwar period. Bennett saw itself as the "Vassar of the South," and its students, known as "Bennett Belles," would never appear in public without their hats, gloves, and pocketbooks. As one student from the class of 1964 explained, "They were trying to make classy people out of us." Yet, as early as 1937, Bennett students had been involved in protests against the city's movie theaters because of the degrading images of blacks in the films shown there, and when the civil rights protests began in earnest in the fifties, "Bennett was the only school in Greensboro that allowed Martin Luther King Jr. to speak. And during the Greensboro sit-ins, Bennett women served as the second line of defense, behind male students from N.C. A&T."[29]

Women students were involved in the integration of the Universities of Alabama, Florida, Georgia, and South Carolina. These women were not welcomed with open arms, but their determination helped paved the way for other African American students to follow. Autherine Lucy and Pollie Ann Myers applied for admission to the University of Alabama in 1952. When their applications were rejected by the board of trustees, the women sued, and in October 1955 the United States Supreme Court ruled that the university could not deny admission on the basis of race alone. The trustees subsequently denied Myers's application because she had married since filing her suit, but they admitted Lucy, without dormitory or cafeteria privileges, in February 1956.[30]

Autherine Lucy had no trouble in her classes, but segregationists in the town organized protests on the night after her admission, and three days later a hostile crowd of almost a thousand gathered outside the building where she was attending classes. The police had to drive her to safety, and another mob appeared outside the president's home that night to protest her presence on the campus. University officials gave in and suspended Lucy for her own protection. Once more she turned to the courts. Her lawyer accused university officials of creating an atmosphere "of riot and discord" so that they could get rid of her. The U.S. District Court ordered Lucy's readmission, but the board of trustees proceeded to expel her permanently for libeling the university's intentions. Lucy married and did not seek readmission to the university, although her daughter matriculated there in 1981.[31]

Despite Governor George Wallace's charades at the "schoolhouse door," the University of Alabama was finally integrated in 1963. One of the two students admitted under the 1963 court order, Vivian Malone, "became the University's first black graduate in 1965." Malone served as a role model for both women and blacks on the campus, and in 1972 the Afro-American Cultural Center at the university was dedicated to her. She was invited back to the campus again in 1976 to speak at a symposium with the theme "Emerging Women."[32]

A woman was also part of the original suit to integrate the University of Florida. Rose Boyd applied for admission to the pharmacy school in 1949, but her application was rejected. When she and four other African American applicants sued, the courts allowed the Florida Board of Control to offer graduate and professional opportunities at all-black Florida Agricultural and Mechanical College instead. Not until 1958 did a federal district judge order the University of Florida to admit qualified African Americans into its graduate and professional schools. The following year, two black women began graduate studies at the university.[33]

A young black man tried unsuccessfully to integrate the University of Georgia in 1950, but his efforts paved the way for the admission of Charlayne Hunter and Hamilton Holmes in 1961. University of Georgia officials had rejected their applications in the fall of 1959 because the school's dormitories were already full, and Holmes and Hunter took their case to court. On 6 January 1961 the university was ordered to enroll the two students immediately. Because the university required all unmarried women younger than twenty-three years of age to live in the dormitories, Georgia authorities reluctantly decided to house Hunter on campus. They provided her with a suite containing a kitchenette in the hope that she would stay away from the university dining halls. She was given no roommate.[34]

The two students registered without incident, but on the night before they were to begin classes, the governor announced that the university must close under the provisions of a 1956 anti-integration law. Crowds of students gathered to protest, and a mob surrounded the dormitory where Hunter was housed, throwing bricks and starting fires. Although Hunter was not injured, the administration (déjà vu—Alabama) decided to withdraw Hunter and Holmes for their own protection. The faculty met the next day and demanded their return; two days later the court ordered the students reinstated. Both went on to earn their degrees from Georgia. In the process, Hunter also integrated the university's dining facilities. In the spring of 1962, another woman, Mary Frances Early, became the school's first black graduate student.[35]

Admission to a previously all-white school was only the first step in the desegregation process. Black women soon found that there were numerous obstacles to be surmounted before they could be integrated into the academic and social life of the institution. When Joanne Smart Drane arrived in Greensboro in 1956, she discovered that she and her roommate, Bettye Davis Tillman—the only other black student admitted to the Woman's College of North Carolina, were given an entire wing of the dormitory "to preclude any white girls using the same bathroom facilities." She joked that she "often wondered how many white girls were denied on-campus housing that year because two black girls had been given an entire section of a dorm and used only one of about eight available rooms."[36]

Social life was often nonexistent for black women at white colleges in the late fifties and early sixties. Drane recalled being invited by two white friends to go shopping and to have lunch. When the three attempted to order their food, however, they were told that "we don't serve colored here." There was no restaurant in all of downtown Greensboro, North Carolina, in 1956 where black and white students could sit down together.[37]

Dating was another problem. Drane never attended a Woman's College dance. "It was one thing to interact socially with persons of the same sex," she noted, "but when males came into the picture, that was something else. The taboos of society, both on campus and off, were straightforward about this. At a dance, my date would have to dance every dance with me and I with him." Drane had to travel to nearby black campuses for social activities.[38]

Community interracial and religious organizations tried to help black women adjust to life on the white campus. Henri Monteith, whose legal action opened the University of South Carolina to blacks, was active in the school's branch of the Student Council on Human Relations and in her senior year became state coordinator for Operation Search, a project designed to encourage African American students throughout the state to enroll in the integrated colleges of South Carolina.[39] Despite her importance to integration efforts in South Carolina, Monteith kept a low profile at the university. For security reasons, she was required to live on campus during her first year, but she occupied the only single room with a private bath at the school. She was never photographed with her class for the yearbook.

Many Southern women worked hard to improve racial relations on their campuses and in their communities in the fifties and sixties and were actively involved in civil rights activities. In February 1960 four African American men from North Carolina's Agricultural and Technical (A&T) College began the sit-ins that would challenge the segregation of public facilities in the region. Other students throughout the South—male and female, black and white—organized their own protests. Three white students from the Woman's College of North Carolina joined black students from A&T and Bennett in the sit-ins in Greensboro; the Women's

Student Government of Duke University passed a resolution supporting civil rights' activities in Durham; and students at Agnes Scott College offered "[s]pecific support" for the "Appeal for Human Rights" issued by African American students in Atlanta.[40]

Student protestors strove to behave like ladies and gentlemen. Women wore dresses, and men wore coats and ties. One white demonstrator recalled that he was careful to sit next to black men rather than black women so as not to incite charges of sexual impropriety. Violence was eschewed. Diane Nash, a student from Fisk who participated in sit-ins in Nashville in the spring of 1960, remembered first attending workshops that taught the nonviolent protest techniques of Mohandas Gandhi.[41]

Women activists, despite their advocacy of passive resistance, were not treated like "ladies." Anne Moody, in her book *Coming of Age in Mississippi*, described the reception that she and other women protestors from Tougaloo College received when they tried to integrate a lunch counter in Jackson, Mississippi. Teachers and students alike were smeared with food, sprayed with paint from a nearby counter, and dragged by their hair across the floor. A woman professor who joined the demonstrators was called a "white nigger" and thrown off her seat at the lunch counter by a high school student.[42]

Some commentators saw the violent treatment of peaceful protestors as a logical consequence of Southern paternalism. Anne Braden—a journalist who was arrested in Jackson, Mississippi, in 1951 for protesting the killing of a black man who had been wrongly accused of rape—recalled the anger of a white policeman when he discovered that she was from Alabama. "You are not fit to be a Southern woman," he told her. Braden shot back, "No, I'm not your kind of Southern woman." The policeman's reaction, Braden concluded, was not unique. It was typical of "all the rulers of the South who treated black people like children and put white women on pedestals and turned on both in fury when they asserted their humanity."[43]

Indeed, women arrested for civil rights activities seldom saw much chivalry in the Southern legal system. Fisk student Diane Nash and Spelman student Ruby Doris Smith spent thirty days at hard labor in a South Carolina prison as the result of a new "jail, no bail" tactic tried in the Rock Hill sit-ins. Nash was jailed again as a consequence of protests in Mississippi, and even though she was pregnant, she refused to appeal her conviction. She was willing to give birth in prison so that other black babies might be born and live free.[44]

Southern college women were involved in less conspicuous efforts for social change as well. One of the groups most active in promoting integration at South Carolina's colleges and universities was the South Carolina Council on Human Relations. In 1960 Elizabeth Ledeen, a volunteer at the Presbyterian Student Center at the University of South Carolina, helped to organize, under the auspices of the council, the first statewide meeting of college students interested in improving racial relations. Ledeen was subsequently hired as student program director by the council, and she set out to conscript student representatives from all the colleges in the state. She wrote to a friend in Virginia that her work in "developing intercollegiate biracial student groups" was not popular among many whites and that her next letter might well be a request for asylum.[45]

The first state conference of the South Carolina Student Council on Human Relations (SCSCHR) was small—only forty students attended and just eight colleges in the state were represented. Within five years, however, the organization boasted more than 4,000 students from twenty-four different colleges.[46] Women were well represented on the SCSCHR from its formation. In 1962 the intercollegiate mailing list included nineteen women and fifteen men students from the University of South Carolina. Black women from Claflin College in Orangeburg served as both officers in and representatives to the organization, and in 1964 an African American woman from Benedict College in Columbia was elected president.[47]

The SCSCHR helped smooth the way for the integration of Clemson and the University of South Carolina in 1963. Harvey Gantt and Henri Monteith participated in SCSCHR group meetings before their court-ordered enrollments at the two universities. Because of the biracial sessions organized by the council, both students knew they had "friends" on campus.[48]

African American students generally found more parental and institutional support for their protest activities than did white students. Professors from historically black colleges participated in civil rights demonstrations in every Southern state. Black women activists often had family members who were interested in social reform. Marianna Davis, a graduate of South Carolina State College who later earned her doctorate in English and became a professor at Benedict College in South Carolina, noted that her grandmother had been a "fighter" and that her mother had served as secretary of the NAACP "when school teachers were not allowed to be a member." She credited both women for whetting her interest in civil rights and the women's movement.[49]

The civil rights activist Ella Baker was an inspiration to students throughout the South. A native of North Carolina and alumna of Shaw University in Raleigh, Baker personified the "participatory democracy" she advocated. Preferring "group-centered leadership" to "leader-centered groups," she rejected the patriarchal culture of the Southern Christian Leadership Conference and encouraged African Americans to create their own grassroots organizations. It was Baker who called the April 1960 conference of students at Shaw that resulted in the founding of the Student Nonviolent Coordinating Committee (SNCC). More than any other civil rights group, SNCC "created the sixties concept of activism."[50]

For many black women in the sixties, civil rights activities were an integral part of student life. When Anne Moody was jailed for joining Dr. Martin Luther King Jr. at a demonstration in Jackson, Mississippi, she found twelve of her classmates already in the cell. She felt sorry for the white women who had been arrested with them because, sent to separate cells, they were "missing out on all the fun we planned to have. Here we were going to school together, sleeping in the same dorm, worshiping together, playing together, even demonstrating together."[51]

Spelman women participated in numerous civil rights protests in Atlanta. Howard Zinn, a white New Yorker who became chair of the department of history and social sciences at Spelman in 1956, was proud when his students in the social science club decided "to undertake some real project involving social change" by challenging the segregation of Atlanta's public libraries. Spelman graduates continued their activism after college. An alumna from South Carolina, Marian Wright Edelman, was a founding member of SNCC and afterward the first African American woman to be called to the bar in Mississippi and the creator of the Children's Defense Fund in Washington, D.C.[52]

White women often lacked similar support for their protest activities. A 1961 graduate of Sweet Briar College in Virginia recalled that she was called on the carpet by the dean of students for engaging in civil rights

activities in the nearby town of Lynchburg. She found the college administration hostile to students' concerns "except when they wanted student support for increased faculty salaries! I really had to fight for my activities,"
she remembered.[53]

Ann Dearsley-Vernon, one of the three white women who joined the
sit-in at Woolworth's begun by black students from nearby A&T in February 1960, was surprised by the negative reactions that her participation
elicited from other whites on the campus and in the community. "The hate
mail directed at the other two girls and myself was so virulent," she contended, "that it was monitored [by the Federal Bureau of Investigation] for
the remainder of the school year." Dearsley-Vernon believed that without the backing of her parents, she "would have been quietly removed from
the rolls." As it was, all three women were confined to the campus for several weeks.[54]

It was not always easy for Southern women to take a stand for civil
rights. "In contrast to portions of the Northern student movement," Sara
Evans—a white South Carolinian who became active in the civil rights
movement while a student at the University of North Carolina—wrote,
"Southern women did not join the civil rights struggle thoughtlessly or
simply as an extension of a boyfriend's involvement. Such a decision often
required a break with home and childhood friends that might never heal."[55]
In her book *Personal Politics*, Evans argued that most Southern women became involved in civil rights through the church: "Although southern
Protestantism in the 1950s was in general as segregated and racist as the
rest of southern society," she asserted, "it also nourished elements of egalitarian idealism."[56]

Mary Edith Bentley, a Randolph-Macon Woman's College student
who was jailed in February 1961 for her participation in a sit-in, viewed
her actions as a natural consequence of her Christian faith. "Some people
thought I had become very political or radicalized," she remembered. But
"none of that was true. I simply had found a deepening and broadening
of the religious concerns I always had."[57] Constance Curry, a white North
Carolinian who became involved in interracial work while a student at
Agnes Scott in the 1950s, traced her activism to an incident in the fourth
grade when she reprimanded a classmate who had insulted one of the black
cafeteria workers: "I have no idea where that brazenness came from except

that, as naive as it sounds, Sunday school lessons and the U.S. Constitution had made deep impressions, and I'd become very conscious of the gap between the values we professed and the reality of our segregated lives."[58] Katharine Lumpkin, too, credited religion for her racial "remaking." Religious arguments, she contended, could be "turned around" so that their "high authority" could "justify the very acts which our Southern teaching had told us were unjustifiable. Under religion's felt demand I could first profane the sacred tabernacle of our racial beliefs and go on profaning it in subsequent years."[59]

Campus religious groups had long worked to improve racial relations in the region. When Alice Spearman Wright, a 1923 graduate of Converse College, was asked why she became involved in the civil rights movement in the fifties, she credited the interracial work she had done with the YWCA at Converse. Religion was an important motivating factor in her life; so was the concept of noblesse oblige. "One of the things that was strongly inculcated [in] us as children in our family," she explained, "was the idea of to whom much [has] been given from him much is expected."[60]

By couching their message in religious terms, black civil rights leaders had awakened many sleeping white consciences. Religious idealism seemed to be the motive force behind most women's efforts to achieve racial justice, and campus religious organizations often took the lead in ameliorating racial inequities in the community. Religion provided strength as well as inspiration. When Charlayne Hunter feared ostracism as the lone black woman on the University of Georgia campus, she was comforted by the words of her priest assuring her of God's presence and by the voice of her grandmother reciting the Twenty-third Psalm.[61]

In 1961 the South Carolina Baptist Students, the National Conference of the Methodist Youth Fellowships, and the Council of Lutheran Student Associations of America all spoke out publicly in favor of integration. One Presbyterian clergyman, when asked about the outside influences that led to the "sit-ins" of the sixties, responded that the Southern "youth movement had its origins not in Moscow but . . . in Carpenters' Hall, Philadelphia, and . . . in the Judean Hills where the carpenter's Son preached glad tidings to the disinherited of the earth."[62]

Jewish students and faculty were especially sensitive to the racist taunts of segregationists. Hunter remembered being visited during her first semester at Georgia by a "delegation" of Jewish girls: "They said they felt bad about how I had been treated, and that because Jews had a history of persecution, too, they could in some small way understand how I must be feeling." Significantly, the history professor selected by the chair to be Hunter's Western civilization teacher was a refugee from Nazi Germany.[63]

College religious groups were involved in various and sundry civil rights activities in the late fifties and early sixties. The YWCA at the University of Texas "initiated a series of pickets at local restaurants"; the Presbyterian Student Center at the University of South Carolina organized some of the first sit-ins in Columbia. When the University of Texas refused to house black women in its dormitories, the Women's Society of Christian Service, an organization affiliated with the Methodist Church, provided a building for them.[64]

In true Southern tradition, campus support for civil rights issues was even justified by appeals to local chauvinism. South Carolinians, for instance, were determined that the integration of their universities would occur more "graciously" than it had in neighboring states. The January 1963 admission of Harvey Gantt to Clemson was described as "integration with dignity," and students at the University of South Carolina behaved equally well toward Henri Monteith. South Carolinians, one freshman woman told a news reporter, were a " 'better breed' than to allow anything untoward to develop concerning Miss Monteith's admission." And, referring to events upstate, she concluded, "If Clemson can, Carolina can."[65] More often than not, however, the region's traditionalism worked against social change on the Southern college campus.

African American women at public colleges sometimes faced the same conservative attitudes toward race, gender, and class as their counterparts at white institutions. Students and faculty at South Carolina State College, for example, had few rights or privileges. State students participated in sit-ins at lunch counters and other civil rights demonstrations during the early sixties (as the story of Joan Mack attests), but the administration was not perceived as encouraging or supporting student activism.[66] In all fairness to the college authorities, their position was awkward at best. As one alumna of the class of 1965 put it, they were "caught between a rock and a hard place . . . because of the civil rights activities." The faculty, staff, and student body were all black (until 1965), but the board of trustees, which approved college policies, was all white (until 1967) as was the state's general assembly (until 1970), which voted college appropriations.[67]

Lewis McMillan, a professor of history at South Carolina State, believed that the general assembly intentionally maintained inferior facilities, personnel, and programs at its black public college. In a scathing critique, *Negro Higher Education in the State of South Carolina*, McMillan concluded that outdated philosophies of education prevented blacks from competing on equal terms with whites and kept colleges from raising the "level of the Negro masses . . . by means of a thoroughgoing 'liberal and practical training.'" Most black colleges, McMillan complained, did nothing to inspire "men and women to live dangerously in the awful work of freeing an enslaved people."[68]

By the late sixties, students at South Carolina State were frustrated by the lack of progress they had made in achieving equal rights and were eager to take action against college and community injustices. Although women students did not organize the protests, the treatment of women faculty and students by the administration and state police helped precipitate demonstrations by students in 1967 and 1968.

The event that touched off the student protests of 1967 was the college's refusal to renew the contracts of three Woodrow Wilson teaching fellows. One of the three was a woman who had been "reprimanded" by the president for having a "male visitor at her quarters one evening." Another fellow, a white man, had frightened authorities with his encouragement of civil rights activities. The crime of all three seemed to have been their interest in student welfare and campus reform. When an ad hoc student action committee demanded their reinstatement in a demonstration in front of the president's home, the three students who had organized the protest were expelled.[69]

Eighty percent of the student body agreed to boycott classes until the suspended students were reinstated. Other college students throughout the state joined the protest. The South Carolina Student Council on Human Relations called for an intercollegiate march from all-black Allen University to the state capitol. The student council president wrote in her flyer to college students throughout the state, "This is the time for students to support other students who are trying to get rid of the chains of suppression."[70]

The governor agreed to meet with a delegation of the marchers and with the assistance of educational leaders from around the state, and the state NAACP legal counsel negotiated a settlement favorable to the students. In the following autumn, students established a campus chapter of the NAACP and, encouraged by SNCC organizer Cleveland Sellers, also set up a more militant, black-power group, the Black Awareness Coordinating Committee. As one woman student and committee member explained, "[U]nless black people have race pride and black unity we will not emerge successfully in this white power structure."[71]

Emboldened by the changes implemented by acting president Manceo Nance, SCSC students decided to expand their efforts for civil rights beyond the campus and into the town of Orangeburg itself. They focused on a nearby bowling alley that had remained segregated. Although the campaign to integrate the facility was led by a male student, a number of women from the campus participated in the demonstrations. In fact, it was the police clubbing of several women students outside the bowling alley on the night of 6 February 1968 that seems to have inflamed student tempers to the exploding point. Two days later the bowling alley was closed, and the SCSC campus and that of adjacent Claflin College were barricaded by the police and the National Guard. "Many students," journalist Jack Bass noted in his analysis of the confrontation, "still were talking angrily about the girls being beaten." The worst was yet to come; police fired into the crowd, injuring thirty students, three fatally. No women were among the students shot, but women students helped drive the more seriously injured to the hospital, and one married student suffered a miscarriage as a result of the incident.[72]

Women students were among the hundreds of demonstrators who marched on Columbia later that year to protest the massacre and the continued second-class status of historically black colleges. Although no one was ever punished for the shooting, the general assembly did approve a $6.5 million bond issue to revitalize the college.[73]

Students at Howard University in Washington, D.C., were also disillusioned with the conservatism of campus life in the sixties. One woman complained about the "provincial mind set" of the administrators and classmates whom she encountered in the fall of 1962. The dean of women "lectured on etiquette and stressed the importance of being 'ladies,' " and most of the women students "were looking for husbands." Another woman who enrolled at the university in 1964 was disappointed that the campus lacked a "black environment." The campus culture was white, the campus politics were white, and even the campus "beauties" were white. In disgust, a woman with a "natural hairstyle" ran for homecoming queen in 1966 to "make a political statement." Her campaign focused on "black politics" and "the movement." To her surprise, she won, and the black power movement took off at Howard.[74]

In March 1967 some forty students interrupted Howard's Charter Day convocation to protest the lack of black studies at the university. Later that month, students demonstrated their opposition to the draft by shouting down the director of the Selective Service, Lewis B. Hershey, when he came to the campus to speak. When the administration appeared to be dragging its feet over promised reforms, students decided to take matters into their own hands. In March 1968 they again disrupted Charter Day ceremonies, this time to demand the establishment of an Afro-American Center at Howard and to call for the resignation of the university president. More than a thousand students participated in the takeover of the administration building that followed the Charter Day protests. Their success had a tremendous impact on black students throughout the South: "I got . . . a new sense of my black self, in terms of culture, in terms of politics, in terms of the rights to demand certain things, the right to feel good about yourself," Paula Giddings wrote.[75]

The civil rights movement encouraged students from various backgrounds to question the hierarchical, paternal nature of Southern society. It revealed the ways in which traditional stereotypes of race, gender, and class were used to foster social, economic, and political dependence. For some women, involvement in civil rights activities led to a growing feminism. For others, the movement's emphasis on religious brotherhood aroused antiwar sentiments. For still others, issues of individual rights led to criticism of *in loco parentis*.

Journalist Anne Braden credited the civil rights struggle for much of the student activism of the sixties and seventies. By challenging the racial premises of Southern society, African Americans had raised questions about other cultural assumptions as well. Sara Evans argued that in the 1960s, as in the 1830s, women's efforts for racial equality made them poignantly aware of lingering sexual injustices, and that their involvement in civil rights activities often led them into feminist issues on campus and in the community at large. Referring to the abolitionist efforts of South Carolina's Grimké sisters in the early nineteenth century, she concluded that it was not incoincidental that "the first voices to link racial and sexual oppression were those of Southern white women." Similarly, Braden believed that the region's racist past made Southerners particularly sensitive to questions of economic and political justice: "Most white Southerners who come to understand the great social issues of our world do so through that long, painful passageway of the struggle with racism. In a society that built its economy, its culture, its very existence on racism, it can be no other way."[76]

237

Women students became more prominent in all sorts of campus protest in the late sixties. At the University of South Carolina (USC), a woman was chair of the Student Mobilization Committee, organized to protest the war in Vietnam. Another woman established an abortion hotline on the campus and served as the first woman president of the student union. Fifteen women were implicated in the occupation of the student center and the takeover of the administration building that followed the May 1970 invasion of Cambodia by American troops.[77]

Southern college women shared in the idealism and pacifism associated in the national mind with campuses such as Berkeley and Columbia. As an editorial in the University of South Carolina yearbook explained: "The distinguishing factor of the sixties is also the same factor which makes this 'generation gap' different from any other—it all comes under the heading of a revolt against the establishment. Young people question materialistic motives and especially the so-called values of a Madison Avenue executive, they want something more—they've had money, they want a new and beautiful world of love and peace and fulfillment." Significantly, the editors found a new "mood" on campus: USC was losing its label as a "party school" and gaining respect for its academic offerings and scholarly accomplishments. One woman activist, a member of the Student Mobilization Committee, believed that the university was becoming "an increasingly freer place for the exchange of ideas among students."[78]

If one were to judge the degree of involvement in campus protest by references to individuals in the college and local newspapers, USC women seemed more inclined than USC men to speak out against the war in Indochina. Rita Fellers, chairman of the Student Mobilization Committee, was the person whom USC students and administrators most often identified with the campus antiwar effort. Characterized by the board of trustees as a "hard core activist," Fellers participated in the May 1970 protests, chaired the Moratorium Rally held at USC in October 1970, led a February 1971 campus march against the war, and traveled to Washington, D.C., in April 1971 to attend an antiwar demonstration.[79]

Women students were associated with the Grimké Sisters Union of Columbia and Charleston, an underground group that distributed radical leaflets and newspapers at university events. One student told a policeman who questioned her that "anyone who dies for this country [is] stupid." Two other women were picked up by military authorities in April 1970 for distributing antiwar literature at nearby Fort Jackson.[80]

Antiwar demonstrations peaked in the South, as in the nation, during the 1969–1970 academic year. Students observed Moratorium Day in the fall with forums, vigils, and marches, and the combined impact of the shootings at Kent State University and the bombing of Cambodia led to extensive campus protests in May 1970. There were major demonstrations at the state universities of Alabama, Georgia, North Carolina, South Carolina, and Texas during the second week in May. "Almost overnight," University of Georgia historian Dyer noted, "the antiwar movement, which had been tame at best by standards elsewhere, suddenly grew in intensity."[81] At the University of South Carolina, the National Guard was called in when protestors occupied the student center and administration building, demanding changes both in university and national governance.[82] White women students participated in all these protests and were pictured prominently in campus and local newspapers.

Prominence in the press, however, did not always correspond to prominence in the protest movements themselves. College authorities certainly believed that most of the campus radicals were Northern men, not Southern women, and they tended to characterize women protestors as "camp followers." One alumna remarked that many of the women associated with antiwar activities at USC got involved because of their boyfriends.[83]

At first, many college administrators simply refused to believe that Southern women had participated in campus protests, blaming "outsiders" for student "problems." The president of Florida State University claimed that his school "had been identified by national radical leaders as a campus in the South on which to focus their efforts." Authorities at Voorhees College in South Carolina attributed disturbances on their campus to "printed activist materials" from Cornell University and North Carolina A&T.[84]

University of South Carolina officials doubted that Southern women were involved in the takeover of their administration building. They were sure that the troublemakers were "Yankees." Much to their chagrin, an investigation revealed that the overwhelming majority of the protesters were Southerners. Of the fifteen women investigated by the university authorities, eight were from South Carolina, three from Virginia, two from the border states of Maryland and Delaware, one (a military dependent) from Hawaii, and only one from New Jersey. All but two had respectable Scholastic Aptitutde Test scores and grade-point-ratio averages; their parents were doctors, judges, teachers, and even military officers. As the chairman of the board of trustees conceded: "Our misbehaving students are not imported. . . . We rear too many here at home."[85]

The president of the Consolidated University of North Carolina came to similar conclusions about the identity of student protesters on North Carolina campuses in the spring of 1970. "To my knowledge," he wrote, "the vast majority who have participated in these demonstrations on our campuses and others are our own sons, daughters, nieces and nephews." And they were inspired, he concluded, not by outside agitators, but by their families and communities: "During all the years before enrolling in the University, these young people have been developing their sense of values, their standards and judgments by what they learned from us as parents in our homes and by what they were taught in our schools and in our churches."[86]

Although traditional conceptions of race, gender, and class had enabled many Southern women to work for social change, these same beliefs made it difficult for others to break with the past. "The South," Sam Wiggins concluded in a 1966 study of higher education in the region, "is different." Southern students had "a respect for tradition and for estab-

lished authority" that was lacking elsewhere in the nation. "Public demonstrations against an institution," he concluded, "are not yet in the Southern
manner."[87]

As Wiggins implied, many students on Southern college campuses
in the sixties and seventies were conservative. At Furman University, a
Baptist college in South Carolina, a chapter of the Young Americans
for Freedom (YAF) was organized to present "facts in opposition to the
Moratorium." The "Gung-Ho Club," an affiliate of the YAF, was one of the
most popular organizations at Newberry, a Lutheran college also in South
Carolina. Students at nearby Clemson University staged a counterdemon-
stration when the school's moratorium committee organized a protest
against U.S. involvement in Vietnam. The antiwar faction wore black armbands, sang peace songs, and carried banners calling for the end of the
war; the pro-war faction "wore red, white and blue armbands, sang 'Dixie'
and displayed signs saying 'Peace Through Victory.' " A similar conflict
between proadministration and antiadministration students at the University of Alabama in May 1970 led to the arrest of some sixty students.
At Pikesville College in Kentucky, conservative students demonstrated
against "long-haired professors, women teachers in miniskirts, and a liberal president who wanted to give students more freedom and make the
curriculum more relevant."[88]

Student criticisms of government policies bothered a number of
Southern women. One graduate of the class of 1971 of Mississippi State
College for Women recalled that she "was upset by the [national] student
unrest and grateful it didn't reach the W[omen's] campus."[89] Limestone
College in South Carolina dedicated its 1970 yearbook to "the men and
women who have served in the Republic of South Vietnam while freeing
the people from the Communists."[90]

The impact of the social protests of the era varied considerably from
campus to campus and from student to student. Hope Morris Florence,
who received her B.A. degree in mathematics from the College of
Charleston in 1970 and her M.A. in mathematics from the University of
South Carolina (USC) in 1972, recalled the culture shock she experienced
when she arrived at USC for her graduate work.[91] Although the College of
Charleston had integrated during Hope's junior year, campus life remained
virtually unchanged. Women always wore nice dresses and hose to class,

carefully fixed their hair and makeup, and carried a pocketbook. There was no dress code: "We just knew how to dress. . . . I didn't know what pants were." Political views were conservative as well: "I didn't know anyone who avoided the draft." Sororities and fraternities were popular, and Hope pledged Chi Omega. She considered herself independent because she dated "fellows from ATO [Alpha Tau Omega], when most Chi Omegas dated Pi Kapps." Students took their studies seriously: "There was never any talk of cutting class." And there were no protests. The university was an entirely different place. Students wore beat-up jeans and sported long, unkempt hair. Most of Hope's fellow graduate students were "interested in their careers and not going to Vietnam." It was difficult to walk across campus and not encounter someone protesting about something.

How does one account for the difference in two institutions only two hours' drive from one another? USC had an enrollment in the thousands; the College of Charleston, in the hundreds. USC had a cosmopolitan student body consisting of both undergraduates and graduates from all over the country who were enrolled in a variety of liberal arts and professional programs; the college was a commuter campus, enrolling students primarily from the Carolina Low Country and granting degrees in the liberal arts and sciences. The college had gone from a municipal to a private institution in an effort to avoid integration and only recently had become a public college. And Charleston was well known as a place that worshiped the past.

Yet Hope's own story illustrates the extent to which even conservative institutions like the College of Charleston had been transformed by two decades of depression and war. When Pat Carter attended the college in the thirties, she believed that her gender, religion, and family background were "handicaps"; her decision to study medicine was viewed as inappropriate for a woman. When Florence's aunt attended the College of Charleston several years after Carter, she, too, found her ethnicity an issue. Yet neither Hope Florence's gender, her Greek heritage, her Orthodox Catholicism, nor her decision to major in mathematics affected her social or academic life at the college. Despite its traditional aura, the College of Charleston was a very different place by the late sixties.

For some Southern women, even attendance at a conservative college could be liberating. Before going to Columbia College in 1968, Rita

Joanne Williams Livingston had lived all her life in Ridgeland, South Carolina, a small town of approximately 1,200 people near the Georgia border, where "everyone knew everyone else's business."[92] Her parents divorced when she was young, and Rita was raised as "a strict Methodist" by her mother, grandmother, and two maiden aunts. When it came time for college, Rita applied to Agnes Scott and Columbia College: "I was not allowed to go to a coed school." Her family preferred Columbia College because it was Methodist and the alma mater of her paternal grandmother. So, in the fall of 1968, the "country girl" headed off to the big city of Columbia.

Columbia College, like the College of Charleston, appeared relatively untouched by the student protests of the fifties and sixties. The college had integrated, but there were still dress regulations and social restrictions. The typical classroom wardrobe was a blouse with a Peter Pan collar and a circle pin, a Villager skirt, and Weejun shoes. Parental permission was necessary to consume alcohol, and students could drink only in the presence of their parents. The only men allowed in the dormitory were fathers and brothers carrying in heavy items, and their entrance was greeted with shouts of "man on the hall!" Religion was an integral part of campus life. Students were required to take twelve credit hours of religious courses for graduation, to complete a community service project, and to attend weekly chapel services. Image was important. The honor code included the phrase, "I will do nothing to embarrass myself, my family, my college, or my church."

Yet, for Rita, college life was anything but stifling: "I was finally out of the control of some very strong women. . . . It took me seven semesters to pull my first-semester average up. I played." Taking the bus from the campus to the city center was in itself an experience: "It was the first time I saw lights that flashed 'walk' and 'don't walk.' " The city colosseum held 12,000 people—"ten times as many people as in my home town." At Columbia College, Rita was able to take classes in and read books on subjects she had never heard of in Ridgeland and to enroll in four study-abroad courses in Europe. A psychology professor took Rita under her wing: "Be brave enough to think for yourself," she exhorted. "No one ever told me that before," Rita recalled. "At Columbia College there were so many different types of people and so many different opinions that I had never seen in Ridgeland. After I got over the initial culture shock, I began to change."

At the height of the antiwar movement, Rita traveled to England for a summer to study Shakespeare at Stratford-upon-Avon. "I had always been conscious about being Southern; that summer made me more aware of being American." Her boyfriend was a pilot in Vietnam, and she was infuriated by the criticisms made of American policies there. "I came as close as I ever did to getting into trouble over a girl wearing an American flag." Fortunately, her professor was able to convince her that Columbia College ladies did not solve problems by "punching out" their antagonists.

The campus culture at Columbia College in the late sixties and early seventies was not all that different from that fifty years before. Freshmen were initiated into college life by sophomores during "Rat Week"; activities such as songfests, skits, and athletic contests were organized to encourage class spirit and cohesion; and relationships with men were carefully monitored. Yet there was lots of mischief as well: the sophomores put sloe gin in the punch at the freshman mixer ("The Dean of Women had a mellow look"); women got around curfews and "sign-ins" by avoiding the dormitory's front entrance ("It was my class that led the administration to place alarms on the side doors"); student playwrights employed allegories and farce to ridicule individuals and policies seen as anachronistic ("Ours was the only class in the history of Columbia College which had to rewrite our entire 'folly' "); and interclass "touch" football games were decidedly physical ("I had several broken ribs one year").

Because Livingston had grown up in a family of working women, it never occurred to her that she would not get a job after graduation. But there was little talk on campus of careers: "We were the last generation to be thought of as wives." Because teaching was seen as an occupation compatible with marriage and motherhood, Rita and most of her cohorts took the National Teacher Examination and acquired teaching certificates. It was only after she had taught in high school for several years that she decided to go to graduate school. When asked about the women's movement at Columbia College, she replied, "There was none." Nonetheless, the school produced "steel magnolias" who could fend for themselves in a rapidly changing world.

Although Rita and her classmates "pushed the rules to the limit," they were careful not to do anything that would reflect badly on themselves, their families, their school, or their church. Looking back on her college years, she was grateful for the college's protective mantle: "In all honesty, coming out of a small high school—there were 49 in my senior class—if I had gone to Carolina, I would have been eaten alive." As the experiences of Rita Livingston at Columbia College and Hope Florence at the College of Charleston suggest, campus images of conformity and complaisance could be deceiving.

African American women students were seldom involved in antiwar protests or in the woman's movement.[93] In part, their absence was a matter of numbers at the large state universities. Despite integration, there were fewer than a hundred black women on most of the previously white campuses in the South. But there were ideological reasons, too, for their disinterest in what were perceived as white, middle-class issues. For most African Americans, racial discrimination remained the real problem. It was race, not sex, that had kept black women out of the universities of the region, and Richard Nixon's "soft" stance on civil rights was considerably more disturbing than his "hard" line on the war. African American women were far more likely to fight for black power or civil rights in the United States than to march for woman power or for peace in Vietnam. Cleveland Sellers, the SNCC organizer who helped South Carolina State students to establish campus branches of NAACP and SNCC, attracted few supporters when he campaigned against the draft.[94]

At the height of the antiwar movement (1969), seventy African American students at Duke University took over the administration building, demanding the establishment of a black-studies program and the creation of a separate dormitory and adviser for black students. Their protests resulted in the creation of the first black-studies program at a major Southern university. Similarly, students at historically black Voorhees College in South Carolina occupied their administration building in 1969, demanding more black faculty, a black-studies program, and a library section on black history.[95]

Black women found it hard at times to identify with the concerns of white women. White women were demanding self-sufficiency and independence, qualities that "racial and class oppression had thrust upon black women." When two white women, Mary King and Casey Hayden, complained in 1964 that sexism in the Student Nonviolent Coordinating Committee (SNCC) limited women to subsidiary positions as typists and clerks, few black women shared their views. African American women such as Ruby Doris Smith, Diane Nash, Donna Richards Moses, Cynthia Washington, and Muriel Tillinghast all played important roles in the running of the operation. Black women's resentment of black men (and of white women) often focused on the role of their "brothers" in the sexual liberation of their white "sisters." As black power advocates called for autonomous black organizations, white women were barred from positions of importance in SNCC because they were white, not because they were women.[96]

Cynthia Washington, a young African American who was an engineering student at George Washington University when she became involved in SNCC in the early sixties, confessed that she could not understand the complaints of white women in SNCC: "It seemed to many of us . . . that white women were demanding a chance to be independent while we needed help and assistance which was not always forthcoming. We definitely started from opposite ends of the spectrum."[97]

Washington's comments revealed the ways in which racial and socioeconomic differences made it difficult for white and black women to come together on many women's issues. The image of a lady had hindered elite, white women's efforts to be independent, but it also had provided them with economic support and political protection that had been denied to poor and black women. Thus, although many black women wanted to continue to focus on racial discrimination, many white women wanted to move on to issues perceived as more relevant to their problems.

Some white students seemed more interested in campus reforms than in national social or political causes. The 1967 student "riot" at the University of Southern Mississippi began with a panty raid, and student grievances included "bad food, crowded dormitories, mandatory meal tickets, stringent social regulations, and the stifling of free expression." The student "sit-in" at Queens College in North Carolina in the winter of 1960 was organized to show support for a proposal to abolish compulsory chapel. At the University of Georgia, even the Students for a Democratic Society concentrated on campus social issues rather than on national political concerns. The aim of the rather small Athens chapter in 1967 was to "force the administration to immediately abolish or revise all regulations governing student conduct." In the following year, some five hundred Georgia students marched for "coed equality," demanding the end of special curfews and regulations for women.[98]

In South Carolina the Moratorium Day protests attracted a large crowd, but many nonradical students were drawn to the symposium, one woman explained, "merely out of curiosity." USC officials who investigated the student protests of May 1970 concluded that the U.S. involvement in Indochina was only one of twenty issues that "politicized a substantial majority of the student body during the Fall and Winter months of the 1969–1970 school year." Other grievances included curriculum revision, coed visitation, the quality of food and the food service, the question of refrigerators in the dorms, concern over false drug busting, fee increases, and the closing of a popular coffeehouse.[99]

Students wanted to liberalize restrictions on the use of drugs and on visitation in the dormitories. Seventy-nine percent of USC students polled at random in 1970 knew "someone who use[d] marijuana, pep pills, barbiturates, heroin, morphine, or LSD," and 47 percent "favored more lenient laws in regard to the use of marijuana." Students asked about dormitory reforms they would like to see implemented mentioned the end of curfews and of sign-outs for women students and more opportunities to entertain members of the opposite sex. One woman told the interviewer: "I'd like a double bed. We need our own bars. I'd have no house mothers."[100]

Regional political issues elicited much more response than national ones. Eighty-three percent of USC students questioned thought that the band should continue to play Dixie at school functions, and 65 percent thought that the Confederate flag should be flown at campus events as well. Responses to the poll were broken down by home state and race. Not surprisingly, fewer Northern students than Southern ones and no black students thought that the song or the flag was appropriate for college activities. The pollsters noted no significant gender differences in the responses.[101]

The abolition of special social regulations was of particular interest to women at Southern schools in the late sixties and early seventies. The attitude of university administrators toward women students had remained paternalistic. Women were subject to more restrictive curfews, dormitory visiting privileges, and dress codes than were men. Students generally and women students especially were, as Southern Mississippi students complained in 1967, "treated as children." They were "told how to dress, where to live, how to act when they have an on-campus date, forced to room in dormitories they dislike." One Furman University student argued that sexual discrimination served as a deterrent "to the establishment of a university-wide community. Furman men and women," he noted, "are not only separated geographically but also by the archaic, ante-bellum morals which govern so many of the rules they live under."[102]

As the war in Vietnam wound down, students focused increasingly on campus concerns. The most serious student "outburst" at the University of Georgia in the mid-seventies occurred over "university policies in housing." Furman University's historian noted that "student interests had shifted to less ideological issues such as reinstatement of social fraternities, interdormitory visitation, coeducational dormitories, drinking regulations, women's due-in hours at night, and the Jesus movement."[103]

Student pressures resulted in a liberalization of social restrictions at most institutions of higher education in the region. Mississippi State College for Women created "rules change forums" in the spring of 1968, which revised campus social regulations. In the following year it closed its "family-style dining hall" and replaced it with a modern cafeteria. The campus government association at Texas Woman's University removed restrictions on casual dress, overnight absences, and automobile and airplane travel from the student handbook in 1969. A "dormitory walkout" by women at the University of Tennessee in the spring of 1969 led the institution to abolish curfews for women older than twenty-one years and for younger students with parental permission. During the 1969–1970 academic year, Sweet Briar College in Virginia liberalized its dress code, and Columbia College in South Carolina granted students "unlimited date nights" and curfew extensions. Auburn University in Alabama retained its curfews for undergraduate women in the 1970–1971 academic year, but curfew times were extended and seniors were given "self-regulated hours." Dress prescriptions were replaced with a general statement that "[w]omen students [were] expected to dress neatly and appropriately at all times and to use their discretion and good judgment in choice of apparel."[104]

Students at Florida State University protested in May 1971 when the Florida Board of Regents banned all dormitory visits by members of the opposite sex. The regents were responding to parental complaints that campus dormitories were becoming "taxpayers' whorehouses." University presidents throughout the state came to the defense of the students and "urged that a uniform policy allowing boy-girl visiting in dorm rooms be enacted to supersede the ban." The regents subsequently revised the visitation policy in August 1971.[105]

A number of denominational colleges also made changes in their social regulations in the late sixties and early seventies. Furman, a Baptist institution, liberalized its dress code and curfew hours for women in the fall of 1969 and allowed students to play cards and listen to the "jukebox" on campus. Trustees removed the prohibitions against dancing on weekends and golfing on Sunday. Erskine, a Presbyterian college in South Carolina, reduced the number of required chapel assemblies to two per week in 1970 and relaxed its "restrictions on dress and use of alcoholic beverages off campus." But not every religious school was willing to abolish its social restrictions. Baylor, a Baptist university in Texas, did not lift its ban on campus dancing until 1996, and even then, the president "warned students against being 'obscene or provocative.' No pelvic gyrations; no excessive closeness; no 'Dirty Dancing.' "[106] Fundamentalist sectarian schools such as Bob Jones in South Carolina and Liberty in Virginia similarly retained their rigid prescriptions on behavior for both men and women into the nineties.[107]

Bob Jones University's restrictions on interracial dating led to a debate over its tax-exempt status in the seventies. In 1970 the all-white school lost its tax-exempt status "as a result of a Mississippi lawsuit that challenged the constitutionality of giving tax exemptions to schools that discriminated against blacks." In 1971 married nonwhite students and in 1976 unmarried nonwhite students were admitted to the university, but the Internal Revenue Service (IRS) refused to reinstate the tax exemption because of the school's rules against interracial dating and marriage. Bob Jones took the case to court on the grounds of religious freedom: "Every class began with a prayer. Every teacher was required to be a born-again Christian who could testify to at least one saving experience with Jesus Christ. Students were not allowed to dance, smoke tobacco, or play cards, and were expected to eschew questionable music and movies." And because "God intended the races to remain separate," they were not allowed to date or marry individuals of another race. Although a number of religious groups filed legal briefs in support of the school and conservatives protested the constitutionality of allowing the IRS to define public policy, the United States Supreme Court ruled 8 to 1 against Bob Jones.[108]

The Bob Jones case was atypical, however. Most predominantly white colleges and universities tried to address the racial concerns of African American students on their campuses. Schools stopped playing "Dixie" and flying the Confederate flag at football games. A black student union was organized at the University of Florida in 1968; at Furman University in March 1972. An "Afro-American Room" was set up in the Texas Union in 1970. African American students at Mississippi State College for Women formed a black social club, Las Amigas, in 1976. The universities of both Florida and Alabama dedicated African American cultural centers in 1972.[109] Women were active in all these organizations.

African American women became more prominent in the social and political life of the white campus in the years after 1970. University of Alabama students elected a black homecoming queen in 1973, who was congratulated by none other than George Wallace. Florida State University chose a black homecoming queen in 1976. An African American woman was elected president of the student government at Queens College in North Carolina in 1972. The University of Florida selected two black women for its "hall of fame" in 1983 and elected a black woman student body president in 1986.[110]

The campus protests of the period also affected administrative policies at Southern colleges and universities. Calls for participatory democracy and academic relevancy reverberated through the Southern halls of ivy. Student representatives were added to faculty committees and boards of trustees, giving young women and men a greater voice than ever before in the formulation of college polity. New courses were introduced that focused on current problems and issues, and the use of teacher evaluation forms allowed students to critique existing academic offerings. Alumnae, too, benefited from the desire to make administrative decisions more democratic. Throughout the South, women and blacks were added to previously all-male and all-white boards of trustees. At Hollins, a woman's college in Virginia, faculty and students voted in 1972 to replace their separate governing bodies with a common college legislature containing representatives from the faculty, alumnae, and student body.[111]

At many Southern institutions, extracurricular activities and curricular offerings began to reflect the concerns raised by the women's movement. Texas Woman's University instituted the Woman's Day Colloquium in 1968 and adopted the theme of "The Liberated Woman" for its campus activities program in the 1971–1972 academic year. The student council decided not to choose "class beauties" for the yearbook, and the campus speakers series included prominent feminists such as Gloria Steinem. In 1974 the university introduced its first women's studies course, "Women in American and World Society."[112]

During the May 1970 demonstrations at the University of Florida, women students and faculty organized a women's ad hoc committee to demand the elimination of practices and policies that discriminated against women. "The Strike Committee and Student Government are calling for the administration to hire more black professors and implement a black studies program under the direction of the Black Student Union," one woman told reporters, but "no one has even considered the crucial demands by women." The following year the president of the University of Florida established the Committee to Study Opportunities for Women and to look into some of the complaints made by the ad hoc committee. As a result of this study, university authorities revoked their antinepotism regulations, reconsidered their promotion and salary policies, and reexamined their admission and financial aid procedures. The enrollment of women subsequently rose from 36 percent of the student body in 1972 to 45 percent in 1986; the percentage of women faculty from 11.9 percent in 1972 to 16.5 percent in 1986. Women's studies courses were introduced in a number of departments and colleges, and in 1979 a women's studies program was established.[113]

Title IX of the Educational Amendments Act of 1972 affected both academic and social activities at Southern schools. The measure barred federal aid from institutions that discriminate against women in such things as admissions, athletic offerings, facilities, financial aid, and employment opportunities. To achieve educational equity and not lose federal funds, coeducational colleges and universities had to expand their intercollegiate athletic programs for women and to allow women to enroll in campus units of the Reserve Officers' Training Corps.[114]

Campus stereotypes of the Southern lady remained remarkably resilient, however. Despite concerns of sexism raised by feminists, traditional images of womanhood continued to adorn school annuals in the seventies. Almost every campus organization had its beauty queen or coed "sponsor." The 1970 yearbook of predominantly white Lander College in South Carolina featured a Miss Lander 1970, a homecoming queen, a best-dressed woman, a Miss Merry Christmas, a May Queen, a Junior and Senior "Cutie," and a Miss Freshman, Sophomore, and so forth. The 1970 yearbook for predominantly black Voorhees College, also in South Carolina, had a similar array of campus beauties, including a Miss Sunday School. Homecoming queens remained popular at coeducational schools throughout the region.[115] Sensitivity to gender issues was not reflected in many college publications until the mid-seventies.

Still other college women used gender stereotypes to effect social change. Activists in the sixties and seventies, like generations of Southern women before them, often employed the protective coloration of "ladyhood." When Gladys Avery Tillett, a graduate of the Woman's College of North Carolina, died at age ninety-two in 1984, commentators attributed her long and successful campaign for racial and sexual equality to her demeanor. Discussing her suffragist activities as a student, one friend remarked that Tillett "knew how to deal with male politicians so they didn't get too mad at her. Always very delicate." Tillett championed controversial causes—religious toleration, labor organization, civil rights, the Equal Rights Amendment—and remained "a lovely lady through it all." An editorial in the *Charlotte Observer* noted that she had "emerged untouched by the bitterness associated with all these public movements. She has been like a woman walking through the eye of a hurricane."[116]

Southern women who wanted social change found that appeals to regional stereotypes or prejudices continued to be useful. Victoria Eslinger, the woman student who set up the abortion hotline on the University of South Carolina campus in 1971, convinced the president of the school that reports of fetuses found in dormitory trash cans tarnished the school's image in the state. The administration agreed to provide a room for the telephone service, provided that the student volunteers were "discreet."

Within a week, the hotline was operating twenty-four hours a day. Students were referred to a doctor at a nearby health clinic for free birth control counseling, and those desiring an abortion were sent to hospitals in New York, where abortions had been legalized in 1970. The student government was persuaded to pay for a birth control handbook that was subsequently distributed free of cost at the student center.[117]

By appealing to the traditional Southern antipathy to government intrusion into the private lives of individuals, one woman was able to effect considerable social change at the University of South Carolina. It probably helped that she was, as the president advised, "discreet." When asked to discuss women's issues on campus, she always looked and sounded the proper Southern lady. She preferred to work through rather than against the system. She planned, she organized, and she coordinated; she did not strike or march or picket.[118]

Employing the protective coloration of "ladyhood" made it difficult, of course, to erase the image itself, and women's use of conservative behavior in support of liberal causes sent a mixed message to the next generation of college women. But Southern women were not the only women in the postwar period whose words and actions often appeared contradictory. Paula Fass, in her examination of the "female paradox" in American education, noted that many college women claimed a "devotion to home and family" while joining the workforce in increasing numbers. Fass warned her fellow educators that, when devising curricular reforms and planning professional programs, they needed to remember that the "direction of women's voices is not always the same as that of their feet."[119]

Such discrepancies also make it difficult to reconstruct the educational experiences of college women in the postwar period. Most white women who attended college in the sixties and seventies remember their college days as times of social pleasantries, not social protest. Although almost every Southern campus had its contingent of "radical" students with visions of a truly New South, an even greater number of students seemed comfortably ensconced in the culture of the Old. In the fall of 1968, the Student Action Party was organized at the University of Southern Mississippi, but most students preferred talking about "the football game against Alabama" or "the new campus coffee house" than about the war in Vietnam. The president of the student body at Florida State University in the 1966–1967 academic year described his campus as "clean-cut" and "traditional." He recalled that "fraternities serenaded the women's dorms; football was exciting; student government campaigns were fun; dress was sharp."[120]

Seventy-three percent of alumnae from the classes of 1955, 1960, 1965, and 1970 at the University of South Carolina who were surveyed in 1989 listed football games, fraternity and sorority parties, and school dances as the most popular student activities. Only one of the respondents belonged to a campus political organization (Student Government). Except for alumnae of the class of 1970, no respondents recalled any campus protests whatsoever, and even two of the graduates of 1970 who had been on campus during the student strike of May 1970 did not remember any student disturbances.[121]

Although more than 60 percent of respondents characterized their classmates as very or fairly well aware of current political and social issues, their responses to other questions suggest that their perceptions were rather myopic. One graduate of the class of 1965, for instance, did not know that the university was integrated. Another admitted honestly that she "avoided political activities and knowledge of current events like the plague." She had "dated a Lebanese student . . . and had *no* idea why he harped on politics all the time. I *never* read the paper or watched T.V. news (too depressing)," she wrote. There were probably a good number of students like her who considered college as " 'time out' from the world around me."[122]

Even at traditionally black institutions where students had been active in civil rights protests throughout the fifties and sixties, students seemed less interested in social and political issues after 1970. Some were simply disillusioned with the consequences of their activism. When the President's Commission on Campus Unrest interviewed students at Jackson State College in Mississippi in 1970, they found that many had come to believe that protest was futile. Mississippi seemed impervious to change. Most young African Americans, the commissioners concluded, were "too busy fighting for their physical, economic, social, and psychological lives to engage in protest." There were others who believed that all the important battles had been fought. The editor of the South Carolina State College yearbook worried that the new generation of students would "expect freedom without responsibility, success without preparation, rewards without work, consideration without being considerate. . . . [Would] they attempt to escape their problems through sexual freedom and psychedelic drugs or pot?"[123]

Antebellum attitudes and behaviors did not disappear altogether from the Southern scene. Fraternities and sororities—and the social and racial exclusiveness associated with them—revived remarkably in the eighties. Even at institutions where women were in the majority, men were more likely to hold campus leadership positions, to dominate classroom discussions, and to major in mathematics and science. Black students experienced similar problems when they integrated previously white institutions. They discovered that they were expected to adopt white, middle-class patterns of culture and were labeled racists if they advocated black nationalism and separatism. Predominantly black colleges still faced many more difficulties than their predominantly white counterparts. Joel Rosenthal, writing on "Southern Black Student Activism" in the *Journal of Negro Education* in 1975, found "the same structural problems of inadequate funds and facilities, white control of Black education, [and] stifling of student and faculty nonconformity," which had led to student protests in the fifties and sixties.[124]

The resurgence of conservatism that occurred on Southern college campuses in the late seventies and early eighties did not mean a return to "yesterday's" views of race, class, and gender, as Susan Farrell's experience at Austin College in Texas in the eighties demonstrates. Austin was a Presbyterian college of approximately 1,200 students, most of whom were "white suburban kids from Houston and Dallas." Although Susan was required to live on campus, she resided in a coeducational dormitory with women on one wing and men on the other. There were visitation policies, but "no one enforced them." For those who wanted more restricted interactions between the sexes, there was an all-women's dormitory, where male visitors had to sign in and out.[125]

The curriculum at Austin College was traditional. A three-semester course entitled "Heritage of Western Culture" (previously "History of Western Man") was required of all students, and the faculty was primarily male. When Susan decided to write her bachelor's essay on Toni Morrison, "none of my professors knew anything about her. . . . I worked with an adjunct who had been to Mount Holyoke." There was a course on women writers, but she elected not to take it "because it was taught by my boyfriend's father." The students took matters into their own hands: "We started consciousness-raising groups." Participants met regularly and discussed a variety of gender issues and personal concerns. "A lot of women identified themselves as feminists."

Extracurricular activities were far less traditional. There were no national sororities and fraternities, and those women who did join the local sororities "weren't quite as smart . . . [and were] more interested in clothes than intellectual life." None of Susan's friends were "sorority girls." Instead, she was involved in the English club, the student activities board, and community service projects. Because the students and staff were "perceived as a privileged group in a poor part of town," Austin College officials "made a big deal about giving back to the community." Although only a few students attended church regularly (and Susan was not one of them), she credited the school's social activism to its Presbyterian heritage. Off campus, Susan was active in local Democratic politics, and a number of her friends were leaders in the state Campaign for Nuclear Disarmament. "We didn't fit the stereotypes of students in the eighties being complacent and politically unaware."

The majority of women at Austin College assumed they would have careers after graduation. Although Susan went on to earn a Ph.D. degree in English from the University of Texas after graduation from Austin in 1985, "I never imagined myself going on to grad school and teaching. . . . I imagined myself as Mary Tyler Moore." Susan's grandmother had been a nurse, and before Susan went off to college, she had told Susan that there were three career options for women: "secretary, nurse, or teacher." Yet Susan's own mother had demonstrated that this was no longer true in the eighties. Mrs. Farrell had dropped out of college to get married, but when Susan was in high school, she enrolled in the University of Texas "Women in Science" program and completed a degree in computer science. Susan's peers, too, felt far less pressure than the preceding generation to marry and have children. And her reference to Mary Tyler Moore suggests that the national media were affecting how Southern college women perceived themselves and their futures.

The civil rights protests of the fifties and early sixties, the antiwar activities of the sixties and early seventies, and the feminist movements of the seventies and early eighties had changed women's educational experience considerably. One 1956 alumna of Texas State College for Women who returned to the university in 1973 was amazed at the differences between students of her day and those of the seventies. After reading the student newspaper, she commented, "I frequently heard the voices of young women, not little girls; of adults, not children." She characterized the change as "one of the [most] heartening developments in education in the past few years" and was pleased to find that "college students are now expected to be adults, fully in control of their own morality and their own style of life."[126] Southern college women had been active in campus and community protests, and even though many had employed the shield of "ladyhood," their very involvement in such "unfeminine" activities had raised important questions about the nature of Southern womanhood. The voices of students by the seventies were indeed those of young women, not children, but their Southern accents were still recognizable.

Accentuating the continuity of Southern life and culture may cause us to discount the significant changes that occurred at Southern colleges in the postwar period. The South was still not Paradise, but by the seventies, many of its cultural demons had been exorcized. If we focus on the women who attended institutions of higher education during these turbulent times, we are struck by the ways in which campus social protest transformed their lives. The civil rights struggles and student protests lessened but did not eliminate regional differences on the basis of race, gender, and class. Indeed, it was an appreciation of this "twoness" and an awareness of the "past in the present" that enabled Southern women to "take control of [their] destiny" in the years after World War II.

7

A Double Focus

A Century of Women's Higher Education
in the South

*T*he history of the higher education of women is part of the larger drama of the history of the twentieth-century South. Both stories contain themes of continuity and change; both reflect the "double consciousness" of the region's peoples and institutions. Just as the debate over change and continuity in the region's history reveals the complex nature of the South's economic, political, and social structure, so too does an analysis of women's collegiate experiences reveal the contested nature of educational developments. Even as we approach the twenty-first century, questions of who should be educated, at what type of school, with what sort of curriculum, and for what purpose remain.

One of the best illustrations of this complex narrative—and its subplots of gender, race, class, place, and time—is the story of Oseola McCarty and the University of Southern Mississippi (USM). On 26 July 1995 McCarty, an eighty-seven-year-old woman from Wayne County, Mississippi, donated $150,000 to USM to be used for scholarships for disadvantaged minority students. Hers was the largest donation ever given to the school by an African American. McCarty's generosity poignantly demonstrated the value Southern women—black and white, rich and poor—have placed on education as a means of individual and community development. Forced to drop out of school in sixth grade to care for an ailing relative, McCarty supported herself for seventy-five years by washing and ironing for Hattiesburg's white elite. By living simply in a modest house left to her by her uncle, she was able to save most of her earnings. "I didn't know how to do it," she explained to an interviewer, "but I wanted to fix up a scholarship at USM so young people could get their education. You can't do [anything] nowadays without an education."[1] Too old to return to school herself, McCarty was nonetheless determined "to help somebody's child go to college." When a reporter asked why she didn't use the money for herself, she replied, "I am spending it on myself."[2] Investing in the next generation was for McCarty, as it was for individuals and communities throughout the twentieth-century South, the best gift one could give oneself.

McCarty was surprised at the media frenzy that followed the announcement of her gift. She was invited to dinner at the White House and awarded the Presidential Citizens Medal, given an honorary doctoral degree by Harvard University, asked to carry the Olympic torch, featured on the front page of the *New York Times*, and honored with medals and awards by the National Urban League, UNESCO (United Nations Educational, Scientific, and Cultural Organization), American Association of Retired Persons, the Aetna Foundation, and the National Federation of Black Women Business Owners, among others.[3] Her story touched so many hearts that money poured in to the scholarship fund from all over the world, enabling the university to begin awarding the scholarship immediately. The interest in the elderly philanthropist was so great that USM set up an Oseola McCarty homepage and established a section for her memorabilia in the school's library. Her portrait was placed in the administration building, the first ever of an African American to be displayed. Impressed by her words as well as her deeds, editors at Longstreet Press in Atlanta published a volume of her sayings entitled *Simple Wisdom for Rich Living*.[4]

When some critics asked why McCarty had left her money to an institution that had not admitted blacks until the 1960s, she replied, "Because it is here." Hattiesburg was her home, and the home of many other African Americans as well. Her gift would enable young blacks who could not afford to leave the area to receive a college education in their own town. She was very much aware of the segregated history of the state and its institutions, but she preferred to work toward an integrated future.[5] As McCarty noted in her book: "Building community is not that hard. It just takes ordinary friendliness."[6] The first recipient of the scholarship, Stephanie Bullock, was an honor graduate of Hattiesburg High School who would have been unable to attend college without the $1,000 award. But friendliness begets friendliness, and Bullock was able to offer McCarty something in return—her family. Bullock's relatives soon were inviting McCarty, whose own kin were all deceased, to family celebrations and treating her as one of their own. Most important, Bullock planned to use her education to better the community from whence she came.[7] Oseola McCarty's gift and the response it evoked represented the very best of the Southern past—its attachment to place and family, its belief in what Stephanie Shaw has called "socially responsible individualism"—and the hope of the Southern future.

McCarty's story is also indicative of the extent to which the South has changed in the twentieth century. The Southern college woman of the nineties has more in common with her contemporaries elsewhere in the nation than with any other generation of Southern women. The economic, political, and cultural gap between the North and the South has narrowed considerably. Civil rights protests and equal rights legislation have ended legal segregation by race and sex; educational opportunity grants and guaranteed student loan programs have made it possible for greater numbers of Southern women to attend college. Industrial development and urban migration have transformed the Cotton Belt into the Sun Belt. Most Southerners, as most Americans, now live in the suburbs. The rural and small-town culture of the past has "yielded to a different scene, one increasingly shaped by business, technology, and a keen focus on tomorrow."[8]

In the sixties, the rate of population growth in the South surpassed that in the country as a whole, and this trend is predicted to continue into the first decades of the twenty-first century. Nearly one-fourth of Americans now live in the Southeast. If Kentucky, Maryland, Oklahoma, and West Virginia are added to the states of the Old Confederacy, the Southern population encompasses more than 34 percent of the national total. Texas, Florida, and North Carolina are among the ten most populous states in the nation.[9]

As a result of these population changes, the South has become more like the rest of the nation demographically. Most Southerners today are city folk. Only the states of Arkansas, Kentucky, Mississippi, and West Virginia are more rural than urban. The racial and ethnic composition of the population is closer to that of the United States as a whole than ever before in its history. Whites make up 83.3 percent of the population of the

United States and 79.2 percent of the South; blacks 12.5 and 18.5 percent, respectively; Hispanics, 9.7 and 8.7 respectively; and other (Native Americans, Asians, and other races) 4.3 and 2.3 percent, respectively.[10]

Economically, the region has made great gains since 1970. The per capita income in 1993 was 92 percent of the U.S. figure. Maryland, Virginia, and Florida all had per capita incomes above the national average. Fourteen million new jobs have been created in the Southeast since 1970, and these jobs are outside the low-skill, low-pay, and extractive industries historically associated with the region: "Fewer Southerners mine coal; more assemble automobiles. Almost nobody picks cotton; thousands work in laboratories." Most of these new jobs required some sort of postsecondary education. As the authors of a 1996 report, *The State of the South*, concluded, when it comes to economic well-being, "[e]ducation doesn't matter just a little. It matters most of all."[11]

The earnings gap between educated blacks and educated whites has almost disappeared. In 1989 college-educated blacks had a median income 90 percent that of college-educated whites; in 1993, 92 percent. Higher education especially pays dividends to black women. The median salary of a black woman with a bachelor's degree was 11 percent higher than that of a similarly educated white woman; with a master's degree, the black woman earned 6 percent more than her white counterpart. One reason for this differential seems to be that educated black women are more likely to be employed full time than are educated white women.[12]

The proportion of women in the college population has increased dramatically since 1960. In 1959 Southern women were only 38 percent of the student population in the region; in 1992, this figure had risen to almost 56 percent. By the early nineties, more than 55 percent of the region's bachelor's degrees and 54 percent of its master's degrees were earned by women. Women were awarded more than 38 percent of the doctorates and 37 percent of the first professional degrees given by Southern schools in the same period. Black women did proportionately better than white women, earning more than 60 percent of the bachelor's, master's, doctoral, and first professional degrees awarded to black students.[13]

White Southern women in the nineties are more likely than their foremothers to attend a coeducational institution. (Coeducational institutions have always enrolled the vast majority of black women.) The admission of women to Virginia Military Institute (VMI) in the fall of 1997 marked the end of publicly funded single-gender education in the region. Equal opportunity legislation has not only forced public men's colleges to open their doors to women but has also required public women's colleges to admit men. For a variety of economic and philosophical reasons, many private single-gender institutions became coeducational in the seventies and eighties as well. There were almost 300 women's colleges in the nation in 1960; fewer than a third of them remain single-gender institutions today.[14]

Coordinate colleges, established in many areas of the South to avoid coeducation, have merged with their male counterparts, and their campuses have been transformed into residential areas. For example, Richmond College, which was founded as a liberal arts college for men by Virginia Baptists in 1830, and Westhampton College, which was founded as a liberal arts college for women by the Baptists in 1914, were combined in 1990 into the School of Arts and Sciences of the University of Richmond. Westhampton describes itself as a "community within a community," providing "the advantages of a major coeducational university" with "the benefits of the small, single-gender, residential college experience." Both Westhampton and Richmond have kept their "own residence hall system, student government, traditions, honor system, judicial system, academic advisers, and student-faculty committees."[15] All classes are coeducational, however, as are most extracurricular activities.

Even in a state such as Virginia, which has four thriving women's colleges—Hollins, Mary Baldwin, Randolph-Macon Woman's, and Sweet Briar—more than 96 percent of women are enrolled in coeducational institutions. Private women's colleges, like private coeducational institutions, find it hard to compete with the larger programs and lower tuition of the public colleges and universities. In Virginia, for example, there are 15 public and 32 private four-year institutions of higher education, but the public schools enroll 76 percent of all students and almost 84 percent of all women.[16] Similar patterns exist throughout the South.

Women's colleges in the region, as those elsewhere in the nation, have found that they must accommodate new definitions of womanhood or lose their clientele. Most have carved a niche for themselves by emphasizing the advantages of their small size—a low faculty-student ratio and a commitment to teaching by the faculty. They also remind students that, at women's colleges, women come first.

Randolph-Macon Woman's College (RMWC) sends a brochure to high school counselors containing a list of "reasons for considering a women's college." There is no reference to preserving women's "gentleness and grace," as in college bulletins before World War II; instead, prospective students are promised "first-class citizenship," "career direction" and "job placement," and "influential role models." They are also urged to consider their future economic well-being: "Studies show that graduates of women's colleges earn proportionately more graduate degrees and considerably higher salaries than their counterparts from coeducational colleges."[17]

On its web page, RMWC promotes its "Education in the Singular." The term "singular" applies not only to the single-gender nature of the institution but also to its individualized education, which includes small classes, opportunities to work one-on-one with faculty, and the ability to schedule one's own examinations. The school's small size and its personal attention to each student's education make it difficult for anyone to fade into the background: "[M]ore than 80 percent of our students hold leadership positions by the time they graduate, while more than 50 percent participate in volunteer activities. Nearly 30 percent of the junior class studies abroad, while 55 percent of all students take part in career-enhancing internships."[18]

Women's colleges in the first half of the twentieth century often denigrated utilitarian curricula and programs, but women's colleges in the nineties use their vocational and preprofessional programs as drawing cards, and their promotional materials extol the career attainments of alumnae of single-gender institutions. Judson College, the only woman's college extant in Alabama, subtitles its academic catalog, "For Women Who Seek Success," and it proudly claims as alumnae the "first woman elected to the Supreme Court of Alabama," the second woman "to be elected state superintendent of education," and the first woman missionary to Japan. Judson's web page includes a feature on "Greater Success at a Women's College," with statistics from the Women's College Coalition enumerating the achievements of women's college graduates nationwide. "While fewer than 4% of all college educated women graduate from women's colleges," the site proclaims, 33 percent of women board members of Fortune 1000 companies and 24 percent of women members of Congress are alumnae of women's colleges. Graduates of women's colleges are more than twice as likely as graduates of coeducational schools to receive doctoral degrees and to enter medical school. While noting that 81 percent of women's college graduates have some form of postcollegiate education, analysts for the Women's College Coalition emphasize that such success has not come at the cost of their family life: "More than three quarters of the alumnae surveyed are or have been married, and half have children."[19]

Hollins College tells applicants that "[w]omen who are going places start at Hollins" and provides a list of names and careers of successful graduates. Students can participate in a "Leaders on the Grow" program, which teaches them leadership skills and enables them to explore career options through internships. All students receive career counseling beginning in their freshman year. A web site entitled "Careers and Life After Hollins" proclaims that "Hollins prepares students for successful lives of fulfilling work through hands-on training, study abroad, community service, and internships aided by an active Career Assistance Network of alumnae." Another Hollins web page focuses on "Real World Experiences," noting that "each year, one third of our students do internships at businesses and organizations in Roanoke and beyond."[20]

A women's studies program is an integral component of the curriculum at most women's colleges. Mary Baldwin includes a women's studies requirement as part of its core curriculum for all degree-seeking students and requires them to "engage in at least one learning activity . . . , such as an externship, which involves primarily the practical application of theoretical concepts and principles."[21] Such classes allow students to examine their culture and history from a woman-centered perspective.

Besides offering courses and programs that focus on women and gender, many institutions have also established various forms of women's leadership training. The Virginia Women's Institute for Leadership (VWIL) at Mary Baldwin College was originally created in 1995 as a parallel experience to cadet life at VMI and combined a liberal arts program with military and leadership training. In addition to the regular Mary Baldwin degree requirements, VWIL students have to take special courses in leadership, mathematics, computer science, foreign language, laboratory science, and physical education and health. They also travel to Lexington once a week to train in the army, navy, or air force Reserve Officers' Training Corps with VMI cadets.[22]

When VMI became coeducational in 1997, officials at Mary Baldwin worried that VWIL would lose its funding and its appeal. Before the United States Supreme Court ruled against VMI, the Virginia General Assembly had approved tuition subsidies of more than $7,000 per student for in-state students in the VWIL program, an amount that was equivalent to that appropriated to VMI for each cadet and that enabled women to attend a private college at the cost of a public one. Although state funding for the program was guaranteed through the 1997–1998 school year, some legislators questioned "whether Mary Baldwin, a private college, should continue to receive state dollars . . . given that state-supported VMI has opened its doors to women."[23] Without the state subsidy, the tuition, room, and board at Mary Baldwin's VWIL program would be considerably more than that of VMI.

VWIL directors were also concerned that women, once they had the option, would choose VMI over VWIL. Despite such fears, interest in VWIL remained high. Three women who were accepted for the class of 2001 at both VMI and VWIL chose VWIL over VMI, and no VWIL students opted to transfer to VMI. And while VMI welcomed a contingent of approximately 30 women in August 1997, VWIL enrolled 45 new freshmen—its largest group so far. One student who chose VWIL over VMI said that she had received more scholarship aid at VWIL; another said that she did not want to shave her hair off. Other women liked the unique blend of women's culture and military tradition. As one VWIL parent explained: "My daughter was interested in this program. . . . It's a better philosophy. At VMI they tear you down to build you back up. Here, they're into team work, building you up from where you are." VWIL's director, Brenda Bryant, told legislators that "the benefit of the program is that it is not Virginia Military Institute in Lexington. This is a program designed by and for women to develop young female students into strong leaders." In a "gender-bound culture," Mary Baldwin's dean of students concluded, the best education for women is often different from the best education for men.[24]

Most women's leadership programs in the region are not connected with military training, however. Agnes Scott College sponsors the Women, Leadership and Social Change Program, centered on the Atlanta community: "Students in the program are challenged to examine the contributions to social change made by women leaders as they experience first hand the pressures and rewards of leadership in internships with Atlanta-based organizations." The University of Richmond offers a similar program, Women Involved in Living and Learning (WILL), which entails courses in women's studies, participation on a student-directed activities board, and the completion of a community internship. Meredith College in Raleigh targets "career-oriented women over 25" for its Women's Leadership Certificate Program. The object of the program is "to develop competent, high-profile leaders who make a positive difference in the community." Judson College's Alabama Women's Leadership Database is aimed at the wider community as well and is designed "to identify and train qualified women who are interested in serving on public boards" in the state.[25]

At the beginning of the twentieth century, professional opportunities for women were rare outside the fields of teaching, nursing, and social work. By the end of the century, however, even small liberal arts colleges offer a wide variety of preprofessional courses and programs. As Texas Woman's University (TWU) explains to prospective students: "TWU was established in 1901 to educate women for the 'industries of the age.' Today, those industries probe genetic engineering and the behavioral sciences, explore microbiology and promote health and the prevention of disease. They also give us the visual and performing arts, the teaching professions, social and family sciences, mass communications, information systems—and much more."[26]

Women's colleges have joined with other, nearby institutions in consortia that enable them to offer a greater variety of courses and programs than their size or facilities might allow. Sweet Briar College, for instance, has a dual-degree engineering program in conjunction with Columbia University and Washington University of St. Louis. Bennett College offers a three-two nursing program and a five-year dual-degree program in electrical and mechanical engineering with North Carolina Agricultural and Technical (A&T) State University. Hollins has a three-two combined degree program in engineering with Virginia Tech (Virginia Polytechnic Institute and State University) and Washington University, as well as a six-year architecture program with the Virginia school. Texas Woman's University, Texas A&M University, and Texas Instruments "have joined forces to offer a cooperative engineering program that allows students to earn two bachelor's degrees simultaneously while preparing for a professional career in engineering."[27]

The expansion of course offerings and career opportunities for college women in the last quarter of the twentieth century is one of the most significant legacies of the civil rights and women's movements. Rita Williams Livingston, a 1972 alumna of Columbia College in South Carolina and the mother of two college students, is amazed at the difference a generation has made: "When I was a student, you took biology if you were going to teach science; now you take it for the pre-med track."[28]

The women's college that has been most successful in attracting new students and steering them into nontraditional majors is Spelman, a historically black institution in Atlanta. Spelman enrolls almost 2,000 students, and approximately 38 percent of them major in the natural sciences. The school is so popular with African American women that it can accept only 33 percent of its first-year applicants. Whereas the average Scholastic Aptitude Test (SAT) score and the average class rank of matriculants have dropped for most women's colleges nationally, they have risen at Spelman. As a consequence, "Spelman is far more selective than other top-quality women's colleges such as Smith, Mount Holyoke, and Bryn Mawr."[29]

Indeed, colleges throughout the region have become more competitive nationally. Duke University, the University of North Carolina–Chapel Hill, the University of Virginia, and the University of Texas–Austin have programs that are consistently ranked among the top twenty in the country. Nineteen of the top 89 research universities and 101 of the 450 best doctoral programs are in the region.[30]

Southern alumnae are recognized nationally for their achievements. Perhaps the most striking example of this recognition was the selection of Ruth J. Simmons as president of Smith College in 1995. Simmons was the youngest of twelve children of a sharecropper family in Texas. She earned her undergraduate degree at historically black Dillard University in New Orleans before going on for her M.A. and Ph.D. degrees at Harvard. At Simmons's inauguration, President Johnnetta Cole of Spelman quipped, "Look indeed, where the Good Lord she has brought us from, for today, a great granddaughter of slaves leads this prestigious institution, and all of American higher education is the better for it."[31]

Have the demographic, economic, social, and political changes since the sixties ended the South's distinctiveness as a region? Is Southern women's educational experience no longer different from that of American women nationally? Are Southern college women less conscious of their "twoness"? Despite the "Americanization of Dixie," heralded by news commentators and regional analysts, surveys at the University of North Carolina by John Shelton Reed and at institutions of higher education nationally by the American Council on Education reveal regional differences in attitudes and experiences among college students. As Reed explains, Southerners resemble "ethnic groups in that they have a sense of group identity based on their shared history and their cultural distinctiveness in the present."[32]

If College of Charleston students are representative of Southern college students regionally—and I think they are—the South, Southerners, and Southern institutions are still perceived as distinctive in the nineties. An overwhelming 91 percent of students surveyed in 1995 thought that Southerners as a group were different from other Americans. Although most saw these differences as ones in which the South compared favorably, they were not so sure that outsiders hold this view of them or their region. Eighty percent believed that "Southerners are looked down upon by other Americans." In the students' minds, the Southern past clouds current portrayals of the Sun Belt.[33]

In a survey of North Carolina undergraduates, Reed found that the traits students identified as Southern—"slow, not fast; generous, not greedy; religious, not materialistic; conservative, not progressive"—were the converse of Northern traits. Yet, when asked to give a list of American traits, they tended to use the same words they had used to describe Northerners. Even more interesting, students' perceptions of themselves as Southern or American or both varied with the situation: "Compared to other Americans, they were Southerners: traditional, easygoing, polite, and so forth. But compared with foreigners, they were Americans—progressive, efficient, and all the rest."[34] The "twoness" remains.

Changes in the racial balance of the population have not eliminated black Southerners' "double consciousness," or what Darlene Clark Hine has called black women's "multi-consciousness." For one thing, although the proportion of blacks in the Southern population has declined substantially in the twentieth century, more than half of all African Americans still live in the South. The vast majority of predominantly black and historically black colleges and universities (HBCUs) are located in the region, and enrollment in these institutions has soared in the last decade, increasing 32 percent between 1982 and 1993. More than 60 percent of students enrolled in HBCUs are African American women.[35]

Predominantly black colleges are more likely to offer courses pertaining to the African American experience than are historically white institutions. Dillard University, for instance, a Methodist college in New Orleans that is 99 percent black and 79 percent female, offers more than twenty courses on various aspects of African American culture. Because most of their students are from African American or African backgrounds, black colleges tend to be less bound by Western standards of culture and perspectives of history than other Southern institutions of higher education. As Vernon Jordan noted in an 1988 essay in *Daedalus*, "[T]he black college represents to black students what other schools traditionally associated with a particular religious outlook or ethnic group represent to other Americans—the availability of the choice of going to a school that embraces their past, their concerns, and their values."[36]

Bennett College in North Carolina supports the Women's Leadership Institute, incorporating the Center for African Women and Women of the African Diaspora, the Center for Women and Family, the Center for Women and Health, the Center for Women and Spirituality, and the Center for Women and Work. Spelman College in Atlanta houses the Women's Research and Resource Center, "the main emphasis of which is curriculum development in women's studies (focusing on women of color), community outreach, and research." Florida Agricultural and Mechanical University contains the Florida Black Archives, Research Center, and Museum. Tougaloo College in Mississippi boasts "one of the most extensive African-American Art Collections in the nation."[37]

Historically black institutions have provided and continue to provide impressive role models. Bennett College was the first institution of higher education in the United States to choose an African American woman as president. Bennett alumnae include Glendora M. Putnam, the first black woman president of the national Young Women's Christian Association; Barbara Hamm, the first African American woman television news director; and Belinda Foster, the first black woman district attorney in North Carolina. The president of Spelman College for much of the nineties was a black Southern woman, Johnnetta Cole. Spelman alumnae include Marian Wright Edleman, founder of the Children's Defense Fund, and Alice Walker, Pulitzer prize–winning author, to name only two. The country's first black woman lawyer graduated from Howard University in Washington, D.C. In fact, Howard claims "the largest concentration of black scholars in any single institution of higher education in the world."[38]

The contributions of black Southerners to the culture of the region remain significant. In an essay entitled "The Southern Writer in the Postmodern World," literary critic Fred Hobson asserts that the region's contemporary black writers, much more than its contemporary white writers, have retained the "old power of southern fiction." Writers such as Ernest Gaines and Alice Walker "tend to be more concerned with community, place, and the past and its legacy—and to ground their fiction more fully in a rich traditional folk culture—than do most of their white counterparts."[39]

The future of the region, the authors of the report *The State of the South* contend, will be determined by the formal—and informal—education of its population. This means changing "old attitudes and mind-sets that have stereotyped blacks, women and rural residents and channeled them into lower-skill, lower-pay jobs." It also requires "universal education beyond high school and a deeper appreciation of the role of higher education in developing the economy."[40]

Are "old attitudes and mind-sets" limiting the horizons of college women as we approach the twenty-first century? Student choices of majors certainly suggest otherwise. The most popular major of first-year college women at black colleges who were surveyed by the American Council on Education in 1995 was "biology (general)," followed by "predent, premed, prevet." At the College of Charleston, freshmen women chose the same majors but reversed their order of preference. These same students, when asked about their probable careers, also listed untraditional choices: at black colleges and at the College of Charleston, the largest group of women planned to become physicians; the second largest group indicated some "other career." Only one-tenth of one percent of women at black colleges and no women at the College of Charleston wanted to become a "home-maker (full-time)."[41]

Gender, race, and class remain, however, factors in determining Southern women's employment and remuneration. Even with advanced degrees, "the incomes of white women, black men and black women lag well behind that of white men." And although black women seem to have closed the income gap with white women—in 1993 the median income of a college-educated black woman was $24,588, compared with $22,234 for a similarly educated white woman—when part-time workers are factored out of the equation, black women earn less than their white counterparts: the median income of a college-educated black woman employed full time was $28,708, compared with $30,539 for similarly employed white women. As the authors of *The State of the South* conclude, "[R]acial and gender gaps within the college-educated segment of society are testimony to the persistence of cultural barriers."[42]

More than forty years after *Brown v. Board of Education*, the debate over "separate and unequal" still engenders bitter controversy. In the 1992 Mississippi case of *U.S. v. Fordice*, the United States Supreme Court ruled 8 to 1 that race-neutral access policies were not sufficient to dismantle the dual system of education dating back to de jure segregation. Although the Justices found against the State of Mississippi, they also rejected the plaintiffs' proposal to remedy existing inequities by adding funding for HBCUs; the idea of "a separate, but 'more equal' system" was too reminiscent of the segregationist past. Instead, they remanded the case back to the district court, asking the State of Mississippi to devise a plan to remedy the inequities in its public colleges and universities. Possible remedies suggested to the state included eliminating program duplication at historically white institutions (HWIs) and HBCUs, adopting a single set of admissions standards for all publicly funded colleges and universities, offering courses that would attract blacks to HWIs and whites to HBCUs, and merging several HWIs and HBCUs.[43]

The suggestion of merging black and white institutions engendered the most controversy. Many feared that such assimilation would mean the end of courses, programs, and community projects that catered specifically to African Americans. When publicly funded women's colleges such as Florida State became coeducational in the years after World War II, female traditions and symbols were replaced by those of the dominant male culture. Critics feared that white culture would similarly dominate schools created by court-mandated racial mergers. Indeed, when the Supreme Court handed down its decision in 1992, Justice Clarence Thomas noted that "[i]t would be ironic, to say the least, if the institutions that sustained blacks during segregation were themselves destroyed in an effort to combat its vestiges."[44]

At the same time that the *Fordice* case seemed to threaten the existence of HBCUs, other rulings suggested that the courts were moving away from the affirmative action policies of the sixties and seventies. In the Maryland case of *Podberesky v. Kirwan* (1995), the United States Court of Appeals for the Fourth Circuit held that the Benjamin Banneker Scholarship Program at the University of Maryland at College Park, a merit-based award for African Americans, violated the Fourteenth Amendment rights of a Hispanic student. In *Texas v. Hopwood* (1996) the Fifth Circuit likewise ruled that the University of Texas Law School could not use different racial standards for admission. Proponents of affirmative action feared that the elimination of race-based preferences would reduce the number of minority students enrolled in HWIs.[45]

The fate of HBCUs in the twenty-first-century South is unclear. Some institutions, such as the Arkansas Agricultural, Mechanical and Normal College, have successfully merged into the historically white university system. Arkansas AM&N (Arkansas Agricultural, Mechanical, and Normal College) was transformed into the University of Arkansas at Pine Bluff in 1972 and as a result received increased state funding for its programs, its physical plant, and its faculty. Other HBCUs have been less fortunate. Since 1976, ten institutions have been forced to close their doors, and still more face problems associated with decades of underfunding. On the other hand, enrollment at HBCUs continues to increase. There were 70,000 students at HBCUs in 1954, more than 200,000 in 1980, and almost 260,000 in 1990.[46]

The chapter on coeducation at the previously single-gender public institutions of the region is likewise incomplete. Although Texas Woman's University (TWU) and Mississippi University for Women (MUW) both admit men to all their programs, neither has changed its name to reflect its coeducational status, and both describe themselves as institutions "primarily for women." MUW's President Clyda Rent introduced a new slogan, "Mississippi University for Women—and Smart Men, Too," but she and alumnae supporters, dubbed "Clyda's Commandos," successfully opposed a plan to make MUW a unit of the University of Southern Mississippi. TWU's web site includes a feature, "Why Smart Women Choose Women's Colleges," on the very same page where it declares that "the university now admits men to all of its programs."[47]

Despite extensive assimilation plans developed by officials at The Citadel and VMI, both institutions faced problems in the fall of 1997. A female "rat" at VMI was suspended for hitting a male cadet, and a male cadet at The Citadel resigned after it was discovered that he had engaged in sexual relations with a female "knob." Such intergender conflicts are obviously not limited to the military schools of the South. Yet a national panel appointed in 1996 to review policies on sexual harassment in the U.S. military blamed some of the sexual conflicts on the single-gender educational background of many of the men. Major General Claudia Kennedy, one of the panelists, concluded "that if she had a daughter who joined the Army, she would want the young woman to serve under an officer who had graduated from a coeducational university instead of a school like the Citadel, which only started admitting women last August [1996]."[48]

Notwithstanding their concerns about racial and gender issues, today's college women are generally optimistic about the future of their region and positive about the characteristics of its residents. Fewer than a fourth of the College of Charleston students surveyed in 1995 planned to leave South Carolina after graduation, and many of these hoped to live in another Southern state. When asked about attributes that distinguished Southerners from other Americans, students replied that Southerners were friendlier, more religious, more attached to their region, more family oriented, more traditional, and more prejudiced. The students' race, sex, or hometown did not affect their responses—except in the case of "prejudice." Whereas 58 percent of all students and of white women thought that "Southerners were more prejudiced than other Americans," only 37 percent of black Southern women at the college agreed with the statement. As one student remarked afterward, "[R]acism may be more subtle in other parts of the country, but it's still racism."[49]

When asked to describe the "typical" Southern woman and man, College of Charleston students gave answers that fit the stereotype of the Southerner in popular culture. The typical woman was characterized as polite, pretty, genteel, friendly, and strong—the "steel magnolia"—whereas the typical man was seen as polite, gentlemanly, industrious, traditional, and "laid back." Blacks and whites differed significantly, however, in the adjectives they chose. Whereas white Southern women at the College gave "gentleman" as their most common descriptor of a Southern man, no Southern black woman did. For black women, the best word to describe Southern males was "hardworking." The most common adjective black women used to describe Southern women was "strong," followed by "family-oriented"; for white women the responses of "polite" and "genteel" were more common than "strong."[50]

College of Charleston women, like other Southerners, tended to see themselves as more conservative than students from other parts of the country. Although 70 percent of the students who identified themselves as liberals, moderates, or conservatives were Southern, only 39 percent of those who claimed to be liberal were. Southerners, on the other hand, made up 85 percent of those who claimed to be conservative. Yet College of Charleston women were less likely than students nationally to agree "strongly or somewhat" with the statement that "[m]arried women [are] best at home." Whereas more than 19 percent of women nationally believed that this is the case, fewer than 17 percent at the college did.[51]

Southern college women, as Southerners generally, are more religious than women in the remainder of the United States. More than 92 percent of College of Charleston freshmen had attended a religious service in the past year, and a third of the women claimed to be "born-again Christians." Among black students, these numbers were even higher. When students at the college were asked how important religion was in their personal life, 74 percent of black Southern women answered "very important" and 26 percent "somewhat important." No respondent indicated that religion was "not important" in her life. Fewer white Southern women were as committed: 36 percent said it was "very important," and 56 percent said it was "somewhat important." Nonetheless, only 8 percent of white women believed that religion was not at all important in their lives.[52]

Denominational colleges continue to proclaim religious principles and values as the foundation of their educational programs. David Potts, of Judson, in his presidential message, tells students: "While Judson seeks to embrace students from diverse backgrounds and religions, the College is unapologetically Christian in her world view. Providing opportunities for service, volunteering, worship, and Bible study are integral to the College and her relevance to society and you." The mission statement of Barber-Scotia College, an HBCU, makes a similar connection between its Christian heritage and the social gospel, declaring "that human dignity is an endowment from God and that all persons have the responsibility for developing their potential to the fullest and for devoting their creative energies toward making a better world."[53]

As such statements suggest, another characteristic of Southerners past and present is their "level of devotion and commitment to local communities" and their use of voluntary associations of private citizens for public service.[54] Southern history is replete with examples of women, black and white, who have used their clubs, sororities, and associations to improve the health, education, and safety of their communities. American college women are generally more likely than American college men to spend time on "household/child care, . . . participating in student clubs/ groups, . . . [and] performing volunteer work." But Southern women seem even more involved in such activities. Approximately 74 percent of freshman women nationally "performed volunteer work" during the past year; 82 percent of women at the College of Charleston did so.[55]

Mission statements of Southern institutions of higher education tend to reflect this sense of responsibility to the world beyond the college gates. Hampton University describes itself as "a comprehensive institution of higher education, dedicated to the promotion of learning, building of character, and preparation of promising students for positions of leadership and service. . . . It is expected," the college catalog proclaims, "that faculty, staff, and students will provide leadership and service to the Hampton University and wider communities." Sweet Briar College designs its academic program to support "its mission to prepare women to be active, responsible members of a world community by integrating the liberal arts and sciences with opportunities for internships, campus and community leadership, and career planning." Tougaloo College has a community service requirement for graduation. Students must complete "60 clock hours" of community work and write a paper describing their project and its benefits. Mary Baldwin College has its own college chapter of Habitat for Humanity, Amnesty International, and Circle K, as well as the campus Volunteer Action Council to coordinate student volunteer efforts on and off campus. Florida A&M University requires its fraternities and sororities to sponsor tutorial services, promote African American culture, and serve as role models. As Spelman Provost Glenda Price explains, "We tell [our students], 'We want you to work in groups. We want you to assume responsibility. We want you to take care of your sisters.' That is a constant refrain on campus."[56]

In addition to traditions of social responsibility, Southern college women have also retained a number of other campus customs and celebrations. Most women's colleges have kept class colors, symbols, and rivalries and the various athletic contests and songfests associated with them. New students receive explanations of college legends, many of them associated with campus dignitaries. At Randolph-Macon Woman's College, new students learn that the campus statue of George Morgan Jones will "raise his sword when a woman who is a virgin walks before him. Since he has not been known to lift his saber, students always walk behind the statue." Another legend is associated with one of the school's gardens: anyone who crosses Mary's Garden rather than using the brick path on its perimeter "will not graduate from the College, will never marry, [and] will see Mary's ghost."[57]

Honor systems have also remained popular on Southern campuses. At Mary Baldwin College, freshmen still sign an honor pledge that requires them not to lie, cheat, or steal and to report any violations to a student-run honor council. "Pride in family and college helps keep students honest," concluded one professor. "So does having a small campus." Mary Baldwin, along with a number of other women's colleges in the region, allows students "to take examinations on their own time with no professors watching." This element of trust extends to all aspects of campus life: "You can leave anything anywhere," one student commented, "and nobody touches it."[58]

Family metaphors continue to be employed to describe student relationships and residence life, especially at women's colleges and HBCUs. "The primary goal of the Campus Life staff," Converse College tells prospective students, "is to ensure that you feel a part of the Converse family." Interclass bonding is encouraged through the Big Sister/Little Sister Program, described in nineties lingo as "a special mentoring tradition." Sherry Adams, an MUW student, claims that the "loving family atmosphere is what stands out to me about 'The W.' No matter what department you go to or who the person is, there is always someone there to depend on." Paquita Herring feels the same about Bennett: "I came here as an only child. Now I have 600 sisters and one mother. And her name is Bennett College." College personnel and facilities are similarly described in familial terms. The Campus Ministry at Xavier, a historically black Catholic university in New Orleans, "[f]osters the development of a campus religious family," and the University Union at Florida A&M (FAMU) serves as "The Living Room" of the campus. And, as in any family, there are rules to be followed. A number of institutions require students to live in campus dormitories for at least their first two years. FAMU's residence halls still have quiet hours. Although coeducational visitation rules have been modified considerably, restrictions remain. Mary Baldwin has a "male guest house" to provide "overnight housing for male visitors," but "[a]t no time are Mary Baldwin students permitted in the Guest House." FAMU does not permit "inter-room visitation," either.[59]

Making generalizations about campus life at Southern colleges and universities in the nineties is complicated by the ways in which students have combined diverse elements of the Old and the New South. Sororities, which had been banned from many schools early in the century because of their elitist associations, are today known for their volunteer efforts and community service projects. Formal dances and balls, once restricted to the "first [white] families" of an area, are especially popular at HBCUs, where they are used to raise money for needy causes. At the University of Mississippi, African Americans have been elected "Colonel Rebel" and "Miss Ole Miss," honorary positions whose names recall the white plantation families who dominated the school's administration and student government since its founding in the mid-nineteenth century. That a black woman could major in pharmacy and star on the basketball team at Ole Miss is, in itself, a mark of how much the Southern university scene had changed in the twentieth century. But that she could be awarded a title associated with the slave-holding aristocracy is even more ironic—and this occurred at an institution that, until 1993, celebrated the victories of its black athletes by playing "Dixie"![60]

The experiences of Cherisse Jones, a 1994 graduate of the College of Charleston and a 1997 recipient of a master's degree in history from the University of Charleston, illustrate a "consciousness of the past in the present" that continues to affect Southern women's education in the nineties. Cherisse was born in Charleston, South Carolina, in December 1970 to a middle-class family. Her father, an engineer, wanted to attend Clemson when he graduated from high school, but because the school was not yet integrated, the state of South Carolina offered him a scholarship to North Carolina A&T. After the integration of the public colleges in South Carolina, he received a master's degree from the University of South Carolina in Columbia. Her mother attended Bennett, a black women's college in Greensboro, North Carolina, and later earned a master's degree in education from The Citadel. Education was very important to the Jones family: "It was not a question of whether I would go to college," Cherisse remembered, "but where."[61]

Unlike her parents, Cherisse grew up attending integrated schools. Although very little black history was taught in the public schools of the South in the seventies and eighties, Cherisse was exposed to great "race" men and women through family stories, books, and activities. Her mother told her about being arrested for her civil rights activities as a student at Bennett. Mrs. Jones had been frightened to tell her mother what had happened—black women from good families did not go to jail—but the older woman responded by telling her daughter how proud she was that she had stood up for what was right. Bennett College officials, to their credit, were also supportive of student involvement in the civil rights movement. Mr. Jones, too, was willing to fight for racial justice: "My dad was instrumental in integrating the library in Georgetown County."

Cherisse's interest in black history was piqued by reading about famous men and women in the *Ebony* encyclopedia that the family purchased when she was a young child. She remembered looking at the pictures and pretending to read the encyclopedia before she entered first grade. "I knew even then I wanted to major in history," she says. In addition, she learned about contemporary black heroes and heroines from articles in black magazines such as *Jet* and *Ebony*.

277

A Double Focus

The Jones family was active in the black church and in fraternal organizations. Mrs. Jones had joined the Alpha Kappa Alpha sorority after
graduation—Bennett, like many other private women's colleges, discouraged fraternal organizations. In addition to sponsoring many municipal
improvement projects, Charleston's chapter of the sorority held a debutante
ball every spring. Cherisse was selected as one of these debutantes in her
senior year of high school. Some seventy young women attended Saturday
lectures on manners, deportment, education, careers, and public service
before donning identical long white dresses and pearls and marching across
the stage at the Charleston Hilton, where, escorted by Citadel cadets
("They rounded up every black cadet they could find"), they were presented to the black elite of the Carolina Low Country.

Cherisse hoped to pay for her college education by joining the army,
but when her parents found out what their seventeen-year-old daughter intended to do, they refused to sign the necessary papers. The Joneses, concerned that Cherisse might not enroll in college if she enlisted in the army
right out of high school, would give their daughter permission to join only
the reserves. Thus, in the summer after her junior year of high school,
Cherisse went off to boot camp. "I was very independent," Cherisse asserted, and "was determined to pay my own way."

Institutions of higher education throughout the nation were integrated when Cherisse went off to college in 1989, but she chose to attend
historically black South Carolina State College. "I wanted to have some of
the black experience I missed in high school." Cherisse was disappointed in
the college, however: "There was too much hand holding." She was thinking of transferring when her unit was called up for active duty in the
Kuwait-Iraq war. She withdrew from class, packed her bags, and left for
Saudi Arabia. "I was too young to realize what danger I was in," she said
afterward. In Saudi Arabia, Cherisse drove an eighteen wheeler that hauled
fuel to the troops, a job that brought her very close to the front lines. At
one point she went to Iraq. Viewing bodies of the villagers along the side of
the road was disconcerting: "How the hell did I get here?" she wondered.

On returning from Saudi Arabia, Cherisse enrolled in the College
of Charleston. She joined Sigma Gamma Rho sorority and began to focus
on African American history. She has been the research assistant at the
Avery Research Center for African American History and Culture, the co-

ordinator of African American Studies, and an active member in the Association for the Study of African American Life and History. After completing her master's thesis on black women's social activism at the turn of the century, she entered the Ph.D. program at Ohio State University. It is ironic (and indicative of the changes that have occurred throughout the South in the last quarter century) that Cherisse studied black history and culture at a school that did not accept its first African American student until 1968!

In many ways, Cherisse fits the picture of the "typical" Southerner described by sociologists such as John Shelton Reed. Family, place, and history are important to her. "I see myself as Southern by birth and by choice. . . . [S]low moving, even tempered, more polite—I can identify with all those things." Although her mother's family was small and her maternal grandmother died when she was only eight years of age, Cherisse remembers her paternal grandmother well. In fact, when asked who her "heroes/heroines" were, she named her paternal grandmother and her mother. Her family ties to the South Carolina Low Country are extensive: "My father is related to every other person in Georgetown."

Cherisse's upbringing was strongly "traditional." Her father was a "Bible reading, Bible quoting type of person." Even though she "kind of hated going to church," she and her other siblings had to attend every Sunday until they were eighteen years of age. Mr. Jones was also very strict when it came to dating. He did not want his daughters marrying a "ne'er do well" or getting pregnant out of wedlock. Cherisse's reputation in the community was important. She was brought up to be a "lady."

Yet the complex nature of Southern womanhood, its "twoness," can also be seen in Cherisse's upbringing. When asked to describe herself, she selects the adjectives "determined" and "persistent." Her parents taught her that "no matter what you did, you had to do it well." Education and hard work were the key to success. By joining the army reserves, Cherisse was able to pay for her own college education and to take care of herself: "I don't know how to be dependent," she admits. Despite the paternalistic environment of Charleston, she sees herself as a "big advocate of women's rights."

What is—as C. Vann Woodward entitled his 1989 study of "the impact of past upon present and present upon past"—"the future of the

Past"?[62] The regional fascination with the past has been a blessing and a curse for women's higher education in the twentieth century. Plantation stereotypes of gender, race, and class have made it difficult for Southern women to assert themselves and to challenge the status quo. Traditional concepts of womanhood have discouraged independent thought and action and have encouraged women to look outward, not inward, for solutions to their problems. Yet the paternalism that characterized Southern culture and Southern institutions also fostered social consciousness, group sensitivity, and community activism. From the campuses of the twentieth-century South emerged women whose words and deeds challenged the most sacred shibboleths of the region.

The "double consciousness" of Southern colleges is clear in their promotional literature. As a brochure for Johnson C. Smith University, a historically black institution in North Carolina, explains: "[M]uch like the Roman god Janus, we have two faces. The first, which looks ever forward, suggests our commitment to provide an exciting, relevant and 'futures oriented' curriculum and program. . . . [O]ur other face, which looks backwards, celebrates the unique heritage about which we are so very proud . . . the immense contributions which have been made by people of African descent." The President of Mississippi University of Women, Clyda Rent, expresses similar sentiments in her message to prospective students: "At the 'W' we keep the best of the past, paying attention to the individual, with faculty who have outstanding credentials and a deep, abiding love for teaching and helping our students reach their potential. At the same time, the 'W' is on the cutting edge of supplying the skills, resources, and approaches that will be necessary for success in the new century." Knowing the trials and tribulations of the past has made the South's people and institutions stronger. As Johnnetta Cole, who recently resigned as president of Spelman College to take a teaching position at Emory University, told an interviewer: "I love the South at its best—so warm, so open, so gracious, and so compassionate. I don't think I could love all that if I didn't know the South in its antithesis—when it's cold, not by weather but by attitudes and behavior."[63]

Southern college women have been part of the great transformation of American higher education that occurred in the second half of the twentieth century, but they have also retained their "ethnic identification" as

Southerners. As the terms "twoness" and "double consciousness" and "multiconciousness" imply, no single-variable model can capture the complexity of Southern women's educational experiences. Southern women continue to be cognizant of the ways in which they are simultaneously American and Southern, Southern and female, female and black/white, and black/white and upper/middle/lower class. They are all too aware of their "shared history and . . . divided heritage."[64] This complexity—of time, of character, and of place—has made and will continue to make the story of Southern women's educational experience distinct.

~Notes~

Introduction: The Past in the Present

1. Despite innumerable efforts to capture its essence, the "South" remains an elusive concept. The region has been defined geographically, climatically, racially, historically, culturally, and even psychologically. For various definitions of the South, see Wilbur J. Cash, *The Mind of the South* (New York: Alfred A. Knopf, 1941); Carl N. Degler, *Place Over Time: The Continuity of Southern Distinctiveness* (Baton Rouge and London: Louisiana State University Press, 1977); John B. Boles, ed., *Dixie Dateline: A Journalistic Portrait of the Contemporary South* (Houston: Rice University Studies, 1983); Louis D. Rubin, Jr., ed., *The American South: Portrait of a Culture* (Baton Rouge and London: Louisiana State University Press, 1980); C. Vann Woodward, *The Burden of Southern History* (Baton Rouge: Louisiana State University Press, 1960); Rupert Vance, *Human Geography of the South: A Study in Regional Resources and Human Adequacy* (Chapel Hill: University of North Carolina Press, 1935); John Shelton Reed, *Southerners: The Social Psychology of Sectionalism* (Chapel Hill: University of North Carolina Press, 1983) and *The Enduring South: Subcultural Persistence in Mass Society* (Lexington, MA: Lexington Books, D. C. Heath, 1972). For the purposes of this study, I have adopted John Shelton Reed's solution in *Enduring South* and let the region define itself. If a particular individual, group, organization, or institution considers itself "Southern," I do as well.

2. Degler, *Place Over Time*, 127; W. E. B. Du Bois, *The Souls of Black Folk: Essays and Sketches* (Chicago: A. C. McClurg, 1903), 3.

3. Dorothy Salem, "National Association of Colored Women," in *Black Women in America: An Historical Encyclopedia*, vol. 2, ed. Darlene Clark Hine (New York: Carlson Publishing, 1993), 845; Darlene Clark Hine, *Speak Truth to Power: Black Professional Class in United States History* (New York: Carlson Publishing, 1996), 34.

4. Allen Tate, "The New Provincialism," *Essays of Four Decades* (Chicago: Swallow Press, 1968), 545; Degler, *Place Over Time*, 1977), 127.

5. *Discourse on Western Planting Written in the Year 1584 by Richard Hakluyt*, ed. Leonard Wood (Cambridge, MA: J. Wilson & Son for the Maine Historical Society, 1877); Charles Reagan Wilson, "History and Manners," *Encyclopedia of Southern Culture*, ed. Charles Reagan Wilson and William Ferris (Chapel Hill and London: University of North Carolina Press, 1989), 583.

6. Cash, *The Mind of the South*, 32, 46.

7. Patrick Gerster, "Religion and Mythology," in *Encyclopedia of Southern Culture*, 1123.

8. C. Vann Woodward, *The Burden of Southern History*, rev. ed. (New York and Toronto: New American Library, 1969; first published in 1960), 27.

9. Jonathan Daniels, *A Southerner Discovers the South* (New York: Macmillan, 1938), 1.

10. Ibid., 335–36.

11. Allen Tate, "*The Fugitive* 1922–1925: A Personal Recollection Twenty Years After," *The Princeton University Library Chronicle* 3 (1942): 83; "The New Provincialism," 545.

12. Howard W. Odum, *Southern Regions of the United States* (Chapel Hill: University of North Carolina Press, 1936), 503.

13. Philander P. Claxton, "Educational Ideals," in *The South in the Building of the Nation: History of the Social Life of the South*, vol. 10, ed. Samuel Chiles Mitchell (Richmond, VA: Southern Historical Publication Society, 1909), 400.

14. Robert Burwell Fulton, "Education in the South Before the War," in *The South in the Building of the Nation*, 198.

15. T. Harry Williams, introduction to *Louisiana State University: A Pictorial Record of the First Hundred Years*, ed. V. L. Bedsole and Oscar Richard (Baton Rouge: Louisiana State University Press, 1959), 16.

16. Grady McWhiney, "Education in the Old South: A Reexamination," in *The Southern Enigma: Essays on Race, Class, and Folk Culture*, ed. Walter J. Fraser, Jr., and Winfred B. Moore, Jr. (Westport, CT: Greenwood Press, 1983), 169, 175, 180–81; *The Education of Henry Adams: An Autobiography* (Cambridge, MA: Riverside Press, 1961; first privately printed and distributed in 1906).

17. Edwin Mims, *The Advancing South: Stories of Progress and Reaction* (New York: Doubleday, Page, 1926), 240.

18. Colyer Meriwether, *The History of Higher Education in South Carolina* (Washington, DC: Government Printing Office, 1889), 103; Rosser H. Taylor, *Ante-Bellum South Carolina: A Social and Cultural History* (Chapel Hill: University of North Carolina Press, 1942), 112.

19. Christie Anne Farnham, *The Education of the Southern Belle: Higher Education and Student Socialization in the Antebellum South* (New York and London: New York University Press, 1994), 7, 2–3.

20. Carol Ruth Berkin, "Women's Life," in *Encyclopedia of Southern Culture*, 1521.

21. See Paula S. Fass, *Outside In: Minorities and the Transformation of American Education* (New York and Oxford: Oxford University Press, 1989), for a discussion of the ways in which "schools have aimed to unify and integrate the nation and to direct the behavior and beliefs of its complex population in regular and socially acceptable ways" (229).

22. Odum, *Southern Regions of the United States*, 109. In a 1909 list of Southern colleges and universities compiled by George H. Denny, President of Washington and Lee University, thirty-three schools were under Methodist control; twenty-one, Baptist control; twenty-one, Presbyterian control; ten, the control of various other Protestant sects; sixteen, Roman Catholic control. Only fifteen private colleges were nonsectarian, whereas eighteen state universities and thirty-three agricultural and mechanical institutions were nondenominational. (George H. Denny, "Universities and Colleges of the South," in *The South in the Building of the Nation*, 256–57.)

23. John P. Marcum, "Population," in *Encyclopedia of Southern Culture*, 556.

24. Elizabeth L. Ihle, "Black Women's Academic Education in the South," Modules III and IV, in *History of Black Women's Education in the South, 1865–Present* (Washington, DC: U.S. Department of Education, 1986).

25. Drew Gilpin Faust, *A Sacred Circle: The Dilemma of the Intellectual in the Old South, 1840–1860* (Baltimore and London: Johns Hopkins University Press, 1977), x; Cash, *The Mind of the South*, 91; Catherine

Clinton, *The Plantation Mistress: Woman's World in the Old South* (New York: Pantheon Books, 1982), 13; William H. Nicholls, *Southern Tradition and Regional Progress* (Chapel Hill: University of North Carolina Press, 1960), 133.

26. Peggy Lamson, *The Glorious Failure: Black Congressman Robert Brown Elliottt and the Reconstruction in South Carolina* (New York: W. W. Norton, 1974), 56–57.

27. Ibid., 72.

28. Louis R. Harlan, "Desegregation in New Orleans Public Schools During Reconstruction," in *The American Historical Review* 67, No. 3 (April 1962): 663–75.

29. Jane E. Smith Browning and John B. Williams, "History and Goals of Black Institutions of Higher Learning," in *Black Colleges in America: Challenge, Development, Survival*, ed. Charles V. Willie and Ronald R. Edmonds (New York: Teachers College, Columbia University Press, 1978), 69.

30. A. Freeman Butts and Lawrence A. Cremin, *A History of Education in American Culture* (New York: Holt, Rinehart and Winston, 1953), 520–21.

31. Denny, "Universities and Colleges of the South," in *The South in the Building of the Nation*, 247; Odum, *Southern Regions of the United States*, 117.

32. Bridget Smith Pieschel and Stephen Robert Pieschel, *Loyal Daughters: One Hundred Years at Mississippi University for Women, 1884–1984* (Jackson: University Press of Mississippi, 1984), 92.

33. Sam P. Wiggins, *Higher Education in the South* (Berkeley, CA: McCutchan Publishing, 1966), 56.

34. Samuel Chiles Mitchell, "Education in the South Since the War," in *The South in the Building of the Nation*, 214.

35. Odum, *Southern Regions of the United States*, 19.

36. Ibid., 101, 19.

37. Ellen Glasgow, *Virginia* (New York: Penguin Books, 1989; first published in 1913), 16, 17.

38. Louise Schutz Boas, *Woman's Education Begins: The Rise of the Women's Colleges* (Norton, MA: Wheaton College Press, 1935), 12.

39. Thomas Woody, *A History of Women's Education in the United States*, 2 vols. (New York: Science Press, 1929).

40. See Thomas G. Dyer, "Higher Education in the South Since the Civil War: Historical Issues and Trends," in *The Web of Southern Social Relations: Women, Family, and Education*, ed. Walter J. Fraser, Jr., R. Frank Saunders, Jr., and Jon L. Wakelyn (Athens: University of Georgia Press, 1985), 127–45.

41. See Barbara Miller Solomon, *In the Company of Educated Women: A History of Women and Higher Education in America* (New Haven and London: Yale University Press, 1985), 21, 45–47, 49, 53–54, 203; Helen Lefkowitz Horowitz, *Campus Life: Undergraduate Cultures From the End of the Eighteenth Century to the Present* (Chicago and London: University of Chicago Press, 1987), 193–219; Lynn D. Gordon, *Gender and Higher Education in the Progressive Era* (New Haven and London: Yale University Press, 1990), 165–88.

42. Stephanie J. Shaw, *What a Woman* Ought *to Be and to Do: Black Professional Women Workers During the Jim Crow Era* (Chicago: University of Chicago Press, 1996), 10, 2.

43. Elizabeth Showalter Muhlenfeld, "Mary Boykin Chesnut: The Writer and Her Work" (Ph.D. diss., University of South Carolina, 1978), 548.

44. Peter H. Wood, *Black Majority: Negroes in Colonial South Carolina from 1670 Through the Stono Rebellion* (New York and London: W. W. Norton, 1974; Eugene Genovese, *Roll, Jordan, Roll: The World the Slaves Made* (New York: Pantheon Books, 1974), 597, 659.

45. Evelyn Brooks Higginbotham, "African-American Women's History and the Metalanguage of Race," in *"We Specialize in the Wholly Impossible": A Reader in Black Women's History*, ed. Darlene Clark Hine, Wilma King, and Linda Reed (New York: Carlson Publishing, 1995), 13–15.

46. Barbara T. Christian, *Alice Walker, "Everyday Use,"* ed. Barbara T. Christian (New Brunswick: Rutgers University Press, 1994), 15.

47. Marjorie Nicolson, "Scholars and Ladies," *Yale Review* 19 (June 1930): 783.

48. Odum, *Southern Regions of the United States*, 507.

49. John B. Boles, "Introduction: The Dixie Difference," in *Dixie*

Dateline: A Journalistic Portrait of the Contemporary South, ed. John B. Boles (Houston: Rice University Studies, 1983), 1.

50. William D. Piersen, *Black Legacy: America's Hidden Heritage* (Amherst: University of Massachusetts Press, 1993), xv.

1. The Forgotten Woman

1. An earlier version of this chapter was published as "Progressivism and the Higher Education of Southern Women," in *The North Carolina Historical Review* 70, No. 3 (July 1993): 302–25.

2. Dewey W. Grantham, *Southern Progressivism: The Reconciliation of Progress and Tradition* (Knoxville: University of Tennessee Press, 1983), 246.

3. C. Vann Woodward, *Origins of the New South, 1877–1913* (Baton Rouge: Louisiana State University Press, 1951), 369–428; Edward L. Ayers, *The Promise of the New South: Life After Reconstruction* (New York: Oxford University Press, 1992), viii, 420–26.

4. Glenda Elizabeth Gilmore, "Gender and Jim Crow: Women and the Politics of White Supremacy in North Carolina, 1898–1920" (Ph.D. diss., University of North Carolina at Chapel Hill, 1992), 358–59, 317.

5. "Illiteracy," in *Population, 1920: General Report and Analytical Tables*, vol. 2 of *Fourteenth Census of the United States, Taken in the Year 1920* (Washington, DC: U.S. Government Printing Office, 1922), 1145–46.

6. Walter H. Page, "The Forgotten Man," typescript of commencement address given at the North Carolina Normal and Industrial Institute, 19 May 1897, University Archives, Jackson Library, University of North Carolina–Greensboro, 4.

7. Elizabeth L. Ihle, "Black Women's Academic Education in the South," Modules III and IV, *History of Black Women's Education in the South, 1865–Present* (Washington, DC: U.S. Department of Education, 1986).

8. Edgar W. Knight, *Education in the South* (Chapel Hill: University of North Carolina Press, 1924), 1, 4, 23.

9. There were 250,000 more illiterate women than men in the region in 1890 (100,000 of these women were white; 150,000 were black). See

Charles D. McIver, "The Southern Educational Problem," typescript of speech in Charles D. McIver Papers, University Archives, Jackson Library, University of North Carolina–Greensboro, 3–5; McIver, "The Education of the White Country Girl: The Great Problem of the South," typescript of speech in Charles D. McIver Papers, 2; William Louis Poteat, "Greetings," in *Meredith College Quarterly Bulletin* 9, No. 2 (January 1916): 48.

10. Grantham, *Southern Progressivism*, 274.

11. William A. Link, *A Hard Country and a Lonely Place: Schooling, Society, and Reform in Rural Virginia, 1870–1920* (Chapel Hill and London: University of North Carolina Press, 1986), 94.

12. Edwin Alderman, "Charles D. McIver of North Carolina," *Sewanee Review* 15 (January 1907): 108.

13. William C. Smith, "Charles Duncan McIver," in *Charles Duncan McIver Memorial Volume*, ed. William C. Smith, Viola Boddie, and Mary Settle Sharpe (Greensboro, NC: n.p., ca. 1907), 280.

14. McIver, "The Education of the White Country Girl," 1–2, 8.

15. Charles D. McIver, "Two Open Fields for Investment in the South," typescript of speech in Charles D. McIver Papers, 10.

16. McIver, "Speech at Columbia, SC, December 1901," typescript of speech in Charles D. McIver Papers, 8.

17. Ibid., 7.

18. Charles Duncan McIver, "Alumni Address," Commencement 1892, *North Carolina University Magazine*, Old Series, vol. 22; New Series, vol. 11; No. 6 (1892): 287.

19. Henry S. Pritchett, "Educational Agencies," in *The South in the Building of the Nation*, vol. 10, ed. Samuel Chiles Mitchell (Richmond, VA: Southern Publication Society, 1909), 392.

20. See H. Leon Prather, *Resurgent Politics and Educational Progressivism in the New South: North Carolina, 1890–1913* (Rutherford, NJ: Fairleigh Dickinson University Press, 1979), 221–27.

21. McIver, "The Education of the White Country Girl," 1.

22. Bridget Smith Pieschel and Stephen Robert Pieschel, *Loyal Daughters: One Hundred Years at Mississippi University for Women, 1884–1984* (Jackson: University Press of Mississippi, 1984), 5–12.

23. Ron Chepesiuk, *Winthrop College: A Centennial Celebration* (Rock

Hill, SC: Winthrop College, 1985), 14–19; E. Thomas Crowson, *The Winthrop Story 1886–1960* (Baltimore: Gateway Press, 1987), 20–26.

24. Crowson, *The Winthrop Story*, 39.

25. "Governor Benjamin R. Tillman's Message Delivered December 4, 1890 to the General Assembly," typescript W403-1A-5, Archives and Special Collections Department, Dacus Library, Winthrop University, 1.

26. Report of the Commissioners Appointed Under Concurrent Resolution of the General Assembly of South Carolina, Relative to the Establishment of a State Industrial School for Women (Columbia, SC: James H. Woodrow, State Printer, 1891), 6.

27. Report of the Commissioners . . . Relative to the Establishment of a State Industrial School for Women, 14, 15.

28. Crowson, *The Winthrop Story*, 56, 77; James P. Kinard, Historical Sketch of Winthrop College The South Carolina College for Women, A Radio Address at WBT, Charlotte, NC, 9 February 1934, in the Series of the South Carolina Economic Association, Being the Fiftieth Consecutive Weekly Broadcast in Educational Series (pamphlet in South Carolina Historical Society), 4; Report of the Commissioners . . . Relative to the Establishment of a State Industrial School for Women, 6, 9.

29. Pieschel and Pieschel, *Loyal Daughters*, 8.

30. Frances Gibson Satterfield, *Charles Duncan McIver* (Greensboro: Woman's College of the University of North Carolina, 1942), 48.

31. Jack Temple Kirby, *Rural Worlds Lost: The American South, 1920–1960* (Baton Rouge: Louisiana State University Press, 1989), 20–21; Mabel Newcomer, *A Century of Higher Education for American Women* (Washington: Zenger, 1959), 58.

32. Satterfield, *Charles Duncan McIver*, 40; William C. Smith, Viola Boddie, and Mary Settle Sharpe, *Charles Duncan McIver Memorial Volume* (Greensboro, NC: n.p., ca. 1907), 245.

33. Betty Anne Ragland Starback, "Dr. Iver and State Normal," *Alumni News* (University of North Carolina at Greensboro) 55, No. 1 (Fall 1966): 6.

34. Starback, "Dr. McIver and State Normal," 21–22.

35. Cornelius J. Heatwole, *A History of Education in Virginia* (New York: Macmillan, 1916), 334, 337; D. B. Johnson, "Normal Education," in *The South in the Building of the Nation*, vol. 10, 298.

36. Heatwole, *A History of Education in Virginia*, 334, 337.

37. Rose Howell Holder, *McIver of North Carolina* (Chapel Hill: University of North Carolina Press, 1957), 130.

38. Faculty Roster, First Annual Catalogue of the State Normal and Industrial School, Greensboro, North Carolina, 1892–1893.

39. Carrie Mullins to President Charles D. McIver, 2 July 1892, Charles D. McIver Papers.

40. President's Report, Report of the Board of Directors of the Normal and Industrial Schools for the Two Scholastic Years Ending September 30, 1894 (Raleigh: Presses of Edwards & Broughton, 1895), 13; Lottie Watkins to President Charles D. McIver, 14 September 1892, Charles D. McIver Papers.

41. Holder, *McIver of North Carolina*, 129.

42. Ibid., 148–56.

43. Woodward, *Origins of the New South*, 437.

44. Thomas Woody, *A History of Women's Education in the United States* (New York: Science Press, 1929), vol. 2, 314–16.

45. Quoted in Brandt V. B. Dixon, *A Brief History of H. Sophie Newcomb Memorial College 1887–1919: A Personal Reminiscence* (New Orleans: Hauser, 1928), 10; The H. Sophie Newcomb Memorial College for Women, Announcement for 1920–1921, *Bulletin of Tulane University of Louisiana* 21, No. 5 (May 1920): 13, 44, 92; Woody, *A History of Women's Education*, vol. 2, 315–16.

46. John P. Dyer, *Tulane: The Biography of a University, 1834–1965* (New York and London: Harper & Row, 1966), 104, 250 [my emphasis].

47. Rosa Catherine Paschal, quoted in Mary Lynch Johnson, *A History of Meredith College* (Raleigh, NC: Meredith College, 1956), 56–57.

48. Quoted in Gail Apperson Kilman, "Southern Collegiate Women, Higher Education at Wesleyan Female College and Randolph-Macon Woman's College, 1893–1907" (Ph.D. diss., History, University of Delaware, 1984), 84.

49. Woody, *A History of Women's Education*, vol. 2, 160–79, 188; Marion Talbot and Lois Kimball Matthews Rosenberry, *The History of the American Association of University Women, 1881–1931* (Boston and New York: Houghton Mifflin, 1931).

50. Lilian A. Kibler, *The History of Converse College* (Spartanburg,

SC: Converse College, 1973), 50; advertisement in *The State* (Columbia, SC), 20 July 1891.

51. Baptist Female University, *Annual Catalogue, 1899–1900*, 23.

52. Johnson, *A History of Meredith College*, 102.

53. John M. McBryde, Jr., "Womanly Education for Woman," *Sewanee Review* 15, No. 4 (October 1907): 472.

54. See Kilman, "Southern Collegiate Women," 142, 146. Kilman found that the majority of students at Wesleyan Female College and Randolph-Macon Woman's College in the years between 1893 and 1907 enrolled for two years or less.

55. *Meredith College Quarterly Bulletin* 3, No. 4 (May 1910): 16.

56. James H. Kirkland, "Higher Education in the South," in *The South in the Building of the Nation*, vol. 10, 233–36.

57. James H. Kirkland, "College Standards—a Public Interest," reprinted from the Proceedings of the Fourteenth Annual Meeting of the Southern Association of College Women, in *Meredith College Quarterly Bulletin* 12, No. 1 (November 1918): 18.

58. "Sketch of the Association of Colleges and Preparatory Schools of the Southern States," *Association of Colleges and Preparatory Schools of the Southern States*, Proceedings of the Fourth Annual Meeting, University of Georgia, November 1–2, 1898, vii.

59. "Minimum College Requirements Adopted by the Executive Committee of the Association of Colleges and Secondary Schools of the Southern States," reprinted in *Meredith College Quarterly Bulletin* 12, No. 1 (November 1918): 15–16.

60. Talbot and Rosenberry, *History of the American Association of University Women*, 46–48.

61. Ibid., 48; *Association of Colleges and Preparatory Schools of the South States*, Proceedings of the Fourth Annual Meeting, vii.

62. Talbot and Rosenberry, *History of the American Association of University Women*, 51–52.

63. Elizabeth Avery Colton, "The Junior College Problem in the South," *Meredith College Quarterly Bulletin* 8, No. 2 (January 1915): 9.

64. Elizabeth Avery Colton, "The Various Types of Southern Colleges for Women," *Meredith College Quarterly Bulletin* 9, No. 4 (May 1916): 3.

65. Elizabeth Avery Colton, "Address to High School Students on Standard Colleges," ca. 1915, handwritten draft, Elizabeth Avery Colton Papers, North Carolina State Archives.

66. Elizabeth Avery Colton, "Southern Colleges for Women," *Meredith College Quarterly Bulletin* 5, No. 2 (January 1912): 18.

67. Ibid., 9.

68. Colton, "The Junior College Problem in the South," 14, 9.

69. Emily Helen Dutton, "History of the Southern Association of College Women," typescript in Library of AAUW Educational Foundation, Washington, DC, 15.

70. Ibid., 16.

71. "Table 7: Per Cent Illiterate in Population 10 Years of Age and Over, by Sex and Principal Population Classes, by Divisions and States: 1920, 1910, and 1900," in *Population, 1920*, 1156.

72. Woodward, *Origins of the New South*, 397; Ayers, *Promise of the New South*, 426; Grantham, *Southern Progressivism*, 269.

73. Pamela Dean, in her study of campus culture at the North Carolina Normal and Industrial College in the early twentieth century, has shown how students learned to use "the language of religion and domesticity . . . to lay to rest the fears raised by the specter of assertive women acting autonomously on the public stage." See Pamela Dean, "Learning to Be New Women: Campus Culture at the North Carolina Normal and Industrial College," *North Carolina Historical Review* 68 (July 1991): 297.

74. Anne Firor Scott, *Natural Allies: Women's Associations in American History* (Urbana: University of Illinois Press, 1992), 90.

75. Woodward, *Origins of the New South*, 406; Ayers, *Promise of the New South*, 420; "Table 7: Per Cent Illiterate in Population."

76. Link, *A Hard Country and a Lonely Place*, 183; J. Morgan Kousser, "Progressivism—for Middle Class Whites Only: North Carolina Education, 1880–1910," *Journal of Southern History* 46, No. 2 (May 1980): 182.

77. Thomas Jesse Jones, *Negro Education: A Study of the Private and Higher Schools for Colored People in the United States*, vol. 2, Department of Interior Bureau of Education Bulletin, 1916, No. 39 (Washington, DC: U.S. Government Printing Office, 1917), 16, 17.

78. Neil R. McMillen, *Dark Journey: Black Mississippians in the Age of Jim Crow* (Urbana and Chicago: University of Illinois Press, ca. 1989; Illini Books ed., 1990), 73–85.

79. Jane E. Smith Browning and John B. Williams, "History and Goals of Black Institutions of Higher Learning," in *Black Colleges in America: Challenge, Development, and Survival*, ed. Charles V. Willie and Ronald R. Edmonds (New York: Columbia University Press, 1978), 73; James D. Anderson, *The Education of Blacks in the South, 1860–1935* (Chapel Hill: University of North Carolina Press, 1988), 84–89.

80. Link, *A Hard Country and a Lonely Place*, 178–79.

81. Henry Allen Bullock, *A History of Negro Education in the South from 1619 to the Present* (Cambridge, MA: Harvard University Press, 1967), 159–60.

82. Jane Bernard-Powers, "Lucy Craft Laney," in *Women Educators in the United States, 1820–1993*, ed. Maxine Schwartz Seller (Westport, CT: Greenwood Press, 1994), 276–82.

83. Olga Skorapa, "Mary McLeod Bethune," in *Women Educators*, 49; Mary McLeod Bethune, "Faith That Moved a Dump Heap," *Who, the Magazine About People* 1, No. 3 (June 1941): 31–35, 54; "Who's Who," in *What the Negro Wants*, ed. Rayford W. Logan (Chapel Hill: University of North Carolina Press, 1944), 345.

84. Marcia G. Synnott, "Nannie Helen Burroughs," *Women Educators*, 72; Evelyn Brooks Barnett, "Nannie Burroughs and the Education of Black Women," in *The Afro-American Woman: Struggles and Images*, ed. Sharon Harley and R. Terborg-Penn (Port Washington, NY: Kennikat Press, 1978), 90–107.

85. Barnett, "Nannie Burroughs and the Education of Black Women," 98–107.

86. Jones, *Negro Education*, vol. 2, 119, 253; Felton G. Clark, *The Control of State-Supported Teacher-Training Programs for Negroes* (New York: Teachers College, Columbia University, 1934), 11.

87. Ihle, "Black Women's Academic Education"; Thomas Jesse Jones, *Negro Education: A Study of the Private and Higher Schools for Colored People in the United States*, vol. 1, Department of the Interior Education Bulletin, 1916, No. 38 (Washington, DC: U.S. Government Printing Office, 1917), 260.

88. Ihle, "Black Women's Academic Education," 3–4; Rayford W. Logan, "The Evolution of Private Colleges for Negroes," *Journal of Negro Education* 27 (Summer 1958): 218; Bullock, *A History of Negro Education in the South*, 186.

89. Clark, *The Control of State-Supported Teacher-Training Programs*, 12, 15; Louis Round Wilson, *Louis Round Wilson's Historical Sketches* (Durham, NC: Moore Publishing, 1976), 125–27.

90. Elizabeth L. Ihle, "Black Women's Vocational Education," Module II, *History of Black Women's Education in the South, 1865–Present* (Washington, DC: U.S. Department of Education, Office of Educational Research and Improvement, Educational Resources Information Center, 1986), 4.

91. McMillen, *Dark Journey*, 86, 101, 99.

92. Jones, *Negro Education*, II, 625.

93. Cynthia Neverdon-Morton, *Afro-American Women of the South and the Advancement of the Race, 1895–1925* (Knoxville: University of Tennessee Press, 1989), 16–25, 32, Barrett quotation on 105.

94. Beverly Guy-Sheftall, "Black Women and Higher Education: Spelman and Bennett Colleges Revisited," *Journal of Negro Education* 51, No. 3 (Summer 1982): 279–80; Jones, *Negro Education*, vol. 2, 222; Beatrice Bowen Butcher, "The Evolution of Negro Women's Schools in the United States" (M.A. diss., School of Education, Howard University, 1936), 25.

95. Beverly Guy-Sheftall and Jo Moore Stewart, *Spelman: A Centennial Celebration 1881–1981* (Charlotte, NC: Delmar, 1981), 27, 29, 58.

96. Neverdon-Morton, *Afro-American Women of the South*, 49–52.

97. U.S. Commissioner of Education, *Report, 1899–1900*, vol. 2 (Washington, DC: U.S. Government Printing Office, 1901), 2506–07.

98. Joe M. Richardson, *A History of Fisk University, 1865–1946* (University, AL: University of Alabama Press, 1980), 9, 42.

99. *Straight Ahead*, The American Missionary Association, Report for the Academic Year 1933–1934 (New York: American Missionary Association, 1934), 10.

100. Richardson, *History of Fisk University*, 49, 21, 97.

101. Mamie Garvin Fields with Karen Fields, *Lemon Swamp and Other Places: A Carolina Memoir* (New York and London: Free Press, 1983), 83–105.

102. Clark, *Control of State-Supported Teacher-Training Programs*, 28; Richardson, *History of Fisk University*, 64; Mary M. Carter, "The Educational Activities of the NACW, 1923–1960" (M.A. diss., Education Department, Howard University, 1962), 68.

103. Jacqueline A. Rouse, "Atlanta's African-American Women's Attack on Segregation, 1900–1920," in *Gender, Class, Race, and Reform in the Progressive Era*, ed. Noralee Frankel and Nancy S. Dye (Lexington: University Press of Kentucky, 1991), 13.

104. Jacqueline Anne Rouse, *Lugenia Burns Hope: Black Southern Reformer* (Athens and London: University of Georgia Press, 1989), 45–89, motto on 66.

105. Gilmore, "Gender and Jim Crow," 359, 422.

106. Henry Allen Bullock, *A History of Negro Education in the South from 1619 to the Present* (Cambridge, MA: Harvard University Press, 1967), 198.

107. "Problems of Educated Woman Acute in Southern States," *New York Age* 22 (July 1922).

108. Ronald K. Goodenow, "Paradox in Progressive Educational Reform: The South and the Education of Blacks in The Depression Years," *Phylon* 39, No. 1 (Spring 1978): 53; Lynn D. Gordon, *Gender and Higher Education in the Progressive Era* (New Haven and London: Yale University Press, 1990), 188.

109. Dwight Oliver Holmes, *The Evolution of the Negro College* (New York: American Missionary Society Press, 1934), 207, 206, 181.

110. James L. Leloudis II, "School Reform in the New South: The Woman's Association for the Betterment of Public School Houses in North Carolina, 1902–1919," *Journal of American History* 69, No. 4 (March 1983): 886–909.

111. Wilbur J. Cash, *The Mind of the South* (New York: Alfred A. Knopf, 1941), 246.

112. Rouse, *Lugenia Burns Hope*, 7, 129, 131.

113. Clark Kerr, in his book *The Great Transformation in Higher Education* (Albany: State University of New York Press, 1991), argues that the first "great transformation" in American higher education occurred between 1870 and 1910. The British university system, with its classical curriculum, denominational affiliation, and hierarchical structure, was re-

placed by the German university system with its scientific curricula, specialized department structure, utilitarian focus, and democratic organization. As a consequence of that change in emphasis, the major research university became increasingly important.

114. Ihle, "Black Women's Academic Education in the South," 2.

2. A Lady, a Scholar, and a Citizen

1. An earlier version of this chapter was published as "Pedagogy and the Pedestal: The Impact of Traditional Views of Woman's Place on the Curricula of Southern Colleges in the Early Twentieth Century," *Journal of Thought* 20, No. 3 (Fall 1985): 263–78.

2. See Dorothy Salem, "National Association of Colored Women," in *Black Women in America: An Historical Encyclopedia*, vol. 2, ed. Darlene Clark Hine (New York: Carlson Publishing, 1993), 842–51.

3. Allen B. Ballard, *The Education of Black Folk: The Afro-American Struggle for Knowledge in White America* (New York: Harper & Row, 1973), 13.

4. Sylvanie Francaz Williams, "The Social Status of the Negro Woman," *Voice of the Negro* 1, No. 7 (July 1904): 299; I. A. Newby, *Black Carolinians: A History of Blacks in South Carolina from 1895 to 1968* (Columbia: University of South Carolina Press, 1973), 109.

5. Nell Battle Lewis, "Negro Slavery Throws Dark Shadow Across the South to Keep Southern Women From Securing Their Freedom," *News and Observer* (Raleigh, NC), 3 May 1925.

6. M. Carey Thomas, "Should the Higher Education of Women Differ From That of Men?" *Educational Review* 21 (January 1901): 10.

7. Emma May Laney, "The Woman's College & Its Alumnae," *The Agnes Scott Alumnae Quarterly* (April 1935): 1.

8. Announcements and Course Offerings, The Georgia State Woman's College, 1938–1939, 4.

9. W. E. B. Du Bois, *The Education of Black People: Ten Critiques 1906–1960*, ed. Herbert Aptheker (Amherst: University of Massachusetts Press, 1973), 32, 10.

10. See College of Charleston Catalogue, 1920–1921, 21.

11. Colin B. Burke, *American Collegiate Populations: A Test of the Tra-*

ditional View (New York and London: New York University Press, 1982), 468; *Charles W. Eliot: The Man and His Beliefs*, ed. William Allan Neilson, vol. 2 (New York and London: Harper & Brothers, 1926), 575.

12. Elizabeth L. Ihle, "The Roots of Industrial Education, Black Women's Vocational Education," Module II, *History of Black Women's Education in the South, 1865–Present* (Washington, DC: U.S. Department of Education, 1986), 2.

13. Alain Locke, quoted in Cynthia Neverdon-Morton, *Afro-American Women of the South and the Advancement of the Race, 1895–1925* (Knoxville: University of Tennessee Press, 1989), 14.

14. Emilie M. McVea, "The Present Curricula of Colleges for Women," *School and Society* 12, No. 300, September 25, 1920, 244; C. J. Hyslup, *Virginia Colleges: A Bulletin of Information for Prospective College Students to Assist Boys and Girls in Answering Many of the Questions Regarding Virginia Colleges and Their Entrance Requirements* (Richmond, VA: State Board of Education, 1935), 23.

15. Queens-Chicora College Bulletin, 1930–1931, 28.

16. Randolph-Macon Woman's College Catalogue, 1940–1941, 21.

17. *Public Higher Education in South Carolina: A Survey Report* (Nashville: Division of Surveys and Field Services, George Peabody College for Teachers, 1946), 163.

18. *Bulletin of Judson College* 18, No. 3 (April 1931), Catalogue No. 1930–1931, 26–27; *Judson College Bulletin* 27, No. 2 (March 1940), Catalogue No. 1940–1941, 5.

19. Amy Thompson McCandless, Interview with Clarissa Kennedy Towell and Edward E. Towell, Charleston, South Carolina, 13 July 1982.

20. Lilian A. Kibler, *The History of Converse College* (Spartanburg, SC: Converse College, 1973), 191; Ellen F. Pendleton, "Changes and Experiments in Colleges for Women," *Journal of the American Association of University Women* 24, No. 3 (April 1913): 115; Joyce Thompson, *Marking a Trail: a History of Texas Woman's University* (Denton: Texas Woman's University Press, 1982), 33–34.

21. Elizabeth Avery Colton, "Southern Colleges for Women," *Meredith College Quarterly Bulletin* 5, No. 2 (January 1912): 4–5.

22. McVea, "The Present Curricula of Colleges for Women," 244;

John P. Dyer, *Tulane: The Biography of a University, 1934–1965* (New York and London: Harper & Row, 1966), 96–97, 181.

23. Cox College Catalogue, 1922–1923, 82.

24. *Bulletin of Judson College* 8, No. 1, Catalogue No. 1920–1921, 68.

25. *Meredith College Quarterly Bulletin, 1920–1921,* 13; "College Curricula and Interests of College Women," *School and Society* 10, No. 245, 6 September 1919, 294–96.

26. Kibler, *History of Converse College,* 192.

27. J. R. McCain, "The President's Page," *The Agnes Scott Alumnae Quarterly* 13, No. 1 (November 1934): 7.

28. Elizabeth Barber Young, *A Study of the Curricula of Seven Selected Women's Colleges of the Southern States* (New York: Teachers College, Columbia University, 1932), 19.

29. "Do You Appreciate the Best in Life?" *Queen's Blues,* Queen's College student newspaper, 28 January 1921, 2.

30. Hyslup, *Virginia Colleges,* 21.

31. Kathleen White Schad, *They Call Me Kay: A Courtship in Letters,* ed. Nancy G. Anderson (Montgomery, AL: Black Belt Press, 1994), 8.

32. Amy Thompson McCandless, Interview with Carlotta Petersen Patton, College of Charleston, 23 March 1985.

33. Emilie M. McVea, "Women's Colleges and the Southern Association," *Proceedings of the Association of Colleges and Secondary Schools of the Southern States* (New Orleans, 1922), 109–10.

34. Hollins College, for example, introduced its first career-oriented course in 1952, when its curriculum underwent a major restructuring. See Frances J. Niederer, *Hollins College: An Illustrated History* (Charlottesville, VA: University Press of Virginia, 1973), 108.

35. Burke, *American Collegiate Populations,* 227; David Wilbur Peters, *The Status of the Married Woman Teacher,* Teachers College, Columbia University, Contributions to Education No. 603 (New York: Columbia University, 1934), 21.

36. Mabel Newcomer, *A Century of Higher Education for American Women* (Washington, DC: Zenger, 1959), 213; Columbia College Yearbook, 1920, Columbia College Archives; John Willig, "Class of '34 (Female) Fifteen Years Later," *New York Times Magazine,* 12 June 1946, 10.

37. Gail Apperson Kilman, "Southern Collegiate Women, Higher

299

Education at Wesleyan Female College and Randolph-Macon Woman's College, 1893–1907" (Ph.D. diss., History, University of Delaware, 1984), 150–51.

38. Ibid., 160–61.

39. Class Notes, *Meredith College Quarterly Bulletin*, Alumnae, No. 33, No. 1 (November 1939): 21–22.

40. *Meredith College Quarterly Bulletin* 21, No. 1 (November 1927): 3.

41. Kilman, "Southern Collegiate Women," 161–62.

42. Burke, *American Collegiate Populations*, 223; quoted in Bridget Smith Pieschal and Stephen Robert Pieschal, *Loyal Daughters: One Hundred Years at Mississippi University for Women, 1884–1984* (Jackson: University Press of Mississippi, 1984), 63.

43. Stephanie Shaw, *What a Woman Ought to Be and to Do: Black Professional Women Workers During the Jim Crow Era* (Chicago and London: University of Chicago Press, 1996), 175–76.

44. Ibid., 69.

45. Glenda Elizabeth Gilmore, *Gender & Jim Crow: Women and the Politics of White Supremacy in North Carolina, 1896–1920* (Chapel Hill and London: University of North Carolina Press, 1996), 161–63; Donna Hollie, "Jeanes Fund and Jeanes Teachers," *Black Women in America: An Historical Encyclopedia, vol. 1, A–L,* ed. Darlene Clark Hine et al. (Bloomington and Indianapolis: Indiana University Press, 1994), 632.

46. Anne Winn Stevens, "Mrs. Nannie Carson" (alias for Mrs. Carrie Hepler), in *American Life Histories: Manuscripts From the Federal Writers' Project, 1936–1940,* first copy, 28 December 1938 [http://lcweb2.loc.gov], 1–17; quotations from 7–8.

47. Ibid., 10–12.

48. Press release, "Enrollment Figures at GSCW Show Trend Toward Careers for Women," 13 November 1939, typescript, Georgia State Department of History and Archives.

49. Marion Vera Cuthbert, *Education and Marginality: A Study of the Negro Woman College Graduate* (New York: American Book-Stratford Press, 1942), 22, 37.

50. Florence Read, *The Story of Spelman College* (Princeton: Princeton University Press, 1961), 192–93.

51. Thomas Jesse Jones, *Negro Education: A Study of the Private and Higher Schools for Colored People in the United States*, vol. 1, Department of the Interior, Bureau of Education Bulletin, 1916, No. 38 (Washington, DC: U.S. Government Printing Office, 1917), 83; Mary Church Terrell, "Progress and Problems of Colored Women," *The Home Mission College Review* 2, No. 4 (March 1929): 43.

52. William Henry Brown, *The Education and Economic Development of the Negro in Virginia* (Charlottesville: Publications of the University of Virginia Phelps-Stokes Fellowship Papers, No. 6, 1923), 130–31.

53. Jane E. Browning and John B. Williams, "History and Goals of Black Institutions of Higher Learning," in *Black Colleges in America: Challenge, Development, Survival*, ed. Charles V. Willie and Ronald R. Edmonds (New York: Columbia University Press, 1978), 82.

54. Cornelius J. Heatwole, *A History of Education in Virginia* (New York: Macmillan, 1916), 351.

55. Henry Allen Bullock, *A History of Negro Education in the South From 1619 to the Present* (Cambridge, MA: Harvard University Press, 1967), 87.

56. Advertisement in *Crisis* 37, No. 1 (January 1930): 4.

57. Gilmore, *Gender & Jim Crow*, 141.

58. Cornelius J. Heatwole, "How Virginia Is Meeting the Emergency," in *National Education Association of the United States Proceedings*, 70th Annual Meeting, 25 June to 1 July 1932, vol. 70, 351; Joe M. Richardson, *A History of Fisk University, 1865–1946* (University, AL: University of Alabama Press, 1980), 61–67.

59. Lucy D. Slowe, "Higher Education of Negro Women," *The Journal of Negro Education* 2, No. 3 (July 1933): 352–58.

60. Buell G. Gallagher, "College Training for the Negro—to What End?" *Opportunity* 15 (September 1937): 275.

61. Bulletin of Bennett College for Women, 1928–1929, 5.

62. Bennett College Bulletin, 1940–1941, 65.

63. Catalog of Spelman College, 1940–1941, 48; Catalog of Spelman College, 1930–1931, 44–47.

64. The Hampton Normal and Agricultural Institute, Bulletin, 1920–1921, 15; Walton C. John, *Hampton Normal and Agricultural Institute:*

301

Its Evolution and Contribution to Education as a Federal Land-Grant College, Department of Interior Bureau of Education Bulletin No. 27 (Washington, DC: U.S. Government Printing Office, 1923), 80.

65. The Benedict Bulletin, 1930–1931, 52; Catalogue of Allen University 1923 and 1924, 17; Annual Catalogue of Claflin College, 1929–1930, 28; Clark University Bulletin, 1916–1917, 9; Catalogue of the State Normal and Industrial School for the Colored Race (North Carolina), 1919–1920, 18.

66. Read, *The Story of Spelman College,* 219.

67. "The Higher Training of Negroes," *The Crisis* 22, No. 3 (July 1921): 108.

68. Florence Read, "Place of the Women's College in the Pattern of Negro Education," *Opportunity* 15 (September 1937): 268.

69. Mildred Dee Moore, "A True Spelman Girl," *Spelman Messenger* (January 1927): 23; see also *Campus Mirror* 15, No. 1 (October 1938), student newspaper of Spelman College [editorial].

70. Jeanne L. Noble, *The Negro Woman's College Education* (New York: Columbia University Press, 1956), 89.

71. Ibid., 24.

72. Lucy D. Slowe, "The Colored Girl Enters College," *Opportunity* 15 (September 1937): 276.

73. Eugene D. Genovese, *Roll, Jordan, Roll: The World the Slaves Made* (New York: Pantheon Books, 1974), 212.

74. Jones, *Negro Education,* vol. 1, 7.

75. Alfonso Elder, "About Negro Education," *Phylon* 2, No. 1 (First Quarter 1941): 68, 72.

76. *The Echo of '20, Being the History of Howard University for the Year 1919–1920* (Washington, DC: Howard University, 1920).

77. Charles Johnson, *The Negro College Graduate* (Chapel Hill: University of North Carolina Press, 1938), 108; Willa B. Player, *Improving College Education for Women at Bennett College: A Report of a Type A Project* (New York and London: Garland Publishing, 1987), 9.

78. Noble, *The Negro Woman's College Education,* 51; Elizabeth L. Ihle, "Black Women's Academic Education in the South," Modules III and IV, *History of Black Women's Education in the South, 1865–Present* (Washington, DC: U.S. Department of Education, 1986), 7.

79. O. C. Carmichael, "The Place of the Woman's College in Higher Education," *Proceedings of the Association of Colleges and Secondary Schools of the Southern States* (Lexington, KY, 1929), 284. [Emphasis added.]

80. Bulletin, Georgia State College for Women, 1939–1940, 25.

81. Bulletin, Georgia State College for Women, 1929, 44.

82. Jack Temple Kirby, *Rural Worlds Lost: The American South 1920–1960* (Baton Rouge and London: Louisiana State University Press, 1989), 20–21.

83. Newcomer, *A Century of Higher Education for American Women*, 58.

84. Annual Catalogue of Limestone College, 1917–1918, 53.

85. Pieschel and Pieschel, *Loyal Daughters*, 104.

86. Thompson, *Marking a Trail*, 34, 84.

87. Ibid., 42–44.

88. Schad, *They Call Me Kay*, 39.

89. East Carolina Teachers College, Catalogue, 1930–1931, 79.

90. *A Beacon for Womanhood: The Bennett Bulletin*, 1935, pamphlet in North Carolina Collection, University of North Carolina-Chapel Hill, n.p.

91. Hyslup, *Virginia Colleges*, 19–20.

92. "Demonstration School," Catalogue of the College of Charleston, 1931–1932, 98–100; Pieschal and Pieschal, *Loyal Daughters*, 77.

93. Young, *A Study of the Curricula*, 160.

94. McVea, "Women's Colleges and the Southern Association," 113.

95. Katherine Blunt, "What Constitutes a Good College for Women," *School and Society* 32, No. 814, 2 August 1930, 138.

96. Bessie Carter Randolph, *The Centennial Celebration of Hollins College* (Hollins College, VA: Hollins College, 1949), 16–17.

97. Young, *A Study of the Curricula*, 163.

98. W. E. B. Du Bois, "The Negro College," *The Crisis* 40, No. 8 (August 1933): 175–77.

99. Neverdon-Morton, *Afro-American Women of the South and the Advancement of the Race, 1895–1925*, 12.

100. Chicora College for Women, Catalogue, 1921–1922.

101. Coker College, Catalogue, 1931–1932, 61.

102. Martha Lou Lemmon Stohlman, *The Story of Sweet Briar College* (Sweet Briar, VA: Sweet Briar College, 1956), 181.

103. Ernest McPherson Lander, *A History of South Carolina, 1865–1960* (Chapel Hill: University of North Carolina Press, 1961), 237; Helen Lefkowitz Horowitz, *Alma Mater: Design and Experience in the Women's Colleges From Their Nineteenth-Century Beginnings to the 1930s* (New York: Alfred A. Knopf, 1984), 287.

104. Lois MacDonald, "Has Education Failed the South?" *Journal of the American Association of University Women* 25, No. 2 (January 1932): 65–86; Mary Murphy, "The Awakening of Economic Consciousness in College Students, Especially Women," *School and Society* 50, No. 1304 (23 December 1939), 834.

105. Amy Thompson McCandless, Interview of Patricia Carter, College of Charleston, June 1982.

106. Shaw, *What a Woman* Ought *to Be and to Do*, 2.

3. Maintaining the Spirit and Tone of Robust Manliness

1. An earlier version of this chapter was published as "Maintaining the Spirit and Tone of Robust Manliness: The Battle Against Coeducation at Southern Colleges and Universities, 1890–1940," in *National Women's Studies Association Journal* 2, No. 2 (Spring 1990): 199–216.

2. Willystine Goodsell, "The Educational Opportunities of American Women—Theoretical and Actual," *Annals of the American Academy* 143 (May 1929): 2–3.

3. Walter B. Kolesnik, *Coeducation: Sex Differences and the Schools* (New York: Vantage Press, 1969), 92.

4. Thomas Woody, *A History of Women's Education in the United States*, vol. 2 (New York: Science Press, 1929), 252–53; W. Le Conte Stevens, *The Admission of Women to Universities* (New York: Association for Promoting the Higher Education of Women in New York, 1883), 5–15.

5. Woody, *A History of Women's Education*, vol. 2, 253.

6. *Thirty-sixth Annual Bulletin of the Mississippi State College for Women* 9, No. 1 (June 1921): 17; *Minority Report: A Liberal Arts College for Women*, Senate Document No. 4 (1930), Virginia State Archives, 15.

7. For a discussion of the relationship between Populism and women's education in South Carolina, see Francis Butler Simkins, *Pitchfork Ben Tillman, South Carolinian* (Gloucester, MA: P. Smith, 1964), 175–81.

8. Arney Childs, "Education of Women at the University of South Carolina," *The Carolina Review* (January 1947): 21.

9. Petition to the Board of Trustees, 23 June 1903. Archives, Robert Scott Small Library, College of Charleston.

10. Francis Butler Simkins, *The Tillman Movement in South Carolina* (Durham: Duke University Press, 1929), 104–05, 82.

11. Childs, "Education of Women at the University of South Carolina," 22.

12. Daniel Walker Hollis, *University of South Carolina: College to University*, vol. 2 (Columbia: University of South Carolina Press, 1956), 160–61.

13. Childs, "Education of Women at the University of South Carolina," 22.

14. Hollis, *University of South Carolina*, vol. 2, 171.

15. Ibid., 173; Childs, "Education of Women at the University of South Carolina," 23.

16. Hollis, *University of South Carolina*, vol. 2, 308; Semi-Annual Report of President Samuel Chiles Mitchell to Board of Trustees, 21 November 1912, University Archives, University of South Carolina.

17. Nell Crawford Flinn, "Co-Education From the Standpoint of a Co-Ed," *The Carolinian* 17, No. 8 (May 1905): 253–55; Faculty Minutes, 6 November 1906, University Archives, University of South Carolina.

18. Maude Moore, "History of the College for Women" (M.A. thesis, Education, University of South Carolina, 1932), 59.

19. Moore, "History of the College for Women," 62; "Committee Told Plan of Merger," *The State* (Columbia, SC), 23 January 1914, 9.

20. Minutes of the Board of Trustees, 1 December 1916, University Archives, University of South Carolina.

21. Supplementary Report to the President (William S. Currell), 10 June 1919, University Archives, University of South Carolina.

22. Hollis, *University of South Carolina*, vol. 2, 333.

23. Ibid.

24. Wright Bryan, *Clemson: An Informal History of the University, 1889–1979* (Columbia, SC: R. L. Bryan, 1979), 140, 192–95.

25. Hazel May Beacham, "Woman's Entrance Brings About Changes at State's University, Asserts Co-Ed," Raleigh *News and Observer*, no date,

clipping in Nell Battle Lewis Papers, North Carolina State Archives; Katerine Granthan, 1927, clipping in Nell Battle Lewis Papers, North Carolina State Archives; Nell Battle Lewis, "Sixty-one Women Students Are Now Seeking Higher Education at the State University," *News and Observer* (Raleigh, NC), 20 March 1921, 1.

26. "Shall Co-eds Have Dormitory Built Here? Representative Student Opinion Says 'No,' " *The Tar Heel*, University of North Carolina student newspaper, editorial, 14 March 1923, 1.

27. George A. Works, "A Recent Plan of Co-ordination," *Journal of Higher Education* 4, No. 3 (March 1933): 141–44.

28. "They Rightfully Belong," *The Tar Heel*, editorial, 8 January 1936, 1.

29. Mary Turner Lane, "The University in Transition: The Female Presence," *Carolina Alumni Review* 72, No. 1 (Fall 1984): 6.

30. Thomas G. Dyer, *The University of Georgia: A Bicentennial History, 1785–1905* (Athens: University of Georgia Press, 1985), 140–41, 170–79; Woody, *A History of Women's Education*, vol. 2, 254.

31. Dyer, *The University of Georgia*, 193–94.

32. R. H. Powell, letter to Dr. S. V. Sanford, President of University of Georgia, 26 June 1943, Coordinate College file, Georgia State Archives.

33. Ibid., 5.

34. Woody, *A History of Women's Education*, vol. 2, 254–55; Armistead C. Gordon, Rector of the University of Virginia, in *The Coordinate College at Charlottesville Affiliated With the University of Virginia: Expert Evidence of This Type of Institution and Its Need by the People of Virginia* (Richmond, 1914), 88–91.

35. *The Co-ordinate College: A Vital Matter*, reprinted from *Virginia Journal of Education* (May 1917), pamphlet in the Virginia State Library, 1–4.

36. *Facts and Conclusions Concerning the Proposed Co-ordinate College*, pamphlet in Virginia State Library, 1917, n.p.; C. C. Claxton, letter in *The Coordinate College at Charlottesville*, 13.

37. [Mrs.] Mary Munford, *Why a Co-ordinate College at Charlottesville Affiliated With the University of Virginia Rather Than a Separate College*, pamphlet in Virginia State Library, 1917, 6.

38. Woody, *A History of Women's Education*, vol. 2, 255.

39. Mary Gathright Newell, "Mary Munford and Higher Education for Women in Virginia," in *Stepping Off the Pedestal: Academic Women in the South*, ed. Patricia A. Stringer and Irene Thompson (New York: MLA of America, 1982), 33; *A Liberal Arts College for Women: Report of the Commission Appointed to Study and Report to the Legislature Upon the Advisability of Establishing a Liberal Arts College for Undergraduate Women at One of the State Teachers Colleges or Elsewhere*, submitted to the General Assembly January 1930, Senate Document No. 4 (Richmond: Division of Purchase and Printing, 1930), 8.

40. *A Liberal Arts College for Women*, Senate Document No. 4, 2–4; *Facts in Regard to Bill Admitting Women to the Graduate and Professional Courses at the University* (Richmond: Whittet and Shepperson, 1918); Duncan Lyle Kinnear, *The First 100 Years: A History of Virginia Polytechnic Institute and State University* (Blacksburg, VA: Virginia Polytechnic Institute, 1972), 263; *Adventures in Teaching: Pioneer Women Educators and Influential Teachers* (n.p.: Virginia Iota State Organization, Delta Kappa Gamma Society, 1963), 17.

41. Virginius Dabney, *Mr. Jefferson's University: A History* (Charlottesville: University Press of Virginia, 1981), 67–68, 162.

42. *A Liberal Arts College for Women*, Senate Document No. 4, 3; *Virginia Colleges: A Bulletin of Information about the State Colleges and the Colleges under Private Control in Virginia* (Richmond: State Board of Education, 1942), 8; Kinnear, *The First 100 Years*, 263–64.

43. *A Liberal Arts College for Women*, Senate Document No. 4, title page.

44. *A Liberal Arts College for Women Co-ordinate with the University of Virginia*, Report of the Commission on a Liberal Arts College for Women, submitted to the General Assembly, January 1932, 3.

45. Virginia, 1944, Acts of Assembly, Chapter 54, Section 833-d, 55.

46. Edward Alvey, *A History of Mary Washington College, 1908–1972* (Charlottesville: University of Virginia Press, 1974), 281–83.

47. Dabney, *Mr. Jefferson's University*, 369, 488.

48. Association of American Colleges, *On Campus With Women* 15, No. 4 (Spring 1986): 11.

49. Julie Young, "Coeducation 1970," *University of Virginia Alumni News* 78, No. 6 (July/August 1990): 10–15.

50. Ibid.

51. Samuel Proctor and Wright Langley, *Gator History: A Pictorial History of the University of Florida* (Gainesville, FL: South Star Publishing, 1986), 18; Martee Wills and Joan Perry Morris, *Seminole History: A Pictorial History of Florida State University* (Gainesville, FL: South Star Publishing, 1987), 38–39.

52. Wills and Morris, *Seminole History*, 41; Proctor and Langley, *Gator History*, 24.

53. Proctor and Langley, *Gator History*, 24–25; Wills and Morris, *Seminole History*, 42.

54. Wills and Morris, *Seminole History*, 45, 51.

55. Proctor and Langley, *Gator History*, 39; Wills and Morris, *Seminole History*, 52.

56. Wills and Morris, *Seminole History*, 55; Proctor and Langley, *Gator History*, 39.

57. Wills and Morris, *Seminole History*, 56–57.

58. Proctor and Langley, *Gator History*, 40, 57–58; "Coed Razzing Becomes History: Tradition Lost in Shuffle," *Alligator*, newspaper of the University of Florida, 11 February 1969.

59. Suzanne Rau Wolfe, *The University of Alabama: A Pictorial History* (University, AL: University of Alabama Press, 1983), 6, 97.

60. Ibid., 97, 103, 128, 155.

61. *Co-Etiquette* [A Handbook for Women Students Published by the Women's Student Government Association of the Alabama Polytechnic Institute], *Alabama Polytechnic Institute Bulletin* 39, No. 3 (November 1943): 5–6.

62. John Hugh Reynolds and David Yancey Thomas, *History of the University of Arkansas* (Fayetteville: University of Arkansas Press, 1910), 48, 51, 93; Harrison Hale, *University of Arkansas, 1871–1948* (Fayetteville: University of Arkansas Alumni Association, 1948), 53, 83.

63. James Riley Montgomery, Stanley J. Folmsbee, Lee Seifert Greene, *To Foster Knowledge: A History of the University of Tennessee, 1794–1970* (Knoxville: University of Tennessee Press, 1984), 148–52; *The University of Tennessee Sesqui-Centennial: A Record of 150 Years of Achievement*

of Public Education on the Higher Level—and an Analysis of Future Problems and Responsibilities (Knoxville: University of Tennessee Press, 1945), 166–67, 61.

64. Eudora Ramsay Richardson, *The Influence of Men Incurable* (Indianapolis and New York: Bobbs-Merrill, 1936), 119.

65. Thomas Chadwick, "Carolina's First Coed Braved Parental Disapproval, Faculty Hostility to Break Barriers," *The State* (Columbia, SC), 26 May 1947.

66. Ibid.

67. Beulah G. Calvo, "Co-Education," *Carolinian* 10 (October 1897): 20–21.

68. Dyer, *University of Georgia*, 170; Woody, *History of Women's Education*, vol. 2, 222.

69. "Co-education: A Report of Organization Committee in the Minutes of the Board of Trustees, May 7, 1919," University Archives, University of South Carolina, Columbia; Karen Petit, "Coeducation: Women Gained Their Place," in *Carolina Heritage: A Pictorial History of the University of South Carolina* (Columbia, SC: Garnet and Black Yearbook/Magazine Network Staff, 1976), 23.

70. From author interviews with thirty-five alumnae who graduated between 1922 and 1940 from the municipal College of Charleston, which became coeducational in 1918.

71. Helen Lefkowitz Horowitz, *Campus Life: Undergraduate Cultures From the End of the Eighteenth Century to the Present* (New York: Alfred A. Knopf, 1987), 68, 202.

72. Lynn D. Gordon, *Gender and Higher Education in the Progressive Era* (New Haven and London: Yale University Press, 1990), 70–72.

73. Barbara Miller Solomon, *In the Company of Educated Women: A History of Women and Higher Education in America* (New Haven and London: Yale University Press, 1985), 58–61.

74. Sally Schwager, " 'Harvard Women': A History of the Founding of Radcliffe College" (Ph.D. diss., Education Department, Harvard University, Cambridge, MA, 1982), 370.

75. Letter of Charles B. Curtis to Grenville Clark, 11 June 1931, "1931 Signing of Diploma Affair," Series 4, File 21, Radcliffe College Records, Radcliffe College Documents (1878–1942).

309

76. Letter of Lida Shaw King, 12 October 1913, in *The Co-ordinate College at Charlottesville Affiliated With the University of Virginia*, 29; letter of Laura Drake Gill, April 1911, in *The Coordinate College at Charlottesville Affiliated With the University of Virginia*, 59.

77. Solomon, *In the Company of Educated Women*, 59; David O. Levine, *The American College and the Culture of Aspiration 1915–40* (Ithaca and London: Cornell University Press, 1986), 124.

78. Woody, *A History of Women's Education*, vol. 2, 282, 256; Solomon, *In the Company of Educated Women*, 50.

79. Karen Petit, "USC's First Dean of Women Looks Back," in *Carolina Heritage*, 26–27.

80. *Facts and Conclusions Concerning the Proposed Co-ordinate College the* [sic] *Women*, pamphlet in the Virginia State Library (1914?), 1; Dyer, *The University of Georgia*, 172; Edwin Alderman, *The Present State of Higher Education in Virginia*, an address delivered before the Virginia Educational Conference at Norfolk, 25 November 1925, pamphlet in the Virginia State Archives, 3.

81. Pat McNeely, "Student Respects Business Rights," *The State* (Columbia, SC), 28 June 1963.

82. Kristin S. Caplice, "The Case for Public Single-Sex Education," *Harvard Journal of Law & Public Policy* 18, No. 1 (Fall 1994): 268.

83. Ibid., 241.

84. *Mississippi University for Women et al. v. Hogan*, 458 U.S. 718 (1982), 718–21.

85. Ibid., 721–22.

86. Ibid., 722–29.

87. Ibid., 745–46.

88. Kit Lively, "Discrimination or Compensation?" *Chronicle of Higher Education*, 12 October 1994.

89. Ibid.

90. Linda L. Meggett, "Citadel Pans TWU Plan to Admit Men," *Post & Courier* (Charleston, SC), 15 December 1994.

91. "Virginia Files Lawsuit on V.M.I. Admissions," *New York Times*, 6 February 1990.

92. Ibid.; Linda Greenhouse, "Supreme Court Roundup," *New York Times*, 25 May 1991; "A Legal Lesson for V.M.I.," *New York Times*, 14 Oc-

tober 1992; "V.M.I.'s Unacceptable Remedy," *New York Times*, 1 October 1993.

93. "Judge Endorses V.M.I. Plan on Excluding Women," *New York Times*, 2 May 1994.

94. "VMI's Mary Baldwin Plan Approved by Federal Judge," *Post & Courier* (Charleston, SC), 1 May 1994.

95. "V.M.I.'s Unacceptable Remedy."

96. "VMI's Mary Baldwin Plan Approved by Federal Judge."

97. George Hackett and Mark Miller, "Manning the Barricades," *Newsweek*, 26 March 1990, 20.

98. Ronald Smothers, "In a Coed Age, the Citadel Stands Fast," *New York Times*, 15 March 1991.

99. Herb Frazier, "Women Sue to Attend The Citadel," *Post & Courier* (Charleston, SC), 12 June 1992; Susan Faludi, "The Naked Citadel," *New Yorker*, 5 September 1994, 62, 69; "After Suit, Citadel Extends a Barrier, to Males," *New York Times*, 6 September 1992.

100. Faludi, "The Naked Citadel," 75.

101. *Shannon Richey Faulkner et al. v. James E. Jones, Jr., et al.*, Civil Action No. 2: 93-488-2, U.S. District Court for the District of South Carolina Charleston Division, 22 July 1994, 2–3.

102. "U.S. Court Orders The Citadel to Allow Woman in Classes," *New York Times*, 13 August 1993; "Citadel to Appeal Ruling Enrolling Woman," *New York Times*, 18 August 1993; Andrew Bergstrom, "Public Forum Sheds Light on Faulkner vs. Citadel Case," *Cougar Pause* (student newspaper of the College of Charleston), 7 October 1993; "Military College Is Ordered to Admit Women," *New York Times*, 18 November 1993.

103. "Citadel Hunts Options in Faulkner case," *Post & Courier* (Charleston, SC), 10 March 1994; "Faulkner, Citadel Go to Court," *Post & Courier* (Charleston, SC), 16 May 1994; *Faulkner vs. Jones* (1994), 16–17.

104. *Faulkner v. Jones* (1994), 4–5.

105. Claudia Smith Brinson, "Wait Year If Faulkner Admitted, Citadel Asks," *The State* (Columbia, SC), 28 June 1994.

106. *Faulkner v. Jones* (1994), 42.

107. Ibid., 18, 28–31, 38–40.

108. Pat Wingert, "Oh, to Be a Knob," *Newsweek*, 22 August 1994,

22; Linda L. Meggett, "Faulkner's Out—Again," *Post & Courier* (Charleston, SC), 13 August 1994; Faludi, "Naked Citadel," 75; Linda L. Meggett, "Faulkner to Receive NAACP Award," *Post & Courier* (Charleston, SC), 18 September 1994.

109. "Citadel Files Appeal in Faulkner Case," *Post & Courier* (Charleston, SC), 20 September 1994; "Plan to Remain a Male School," *New York Times*, 7 October 1994; Linda L. Meggett, "Citadel Training Plan Questioned," *Post & Courier* (Charleston, SC), 8 October 1994.

110. Linda L. Meggett, "Girl With Citadel Ties Wants in Corps," *Post & Courier* (Charleston, SC), 1 September 1995.

111. Caplice, "The Case for Public Single-Sex Education," 233, 262, 273.

112. Beth Willinger, "Single Gender Education and the Constitution," *Loyola Law Review* (New Orleans) 40 (Summer 1994): 258; Sara L. Mandelbaum, in Willinger, "Single Gender Education and the Constitution," 270.

113. *United States, Petitioner v. Virginia et al.* and *Virginia, et al., Petitioners v. United States*, 116 S. CT. 2264, 26 June 1996, 28, 23, 80.

114. Sybil Fix, "Citadel Drops Gender Rule," *Post & Courier* (Charleston, SC), 29 June 1996.

115. Sybil Fix, "Women at The Citadel: What Went Wrong?" *Post & Courier* (Charleston, SC), 9 March 1997; Peter Applebome, "Citadel's President Insists Coeducation Will Succeed," *New York Times*, 14 January 1997.

116. "24 Women Accepted at Citadel for Fall," *New York Times*, 31 January 1997.

117. Adam Nissiter, "Woman Who Left the Citadel Tells of Brutal Hazing Ordeal," *New York Times*, 18 February 1997.

118. "The Citadel's Culture of Abuse," *New York Times*, 14 January 1997.

119. "Citadel Offers Detailed Plan for Women," *New York Times*, 23 May 1997; Sybil Fix, "School Sets New Tone for Corps of Cadets," *Post & Courier* (Charleston, SC), 24 August 1997.

120. "V.M.I. Board Won't Rush Coeducation," *New York Times*, 15 July 1996.

121. Mike Allen, "Defiant V.M.I. to Admit Women, But Will Not

Ease Rules for Them," *New York Times*, 22 September 1996; First Quarterly Report, United States District Court for the Western District of Virginia Roanoke Division, United States of America, *Plaintiff, v. Commonwealth of Virginia, et al., Defendants*, C.A. No. 90-0126-R, December 1996; "VMI Files First Report on Assimilation of Women," [http://www.vmi.edu/PR/release1.htm].

313

122. "Assimilation Plan," Status Report 8, 19 June 1997 [http://www.vmi.edu/PR/plan8.htm]; "VMI Coeducation Recrutiment Initiatives: VMI Hires Female Admissions Officer," [http://www.vmi.edu/PR/coed.htm].

123. Sybil Fix, "Alumnus Battles Change," *Post & Courier* (Charleston, SC), 13 November 1997; Sybil Fix, "Alumni Get in Step With Citadel," *Post & Courier*, 15 November 1997.

124. Sybil Fix, "SMI: Southern, Military and Politically Incorrect," *Post & Courier* (Charleston, SC), 2 September 1997.

125. Larry Evans, "School Might as Well Offer a Major in Secession Science," *The Free Lance-Star* (Fredericksburg, VA), 23 August 1997; "Paranoia the New National Pastime," Opinion, *The Philadelphia Daily News*, 22 August 1997; Cody Ann Michaels, "Cody's Column: Where the Boys Are," [http://www.gts.net/cody/where__the__boys.html].

126. Sybil Fix, "Citadel's Change to Coed Unlikely to Be Traumatic," *Post & Courier* (Charleston, SC), 30 June 1996.

127. Judith R. Shapiro, "What Women Can Teach Men," *New York Times*, 23 November 1994.

4. Peerless Standards of Unsullied Honor

1. An earlier version of this chapter was published as "Preserving the Pedestal: Restrictions on Social Life at Southern Colleges for Women, 1920–1940," in *History of Higher Education Annual* 7 (1987): 45–67.

2. Paula S. Fass, *The Damned and the Beautiful: American Youth in the 1920s* (New York: Oxford University Press, 1977), 47, 54.

3. Ibid., 375.

4. George B. Tindall, "The South and the Savage Ideal," in *The Emergence of the New South 1913–1946* (Baton Rouge: Louisiana State University Press, 1967), 184–218.

5. Anne Firor Scott, *The Southern Lady: From Pedestal to Politics, 1830–1930* (Chicago: University of Chicago Press, 1970), 166, 180.

6. Catherine Clinton, "Equally Their Due: The Education of the Planter Daughter in the Early Republic," *Journal of the Early Republic* 2 (April 1982): 59.

7. Anne Firor Scott, *Making the Invisible Woman Visible* (Urbana and Chicago: University of Illinois Press, 1984), 223.

8. Clinton, "Equally Their Due," 59.

9. Scott, *The Southern Lady*, 228, 226; Catherine Clinton, *The Plantation Mistress: Woman's World in the Old South* (New York: Pantheon Books, 1982), chapters 11 and 12.

10. Patricia A. Stringer and Irene Thompson, eds., *Stepping Off the Pedestal: Academic Women in the South* (New York: Modern Language Association of America, 1982), 2.

11. Deborah Gray White, "Jezebel and Mammy: The Mythology of Female Slavery," in *Ar'n't I a Woman? Female Slaves in the Plantation South* (New York and London: W. W. Norton, 1985), 27–61; see also Paula Giddings, *When and Where I Enter: The Impact of Black Women on Race and Sex in America* (New York: Bantam Books, 1984), 85.

12. Scott, *The Southern Lady*, 7; Fass, *The Damned and the Beautiful*, 137; Tindall, *The Emergence of the New South*, 196.

13. Helen Lefkowitz Horowitz, *Alma Mater: Design and Experience in the Women's Colleges From Their Nineteenth Century Beginnings to the 1930s* (New York: Alfred A. Knopf, 1984), 39.

14. Barbara Solomon, *In the Company of Educated Women* (New Haven and London: Yale University Press, 1985), 101; Fass, *The Damned and the Beautiful*, 332, 294, 196.

15. Elaine Kendall, *"Peculiar Institutions": An Informal History of the Seven Sister Colleges* (New York: G. P. Putnam's Sons, 1976), 171–73.

16. Horowitz, *Alma Mater*, 287; Martha Lou Lemmon Stohlman, *The Story of Sweet Briar College* (Sweet Briar, VA: Alumnae Association of Sweet Briar College, 1956), 140.

17. Robert Simpson, *Coker College: The Diamond Jubilee History* (1983), pamphlet in the South Caroliniana Library, University of South Carolina, 18.

18. Lilian A. Kibler, *The History of Converse College* (Spartanburg, SC: Converse College, 1973), 229; Mary Baldwin College Catalog, 1930–1931, 26; Wesleyan College Catalog for 1919–1920, 85.

19. Asheville Normal and Associated Schools, Catalog 1925–1926, 15; Chicora College for Women, Catalog, 1921–1922, 51; Columbia College, Catalog, 1919–1920, 52; Bulletin, Georgia State College for Women 25, No. 9 (May 1940): 46; Frances J. Niederer, *Hollins College: An Illustrated History* (Charlottesville: University of Virginia Press, 1973), 60; Simpson, *Coker College*, 18; Kibler, *The History of Converse College*, 229; Cox College Bulletin, 1922–1923, 31; North Carolina College for Women, Catalog 1920–1921, 160; Queens College Bulletin, Catalog Number 1919, 69–70; Louise Manly, *The History of Judson College* (Atlanta: n.p., ca. 1913), 117.

20. *Co-Etiquette* [A Handbook for Women Students Published by the Women's Student Government Association of the Alabama Polytechnic Institute] 39, No. 3 (November 1943): 20, 22, 25, 29; *Co-Etiquette* 40, No. 12 (August 1945): 22; Chester M. Morgan, *Dearly Bought, Deeply Treasured: The University of Southern Mississippi* (Jackson and London: University Press of Mississippi, 1987), 24.

21. Amy Thompson McCandless, Interview of Pierrine Smith Byrd, Greenwood, South Carolina, July 1982.

22. W. E. B. Du Bois, *The Education of Black People: Ten Critiques 1906–1960*, ed. Herbert Aptheker (Amherst: University of Massachusetts Press, 1973), 41; Joe M. Richardson, *A History of Fisk University, 1865–1946* (University, AL: University of Alabama Press, 1980), 85–88; *H: The Students' Handbook*, Howard University 1936–1937 (Washington, DC: Howard University, 1936), 38; Florence Read, *The Story of Spelman College* (Princeton, NJ: Princeton University Press, 1961), 219.

23. Annual Catalog of Benedict College, 1920–1921, 13; Howard University Bulletin, 1940–1941, 69; *Howard University Student Manual: Regulations and Requirements of the Academic Faculty for the Information of Teachers and Students* (Washington, DC: Howard University, 1929), 21–28.

24. Amy Thompson McCandless, Interview of Marlene Linton O'Bryant Seabrook, College of Charleston, 31 May 1996.

25. Linda L. Meggett, "S.C. State Allows Co-ed Visits," *Post & Courier* (Charleston, SC), 29 January 1996.

26. Stephanie Shaw, *What a Woman* Ought *to Be and to Do: Black Professional Women Workers During the Jim Crow Era* (Chicago and London: University of Chicago Press, 1996), 83, 14.

27. *Conversationalist*, 1940, yearbook of Judson College, 126.

28. Horowitz, *Alma Mater*, 289.

29. Janette Anne Cox Mishoe, "Winthrop in Uniform 1895–1955" (M.A. thesis, Winthrop College, 1970), 18.

30. Stohlman, *The Story of Sweet Briar College*, 174; Roberta D. Cornelius, *The History of Randolph-Macon Woman's College* (Chapel Hill: University of North Carolina Press, 1951), 241; Richardson, *History of Fisk University*, 107.

31. Kibler, *The History of Converse College*, 297–98; Mississippi State College for Women, Student Government Handbook, 1937–1938, 27; Martee Wills and Joan Perry Morris, *Seminole History: A Pictorial History of Florida State University* (Jacksonville, FL: South Star Publishing, 1987), 50–51.

32. Stohlman, *The Story of Sweet Briar College*, 90–91, 118.

33. Wills and Morris, *Seminole History*, 48; Cornelius, *The History of Randolph-Macon Woman's College*, 241; Kibler, *The History of Converse College*, 298.

34. Mildred Morse McEwen, *Queens College Yesterday and Today* (Charlotte, NC: Queens College Alumnae Association, 1980), 246.

35. Questionnaire response, Class of 1938, Wesleyan College. In the spring of 1983 the author wrote to the alumnae offices of women's colleges in Virginia, North Carolina, South Carolina, and Georgia, requesting permission to administer a questionnaire to graduates celebrating their fiftieth, forty-fifth, fortieth, and thirty-fifth reunions. Five institutions—Hollins, Queens, Salem, Sweet Briar, and Wesleyan—agreed to participate in the survey. In May the questionnaire was mailed to 500 women chosen randomly from the classes of 1923, 1928, 1933, and 1938. Two hundred four usable responses were received. Although some respondents signed their names, most questionnaires are identifiable only by institution and years of attendance.

36. Janet Mayo, "The Authority to Govern and the Right to Dance on Campus at Centenary College," *Journal of North Louisiana Historical Association* 9, No. 4 (1978): 205, 307, 210, 212.

37. Kathleen White Schad, *They Call Me Kay: A Courtship in Letters* (Montgomery, AL: Black Belt Press, 1994), 211–12, 255.

38. Clarence A. Bacote, *The Story of Atlanta University: A Century of Service, 1865–1965* (Atlanta: Atlanta University, 1969), 251; Richardson, *History of Fisk University*, 84–85.

39. Fass, *The Damned and the Beautiful*, 300; Solomon, *In the Company of Educated Women*, 101.

40. Kibler, *The History of Converse College*, 227.

41. Cornelius, *The History of Randolph-Macon Woman's College*, 241; Winthrop College Catalog, 1939–1940, 83; Georgia State College for Women Bulletin 14, No. 1 (January 1929): 176; Chicora College for Women Catalog, 1922–1923, 52.

42. Questionnaire response: Class of 1928, Wesleyan College; Class of 1933, Salem College; Class of 1928, Queens College.

43. Fass, *The Damned and the Beautiful*, 317.

44. Simpson, *Coker College*, 19.

45. Questionnaire response: Class of 1938, Hollins College.

46. *Co-Etiquette* [W.S.G.A. Handbook of Rules and Regulations For Women Students, 1963–1964] (Auburn: Women's Student Government Association, 1963), 26, 28.

47. Editors of *Fortune*, "Youth in College," in *American Points of View 1936*, ed. William H. Cordell and Kathryn Coe Cordell (New York: Doubleday, Doran, 1937), 299.

48. Asheville Normal and Associated Schools, Catalog 1925–1926, 17; Winthrop College Catalog, 1930–1940, 85; Georgia State College for Women Bulletin 14, No. 1 (January 1929): 176; Bulletin of Georgia State Teachers College 17, No. 1 (March 1929): 16.

49. The Fifty-sixth Annual Bulletin of Mississippi State College for Women, Register 1940–1941, vol. 56, No. 2 (May 1941): 185–86.

50. Coker College Catalog, 1932–1933, 36.

51. Cox College Bulletin, 1922–1923, 32; Catalog of Columbia College, 1919–1920, 47; Hollins College Catalog, 1920–1921, 65.

52. Questionnaire response: Class of 1933, Wesleyan College.

53. Clark University Bulletin, 1922–1923 and 1923–1924, 17; Morris Brown University Bulletin, 1923–1924, 30; Annual Catalog of Claflin College, 1929–1930, 26.

54. Bulletin of Bennett College for Women, 1933–1934, 83; Annual Circular of Spelman Seminary for Women and Girls, 1920–1921, 31.

55. Coker College Catalog, 1921–1922, 31–32; Hollins College Catalog, 1920–1921, 64; Agnes Scott College Bulletin, Catalog 1940–1941, 17.

56. Gilman M. Ostrander, "The Revolution in Morals," in *The Twenties: The Critical Issues*, ed. Joan Hoff Wilson (Boston: Little, Brown, 1972), 128–39; and George E. Mowry, *The Twenties: Fords, Flappers, and Fanatics* (Englewood Cliffs, NJ: Prentice-Hall, 1963), 173.

57. Kendall, *"Peculiar Institutions,"* 175–79.

58. Randolph-Macon Woman's College, Catalog, 1920–1921, 19.

59. C. J. Hyslup, *Virginia Colleges* [A Bulletin of Information for Prospective College Students to Assist Boys and Girls in Answering Many of the Questions Regarding Virginia Colleges and Their Entrance Requirements] (Richmond: State Board of Education, 1935), pamphlet in the Virginia State Library, 21.

60. Catalog of Columbia College, 1919–1920, 46; Queens College Bulletin, Catalog No. 1919, 67; Cox College Bulletin, 1922–1923, 23; Bulletin of Flora Macdonald College 1940–1941, 22.

61. McEwen, *Queens College Yesterday and Today*, 122.

62. Schad, *They Call Me Kay*, 212, 21, 41, 14.

63. Beverly Guy-Sheftall and Jo Moore Stewart, *Spelman: A Centennial Celebration, 1881–1981* (Charlotte, NC: Delmar, 1981), 48.

64. See Clarence Stephen Marsh, ed., *American Universities and Colleges* (Washington, DC: American Council on Education, 1940), for a breakdown on religious affiliations of American schools; Georgia State Woman's College, Announcements and Course Offerings, 1939–1940, 15; Morgan, *Dearly Bought, Deeply Treasured*, 25; Winthrop College Catalog, 1920–1921, 106.

65. Judson College Bulletin, Catalog Number 1940–1941, 67; Randolph-Macon Woman's College, Catalog, 1920–1921, 19.

66. Wesleyan College Catalog for 1919–1920, 14; Bulletin of Judson College, Catalog Number 1930–1931, 25; Queens College Bulletin, Catalog Number 1919, 11; Chicora College for Women Bulletin, Catalog 1921–1922, 47; Columbia College Catalog 1924–1925, 24–25.

67. Morgan, *Dearly Bought, Deeply Treasured*, 23.

68. "Winthrop Girls Get Good Fare," *Winthrop Weekly News* 7, No. 17, 9 January 1920.

69. Schad, *They Call Me Kay*, 8, 91, 15, 420.

70. *Co-Etiquette*, 1943, 2; Student Government Handbook for Mississippi State College for Women, 1920–1921, 16.

71. *Life at Converse*, Bulletin of Converse College 51, No. 3 (July 1940), pamphlet in South Caroliniana Library, University of South Carolina, n.p.; *Salem Academy and College*, brochure, ca. 1914, in Mary Jeffreys Rogers Collection, North Carolina State Archives.

72. Howard University Bulletin, 1920–1921, 37; Catalog of Livingstone College, 1925–1926, 9.

73. Judson College Bulletin, Catalog Number 1940–1941, Vol. 27, No. 2 (March 1940): 67; Catalog of Columbia College, 1930–1931, 2.

74. Bulletin of Limestone College 2, No. 1 (February 1932): 112.

75. Fass, *The Damned and the Beautiful*, 145.

76. Catalog of Columbia College, 1930–1931, 5; "Investiture," *Silhouette*, Agnes Scott College Annual, 1921, n.p.

77. Amy Thompson McCandless, Interview with Anne Leigh Hawkes, Charleston, South Carolina, 2 August 1996.

78. *MEH LADY* [The Senior Class of 1923 presents the Year Book of M.S.C.W.], vol. 14, Mississippi State College for Women, 210.

79. Schad, *They Call Me Kay*, 9, 16–17, 19, 422, 142, 549.

80. Ibid., 451, 183, 492.

81. Joyce Thompson, *Marking A Trail: A History of Texas Woman's University* (Denton, TX: Texas Woman's University Press, 1982), 36, 52; Bridget Smith Pieschel and Stephen Robert Pieschel, *Loyal Daughters: One Hundred Years at Mississippi University for Women, 1884–1984* (Jackson: University Press of Mississippi, 1984), 78; *The Comet* [1922 yearbook of the College of Charleston], n.p.

82. Annadell Craig Lamb, *The History of PHI MU: The First 130 Years* (Atlanta: Phi Mu Fraternity, 1982), 1, 32–33, 223, 273.

83. For the history of AKA, see Marjorie H. Parker, *Alpha Kappa Alpha through the Years, 1908–1988* (Chicago: The Mobium Press, 1990); for Delta, see Paula Giddings, *In Search of Sisterhood: Delta Sigma Theta and the Challenge of the Black Sorority Movement* (New York: William Morrison, 1988); for Sigma, see Pearl Schwartz White, *Behind These Doors—a Legacy:*

The History of Sigma Gamma Rho Sorority (Chicago: Sigma Gamma Rho Sorority, 1974) and *The Legacy Continues: The History of Sigma Gamma Rho Sorority, 1974–1994*, vol. 2 (Chicago: Sigma Gamma Rho Sorority, 1994); for Zeta, see Ola Adams, *Zeta Phi Beta Sorority, 1920–1965* (Washington, DC: Zeta Phi Beta Sorority, 1965).

84. Parker, *Alpha Kappa Alpha Through the Years*, 118–20, 162.

85. Giddings, *In Search of Sisterhood*, 323.

86. Calvin B. Lee, *The Campus Scene, 1900–1970: Changing Styles in Undergraduate Life* (New York: David McKay, 1970), 4–5; Wright Bryan, *Clemson: An Informal History of the University, 1889–1979* (Columbia, SC: R. L. Bryan, 1979), 189.

87. Lamb, *The History of PHI MU*, 180.

88. Mary Wilson Gee, *Yes, Ma'am, Miss Gee* (Charlotte, NC: Heritage House, 1957), 167; Stohlman, *The Story of Sweet Briar College*, 122; Niederer, *Hollins College*, 85.

89. Richardson, *History of Fisk University*, 88; Read, *The Story of Spelman College*, 250.

90. Richardson, *History of Fisk University*, 88; Morgan, *Dearly Bought, Deeply Treasured*, 82.

91. Lamb, *The History of PHI MU*, 65.

92. Giddings, *In Search of Sisterhood*, 18.

93. Charlayne Hunter-Gault, *In My Place* (New York: Farrar Straus Giroux, 1992), 148.

94. Giddings, *In Search of Sisterhood*, 151, 153.

95. Ibid., 44, 81, 16; Hunter-Gault, *In My Place*, 147–49; Lamb, *The History of PHI MU*, 184.

96. Parker, *Alpha Kappa Alpha Through the Years*, 183–93; *Alpha Kappa Alpha Sorority, Inc.: Service With a Global Perspective*, Programmatic Thrust, July 1986 (Chicago: AKA Sorority, 1986), 1; Lamb, *The History of PHI MU*, 185–201.

97. Giddings, *In Search of Sisterhood*, 324.

98. Amy Thompson McCandless, Interview of Patricia Carter, College of Charleston, June 1982.

99. Amy Thompson McCandless, Interview of Esther Finger Addlestone, Sumter, South Carolina, June 1982.

100. Generally speaking, women's colleges were the first to institute

student governments. See Mabel Newcomer, *A Century of Higher Education for American Women* (Washington, DC: Zenger, 1959), 243.

101. Cornelius, *The History of Randolph-Macon Woman's College*, Bulletin of Limestone College 2, No. 1 (February 1932): 108; Kibler, *The History of Converse College*, 220.

102. Simpson, *Coker College*, 7.

103. Cox College Bulletin, 1922–1923, 23; Chicora College for Women Catalog, 1922–1923, 105; Mary Baldwin College Catalog, 1930–1931, 22; Hyslup, *Virginia Colleges*, 21; Agnes Scott College Bulletin, Catalog 1940–1941, 125.

104. The Thirty-sixth Annual Bulletin of Mississippi State College for Women, 1921, 97.

105. *Co-Etiquette*, 1943, 51, 15.

106. Morgan, *Dearly Bought, Deeply Treasured*, 28.

107. Catalog of Columbia College, 1930–1931, 30.

108. W. Carson Ryan, Jr., "What Do We Know About Women's College Athletics?" *Journal of the American Association of University Women* 23, No. 4 (June 1930): 180.

109. Linda Gage Roth, "Are Sports HARMFUL to Women?" *Forum* 81 (May 1929): 315.

110. Margaret M. Duncan and Velda P. Cundiff, *Play Days for Girls and Women* (New York: A. S. Barnes, 1929), v.

111. *Daily Tar Heel*, University of North Carolina student newspaper, 24 November 1934 and 23 November 1934.

112. "Athletics," Bulletin of Flora Macdonald College (April 1925): 5; *The Edelweiss*, 1930 yearbook of Queens College, 156; *Campus Mirror*, student newspaper of Spelman College, May–June 1938, 18.

113. *Conversationalist*, 1940 yearbook of Judson College, 138.

114. *Queens Blues*, student newspaper of Queens College, 20 January 1934; *Campus Mirror*, student newspaper of Spelman College, 15 May 1931; Oliver K. Cornwell and Jesse F. Williams, Survey Report on Health and Physical Education, University of Georgia, 1943, typescript, Georgia State Department of Archives and History, Record Group 33, Subgroup 1, Series 51; Mary Baldwin College Catalog, 1930–1931, 89; *Garnet and Black*, 1930 yearbook of the University of South Carolina, 237.

115. Stohlman, *The Story of Sweet Briar College*, 140–41.

321

116. Questionnaire response: Class of 1938, Salem College; Class of 1928, Wesleyan College; Class of 1938, Hollins College.

117. Questionnaire response: Class of 1933, Wesleyan College; Niederer, *Hollins College*, 60.

118. Richardson, *History of Fisk University*, 84–104.

119. Ibid., 108.

120. Ibid., 90.

121. Ibid., 98–99.

122. Edward Alvey, *A History of Mary Washington College, 1908–1972* (Charlottesville: University of Virginia Press, 1974), 185–87.

123. Alvey, *A History of Mary Washington College*, 186–87.

124. Anne Firor Scott, "After Suffrage: Southern Women in the Twenties," *Journal of Southern History* 80 (August 1964): 302.

125. Questionnaire response: Class of 1928, Wesleyan College; Class of 1933, Salem College.

126. Questionnaire response: Class of 1933 and Class of 1938, Wesleyan College.

127. David O. Levine, *The American College and the Culture of Aspiration, 1915–1940* (Ithaca and London: Cornell University Press, 1986), 123, 114.

128. Estelle Freedman, "The New Woman: Changing Views of Women in the 1920s," *The Journal of American History* 61 (September 1974): 393.

129. Solomon, *In the Company of Educated Women*, 92, 165; Newcomer, *A Century of Higher Education*, 107.

130. Persis Cope, "The Women of 'Who's Who': A Statistical Study," *Social Forces* 7 (December 1928): 216–17.

131. Time, Inc., *The U.S. College Graduate* (New York: Time, 1941), 13, 16.

132. See Solomon, *In the Company of Educated Women*, 119, for statistics that led to the public concerns of the 1890s.

133. "Economic Status of University Women," *Monthly Labor Review* (February 1940): 346.

134. William H. Chafe, *The American Woman: Her Changing Social, Economic, and Political Roles, 1920–1970* (New York: Oxford University

Press, 1972), 107; Marion Cuthbert, "Problems Facing Negro Young Women," *Opportunity* (February 2, 1936), 48.

135. For a feminist criticism of orthodox Freudianism, see Dee Garrison, "Karen Horney and Feminism," *Signs: Journal of Women in Culture and Society* 6 (Summer 1981): 672–91.

136. Sandra Gilbert, "Soldier's Heart: Literary Men, Literary Women, and the Great War," *Signs: Journal of Women in Culture and Society* 8 (Spring 1983): 422–50.

137. John Shelton Reed, "The Same Old Stand?" in *Why the South Will Survive by Fifteen Southerners* (Athens: University of Georgia Press, 1981), 18.

138. Geoffrey Perrett, *America in the Twenties: A History* (New York: Simon and Schuster, 1982), 243.

139. Perrett, *America in the Twenties*, 73, 84–88.

140. Robert Bone, "The Negro Renaissance," in *The Twenties: The Critical Issues*, 121, 126.

141. Tindall, *Emergence of the New South*, 560–61.

142. Ostrander, "The Revolution in Morals," 130.

143. Wills and Morris, *Seminole History*, 47.

144. James Weinstein, "Radicalism in the Midst of Normalcy," in *The Twenties: The Critical Issues*, 26; Reed, "The Same Old Stand?" 25.

145. Tindall, *Emergence of the New South*, 599, 493, 618.

146. William R. Taylor, *Cavalier and Yankee: The Old South and American National Character* (New York: G. Braziller, 1961), 146.

147. Scott, *Making the Invisible Woman Visible*, 301.

148. "To the Alumnae of St. Mary's School," 1 June 1936, Nell Battle Lewis Papers, North Carolina State Archives.

149. Of the 204 women surveyed in 1983, 143 (70 percent) made comments of this nature.

150. Questionnaire response: Class of 1938, Hollins College.

151. Shirley Abbott, *Womenfolks: Growing Up Down South* (New Haven: Ticknor & Fields, 1983), 167.

152. Shaw, *What a Woman Ought to Be and to Do*, 2, 10.

153. Solomon, *In the Company of Educated Women*, 100; Fass, *The Damned and the Beautiful*, 180.

154. Solomon, *In the Company of Educated Women*, 162; Fass, *The Damned and the Beautiful*, 180.

5. Tomorrow and Yesterday

1. National Emergency Council, *Report on Economic Conditions in the South* (Washington, DC: U.S. Government Printing Office, 1938), 1.

2. David Goldfield, *Promised Land: The South since 1945* (Arlington Heights, IL: Harland Davidson, 1987), 4–7.

3. Ibid., 50.

4. George B. Tindall, *The Emergence of the New South, 1913–1945* (Baton Rouge: Louisiana State University Press, 1967), 561.

5. "Higher Education for Negroes," *School Life* 24, No. 2 (November 1938): 42; Joe M. Richardson, *A History of Fisk University, 1865–1946* (University, AL: University of Alabama Press, 1980), 79; Clarence A. Bacote, *The Story of Atlanta University: A Century of Service, 1865–1965* (Atlanta: Atlanta University Press, 1969), 258, 266; Henry Allen Bullock, *A History of Negro Education in the South from 1619 to the Present* (Cambridge, MA: Harvard University Press, 1967), 142.

6. Bacote, *The Story of Atlanta University*, 266–67.

7. *Facing Facts: The American Missionary Association*, Report for the academic year 1934–1935 (New York: American Missionary Association, 1935), 44–46.

8. Jackson Davis, "The Outlook for the Professional and Higher Education of Negroes," *The Journal of Negro Education* 2, No. 4 (October 1933): 406; D. O. W. Holmes, "The Negro College Faces the Depression," *The Journal of Negro Education* 2, No. 1 (January 1933): 24.

9. "Educational Mergers and Consolidations," *The Journal of Negro Education* 1, Nos. 3 and 4 (October 1932): 445.

10. Charles H. Thompson, "The Socio-Economic Status of Negro College Students," *The Journal of Negro Education* 2, No. 1 (January 1933): 34.

11. Holmes, "The Negro College Faces the Depression," 20.

12. Thompson, "The Socio-Economic Status of Negro College Students," 34.

13. "To College—in Spite of Handicaps," *Spelman Messenger* 57, No. 1 (November 1940): 5–6.

14. *The Eighty-sixth Annual Report of the American Missionary Association*, Report for the academic year 1931–1932 (New York: American Missionary Association, 1933), 29; *Eighty-seventh Year: The American Missionary Association*, Report for the academic year 1932–1933 (New York: American Missionary Association, 1933), 41; *Ninety Years After: The American Missionary Association*, Report for the academic year 1935–1936 (New York: American Missionary Association, 1936), 32.

15. "Current Events of Importance in Negro Education: The Effect of the Depression Upon Educational Activities Among Negroes," *The Journal of Negro Education* 2, No. 1 (January 1933): 106, 97.

16. Rena Chambers Harrell, "Our Mother and Our Queen: A History of Queens College," typescript, Archives, Queens College Library, 71–73.

17. Alfred Sandlin Reid, *Furman University: Toward a New Identity 1925–1975* (Durham, NC: Duke University Press, 1976), 53–57.

18. Malcolm M. Willey, *Depression, Recovery and Higher Education*, A Report by Committee Y of the American Association of University Professors (New York and London: McGraw-Hill, 1937), 335; Hugh Talmage Lefler and Albert Ray Newsome, *North Carolina: The History of a Southern State* (Chapel Hill: University of North Carolina Press, 1953), 555.

19. Ron Chepesiuk, *Winthrop College: A Centennial Celebration* (Rock Hill, SC: Winthrop College, 1985), 57–59; Report of the Board of Trustees of Winthrop College, South Carolina College for Women to the General Assembly, 1 July 1934–30 June 1935 (Columbia: Joint Committee on Printing, General Assembly of South Carolina, 1935), 8–12; Report of President Shelton Phelps to the Board of Trustees, 26 October 1934, Archives and Special Collections Department, Dacus Library, Winthrop University, W402-6.

20. "The Schools *vs.* the Depression: A Brief," *The Alumnae News* (Woman's College of North Carolina), 21, No. 3 (February 1933): 9.

21. Bridget Smith Pieschel and Stephen Robert Pieschel, *Loyal Daughters: One Hundred Years at Mississippi University for Women, 1884–1984* (Jackson: University Press of Mississippi, 1984), 92.

22. Ibid., 94; Chester M. Morgan, *Dearly Bought, Deeply Treasured: The University of Southern Mississippi, 1912–1987* (Jackson and London: University Press of Mississippi, 1987), 53.

23. Martee Wills and Joan Perry Morris, *Seminole History: A Pictorial History of Florida State University* (Jacksonville, FL: South Star Publishing, 1987), 49–50.

24. Joyce Thompson, *Marking a Trail: A History of Texas Woman's University* (Denton, TX: Texas Woman's University Press, 1982), 77–78.

25. Minutes, Board of Trustees, Queens-Chicora College, Charlotte, SC, 17 November 1931, Archives, Queens College Library, 3.

26. Lilian A. Kibler, *The History of Converse College* (Spartanburg, SC: Converse College, 1973), 279.

27. "College Board Reduces Rate," newspaper clipping, file C72, 1932/33, Columbia College [South Carolina] Archives.

28. Walter Carroll Taylor, *History of Limestone College* (Gaffney, SC: Limestone College, 1937), 88.

29. "The Admission of Men Students," *Alumnae News* (Woman's College of North Carolina), 21, No. 2 (November 1932): 14.

30. A. Monroe Stowe, "Enrollment of American Colleges for Women in Years of Depression," *School and Society* 36, No. 940 (31 December 1932), 863–64.

31. *State Agricultural and Mechanical College Extension Work Bulletin*, 38th Annual Report for Year Ending 30 June 1934, vol. 224, No. 1 (January 1935): 9.

32. Chepesiuk, *Winthrop College*, 59; Daniel W. Hollis, "A Brief History of the University," in *Remembering the Days: An Illustrated History of the University of South Carolina* (Columbia: Institute for Southern Studies, University of South Carolina, 1982), xxvi; Kibler, *The History of Converse College*, 292.

33. Fred J. Kelly, "How Education Is Faring," *The American Journal of Sociology* 40 (May 1933): 820; Clarence Stephen Marsh, ed., *American Universities and Colleges* (Washington, DC: American Council on Education, 1940), 469.

34. Suzanne Rau Wolfe, *The University of Alabama: A Pictorial History* (University, AL: University of Alabama Press, 1983), 171; Archibald Henderson, *The Campus of the First State University* (Chapel Hill: Univer-

sity of North Carolina Press, 1949), 288–90; Thompson, *Marking a Trail*, 79.

35. *Eighty-seventh Year, The American Missionary Association*, 43.

36. *Facing Facts: The American Missionary Society*, 60; Richardson, *History of Fisk University*, 127.

37. *Facing the Facts: The American Missionary Society*, 62; Richardson, *History of Fisk University*, 126; *Ninety Years After: The American Missionary Society*, 34.

38. Ambrose Caliver, "Problems of Vocational Guidance of Negroes," *School Life* 24, No. 10 (July 1939): 307–08.

39. Report and Recommendations of the Commission to Study Public Schools and Colleges for Colored People in North Carolina, Authorized by the General Assembly in Resolution No. 28, 10 March 1937 (Raleigh, NC: State Capitol, 1938), 41; Leon Eubanks, "Negro Education in the Deep South," *School and Society* 53, No. 1362 (1 February 1941), 152–53.

40. Lois MacDonald, "Has Education Failed the South?" *The Journal of the American Association of University Women* 25, No. 2 (January 1932): 67.

41. Kathryn McHale, "Education for Women," *The Journal of Higher Education* 6, No. 9 (December 1935): 459–69; Eunice Fuller Barnard, "Girl Graduate, 1936," *Independent Woman* (July 1936): 222.

42. Chase Going Woodhouse, "The Status of Women," *The American Journal of Sociology* 35 (May 1930): 1092.

43. Agnes Riedmann, "Margaret Jarman Hagood," *Women in Sociology: A Bio-Bibliographical Sourcebook*, ed. Mary Jo Deegan (Westport, CT: Greenwood Press, 1991), 157–63.

44. Margaret Jarman Hagood, *Mothers of the South: Portraiture of the White Tenant Farm Woman*, with introduction by Anne Firor Scott (Charlottesville and London: University Press of Virginia, 1996; first published, 1939), 4.

45. Ibid., 68–69.

46. Ibid., 150, 153.

47. Ethel Deal, "Henrietta Pendleton," *American Life Histories: Manuscripts From the Federal Writers' Project, 1936–1940*, [http://lcweb2.loc.gov], 3–4; Geneva Tonsill, "I Managed to Carry On," *American Life*

Histories, 2; Barbara Berry Darsey, "Mary Taylor," *American Life Histories*, 5; Paul [Diggs?], "Charles and Lucinda Robinson," *American Life Histories*, 3.

48. Geneva Tonsill, "Unable to Stage a Comeback," *American Life Histories: Manuscripts From the Federal Writers' Project, 1936–1940*, [http://lcweb2.loc.gov], 8; Geneva Tonsill, "I Managed to Carry On," *American Life Histories*, 5–6; Muriel A. Mann, "Mrs. Martin, Public Health Nurse," *American Life Histories*, 8.

49. Frances J. Niederer, *Hollins College: An Illustrated History* (Charlottesville, VA: University Press of Virginia, 1973), 121; *Ninety Years After: The American Missionary Association*, 30; Jane E. Smith Browning and John B. Williams, "History and Goals of Black Institutions of Higher Learning," in *Black Colleges in American: Challenge, Development, Survival*, ed. Charles V. Villie and Ronald R. Edmonds (New York: Columbia University Press, 1978), 85.

50. Martin Duberman, *Black Mountain: An Exploration in Community* (New York: E. P. Dutton, 1972), 49, 78, 92.

51. Alzada Comstock, "The College Girl: 1933 Model," *Current History*, 181–83.

52. Quoted in Paul Giddings, *In Search of Sisterhood: Delta Sigma Theta and the Challenge of the Black Sorority Movement* (New York: William Morrow, 1988), 143.

53. Giddings, *In Search of Sisterhood*, 128, 150, 182; Annadell Craig Lamb, *The History of PHI MU: The First 130 Years* (Atlanta: Phi Mu Fraternity, 1982), 60; Marjorie H. Parker, *Alpha Kappa Alpha Through the Years 1908–1988* (Chicago: Mobium Press, 1990), 183–93.

54. Stephanie Shaw, *What a Woman Ought to Be and to Do: Black Professional Women Workers During the Jim Crow Era* (Chicago and London: University of Chicago Press, 1996), 191–201.

55. Tindall, *The Emergence of the New South*, 498–99; "The Brightest and the Best," *Alumni News* (University of North Carolina–Greensboro) 63, No. 4 (Summer 1975): 4.

56. Tindall, *The Emergence of the New South*, 561.

57. Ibid., 562–63.

58. Raymond Walters, "Recent Trends in Collegiate Enrollment," *School and Society* 50, No. 1289 (9 September 1939): 329–30.

59. Martin D. Jenkins, "Enrollment in Institutions of Higher Education for Negroes, 1940–1941," *The Journal of Negro Education* (1941): 722–23.

60. John B. Boles, ed., *Dixie Dateline: A Journalistic Portrait of the Contemporary South* (Houston: Rice University Studies, 1983), 17; see also Charles Reagan Wilson, "History and Manners," *Encyclopedia of Southern Culture,* ed. Charles Reagan Wilson and William Ferris (Chapel Hill and London: University of North Carolina Press, 1989), 592.

61. William H. Chafe, *The Paradox of Change: American Women in the Twentieth Century* (New York and Oxford: Oxford University Press, 1991), 172.

62. Minutes, Meeting of South Carolina Association of Colleges, 30 November 1940, Association of SC Colleges (11 MSS [t], 2), South Caroliniana Library, University of South Carolina.

63. *Higher Education and National Defense,* Bulletin No. 22 (Washington, DC: American Council on Education, 1942), F23.

64. Giddings, *In Search of Sisterhood,* 197.

65. Niederer, *Hollins College,* 122; Pieschel and Pieschel, *Loyal Daughters,* 104; Reid, *Furman University,* 117; Wills and Morris, *Seminole History,* 54; Richardson, *History of Fisk University,* 133.

66. Wolfe, *The University of Alabama,* 176.

67. Wills and Morris, *Seminole History,* 55; Richardson, *History of Fisk University,* 133–34; Thompson, *Marking a Trail,* 105.

68. Thompson, *Marking a Trail,* 103–04.

69. Ibid., 104–05.

70. Ibid., 106–09.

71. Ibid., 104–19.

72. Reid, *Furman University,* 114, 117; *Co-Etiquette: A Handbook for Women Students* (published by the Women's Student Government Association of the Alabama Polytechnic Institute) 39, No. 3 (November 1943): 9.

73. Hollis, "A Brief History of the University," xxvi; Enrollment of Colleges in Georgia, typescript, Georgia Department of Archives and History, Record Group No. 33, Sub Group No. 1, Series 36; Morgan, *Dearly Bought, Deeply Treasured,* 73; Tommy Thompson, *Auburn: A University Portrait* (Louisville, KY: Harmony House, 1988), 109; Pieschel and Pieschel, *Loyal Daughters,* 105.

329

74. Barbara Solomon, *In the Company of Educated Women* (New Haven and London: Yale University Press, 1985), 190.

75. Quoted in Lamb, *The History of PHI MU*, 61; Thomas Crowson, *The Winthrop Story, 1886–1960* (Baltimore: Gateway Press, 1987), 20–26.

76. Sara M. Evans, *Born for Liberty: A History of Women in America* (New York: The Free Press, 1989), 219, 225.

77. Niederer, *Hollins College*, 108.

78. Diane Puthoff Brandstadter, "Developing the Coordinate College for Women at Duke University: The Career of Alice Mary Baldwin, 1924–1947" (Ph.D. diss., History, Duke University, 1977), 136–37.

79. Morgan, *Dearly Bought, Deeply Treasured*, 74; Wolfe, *The University of Alabama*, 176; Reid, *Furman University*, 115–19.

80. John Littlepage Lancaster, "College Enrollment in Virginia," typescript (Charlottesville, VA: Bureau of Population and Economic Research, University of Virginia, May 1947), 29.

81. "Educate a Woman," *Alumnae News* (Woman's College of North Carolina) 31, No. 2 (November 1942): 2.

82. Goldfield, *Promised Land*, 40; Rayford W. Logan, *What the Negro Wants* (Chapel Hill: University of North Carolina Press, 1944).

83. David D. Jones, "The War and the Higher Education of Negro Women," *The Journal of Negro Education* 11, No. 3 (July 1942): 329–37.

84. Nora R. Tucker and Thomasina W. Norford, "Ten Years of Progress: The Negro Women in the Labor Force," in *Women United: Souvenir Year Book, Sixteenth Anniversary* (National Council of Negro Women), 41; Susan M. Hartmann, *The Home Front and Beyond: American Women in the 1940s* (Boston: Twayne Publishers, 1982), 105.

85. Kathleen White Schad, *They Call Me Kay: A Courtship in Letters*, ed. Nancy G. Anderson (Montgomery, AL: Black Belt Press, 1994), x–xii.

86. Ibid., 17, 22, 31.

87. Ibid., 39, 435, 407.

88. Ibid., 12, 23–24.

89. Ibid., 211, 212.

90. Ibid., 212, 213, 221–22.

91. Ibid., 267–68.

92. Ibid., 322, 325.

93. Ibid., 327, 344.

94. Ibid., 108–09, 429, 431.

95. Ibid., 78, 81.

96. Ibid., 200, 13, 368.

97. Ibid., 184, 283, 435, 431.

98. Ibid., 511, 557.

99. Ibid., 485.

100. Ibid., 417–18, 442, 567, 601.

101. Hartmann, *The Home Front*, 106–08; Sherna Berger Gluck, *Rosie the Riveter Revisited: Women, the War, and Social Change* (New York: New American Library, 1987), 17.

102. "Institutions of Higher Education—1949 Fall Enrollment of Total, First-Time Students, and Veterans, by Sex, by States and Other Areas" (No. 151) and "Institutions of Higher Education—Fall Enrollment, by Type of Institution: 1947, 1948, 1949" (No. 150), in *Statistical Abstracts of the United States* (Washington, DC: U.S. Department of Commerce, 1950), 125, 124.

103. Morgan, *Dearly Bought, Deeply Treasured*, 79.

104. Reid, *Furman University*, 126.

105. Jerold J. Savory, *Columbia College: The Ariail Era* (Columbia: R. L. Bryan, 1979), 137.

106. Wills and Morris, *Seminole History*, 55–56; Samuel Proctor and Wright Langley, *Gator History* (Gainesville, FL: South Star Publishing, 1986), 39.

107. *Public Higher Education in South Carolina: A Survey Report* (Nashville, TN: Division of Surveys and Field Services, George Peabody College for Teachers, 1946), 164.

108. "Institutions of Higher Education—1949" (No. 151), in *Statistical Abstracts of the United States* (1950), 125.

109. Solomon, *In the Company of Educated Women*, 191.

110. Tindall, *The Emergence of the New South*, 565–67.

111. Logan, *What the Negro Wants*, 7.

112. Goldfield, *Promised Land*, 42–43.

113. Quoted in ibid., 57.

114. Tindall, *The Emergence of the New South*, 731.

6. The Voices of the Future

1. Educator Clark Kerr labeled the period from 1960 to 1980 the "second great transformation" in American higher education. In these two decades the educational system became overwhelmingly public, increasingly dominated by professional schools, and heavily reliant on federal assistance. American campuses also witnessed the "largest series of student revolts in American history" as students fought for civil rights, protested against the war in Vietnam, and argued for social and sexual equality. See Clark Kerr, *The Great Transformation in Higher Education, 1960–1980* (Albany: State University of New York, 1991), xii–xiii.

2. Amy Thompson McCandless, Interview of Joan Gladden Mack, College of Charleston, 20 May 1996.

3. Arnold Shankman, "A Jury of Her Peers: The South Carolina Woman and Her Campaign for Jury Service," *South Carolina Historical Magazine* 81, No. 2 (April 1980): 119, 102.

4. Walter B. Edgar, *South Carolina in the Modern Age* (Columbia: University of South Carolina Press, 1992), 99.

5. Quoted in Charlayne Hunter-Gault, *In My Place* (New York: Farrar Straus Giroux, 1992), 141.

6. Hunter-Gault, *In My Place*, 144.

7. "Results of the 1954 Alumnae Questionnaire," Part II, *Alumnae News* (Woman's College of North Carolina) 44, No. 4 (July 1956): 17; "Results of the 1954 Alumnae Questionnaire," Part I, *Alumnae News* 44, No. 3 (April 1956): 12.

8. Hunter-Gault, *In My Place*, 148.

9. Laurence R. Marcus and Benjamin D. Stickney, *Race and Education: The Unending Controversy* (Springfield, IL: Charles C Thomas, Publisher, 1981), 289; A. Freeman Butts and Lawrence A. Cremin, *A History of Education in American Culture* (New York: Holt, Rinehart and Winston, 1953), 520–21.

10. William H. Robinson, "Desegregation in Higher Education in the South," *School and Society* 88, No. 2174 (7 May 1960): 238.

11. Chester C. Travelstead, "Turmoil in the Deep South," *School and Society* 83, No. 2984 (28 April 1956): 146.

12. E. Thomas Crowson, *The Winthrop Story, 1886–1960* (Baltimore: Gateway Press, 1967), 487.

13. Katharine DuPre Lumpkin, *The Making of a Southerner* (Athens: University of Georgia Press, 1992; 1st ed., 1946), 235; Jacqueline Dowd Hall, panel on "Gendering Historiography," Tenth Berkshire Conference on the History of Women, 8 June 1996.

14. Samuel Proctor and Wright Langley, *Gator History: A Pictorial History of the University of Florida* (Gainesville, FL: South Star Publishing, 1986), 47; Martee Wills and Joan Perry Morris, *Seminole History: A Pictorial History of Florida State University* (Jacksonville, FL: South Star Publishing, 1987), 64.

15. Bridget Smith Pieschel and Stephen Robert Pieschel, *Loyal Daughters: One Hundred Years at Mississippi University for Women, 1884–1984* (Jackson, MS: University Press of Mississippi, 1984), 107.

16. "Winthrop Student Body Quits National Group," *The State* (Columbia, SC), 11 August 1960.

17. Suzanne Rau Wolfe, *The University of Alabama: A Pictorial History* (University, AL: University of Alabama Press, 1983), 200–01; Russell H. Barrett, *Integration at Ole Miss* (Chicago: Quadrangle Books, 1965), 215.

18. James Riley Montgomery, Stanley J. Folmsbee, and Lee Seifert Greene, *To Foster Knowledge: A History of The University of Tennessee 1794–1970* (Knoxville: University of Tennessee Press, 1984), 74, 88, 101, 199, 228–29, 268.

19. Joe B. Frantz, *Forty-Acre Follies* (Austin: Texas Monthly Press, 1983), 199, 204, 213.

20. Ibid., 207–08.

21. Constance Curry, *Silver Rights* (Chapel Hill, NC: Algonquin Books, 1995), 21.

22. Questionnaire response: South Carolina State College, Class of 1955. The survey was mailed by the author to 100 graduates of the classes of 1955, 1960, 1965, and 1970 in July 1989. Alumnae were asked to describe the relationship between the college and the town and the feeling of administrators of the college to student concerns.

23. For a discussion of the relationship between pedestal ideology

333

and campus activities, see Amy Thompson McCandless, "Preserving the Pedestal: Restrictions on Social Life at Southern Colleges for Women, 1920–1940," *History of Higher Education Annual* 7, 1987, 467.

24. Proctor and Langley, *Gator History*, 47; Henry Hampton and Steve Fayer with Sarah Flynn, *Voices of Freedom: An Oral History of the Civil Rights Movement From the 1950s through the 1980s* (New York: Bantam Books, 1990), 430.

25. Amy Thompson McCandless, Interview of Marlene Linton O'Bryant Seabrook, College of Charleston, 31 May 1996.

26. *Co-etiquette* [W.S.G.A. Handbook of Rules and Regulations for Women Students, 1963–1964] (Auburn: Women's Student Government Association, 1963), 15–43.

27. *AWS Coetiquette*, 1968–1969 (Auburn: Auburn Women Student's Association, 1968), 21.

28. Joanne Smart Drane, "The Way It Was . . . ," *Alumni News* (University of North Carolina–Greensboro), 68, No. 3 (Spring 1980): 9.

29. Ernie Suggs, "Fighting to Survive: Single-Sex Option" [www.herald-sun.com/hbcu/docs/single__sex.html].

30. Thomas Dyer, *The University of Georgia: A Bicentennial History, 1785–1985* (Athens: University of Georgia Press, 1985), 329, 334; Proctor and Langley, *Gator History*, 47–48; "From the Past: A Brief History of the South Carolina Student Council on Human Relations," 17 February 1968, typed manuscript, Student Council File, 1966–1967, South Caroliniana Library, University of South Carolina; Wolfe, *The University of Alabama*, 185, 200.

31. Wolfe, *The University of Alabama*, 200–03.

32. Ibid., 212–13.

33. Proctor and Langley, *Gator History*, 47–49.

34. Dyer, *The University of Georgia*, 311, 323–30.

35. Ibid., 331–34.

36. Drane, "The Way It Was . . . ," 10.

37. Ibid., 11.

38. Ibid., 30.

39. Form letter: Henri Monteith to Prospective Students, 13 December 1965, South Carolina Council on Human Relations, Student

Council File, 1965, South Caroliniana Library, University of South Carolina.

40. Newsletter: Southern Project, U.S. National Student Association, April 1960, Files on Civil Disorders and Civil Rights, South Caroliniana Library, University of South Carolina.

41. David W. MacDougall, "Reflections on Charleston's Sit-in at Kress," *News and Courier* (Charleston, SC), 1 April 1990; Merrill Proudfoot, *Diary of a Sit-in* (Chapel Hill: University of North Carolina Press, 1962), 104; Hampton and Fayer, *Voices of Freedom*, 55.

42. Anne Moody, *Coming of Age in Mississippi* (New York: Dial Press, 1968), 236–39.

43. Anne Braden, "A Second Open Letter to Southern White Women," *Southern Exposure* 4, No. 4 (1976): 51.

44. Paula Giddings, *When and Where I Enter: The Impact of Black Women on Race and Sex in America* (New York: Bantam Books, 1984), 278–79.

45. Mrs. Elizabeth Ledeen to Mrs. Elizabeth McWhorter, 27 March 1961, South Carolina Council on Human Relations, Student Council File, 1961, South Caroliniana Library, University of South Carolina.

46. History: South Carolina Council on Human Relations, Student Council File, 1965, South Caroliniana Library, University of South Carolina.

47. Mrs. Alice N. Spearman, Executive Director, to Miss Mary Ann Eaddy, Benedict College, 14 October 1964, South Carolina Council on Human Relations, Student Council File, 1964, South Caroliniana Library, University of South Carolina.

48. "From the Past: A Brief History of the South Carolina Student Council on Human Relations."

49. Interview with Dr. Marianna Davis, in *Women Leaders in South Carolina: An Oral History*, ed. Ronald J. Chepesiuk, Ann Y. Evans, and Thomas S. Morgan (Rock Hill, SC: Winthrop College Archives and Special Collections, 1984), 73.

50. Carol Mueller, "Ella Baker and the Origins of 'Participatory Democracy,'" in *Women in the Civil Rights Movement: Trailblazers and Torchbearers, 1941–1965*, ed. Vicki L. Crawford, Jacqueline Anne Rouse, and

335

Barbara Woods (New York: Carlson Publishing, 1990), 51–70; Charles Payne, "Two Shining Lights: Septima Clark and Ella Baker," Public Lecture, College of Charleston, 20 March 1996.

51. Moody, *Coming of Age in Mississippi*, 244.

52. Howard Zinn, "Reflections of a White Professor at Spelman College in the 1950s," *The Journal of Blacks in Higher Education* 7 (Spring 1995): 98–99; Elizabeth L. Ilhe, "Black Women's Academic Education in the South," Modules III and IV, *History of Black Women's Education in the South, 1865–Present* (Washington, DC: U.S. Department of Education, 1986), 9.

53. Questionnaire response: Sweet Briar College, Class of 1961.

54. Ann Dearsley-Vernon, "A White at the Woolworth Sit-in," *Alumni News* (University of North Carolina–Greensboro) 58, No. 3 (Spring 1980): 7–8.

55. Sara Evans, "Women's Consciousness and the Southern Black Movement," *Southern Exposure* 4, No. 4 (1976): 11.

56. Sara Evans, *Personal Politics: The Roots of Women's Liberation in the Civil Rights Movement and the New Left* (New York: Alfred A. Knopf, 1979), 29.

57. Interview with Mary Edith Bentley Abu-Saba, Class of 1961, in *Portraits R-MWC Graduates*, college brochure, n.p.

58. Curry, *Silver Rights*, 22.

59. Lumpkin, *The Making of a Southerner*, 238.

60. Interview with Alice Spearman Wright, in *Women Leaders in South Carolina*, 44.

61. Hunter-Gault, *In My Place*, 193, 201.

62. "SC Baptist Students Vote in Favor of Integration," *News and Courier* (Charleston, SC), 3 December 1961; Tom McMahan, "SC Baptist Students Ask Study of De-Segregation," *Record* (Columbia, SC), 6 December 1961; Proudfoot, *Diary of a Sit-in*, ix.

63. Hunter-Gault, *In My Place*, 199, 195.

64. Evans, *Personal Politics*, 33; History: South Carolina Council on Human Relations, Student Council File, 1965, South Caroliniana Library, University of South Carolina; Frantz, *Forty-Acre Follies*, 208.

65. Douglas Mauldin, "No Trouble Seen Over Negro Girl," *The Greenville News*, 12 July 1963; George McMillan, "Integration with Dig-

nity: The Inside Story of How South Carolina Kept the Peace," *Saturday Evening Post* (16 March 1963): 16–20.

66. John F. Potts, *A History of South Carolina State College* (Columbia: R. L. Bryan, 1978), 122, 146.

67. Questionnaire response: Class of 1964, South Carolina State College; Jack Bass and Paul Clancy, "The Militant Mood in Negro Colleges," *The Reporter* 38, No. 10 (16 May 1968): 21.

68. Lewis K. McMillan, *Negro Higher Education in the State of South Carolina* (Orangeburg, SC: n.p., 1952), 200, 81.

69. Jack Bass and Jack Nelson, *The Orangeburg Massacre*, 2d ed. (Macon, GA: Mercer University Press, 1984), 5; Edna Smith, chairman of S.C. Student Council on Human Relations, "Support for a Cause," flyer in Student Council File, n.d., South Carolina Council on Human Relations, South Caroliniana Library, University of South Carolina; Potts, *A History of South Carolina State College*, 112.

70. Edna Smith, "Support for a Cause."

71. Bass and Nelson, *The Orangeburg Massacre*, 6–7.

72. Ibid., 45, 76.

73. Ibid., 187–88.

74. Hampton and Fayer, *Voices of Freedom*, 429–35.

75. Ibid., 444–47.

76. Braden, "A Second Open Letter to Southern White Women," 51; Evans, *Personal Politics*, 25.

77. Papers of President Thomas F. Jones, Accession 331, Box 2, Student Unrest 1969–1971, University Archives, University of South Carolina; Partial Timeline of Women's Studies at USC [*sic*], Department of Women's Studies, University of South Carolina, typescript, ca. 1987.

78. *Garnet and Black*, yearbook of the University of South Carolina, 1970, 472, 474, 37.

79. Papers of Thomas F. Jones, Accession 331, Box 2, Student Unrest 1969–1971, University Archives, University of South Carolina; Chuck Keefer, "Students Protest U.S. Offensive," *The Gamecock* (newspaper of the University of South Carolina), 12 February 1971; Charles Fellenbaum, "SMC to demonstrate to close Washington," *The Gamecock*, 28 April 1971.

80. Papers of Thomas F. Jones, Accession 331, Box 2, Student Unrest 1969–1971, University Archives, University of South Carolina.

81. Almetris Marsh Duren and Louise Iscoe, *Overcoming: A History of Black Integration at the University of Texas at Austin* (Austin: The University of Texas at Austin Press, 1979), 25; *Garnet and Black*, yearbook of the University of South Carolina, 1970; Wolfe, *The University of Alabama*, 225; Dyer, *The University of Georgia*, 349.

82. "The Months of May," a special report included in the summer of 1970 issue of the *University of South Carolina Magazine*, prepared by the Alumni Association—Educational Fund, Caroliniana Library, University of South Carolina.

83. Amy Thompson McCandless, Interview of Victoria L. Eslinger (B.A., 1969, University of South Carolina, and J.D., 1973, University of South Carolina), Columbia, SC, 16 September 1989.

84. Wills and Morris, *Seminole History*, 70; Robert J. Blanton, *The Story of Voorhees College From 1897 to 1982* (New York: Exposition Press, 1983), 186.

85. Papers of President Thomas F. Jones, Student Unrest 1969–1971, Accession 331, Box 2, University Archives, University of South Carolina; Ginny Carroll, "Board Unanimously Endorses Dr. Jones," *The State* (Columbia, SC), 8 July 1970.

86. William C. Friday, "President Friday Speaks Firmly on University Policy," *Alumni News* (University of North Carolina at Greensboro), 58, No. 4 (Summer 1970): 3.

87. Sam P. Wiggins, *Higher Education in the South* (Berkeley, CA: McCutchan Publishing, 1966), 110, 112, 113.

88. *Bonhomie*, yearbook of Furman University, 1970, 72; *1970 Newberrian*, yearbook of Newberry College, 1970, 185; Joseph C. Ellers, *Getting to Know Clemson University Is Quite an Education: Determination Makes the Dream Come True* (Clemson, SC: Clemson University Press, 1987), 124; Wolfe, *The University of Alabama*, 225; Calvin B. T. Lee, *The Campus Scene, 1900–1970: Changing Styles in Undergraduate Life* (New York: David McKay, 1970), 139.

89. Pieschel and Pieschel, *Loyal Daughters*, 194.

90. *Calciid*, yearbook of Limestone College, Gaffney, SC: Limestone College, 1970, 197.

91. Amy Thompson McCandless, Interview of Hope Morris Florence, College of Charleston, 9 October 1997.

92. Amy Thompson McCandless, Interview of Rita Joanne Williams Livingston, College of Charleston, 7 October 1997.

93. Irving Louis Horowitz and William H. Friedland, *The Knowledge Factory: Student Power and Academic Politics in America* (Chicago: Aldine Publishing, 1970), 189.

94. Bass and Nelson, *The Orangeburg Massacre*, 6–7.

95. Lee, *The Campus Scene*, 149; mimeographed handout, Voorhees College, file on Civil Disorders and Civil Rights, South Caroliniana Library, University of South Carolina.

96. Alice Echols, *Daring to Be Bad: Radical Feminism in America 1967–1975* (Minneapolis: University of Minnesota Press, 1989), 32; Giddings, *When and Where I Enter,* 302.

97. Cynthia Washington, "We Started From Different Ends of the Spectrum," *Southern Exposure* 4, No. 4 (1976): 14.

98. Chester M. Morgan, *Dearly Bought, Deeply Treasured: The University of Southern Mississippi, 1912–1987* (Jackson and London: University Press of Mississippi, 1989), 129; Mildred Morse McEwen, *Queens College Yesterday and Today* (Charlotte, NC: Queens College Alumnae Association, 1980), 176; Dyer, *The University of Georgia,* 347–48.

99. "The Months of May," background, in *University of South Carolina Magazine (summer 1970).*

100. *Garnet and Black*, yearbook of the University of South Carolina, 1970, 22–25, 38–39, 230–33.

101. Ibid., 46–49.

102. *Bonhomie*, yearbook of Furman University, 1970, 20.

103. Dyer, *The University of Georgia,* 351–52; Alfred Sandlin Reid, *Furman University: Toward a New Identity, 1925–1975* (Durham, NC: Duke University Press, 1976), 249.

104. Pieschel and Pieschel, *Loyal Daughters,* 136–38; Joyce Thompson, *Marking a Trail: A History of the Texas Woman's University* (Denton, TX: Texas Woman's University Press, 1982), 190; Montgomery et al., *To Foster Knowledge,* 288; Michael D. Richards, "The Spring of Seventy at Sweet Briar," *Sweet Briar College Alumnae Magazine* 59, No. 3 (Spring 1986): 15; *Columbian*, yearbook of Columbia College, 1971; *The Feminine Approach: A.W.S. Handbook for Women Students* (Auburn: Auburn Women Students Association, 1970).

105. Wills and Morris, *Seminole History*, 165.

106. "After 151 Years, Dance Ban Ends at Baylor," *New York Times*, 19 April 1996.

107. Reid, *Furman University*, 230–31; *Arrow 70*, yearbook of Erskine College, 1970, 21, 77; see also volumes of *Vintage*, yearbook of Bob Jones University.

108. Raymond Wolters, *Right Turn: William Bradford Reynolds, the Reagan Administration, and Black Civil Rights* (New Brunswick, NJ: Transaction Publishers, 1996), 468–81.

109. Proctor and Langley, *Gator History*, 53–54; Reid, *Furman University*, 247; Duren and Iscoe, *Overcoming*, 24; Pieschel and Pieschel, *Loyal Daughters*, 136; Wolfe, *The University of Alabama*, 213.

110. Wolfe, *The University of Alabama*, 227; Wills and Morris, *Seminole History*, 74; McEwen, *Queens College*, 172; "Celebrating 40 Years of Coeducation at the University of Florida," flyer (chronology in UF.40), University Archives, University Libraries, University of Florida.

111. Frances J. Niederer, *Hollins College: An Illustrated History* (Charlottesville, VA: University Press of Virginia, 1973), 182.

112. Thompson, *Marking a Trail*, 192–97.

113. "UF Women Demand More Services, Rights," *St. Pete Times*, 16 May 1970; "The Status of Women at the University of Florida," typescript, University Archives, University Libraries, University of Florida, 3; "Celebrating 40 Years of Coeducation at the University of Florida" (chronology in UF.40).

114. Susan M. Hartmann, *From Margin to Mainstream: American Women and Politics Since 1960* (New York: Alfred A. Knopf, 1989), 109–10.

115. *Naiad*, yearbook of Lander College, 1970; *Tiger*, yearbook of Voorhees College, 1970.

116. Harold Warren, "Gladys Avery Tillett, Pioneer Suffragist, Political Activist, Dies," *Charlotte Observer*, 23 September 1984.

117. McCandless, Interview of Victoria L. Eslinger.

118. Ibid.

119. Paula S. Fass, *Outside In: Minorities and the Transformation of American Education* (New York and Oxford: Oxford University Press, 1989), 157, 165.

120. Morgan, *Dearly Bought, Deeply Treasured*, 131; Wills and Morris, *Seminole History*, 69.

121. Morgan, *Dearly Bought, Deeply Treasured*, 131; Wills and Morris, *Seminole History*, 69; Questionnaire responses: classes of 1955, 1960, 1965, and 1970, University of South Carolina.

122. Questionnaire responses: classes of 1955, 1960, 1965, and 1970, University of South Carolina.

123. *The Bulldog*, yearbook of South Carolina State College, 1970, 6; U.S. President's Commission on Campus Unrest, Campus Report (Washington, DC: U.S. Government Printing Office, 1970), 445.

124. Joel Rosenthal, "Southern Black Student Activism: Assimilation vs. Nationalism," *The Journal of Negro Education* 44, No. 2 (Spring 1975): 129.

125. Amy Thompson McCandless, Interview of Susan Farrell, College of Charleston, 23 September 1997.

126. Gloria Barboza, Interview of Shirley Abbott Tomkievicz, Class of 1956, in "Changes Seen in TWU Students," *The Daily Lass-O* (student newspaper of Texas Woman's University), 1 May 1973.

7. A Double Focus

1. Sharon Wertz, "Miss McCarty's Gift Keeps on Giving, A Year Later," news from the University of Southern Mississippi.

2. "Miss McCarty Goes to Washington," news from the University of Southern Mississippi [http://www.pr.usm.edu/oolawash.htm].

3. Wertz, "Miss McCarty's Gift Keeps on Giving."

4. "Book Shares McCarty's 'Simple Wisdom' " [http.//www.pr.usm.edu/oolabook.htm]; Rick Bragg, "She Opened World to Others; Her World Has Opened, Too," *New York Times*, 12 November 1996.

5. Maxie Dunnam, "Oseola McCarty: Something Beautiful" [http://www.ats.wilmore.ky.us/apr15.html].

6. Quoted in Bragg, "She Opened World to Others."

7. Wertz, "Miss McCarty's Gift Keeps on Giving, A Year Later."

8. "Our Changing Region: Southerners Who Are Making a Difference," *Southern Living* 25, No. 6 (June 1990): 47, 83.

9. C. E. Bishop, project director, *The State of the South: A Report to the Region and Its Leadership* (Chapel Hill, NC: MDC, April 1996), 2.

10. U.S. Bureau of the Census, *Current Population Reports*, Series P-25, No. 1111, Population Projections for States by Age, Sex, Race and Hispanic Origin: 1993 to 2020 (Washington, DC: U.S. Government Printing Office, 1994).

11. Bishop, *The State of the South*, 2, 13, 53.

12. "Books Matter: College-educated Blacks Now Earn 92 Percent of the Income of White College Graduates," *Journal of Blacks in Higher Education* 5 (Autumn 1994): 12–13.

13. Center for Education Statistics, *Statistical Abstract of the United States*, 1960 (Washington, DC: U.S. Department of Commerce, 1960); Joseph L. Marks, *SREB Fact Book on Higher Education 1994/1995* (Atlanta: Southern Regional Education Board, 1994/1995), 64–66; "Higher Education Gains by Black Women Are Across the Board," *The Journal of Blacks in Higher Education* 6 (Winter 1994/95): 49.

14. "Spelman's Increasing Selectivity Bucks the Trend for Women's Colleges," *The Journal of Blacks in Higher Education* 6 (Winter 1994/95): 40.

15. "Westhampton College" [www.richmond.edu/Student-Affairs/wcollege/wcollege.htm].

16. Marks, *SREB Fact Book on Higher Education 1994/1995*, 44, 46, 54.

17. The reference to woman's "gentleness and grace" comes from Randolph-Macon's original statement of purpose; "Counselor," a brochure provided by the admissions office, Randolph-Macon Woman's College, n.d.

18. "Education in the Singular" [www.rmwc.edu/About/singular.html].

19. Judson College Catalog 1988–1990: "For Women Who Seek Success," 1; "Greater Success at a Women's College" [http://home.judson.edu/why.html].

20. Hollins: "Women Who Are Going Places Start at Hollins," college brochure, n.d.; "Hollins Success: Start at Hollins and Step Into Your Future," college brochure, n.d.; "Careers and Life After Hollins" [www.hollins.edu/html/careers__life.htm]; "Real World Experiences" [www.hollins.edu/html/real__world.htm].

21. "Academics" [www.mbc.edu/academic/undergraduate/trad/

trad.htm]; "Virginia Women's Institute for Leadership" [www.mbc.edu/academic/undergraduate/vwil/program.htm].

22. Andrew Cain, "Mary Baldwin's Cadets Shun VMI," *The Washington Times*, 6 May 1997; Alison Freehling, "Virginia Women Learning to Lead Apart From VMI," *Daily Press* (Newport News, VA), 22 June 1997.

23. Alison Freehling, "State Continues Funds for VWIL Program," *Daily Press* (Newport News, VA), 22 June 1997.

24. Dan McCauley, "Quietly, VWIL's 'Nulls' Report for Duty," *News-Record* (Harrisonburg, VA), 19 August 1997; Michael Hewlett, "Leadership on Display at MBC," *Staunton News Leader* (Staunton, VA), 6 May 1997.

25. "Women, Leadership and Social Change" [www.scottlan.edu/academic/wl&sc/deptpage.htm]; "WILL [Women Involved in Living and Learning]" [www.urich.edu/WILL/]; "Women's Leadership Certificate Program" [www.meredith.edu/3__certi2.html]; "Alabama Women's Leadership Database" [http://home.judson.edu/women.html].

26. "Information" [www.twu.edu/info/Top.html].

27. "Academics" [www.sbc.edu/academics/facts.html]; "Bennett College" [www.collegeedge.com/details/ . . . /d4__1127.stm#Student-BodyStatistics]; "Hollins College" [www.collegeedge.com/details/college/3/80/d4__1180.stm]; "Information" [www.twu.edu/info/Top.html].

28. Amy Thompson McCandless, Interview of Rita Williams Livingston, College of Charleston, 7 October 1997.

29. "*U.S. News and World Report*'s Reckless Downgrading of Spelman College," *The Journal of Blacks in Higher Education* 5 (Autumn 1994): 25; Ernie Suggs, "Fighting to Survive: Single-Sex Option" [www.herald-sun.com/hbcu/docs/single__sex.html]; "Spelman's Increasing Selectivity Bucks the Trend for Women's Colleges," 40.

30. Bishop, *The State of the South*, 61.

31. Johnnetta Cole, quoted in "Ruth J. Simmons President-Elect, Smith College," *The Journal of Blacks in Higher Education* 6 (Winter 1994/1995): 114; "Sister President: Ruth J. Simmons," *The Journal of Blacks in Higher Education* 10 (Winter 1995/1996): 51.

32. John Shelton Reed, *My Tears Spoiled My Aim and Other Reflections on Southern Culture* (Columbia and London: University of Missouri Press, 1993), 6.

33. Amy Thompson McCandless, survey of Southern college students, College of Charleston, fall 1995. In November 1995 a total of 217 students in the introductory Western Civilization course at the College of Charleston were given a questionnaire designed to ascertain their views and attitudes toward various regional, political, and social phenomena. The classes surveyed are required for all candidates for a bachelor's degree regardless of major. The sample had slightly fewer women (64 percent versus 66 percent), whites (84 percent versus 87 percent), and Southerners (69 percent versus 77 percent) and slightly more blacks (13 percent versus 9 percent) than the College of Charleston as a whole, but, generally speaking, the demographic profile of the respondents mirrored that of the college population.

34. Reed, *My Tears Spoiled My Aim*, 46.

35. Marks, *SREB Fact Book 1994/95*, 18, 44–45, 48–49; "Trends in Black Enrollment in Higher Education," *The Journal of Blacks in Higher Education* 7 (Spring 1995): 56.

36. Dillard University, 1989–1991 Bulletin; Vernon E. Jordan, Jr., "Blacks and Higher Education: Some Reflections," *Daedalus* 117, No. 3 (Summer 88): 281.

37. "Women's Leadership Institute" [www.bennett.edu/wli/wli. html]; "Spelman" [www.eyeonwomen.com/spelman.htm]; "Florida Black Archives, Research Center and Museum" [www.famu.edu/archives/index. html]; "Student, Community and Campus Life" [www.tougaloo.edu/ studentcom.html].

38. Suggs, "Fighting to Survive: Single-Sex Option"; "Howard University: Opportunity, Discovery, Challenge," college brochure, n.d., 12.

39. Fred Hobson, *The Southern Writer in the Post Modern World* (Athens and London: The University of Georgia Press, 1991), 93, 92.

40. Bishop, *The State of the South*, 77, 79.

41. Cooperative Institutional Research Program, Freshman Survey Institutional Summary for 1995, Office of Student Affairs, College of Charleston; Linda J. Sax, Alexander W. Astin, William S. Korn, and Kathryn M. Mahoney, *The American Freshman: National Norms for 1995* (Los Angeles, CA: Higher Education Research Institute, Graduate School of Education and Information Studies, University of California, December 1995), 61–63.

42. Bishop, *The State of the South*, 31; "Do the Strong Income Gains of Educated Black Women Point to an End to Racism?" *The Journal of Blacks in Higher Education* 11 (Spring 1996): 19.

43. *U.S. v. Fordice*, 112 S. Ct. 2727 (1992); Peter Applebome, "College Segregation Persists, Study Says," *New York Times*, 18 May 1995.

44. *U.S. v. Fordice*, 112 S. Ct. 2746 (1992); "HBCU [Historically Black Colleges and Universities] Home Page" [http://eric-web.tc.columbia.edu/hbcu/index.html].

45. *Podberesky v. Kirwan*, 115 S. Ct. 2001 (22 May 1995); Nadine Cohodas, *The Band Played Dixie: Race and the Liberal Conscience at Ole Miss* (New York: Free Press, 1997), 258–59.

46. "University of Arkansas at Pine Bluff" [www.uabp.edu/general_info.html]; Ernie Suggs, "Fighting to Survive: Historically Black Colleges and Universities Face the 21st Century" [www.herald-sun.com/hbcu/]; "HBCU Home Page."

47. Nancy Dorman-Hickson, "Women of Substance: Two Strong but Gentle Women Crusade for Education," *Southern Living* 32, No. 9 (September 1997): 108–10; "Why Smart Women Choose Women's Colleges" [www.twu.edu/info/choose.html].

48. "V.M.I. Expels Woman for Hitting Male Student," *New York Times*, 10 September 1997; "Citadel Cadet Resigns Amid Sexual Accusations," *New York Times*, 24 November 1997; Eric Schmitt, "Role of Women in the Military Is Again Bringing Debate," *The New York Times Books*, 29 December 1996 [www.nytimes.com].

49. McCandless, questionnaire of Southern college students.

50. Ibid.

51. Freshman Survey Institutional Summary for 1995; Sax et al., *The American Freshman: National Norms for Fall 1995*.

52. McCandless, questionnaire of Southern college students.

53. "President's Message" [http://home.judson.edu/preslet.html]; "Barber-Scotia College" [web.fie.com/htbin/Molis/MolisDetail?FICE=002909&PART=A].

54. Reed, *My Tears Spoiled My Aim*, 73.

55. Freshman Survey Institutional Summary for 1995; Sax et al., *The American Freshman: National Norms for Fall 1995*.

56. "Hampton University" [www.cs.hamptonu.edu/relations/

overview.html]; "Sweet Briar College" [www.petersons.com/sites/ ugradinc/725400ug.html]; "Student Life" [www.mbc.edu/student/ handbook/residenc.htm]; "Traditions" [www.famu.edu/activities/s__us. html#traditions]; quoted in Suggs, "Fighting to Survive: Single-Sex Option."

57. "Student Life" [www.rmwc.edu/Studentlife/Traditions.html].

58. Robert Greene, "Mary Baldwin Students Give Honor System Close, Lively Look," *Richmond Times Dispatch*, 20 February 1997.

59. "Campus Life" [www.converse.edu/campus.htm]; "Mississippi University for Women" [www.muw.edu/home.html]; quoted in Suggs, "Fighting to Survive: Single-Sex Option"; "Student Services" [www.xula. edu/SLStudentServices.html]; "Activities" [www.famu.edu/activities/ sa__us.html#traditions]; "Housing" [www.famu.edu/admin/housing. html#Education]; "Residence Life" [www.mbc/students/handbook/ residenc.htm].

60. Cohodas, *The Band Played Dixie*, 185, 245, 251.

61. Amy Thompson McCandless, Interview of Cherisse Jones, College of Charleston, 7 May 1996.

62. C. Vann Woodward, *The Future of the Past* (New York: Oxford University Press, 1989), xi–xii.

63. "A Proud Heritage—an Exceptional Future," Johnson C. Smith University, college brochure, n.d., 1; Clyda Rent, "Welcome to Mississippi University for Women" [www.muw.edu/pres2.html]; Andria Scott Hurst, "Women of Substance: Two Strong but Gentle Women Crusade for Education," *Southern Living* 32, No. 9 (September 1997): 108–10.

64. Cohodas, *The Band Played Dixie*, 259.

∼Selected Bibliography∼

Oral Histories

Addlestone, Esther Finger. Interview by Amy Thompson McCandless, Sumter, SC, June 1982.

Byrd, Pierrine Smith. Interview by Amy Thompson McCandless, Greenwood, SC, July 1982.

Carter, Patricia. Interview by Amy Thompson McCandless, College of Charleston, Charleston, SC, June 1982.

Davis, Dr. Marianna. Interview in *Women Leaders in South Carolina: An Oral History.* Ronald J. Chepesiuk, Ann Y. Evans, and Dr. Thomas S. Morgan, eds. Rock Hill, SC: Winthrop College Archives and Special Collections, 1984.

Eslinger, Victoria L. Interview by Amy Thompson McCandless, Columbia, SC, 16 September 1989.

Farrell, Susan. Interview by Amy Thompson McCandless, College of Charleston, 23 September 1997.

Florence, Hope Morris. Interview by Amy Thompson McCandless, College of Charleston, 9 October 1997.

Hawkes, Anne Leigh. Interview by Amy Thompson McCandless, Charleston, SC, 2 August 1996.

Jones, Cherisse. Interview by Amy Thompson McCandless, College of Charleston, 7 May 1996.

Livingston, Rita Joanne Williams. Interview by Amy Thompson McCandless, College of Charleston, 7 October 1997.

Mack, Joan Gladden. Interview by Amy Thompson McCandless, College of Charleston, 20 May 1996.

McCandless, Amy Thompson. Renaissance 200 Celebration, College of Charleston. Interviews with thirty-five alumnae who graduated between 1922 and 1940, March 1985.

Patton, Carlotta Petersen. Interview by Amy Thompson McCandless, College of Charleston, 23 March 1985.

Seabrook, Marlene Linton O'Bryant. Interview by Amy Thompson McCandless, Charleston, SC, 31 May 1996.

Selected Bibliography

Towell, Clarissa Kennedy and Edward E. Towell. Interview by Amy Thompson McCandless, Charleston, SC, 13 July 1982.

Libraries and Archives

Archives and Special Collections Department, Dacus Library, Winthrop University, Rock Hill, SC
The Arthur and Elizabeth Schlesigner Library on the History of Women in America, Radcliffe College, Cambridge, MA
Avery Research Center for African American History and Culture, College of Charleston, Charleston, SC
Columbia College Archives, Columbia, SC
Georgia State Department of Archives and History, Atlanta, GA
Judson College Archives, Marion, AL
Library of AAUW Educational Foundation, Inc., Washington, DC
McCain Library and Archives, The University of Southern Mississippi, Hattiesburg, MS
Moorland-Spingarn Research Center, Howard University, Washington, DC
North Carolina Collection, University of North Carolina–Chapel Hill, Chapel Hill, NC
North Carolina Division of Archives and History, Raleigh, NC
Queens College Library, Archives, Charlotte, NC
South Carolina Historical Society, Charleston, SC
South Caroliniana Library, University of South Carolina, Columbia, SC
Special Collections, Robert Scott Small Library, College of Charleston, Charleston, SC
University Archives, Walter Clinton Jackson Library, University of North Carolina–Greensboro, Greensboro, NC
University Archives, University Libraries, University of Florida, Gainesville, FL
Virginia State Archives, Richmond, VA

College Materials

Please note that the names of many of the institutions and their publications changed with time. Only one representative title is given below;

specific titles for individual years are provided in the endnotes. College
web sites, when available, were used for current materials.
Agnes Scott College (Decatur, GA)
  Agnes Scott Alumnae Quarterly
  Bulletin
  Silhouette. Annual of Agnes Scott College
Agricultural and Technical College of North Carolina (Greensboro, NC)
  *Annual Catalog of the Negro Agricultural and Technical College of North
  Carolina*
  Bulletin
Allen University (Columbia, SC)
  Catalog
Appalachian State Teachers College (Boone, NC)
  Bulletin
Asheville Normal and Associated Schools (Asheville, NC)
  Catalog
Auburn University (Auburn, AL)
  Co-Etiquette: A Handbook for Women Students
Benedict College (Columbia, SC)
  Annual catalog
  The Benedict Bulletin
Bennett College (Greensboro, NC)
  A Beacon for Womanhood
  Bulletin
Bob Jones University (Greenville, SC)
  Vintage. Yearbook of Bob Jones University
Bridgewater College (Bridgewater, VA)
  Catalog
Cherokee Indian Normal School (Pembroke, NC)
  Bulletin and Outlined Course of Study
  Pembroke State College for Indians Catalog
Chicora College for Women (Columbia, SC); see also Queens College
  Catalog
Claflin College (Orangeburg, SC)
  Annual catalog
Clark University (Atlanta, GA)
  Bulletin

Selected Bibliography

Coker College (Hartville, SC)
    Catalog
    Quarterly bulletin
College of Charleston (Charleston, SC)
    Catalog
    The Comet. Yearbook of the College of Charleston
    Cougar Pause. Student newspaper of College of Charleston
Columbia College (Columbia, SC)
    Catalog
    Columbian. Yearbook of Columbia College
Converse College (Spartanburg, SC)
    Bulletin
Cox College (College Park, GA)
    Bulletin
Dillard University (New Orleans, LA)
    Bulletin
Duke University (Durham, NC)
    Trinity College and the Woman's College annual catalog
East Carolina Teacher's College (Greenville, NC)
    Catalog
Erskine College (Due West, SC)
    Arrow 70. Yearbook of Erskine College
Fayetteville State Teachers College (Fayetteville, NC)
    Announcements
    Catalogue of the State Normal and Industrial Schol for the Colored Race
Flora Macdonald College (Red Springs, NC)
    Bulletin of Flora Macdonald College
Furman University (Greenville, SC)
    Bonhomie. Yearbook of Furman University
    Bulletin: Greenville Female College
Georgia State College for Women (Milledgeville, GA)
    Bulletin
Georgia State Teachers College (Athens, GA)
    Bulletin
The Georgia State Woman's College (Valdosta, GA)
    Announcements and course offerings
    Bulletin

H. Sophie Newcomb Memorial College for Women (New Orleans, LA)
   Bulletin
Hampton Normal and Agricultural Institute (Hampton, VA)
   Bulletin
Hollins College (Roanoke, VA)
   Catalog
   Hollins Success: Start at Hollins and Step Into Your Future. Brochure
   Hollins: Women Who Are Going Places Start at Hollins. Brochure
Howard University (Washington, DC)
   Bulletin
   Echo. Yearbook of Howard University
   H: The Students' Handbook
   Howard University: Opportunity, Discovery, Challenge. Brochure
   Howard University Student Manual
Johnson C. Smith University (Charlotte, NC)
   Proud Heritage—an Exceptional Future. Brochure
Judson College (Marion, AL)
   Bulletin
   Catalog
   Conversationalist. Yearbook of Judson College
Lander College (Greenwood, SC)
   Naiad. Yearbook of Lander College
Limestone College (Gaffney, SC)
   Annual catalog
   Bulletin
   Calciid. Yearbook of Limestone College
Livingstone College (Salisbury, NC)
   Catalog
Mary Baldwin College (Staunton, VA)
   Catalog
Meredith College (Raleigh, NC)
   Baptist Female University, annual catalog
   Meredith College Quarterly Bulletin
Mississippi State College for Women (Columbus, MS)
   Annual bulletin
   MEH LADY. Yearbook of Mississippi State College for Women
   Mississippi State College for Women, Student Government Handbook

351

Selected Bibliography

Morris Brown University (Atlanta, GA)
    Bulletin
Morris College (Sumter, SC)
    Catalog
Newberry College (Newberry, SC)
    1970 Newberrian
North Carolina College for Negroes (Durham, NC)
    Annual catalog
Queens College (Charlotte, NC)
    Conversationalist. Student newspaper of Queens College
    The Edelweiss. Yearbook of Queens College
    Queens Blues. Student newspaper
    Queens-Chicora College Bulletin
Randolph-Macon Woman's College (Lynchburg, VA)
    Catalog
    Counselor. College brochure
Salem College (Winston-Salem, NC)
    The Alumnae Record
    Brochure
    Catalog
Shaw University (Raleigh, NC)
    The Shaw Bulletin
South Carolina State College (Orangeburg, SC)
    The Bulldog. Yearbook of South Carolina State College
Spelman College (Atlanta, GA)
    Annual circular of Spelman Seminary for Women and Girls
    Campus Mirror
    Catalog
    Spelman Messenger. Newpaper of Spelman College
Sweet Briar College (Sweet Briar, VA)
    Catalog
    Sweet Briar College Alumnae Magazine
Texas Woman's University (Denton, TX)
    The Daily Lass-O. Student newspaper of Texas Woman's University
University of Florida (Gainesville, FL)
    Alligator

UF 40: Celebrating 40 Years of Coeducation at the University of Florida.
    Flyer
University of North Carolina (Chapel Hill, NC)
    Carolina Alumni Review
    North Carolina University Magazine
    The Tar Heel. Student newspaper of the University of North Caro-
    lina–Chapel Hill
    University of North Carolina Record
University of South Carolina (Columbia, SC)
    Bulletin
    Carolinian. Alumni magazine
    Catalog
    The Carolina Review. Literary magazine of the University of South
    Carolina
    The Gamecock. Student newspaper of the University of South Caro-
    lina
    Garnet and Black. Yearbook of the University of South Carolina
University of Virginia (Charlottesville, VA)
    University of Virginia Alumni News
Virginia Union University (Richmond, VA)
    Bulletin
Voorhees College (Denmark, SC)
    Tiger. Yearbook of Voorhees College.
Westhampton College (Richmond, VA)
    Catalog
Wesleyan College (Macon, GA)
    Catalog
Western Carolina Teachers College (Cullowhee, NC)
    Bulletin
Winston-Salem Teachers College (Winston-Salem, NC)
    Bulletin
Winthrop College (Rock Hill, SC)
    Catalog
    Winthrop Weekly News
Woman's College of North Carolina (Greensboro, NC)
    Alumnae News

Catalog, North Carolina College for Women
First annual catalog, State Normal and Industrial School

354   **Selected Other Sources**

Abbott, Shirley. *Womenfolks: Growing Up Down South.* New Haven: Ticknor & Fields, 1983.

Adams, Henry. *The Education of Henry Adams: An Autobiography.* Cambridge, MA: Riverside Press, 1961; first privately printed and distributed in 1906.

Adams, Ola. *Zeta Phi Beta Sorority, 1920–1965.* Washington, DC: Zeta Phi Beta Sorority, 1965.

Adventures in Teaching: Pioneer Women Educators and Influential Teachers. N.p.: Virginia Iota State Organization, Delta Kappa Gamma Society, 1963.

Alderman, Edwin. *The Present State of Higher Education in Virginia.* Address delivered before the Virginia Educational Conference at Norfolk, 25 November 1925. Pamphlet in the Virginia State Archives.

Alpha Kappa Alpha Sorority, Inc.: Service With A Global Perspective. Programmatic Thrust, July 1986. Chicago. AKA Sorority, 1986.

Alvey, Edward. *A History of Mary Washington College, 1908–1972.* Charlottesville: University of Virginia Press, 1974.

The American South: Portrait of a Culture. Edited by Louis D. Rubin, Jr. Baton Rouge and London: Louisiana State University Press, 1980.

American Universities and Colleges. Edited by Clarence Stephen Marsh. Washington, DC: American Council on Education, 1940.

Ayers, Edward L. *The Promise of the New South: Life After Reconstruction.* New York: Oxford University Press, 1992.

Bacote, Clarence A. *The Story of Atlanta University: A Century of Service, 1865–1965.* Atlanta: Atlanta University, 1969.

Ballard, Allen B. *The Education of Black Folk: The Afro-American Struggle for Knowledge in White America.* New York: Harper & Row, 1973.

Barrett, Russell H. *Integration at Ole Miss.* Chicago: Quadrangle Books, 1965.

Bass, Jack, and Jack Nelson. *The Orangeburg Massacre.* 2d edition. Macon, GA: Mercer University Press, 1984.

Bishop, C. E. *The State of the South: A Report to the Region and Its Leadership.* Chapel Hill: MDC, April 1996.

Blanton, Robert J. *The Story of Voorhees College From 1897 to 1982.* New York: Exposition Press, 1983.

Boas, Louise Schutz. *Woman's Education Begins: The Rise of the Women's Colleges.* Norton, MA: Wheaton College Press, 1935.

Boles, John B., ed. *Dixie Dateline: A Journalistic Portrait of the Contemporary South.* Houston: Rice University Studies, 1983.

Brandstadter, Diane Puthoff. "Developing the Coordinate College for Women at Duke University: The Career of Alice Mary Baldwin, 1924–1947." Ph.D. dissertation, History, Duke University, 1977.

Brown, William Henry. *The Education and Economic Development of the Negro in Virginia.* Charlottesville: Publications of the University of Virginia Phelps-Stokes Fellowship Papers No. 6, 1923.

Browning, Jane E. Smith, and John B. Williams. "History and Goals of Black Institutions of Higher Learning." *Black Colleges in America: Challenge, Development, Survival.* Edited by Charles V. Villie and Ronald R. Edmonds. New York: Columbia University Press, 1978.

Bryan, Wright. *Clemson: An Informal History of the University 1889–1979.* Columbia, SC: R. L. Bryan, 1979.

Bullock, Henry Allen. *A History of Negro Education in the South From 1619 to the Present.* Cambridge, MA: Harvard University Press, 1967.

Burke, Colin B. *American Collegiate Populations: A Test of the Traditional View.* New York and London: New York University Press, 1982.

Butcher, Beatrice Bowden. "The Evolution of Negro Women's Schools in the United States." M.A. thesis, School of Education, Howard University, 1936.

Butts, A. Freeman, and Lawrence A. Cremin. *A History of Education in American Culture.* New York: Holt, Rinehart and Winston, 1953.

Carmichael, O. C. "The Place of the Woman's College in Higher Education." *Proceedings of the Association of Colleges and Secondary Schools of the Southern States.* Lexington, KY: 1929.

Carter, Mary M. "The Educational Activities of the NACW, 1923–1960." M.A. thesis, Education Department, Howard University, 1962.

Cash, Wilbur J. *The Mind of the South.* New York: Alfred A. Knopf, 1941.

Selected Bibliography

Chafe, William H. *The American Woman: Her Changing Social, Economic, and Political Roles, 1920–1970.* New York: Oxford University Press, 1972.

——. *The Paradox of Change: American Women in the Twentieth Century.* New York and Oxford: Oxford University Press, 1991.

Charles W. Eliot: The Man and His Beliefs. Edited by William Allan Neilson. Vol. II. New York and London: Harper & Brothers, 1926.

Chepesiuk, Ron. *Winthrop College: A Centennial Celebration.* Rock Hill, SC: Winthrop College, 1985.

Christian, Barbara T. *Alice Walker, "Everyday Use."* New Brunswick: Rutgers University Press, 1994.

Clark, Felton G. *The Control of State-supported Teacher-Training Programs for Negroes.* New York: Teachers College, Columbia University, 1934.

Cohodas, Nadine. *The Band Played Dixie: Race and the Liberal Conscience at Ole Miss.* New York: Free Press, 1997.

Colton, Elizabeth Avery. "Address to High School Students on Standard Colleges." Ca. 1915. Handwritten draft, Elizabeth Avery Colton Papers, North Carolina State Archives.

Cooperative Institutional Research Program, Freshman Survey Institutional Summary for 1995, Office of Student Affairs, College of Charleston.

Co-ordinate College: A Vital Matter, The. Reprinted from *Virginia Journal of Education* (May 1917). Pamphlet in the Virginia State Library: 1–4.

Cornelius, Roberta D. *The History of Randolph-Macon Woman's College.* Chapel Hill: University of North Carolina Press, 1951.

Crowson, Thomas. *The Winthrop Story 1886–1960.* Baltimore: Gateway Press, 1987.

Curry, Constance. *Silver Rights.* Chapel Hill, NC: Algonquin Books, 1995.

Cuthbert, Marion Vera. *Education and Marginality: A Study of the Negro Woman College Graduate.* New York: American Book–Stratford Press, 1942.

Dabney, Virginius. *Mr. Jefferson's University: A History.* Charlottesville: University Press of Virginia, 1981.

Daniels, Jonathan. *A Southerner Discovers the South.* New York: Macmillan, 1938.

Degler, Carl N. *Place Over Time: The Continuity of Southern Distinctiveness.* Baton Rouge and London: Louisiana State University Press, 1977.

Dixie Dateline: A Journalistic Portrait of the Contemporary South. Edited by John B. Boles. Houston: Rice University Studies, 1983.

Dixon, Brandt V. B. *A Brief History of H. Sophie Newcomb Memorial College 1887–1919: A Personal Reminiscence.* New Orleans: Hauser, 1928.

Duberman, Martin. *Black Mountain: An Exploration in Community.* New York: E. P. Dutton, 1972.

Du Bois, W. E. B. *The Education of Black People: Ten Critiques 1906–1960.* Edited by Herbert Aptheker. Amherst: University of Massachusetts Press, 1973.

Duncan, Margaret M., and Velda P. Cundiff. *Play Days for Girls and Women.* New York: A. S. Barnes, 1929.

Duren, Almetris Marsh, and Louise Iscoe. *Overcoming: A History of Black Integration at the University of Texas at Austin.* Austin: University of Texas at Austin Press, 1979.

Dutton, Emily Helen. "History of the Southern Association of College Women." Typescript in Library of AAUW Educational Foundation, Washington, DC.

Dyer, John P. *Tulane: The Biography of a University, 1834–1965.* New York and London: Harper & Row, 1966.

Dyer, Thomas G. "Higher Education in the South Since the Civil War: Historical Issues and Trends." In *The Web of Southern Social Relations: Women, Family, and Education.* Edited by Walter J. Fraser, Jr., R. Frank Saunders, Jr., and Jon L. Wakelyn. Athens: University of Georgia Press, 1985.

———. *The University of Georgia: A Bicentennial History, 1785–1985.* Athens: University of Georgia Press, 1985.

Echols, Alice. *Daring to Be Bad: Radical Feminism in America 1967–1975.* Minneapolis: University of Minnesota Press, 1989.

Eckleberry, R. H. *The History of the Municipal University in the United States.* Bulletin, 1932, No. 2. Washington, DC: U.S. Government Printing Office, 1932.

Editors of *Fortune.* "Youth in College." *American Points of View 1936.* Edited by William H. Cordell and Kathryn Coe Cordell. New York: Doubleday, Doran, 1937.

Selected Bibliography

The Education of Henry Adams: An Autobiography. By Henry Adams. Cambridge: Riverside Press, 1961; first privately printed and distributed in 1906.

The Eighty-seventh Year: The American Missionary Association. Report for the Academic Year 1932–1933. New York: American Missionary Association, 1933.

The Eighty-sixth Annual Report of the American Missionary Association. Report for the Academic Year 1931–1932. New York: American Missionary Association, 1932.

Ellers, Joseph C. *Getting to Know Clemson University Is Quite an Education: Determination Makes the Dream Come True.* Clemson, SC: Clemson University Press, 1987.

The Enduring South: Subcultural Persistence in Mass Society. By John Shelton Reed. Lexington, MA: Lexington Books, D. C. Heath, 1972.

Evans, Sara M. *Born for Liberty: A History of Women in America.* New York: Free Press, 1989.

———. *Personal Politics: The Roots of Women's Liberation in the Civil Rights Movement and the New Left.* New York: Alfred A. Knopf, 1979.

Facing Facts: The American Missionary Association. Report for the Academic Year 1934–1935. New York: American Missionary Association, 1935.

Facts and Conclusions Concerning the Proposed Co-ordinate College the [sic] *Women.* Pamphlet in the Virginia State Library, 1914(?).

Facts and Conclusions Concerning the Proposed Co-ordinate College. Pamphlet in the Virginia State Library, 1917.

Facts in Regard to Bill Admitting Women to the Graduate and Professional Courses at the University. Richmond, VA: Whittet and Sheperson, 1918.

Farnham, Christie Anne. *The Education of the Southern Belle: Higher Education and Student Socialization in the Antebellum South.* New York and London: New York University Press, 1994.

Fass, Paula S. *The Damned and the Beautiful: American Youth in the 1920s.* New York: Oxford University Press, 1977.

———. *Outside In: Minorities and the Transformation of American Education.* New York and Oxford: Oxford University Press, 1989.

Fields, Mamie Garvin, with Karen Fields. *Lemon Swamp and Other Places: A Carolina Memoir.* New York and London: Free Press, 1983.

Frantz, Joe B. *Forty-Acre Follies*. Austin: Texas Monthly Press, 1983.

"From the Past: A Brief History of the South Carolina Student Council on Human Relations." 17 February 1968. Typed manuscript, Student Council File, 1966–1967, South Caroliniana Library, University of South Carolina.

Gee, Mary Wilson. *Yes, Ma'am, Miss Gee*. Charlotte, NC: Heritage House, 1957.

Genovese, Eugene. *Roll, Jordan, Roll: The World the Slaves Made*. New York: Pantheon Books, 1974.

Giddings, Paula. *In Search of Sisterhood: Delta Sigma Theta and the Challenge of the Black Sorority Movement*. New York: William Morrison, 1988.

———. *When and Where I Enter: The Impact of Black Women on Race and Sex in America*. New York: Bantam Books, 1984.

Gilmore, Glenda Elizabeth. *Gender and Jim Crow: Women and the Politics of White Supremacy in North Carolina, 1896–1920*. Chapel Hill: University of North Carolina Press, 1996.

Glasgow, Ellen. *Virginia*. New York: Penguin Books, 1989; first published in 1913.

Gluck, Sherna Berger. *Rosie the Riveter Revisited: Women, the War, and Social Change*. New York: New American Library, 1987.

Goldfield, David. *Promised Land: The South since 1945*. Arlington Heights, IL: Harland Davidson, 1987.

Gordon, Armistead C., Rector of the University of Virginia. *The Coordinate College at Charlottesville Affiliated with the University of Virginia: Expert Evidence of This Type of Institution and Its Need by the People of Virginia*. Richmond: N.p., 1914.

Gordon, Lynn D. *Gender and Higher Education in the Progressive Era*. New Haven and London: Yale University Press, 1990.

"Governor Benjamin R. Tillman's message delivered December 4, 1890 to the General Assembly." Typescript W403-1A-5, Archives and Special Collection Department, Dacus Library, Winthrop University.

Grantham, Dewey W. *Southern Progressivism: The Reconciliation of Progress and Tradition*. Knoxville: University of Tennessee Press, 1983.

Guy-Sheftall, Beverly, and Jo Moore Stewart. *Spelman: A Centennial Celebration, 1881–1981*. Charlotte, NC: Delmar, 1981.

Hale, Harrison. *University of Arkansas, 1871–1948.* Fayetteville, University of Arkansas Alumni Association, 1948.

Hampton, Henry, and Steve Fayer with Sarah Flynn. *Voices of Freedom: An Oral History of the Civil Rights Movement from the 1950s through the 1980s.* New York: Bantam Books, 1990.

Harrell, Rena Chambers. "Our Mother and Our Queen: A History of Queens College." Typescript, Archives, Queens College Library.

Hartmann, Susan M. *From Margin to Mainstream: American Women and Politics Since 1960.* New York: Alfred A. Knopf, 1989.

———. *The Home Front and Beyond: American Women in the 1940s.* Boston: Twayne Publishers, 1982.

Heatwole, Cornelius J. *A History of Education in Virginia.* New York: Macmillan, 1916.

Henderson, Archibald. *The Campus of the First State University.* Chapel Hill: University of North Carolina Press, 1949.

Higher Education and National Defense. Bulletin No. 22. Washington, DC: American Council on Education, 1942.

Hine, Darlene Clark. *Speak Truth to Power: Black Professional Class in United States History.* New York: Carlson Publishing, 1996.

Holder, Rose Howell. *McIver of North Carolina.* Chapel Hill: University of North Carolina Press, 1957.

Hollis, Daniel Walker. "A Brief History of the University." *Remembering the Days: An Illustrated History of the University of South Carolina.* Columbia: Institute for Southern Studies, University of South Carolina, 1982.

———. *University of South Carolina: College to University.* Vol. II. Columbia: University of South Carolina Press, 1956.

Holmes, Dwight Oliver. *The Evolution of the Negro College.* New York: American Missionary Society Press, 1934.

Horowitz, Helen Lefkowitz. *Alma Mater: Design and Experience in the Women's Colleges From Their Nineteenth Century Beginnings to the 1930s.* New York: Knopf, 1984.

———. *Campus Life: Undergraduate Cultures From the End of the Eighteenth Century to the Present.* Chicago and London: University of Chicago Press, 1987.

Horowitz, Irving Louis, and William H. Friedland. *The Knowledge Factory:*

Student Power and Academic Politics in America. Chicago: Aldine Publishing, 1970.

Hunter-Gault, Charlayne. *In My Place.* New York: Farrar Straus Giroux, 1992.

Hyslup, C. J. *Virginia Colleges: A Bulletin of Information for Prospective College Students to Assist Boys and Girls in Answering Many of the Questions Regarding Virginia Colleges and Their Entrance Requirements.* Richmond: State Board of Education, 1935. Pamphlet in the Virginia State Library.

Ihle, Elizabeth L. *Black Girls and Women in Elementary Education: History of Black Women's Education in the South, 1865–Present.* Module I (instructional module for educators). Washington, DC: U.S. Department of Education, Office of Educational Research and Improvement, Educational Resources Information Center, 1986.

———. *Black Women's Academic Education in the South: History of Black Women's Education in the South, 1865–Present.* Modules III and IV (instructional modules for educators). Washington, DC: U.S. Department of Education, Office of Educational Research and Improvement, Educational Resources Information Center, 1986.

———. *Black Women's Vocational Education: History of Black Women's Education in the South, 1865–Present.* Module II (instructional module for educators). Washington, DC: U.S. Department of Education, Office of Educational Research and Improvement, Educational Resources Information Center, 1986.

John, Walton C. *Hampton Normal and Agricultural Institute: Its Evolution and Contribution to Education as a Federal Land-Grant College.* U.S. Department of the Interior Bureau of Education Bulletin No. 27. Washington, DC: U.S. Government Printing Office, 1923.

Johnson, Charles. *The Negro College Graduate.* Chapel Hill: University of North Carolina Press, 1938.

Johnson, Mary Lynch. *A History of Meredith College.* Raleigh, NC: Meredith College, 1956.

Jones, Thomas Jesse. *Negro Education: A Study of the Private and Higher Schools for Colored People in the United States.* Vols. I and II. U.S. Department of the Interior Bureau of Education Bulletin, 1916, No. 39. Washington, DC: U.S. Government Printing Office, 1917.

Kendall, Elaine. *"Peculiar Institutions": An Informal History of the Seven Sister Colleges.* New York: G. P. Putnam's Sons, 1976.

Kerr, Clark. *The Great Transformation in Higher Education.* Albany: State University of New York Press, 1991.

362

Kibler, Lilian A. *The History of Converse College.* Spartanburg, SC: Converse College, 1973.

Kilman, Gail Apperson. "Southern Collegiate Women, Higher Education at Wesleyan Female College and Randolph-Macon Woman's College, 1893–1907." Ph.D. dissertation, History, University of Delaware, 1984.

Kinard, James P. *Historical Sketch of Winthrop College, the South Carolina College for Women.* A Radio Address at WBT, Charlotte, NC, February 9, 1934, in the Series of the South Carolina Economic Association, Being the Fiftieth Consecutive Weekly Broadcast in Educational Series. Pamphlet in the South Carolina Historical Society.

Kinnear, Duncan Lyle. *The First 100 Years: A History of Virginia Polytechnic Institute and State University.* Blacksburg: Virginia Polytechnic Institute, 1972.

Kirby, Jack Temple. *Rural Worlds Lost: The American South 1920–1960.* Baton Rouge and London: Louisiana State University Press, 1989.

Knight, Edgar W. *Education in the South.* Chapel Hill: University of North Carolina Press, 1924.

Kolesnik, Walter B. *Coeducation: Sex Differences and the Schools.* New York: Vantage Press, 1969.

Lamb, Annadell Craig. *The History of Phi Mu: The First 130 Years.* Atlanta: Phi Mu Fraternity, 1982.

Lancaster, John Littlepage. *College Enrollment in Virginia.* Typescript. Charlottesville: Bureau of Population and Economic Research, University of Virginia, May 1947.

Lee, Calvin B. *The Campus Scene, 1900–1970: Changing Styles in Undergraduate Life.* New York: David McKay, 1970.

Lefler, Hugh Talmage, and Albert Ray Newsome. *North Carolina: The History of a Southern State.* Chapel Hill: University of North Carolina Press, 1953.

Levine, David O. *The American College and the Culture of Aspiration 1915–1940.* Ithaca and London: Cornell University Press, 1986.

A Liberal Arts College for Women. Report of the Commission Appointed to Study and Report to the Legislature Upon the Advisability of Establishing a Liberal Arts College for Undergraduate Women at One of the State Teachers Colleges or Elsewhere. Submitted to the General Assembly, January 1930, Senate Document No. 4. Richmond: Division of Purchase and Printing, 1930.

A Liberal Arts College for Women Co-ordinate With the University of Virginia. Report of the Commission on a Liberal Arts College for Women, submitted to the Virginia General Assembly, January 1932.

Link, William A. *A Hard Country and a Lonely Place: Schooling, Society, and Reform in Rural Virginia, 1870–1920.* Chapel Hill and London: University of North Carolina Press, 1986.

Logan, Rayford W. *What the Negro Wants.* Chapel Hill: University of North Carolina Press, 1944.

Lumpkin, Katharine DuPre. *The Making of a Southerner.* Athens: University of Georgia Press, 1992; first edition, 1946.

Marcus, Laurence R., and Benjamin D. Stickney. *Race and Education: The Unending Controversy.* Springfield, IL: Charles C Thomas, Publisher, 1981.

Marks, Joseph L. *SREB Fact Book on Higher Education 1994–1995.* Atlanta: Southern Regional Education Board, 1994–1995.

McCandless, Amy Thompson. Questionnaire: Classes of 1923, 1928, 1933, and 1938 of Hollins, Queens, Salem, Sweet Briar, and Wesleyan colleges. Spring 1983.

———. Survey of Alumnae from Hollins College, Queens College, Salem College, Sweet Briar College, and Wesleyan College, classes of 1928, 1933, and 1938.

———. Survey of Alumnae from South Carolina State College and the University of South Carolina, classes of 1955, 1960, 1965, and 1970. Summer 1991.

———. Survey of Southern College Students, College of Charleston. Fall 1995.

McEwen, Mildred Morse. *Queens College Yesterday and Today.* Charlotte, NC: Queens College Alumnae Association, 1980.

McMillan, Lewis K. *Negro Higher Education in the State of South Carolina.* Orangeburg, SC: N.p., 1952.

McMillen, Neil R. *Dark Journey: Black Mississippians in the Age of Jim Crow.* Urbana and Chicago: University of Illinois Press, ca. 1989; Illini Books, 1990.

McVea, Emilie M. "Women's Colleges and the Southern Association." In *Proceedings of the Association of Colleges and Secondary Schools of the Southern States.* New Orleans: 1922.

McWhiney, Grady. "Education in the Old South: A Reexamination." *The Southern Enigma: Essays on Race, Class, and Folk Culture.* Edited by Walter J. Fraser, Jr., and Winfred B. Moore, Jr. Westport, CT: Greenwood Press, 1983.

Meriwether, Colyer. *The History of Higher Education in South Carolina.* Washington, DC: U.S. Government Printing Office, 1889.

Mims, Edwin. *The Advancing South: Stories of Progress and Reaction.* New York: Doubleday, Page, 1926.

Minority Report: A Liberal Arts College for Women. Senate Document No. 4 (1930), Virginia State Archives.

Mishoe, Janette Anne Cox. "Winthrop in Uniform, 1895–1955." M.A. thesis, Education, Winthrop College, 1970.

Mississippi University for Women et al. v. Hogan. 458 U.S. 718 (1982).

Mitchell, Samuel Chiles, ed. *The South in the Building of the Nation: History of the Social Life of the South.* Vol. 10. Richmond, VA: Southern Historical Publication Society, 1909.

Montgomery, James Riley, Stanley J. Folmsbee, and Lee Seifert Greene. *To Foster Knowledge: A History of the University of Tennessee, 1794–1970.* Knoxville: University of Tennessee Press, 1984.

Moody, Anne. *Coming of Age in Mississippi.* New York: Dial Press, 1968.

Moore, Maude. "History of the College for Women." M.A. thesis, Education, University of South Carolina, 1932.

Morgan, Chester M. *Dearly Bought, Deeply Treasured: The University of Southern Mississippi.* Jackson and London: University Press of Mississippi, 1987.

Mowry, George E. *The Twenties: Fords, Flappers, and Fanatics.* Englewood Cliffs, NJ: Prentice-Hall, 1963.

Mueller, Carol. "Ella Baker and the Origins of 'Participatory Democracy.' " *Women in the Civil Rights Movement: Trailblazers and Torch-*

bearers, 1941–1965. Edited by Vicki L. Crawford, Jacqueline Anne Rouse, and Barbara Woods. New York: Carlson Publishing, 1990.

Muhlenfeld, Elizabeth Showalter. "Mary Boykin Chesnut: The Writer and Her Work." Ph.D. dissertation, University of South Carolina, 1978.

Munford, Mrs. Mary. *Why a Co-ordinate College at Charlottesville Affiliated With The University of Virginia Rather Than a Separate College.* Pamphlet in Virginia State Library. Charlottesville, VA: Co-ordinate College League, 1916.

National Emergency Council. *Report on Economic Conditions in the South.* Washington, DC: Government Printing Office, 1938.

Neverdon-Morton, Cynthia. *Afro-American Women of the South and the Advancement of the Race, 1895–1925.* Knoxville: University of Tennessee Press, 1989.

Newby, I. A. *Black Carolinians: A History of Blacks in South Carolina from 1895 to 1968.* Columbia: University of South Carolina Press, 1973.

Newcomer, Mable. *A Century of Higher Education for American Women.* Washington: Zenger, 1959.

Nicholls, William H. *Southern Tradition and Regional Progress.* Chapel Hill: University of North Carolina Press, 1960.

Niederer, Frances J. *Hollins College: An Illustrated History.* Charlottesville: University of Virginia Press, 1973.

Ninety Years After: The American Missionary Association. Report for the Academic Year 1935–1936. New York: American Missionary Association, 1936.

Noble, Jeanne L. *The Negro Woman's College Education.* New York: Columbia University, 1956.

Odum, Howard W. *Southern Regions of the United States.* Chapel Hill: University of North Carolina Press, 1936.

Page, Walter H. "The Forgotten Man." Typescript of commencement address given at the North Carolina Normal and Industrial Institute, 19 May 1897. University Archives, Jackson Library, University of North Carolina–Greensboro.

Parker, Marjorie H. *Alpha Kappa Alpha Through the Years, 1908–1988.* Chicago: Mobium Press, 1990.

Selected Bibliography

Perrett, Geoffrey. *America in the Twenties: A History.* New York: Simon and Schuster, 1982.

Peters, David Wilbur. *The Status of the Married Woman Teacher.* Teachers College, Columbia University, Contributions to Education No. 603. New York: Columbia University, 1934.

Piersen, William D. *Black Legacy: America's Hidden Heritage.* Amherst: University of Massachusetts Press, 1993.

Pieschal, Bridget Smith, and Stephen Robert Pieschal. *Loyal Daughters: One Hundred Years at Mississippi University for Women, 1884–1984.* Jackson: University Press of Mississippi, 1984.

Player, Willa B. *Improving College Education for Women at Bennett College: A Report of a Type A Project.* New York and London: Garland Publishing, 1987.

Potts, John F. *A History of South Carolina State College.* Columbia: R. L. Bryan, 1978.

Prather, H. Leon. *Resurgent Politics and Educational Progressivism in the New South: North Carolina, 1890–1913.* Rutherford, NJ: Fairleigh Dickinson University Press, 1979.

President's Report. Report of the Board of Directors of the Normal and Industrial Schools for the Two Scholastic Years Ending September 30, 1894. Raleigh: Presses of Edwards & Broughton, 1895.

Proctor, Samuel, and Wright Langley. *Gator History: A Pictorial History of the University of Florida.* Gainesville, FL: South Star Publishing, 1987.

Proudfoot, Merrill. *Diary of a Sit-in.* Chapel Hill: University of North Carolina Press, 1962.

Public Higher Education in South Carolina: A Survey Report. Nashville, TN: Division of Surveys and Field Services, George Peabody College for Teachers, 1946.

Randolph, Bessie Carter. *The Centennial Celebration of Hollins College.* Hollins College, VA: Hollins College, 1949.

Read, Florence. *The Story of Spelman College.* Princeton, NJ: Princeton University Press, 1961.

Reed, John Shelton. *The Enduring South: Subcultural Persistence in Mass Society.* Lexington, MA: Lexington Books, D. C. Heath, 1972.

———. *My Tears Spoiled My Aim and Other Reflections on Southern Culture.* Columbia and London: University of Missouri Press, 1993.

———. *Southerners: The Social Psychology of Sectionalism.* Chapel Hill: University of North Carolina Press, 1983.

Reid, Alfred Sandlin. *Furman University: Toward a New Identity 1925–1975.* Durham: Duke University Press, 1976.

Report of the Board of Trustees of Winthrop College, the South Carolina College for Women, to the General Assembly, 1 July 1934–30 June 1935. Columbia: Joint Committee on Printing, General Assembly of South Carolina, 1935.

Report of the Commissioners Appointed Under Concurrent Resolution of the General Assembly of South Carolina, Relative to the Establishment of a State Industrial School for Women. Columbia, SC: James H. Woodrow, State Printer, 1891.

Report and Recommendations of the Commission to Study Public Schools and Colleges for Colored People in North Carolina. Authorized by the General Assembly in Resolution No. 28, 10 March 1937. Raleigh, NC: State Capitol, 1938.

Reynolds, John Hugh, and David Yancey Thomas. *History of the University of Arkansas.* Fayetteville: University of Arkansas Press, 1910.

Richardson, Eudora Ramsey. *The Influence of Men Incurable.* Indianapolis and New York: Bobbs-Merrill, 1936.

Richardson, Joe M. *A History of Fisk University, 1865–1946.* University, AL: University of Alabama Press, 1980.

Rouse, Jaqueline A. *Lugenia Burns Hope: Black Southern Reformer.* Athens and London: University of Georgia Press, 1989.

Rubin, Louis D., Jr., ed. *The American South: Portrait of a Culture.* Baton Rouge and London: Louisiana State University Press, 1980.

Satterfield Frances Gibson. *Charles Duncan McIver.* Greensboro: Woman's College of the University of North Carolina, 1942.

Savory, Jerold J. *Columbia College: The Ariail Era.* Columbia: R. L. Bryan, 1979.

Schad, Kathleen White. *They Call Me Kay: A Courtship in Letters.* Edited by Nancy G. Anderson. Montgomery, AL: Black Belt Press, 1994.

Schwager, Sally. " 'Harvard Women': A History of the Founding of Radcliffe College." Ph.D. dissertation, Education Department, Harvard University, 1982.

Scott, Anne Firor. *Making the Invisible Woman Visible.* Urbana and Chicago: University of Illinois Press, 1984.

——. *Natural Allies: Women's Associations in American History.* Urbana: University of Illinois Press, 1992.

——. *The Southern Lady: From Pedestal to Politics, 1830–1930.* Chicago: University of Chicago Press, 1970.

Shannon Richey Faulkner et al. v. James E. Jones, Jr., et al. Civil Action No. 2: 93-488-2, U.S. District Court for the District of South Carolina, Charleston Division, 22 July 1994.

Shaw, Stephanie J. *What A Woman Ought to Be and to Do: Black Professional Women Workers During the Jim Crow Era.* Chicago: University of Chicago Press, 1996.

Simkins, Francis Butler. *Pitchfork Ben Tillman, South Carolinian.* Gloucester, MA: P. Smith, 1964.

Simpson, Robert. *Coker College: The Diamond Jubilee History (1983).* Pamphlet in the South Caroliniana Library, University of South Carolina.

"Sketch of the Association of Colleges and Prepatory Schools of the Southern States." In *Association of Colleges and Prepatory Schools of the Southern States.* Proceedings of the Fourth Annual Meeting, University of Georgia, November 1–2, 1898.

Smith, William C., Viola Boddie, and Mary Settle Sharpe, eds. *Charles Duncan* [memorial volume]. Greensboro, NC: J. J. Stone, 1907.

Solomon, Barbara Miller. *In the Company of Educated Women: A History of Women and Higher Education in America.* New Haven and London: Yale University Press, 1985.

The South in the Building of the Nation: History of the Social Life of the South. Vol. 10. Edited by Samuel Chiles Mitchell. Richmond, VA: Southern Historical Publication Society, 1909.

Southern Project, United States National Student Association. Files on Civil Disorders and Civil Rights, South Caroliniana Library, University of South Carolina.

"The Status of Women at the University of Florida." Typescript, University Archives, University Libraries, University of Florida, 6 April 1972.

Stevens, W. Le Conte. *The Admission of Women to Universities.* New York: Association for Promoting the Higher Education of Women in New York, 1883.

Stohlman, Martha Lou Lemmon. *The Story of Sweet Briar College.* Sweet Briar, VA: Alumnae Association of Sweet Briar College, 1956.

Straight Ahead. The American Missionary Association, Report for the Academic Year 1933–1934. New York: American Missionary Association, 1934.

Stringer, Patricia A., and Irene Thompson, eds. *Stepping Off the Pedestal: Academic Women in the South.* New York: Modern Language Association of America, 1982.

Talbot, Marion, and Lois Kimball Matthews Rosenberry. *The History of the American Association of University Women, 1881–1931.* Boston and New York: Houghton Mifflin, 1931.

Taylor, Walter Carroll. *History of Limestone College.* Gaffney, SC: Limestone College, 1937.

Taylor, William R. *Cavalier and Yankee: The Old South and American National Character.* New York: G. Braziller, 1961.

Thompson, Joyce. *Marking a Trail: A History of Texas Woman's University.* Denton: Texas Woman's University Press, 1982.

Thompson, Tommy. *Auburn: A University Portrait.* Louisville, KY: Harmony House, 1988.

The Twenties: The Critical Issues. Edited by Joan Hoff Wilson. Boston: Little, Brown, 1972.

Tucker, Nora R., and Thomasina W. Norford. "Ten Years of Progress: The Negro Women in the Labor Force." In *Women United: Souvenir Year Book, Sixteenth Anniversary, National Council of Negro Women, Inc.* Washington, DC: National Council of Negro Women, 1951.

United States, Petitioner v. Virginia et al., and Virginia et al., Petitioners v. United States. 116 S. CT. 2264, 26 June 1996.

The University of Tennessee Sesqui-Centennial: A Record of 150 Years of Achievement of Public Education on the Higher Level—and an Analysis of Future

369

Problems and Responsibilities. Knoxville: University of Tennessee Press, 1945.

U.S. Commissioner of Education. *Report 1899–1900.* Vol. 2. Washington, DC: U.S. Government Printing Office, 1901.

U.S. President's Commission on Campus Unrest. Campus Report. Washington, DC: U.S. Government Printing Office, 1970.

Vance, Rupert. *Human Geography of the South: A Study in Regional Resources and Human Adequacy.* Chapel Hill: University of North Carolina Press, 1935.

Virginia Colleges: A Bulletin of Information About the State Colleges and the Colleges Under Private Control in Virginia. Richmond: State Board of Education, 1942.

White, Pearl Schwartz. *Behind These Doors—a Legacy: The History of Sigma Gamma Rho Sorority.* Chicago: Sigma Gamma Rho Sorority, 1974.

——. *The Legacy Continues: The History of Sigma Gamma Rho Sorority, 1974–1994.* Vol. 2. Chicago: Sigma Gamma Rho Sorority, 1994.

Wiggins, Sam P. *Higher Education in the South.* Berkeley, CA: McCutchan Publishing, 1966.

Willey, Malcolm M. *Depression, Recovery and Higher Education.* A Report by Committee Y of the American Association of University Professors. New York and London: McGraw-Hill, 1937.

Williams, T. Harry. *Introduction to Louisiana State University: A Pictorial Record of the First Hundred Years.* Edited by V. L. Bedsole and Oscar Richard. Baton Rouge: Louisiana State University Press, 1959.

Wills, Martee, and Joan Perry Morris. *Seminole History: A Pictorial History of Florida State University.* Gainesville: South Star Publishing, 1987.

Wilson, Joan Hoff, ed. *The Twenties: The Critical Issues.* Boston: Little, Brown, 1972.

Wolfe, Suzanne Rau. *The University of Alabama: A Pictorial History.* University, AL: University of Alabama Press, 1983.

Wolters, Raymond. *Right Turn: William Bradford Reynolds, the Reagan Administration, and Black Civil Rights.* New Brunswick, NJ: Transaction Publishers, 1996.

Women Educators in the United States, 1820–1993. Edited by Maxine Schwartz Seller. Westport, CT: Greenwood Press, 1994.

Woodward, C. Vann. *The Burden of Southern History.* Baton Rouge: Louisiana State University Press, 1960.

———. *The Future of the Past.* New York: Oxford University Press, 1989.

Woody, Thomas. *A History of Women's Education in the United States.* 2 vols. New York: Science Press, 1929.

Young, Elizabeth Barber. *A Study of the Curricula of Seven Selected Women's Colleges of the Southern States.* New York: Teachers College, Columbia University, 1932.

371

~Index~

Index

377

Index

Index

Index

385

Index

Index